Ilya Talev

Some Problems of the Second South Slavic Influence in Russia

SLAVISTISCHE BEITRÄGE

BEGRÜNDET VON ALOIS SCHMAUS

HERAUSGEGEBEN VON HENRIK BIRNBAUM UND JOHANNES HOLTHUSEN

REDAKTION: PETER REHDER

Band 67

ILYA TALEV

SOME PROBLEMS OF THE SECOND SOUTH SLAVIC INFLUENCE IN RUSSIA

VERLAG OTTO SAGNER · MÜNCHEN

1973

A Ph. D. dissertation, originally entitled: "The Impact of Middle Bulgarian on the Russian Literary Language (Post-Kievan Period)", defended on January 5, 1972 at the University of California, Los Angeles before the following Committee:

Professor Dean S. Worth, Chairman
Professor Henrik Birnbaum
Professor Thomas Eekman
Professor Richard Hovannisian
Professor Raimo Anttila

ISBN 3 87690 076 X

Copyright by Verlag Otto Sagner, München 1973
Abteilung der Firma Kubon und Sagner, München
Druck: Alexander Großmann
8 München 19, Ysenburgstraße 7^{I}

T A B L E   O F   C O N T E N T S

A B B R E V I A T I O N S

AfSlPh - Archiv für slavische Philologie, Vienna-Berlin.

AIPHOS - Annuaire de l'Institut de Philologie et d'histoire
orientales et slaves, Brussels-New York.

Annals UAASUS - Annals of the Ukrainian Academy of Arts and
Sciences in the United States, Chicago.

AN SSSR - Akademija Nauk, SSSR.

BAI - Bəlgarski Arxeologičeski Institut.

BAN - Bəlgarska Akademija na Naukite.

Bgrd. - Beograd Library copy of Akir the Wise.

BəlgEz - Bəlgarski ezik. Organ na Instituta za bəlgarski
ezik pri BAN, Sofia.

BəlgIstBibl - Bəlgarska istoričeska biblioteka (S. Slavčev,
ed.), Sofia.

CSP - Canadian Slavonic Papers, Toronto.

EL - Ezik i literatura. Organ i izdanie na družestvoto na
filolozite-slavisti v Bəlgarija, Sofia.

GB - Gosudarstvennaja biblioteka SSSR imeni V. I. Lenina,
Moscow.

GodSU - Godišnik na Sofijskija universitet, Sofia.

GodSU, Filosof.ist.fak.- Godišnik na Sofijskija universitet,
filosofsko-istoričeski fakultet, Sofia.

GodSU, Ist.fil.fak. - Godišnik na Sofijskija universitet,
istoriko-filologičeski fakultet, Sofia.

GPB - Gosudarstvennaja publicnaja biblioteka, Leningrad.

IAG - King Ioan Aleksandər's <u>Four</u> <u>Gospels</u> of 1355-1356. A
microfilm from the original manuscript, kept in
the British Museum under the number 39627 (Parham
Collection, MS XLV).

IBE - Institut po bəlgarski ezik, BAN.

IBL - Institut za bəlgarska literatura, BAN.

II - Institut za istorija, BAN.

IJa - Institut jazykoznanija, AN SSSR.

IJSLP - <u>International</u> <u>Journal</u> <u>of</u> <u>Slavic</u> <u>Linguistics</u> <u>and</u>
<u>Poetics</u>, Hague.

IS - Institut slavjanovedenija, AN SSSR.

ISSt - <u>Indiana</u> <u>Slavic</u> <u>Studies</u>, Bloomington.

IstPr - <u>Istoričeski</u> <u>pregled</u>, Sofia.

IzvBAI - <u>Izvestija</u> <u>na</u> <u>Bəlgarskija</u> <u>arxeologičeski</u> <u>institut</u>,
<u>BAN</u>, Sofia.

IzvIBE - <u>Izvestija</u> <u>na</u> <u>Instituta</u> <u>po</u> <u>bəlgarski</u> <u>ezik</u>, <u>BAN</u>,
Sofia.

IzvIBL - <u>Izvestija</u> <u>na</u> <u>Instituta</u> <u>za</u> <u>bəlgarska</u> <u>literatura</u>,
<u>BAN</u>, Sofia.

IzvII - <u>Izvestija</u> <u>na</u> <u>Instituta</u> <u>za</u> <u>istorija</u>, BAN, Sofia.

IzvOLJa - <u>Izvestija</u> <u>Otdelenija</u> <u>literatury</u> <u>i</u> <u>jazyka</u> AN <u>SSSR</u>,
Moscow.

IzvORJaS - <u>Izvestija</u> <u>Otdelenija</u> <u>russkogo</u> <u>jazyka</u> <u>i</u> <u>sloves-</u>
<u>nosti</u> <u>AN</u> <u>SSSR</u> (<u>Russia</u>), Leningrad (St. Petersburg,
Petrograd).

JF - <u>Južnoslovenski</u> <u>filolog</u>, Beograd.

Mar. - Codex Marianus. Published by V. Jagić as: Quattuor
    evangeliorum versionis palaeoslovenicae Codex
    Marianus glagoliticus (Mariinskoe četveroevangelie
    s primečanijami i priloženijami), Berlin - St.
    Petersburg, 1883 (Photoreprint: Graz, 1960),
    xxx + 607 pp.

MSFL - Matica srpska za filologiju i lingvistiku, Novi Sad.

ODRL - Otdel drevnerusskoj literatury Instituta russkoj
    literatury AN SSSR (Puškinskij dom).

OLJa - Otdelenie literatury i jazyka AN SSSR.

ORJaS - Otdelenie russkogo jazyka i slovesnosti AN SSSR
    (Russia).

OSlP - Oxford Slavonic Papers, Oxford.

Ostr. - Ostromir Gospel. Published by A. Vostokov as:
    Ostromirovo evangelie 1056-1057 g. S priloženiem
    grečeskogo teksta evangelij i s grammatičeskimi
    ob"jasnenijami, St. Petersburg, 1843 (Photoedi-
    tion: Wiesbaden, 1964), viii + 294 + 320 pp.

PamDPI - Pamjatniki drevnej pis'mennosti i iskusstva,
    St. Petersburg.

Period.SpBAN - Periodičesko spisanie na Bəlgarskata Aka-
    demija na Naukite, Sofia.

RÉS - Revue des Études Slaves, Paris.

RFV - Russkij filologičeskij vestnik, Warsaw.

RJaŠ - Russkij jazyk v škole, Moscow.

Sav. - Savvina kniga. Published by V. Ščepkin as:

Savvina kniga (Pamjatniki staroslavjanskogo jazyka, I, 2), St. Petersburg, 1903 (Photoreprint:
Graz, 1959), vii + 235 pp.

SbBAN – Sbornik na Bəlgarskata Akademija na Naukite, Sofia.

SbNUNK – Sbornik za narodni umotvorenija, nauka i knižnina,
Sofia.

SbORJaS – Sbornik Otdelenija russkogo jazyka i slovesnosti
AN SSSR (Russia), Leningrad (St. Petersburg,
Petrograd).

SEEJ – Slavic and East European Journal, Bloomington, Ind.
and Madison, Wis.

SEER – Slavic and East European Review, London.

Slavia – Slavia. Časopis pro slovanskou filologii, Prague.

SlMov – Slov'jans'ke movoznavstvo, Kiev.

SRev – Slavic Review. American Quarterly of Soviet and
East European Studies, Seattle.

Solov. – Soloveckij Monastery copy of Akir the Wise.

SpBAN – Spisanie na Bəlgarskata Akademija na Naukite, Sofia.

Supr. – Codex Suprasliensis. Published by S. Sever'janov as:
Suprasl'skaja rukopis' (= Pamjatniki staroslavjanskogo jazyka, II), St. Petersburg, 1904 (Photoedition: Graz, 1956), iv + 570 pp.

Trudy GPB – Trudy Gosudarstvennoj publičnoj biblioteki,
Leningrad.

Trudy IJa – Trudy Instituta jazykoznanija AN SSSR, Moscow.

Trudy ODRL – Trudy Otdela drevnerusskoj literatury Instituta

russkoj literatury AN SSSR (Puškinskij dom),
Leningrad.

UčZapIS - Učenye zapiski Instituta slavjanovedenija AN SSSR,
Moscow-Leningrad.

VJaz - Voprosy jazykoznanija, Moscow.

Word - Word. Journal of the Linguistic Circle of New York,
New York.

ZbMSFL - Zbornik Matice srpske za filologiju i lingvistiku,
Novi Sad.

Zogr. - Codex Zographensis. Published by V. Jagić as:
Quattuor evangeliorum codex glagoliticus olim
Zographensis nunc Petropolitanus, characteribus
cyrillicis transcriptum notis criticis prolegomenis appendicibus auctum, Berlin, 1879 (Photoreprint: Graz, 1954), xlv + 175 + iii pp.

ŽMNP - Žurnal Ministerstva narodnogo prosveščenija, St.
Petersburg.

Chapter One

THE SECOND SOUTH SLAVIC INFLUENCE ON RUSSIAN

1.1. In May, 1894, at the annual meeting of the
Archeological Institute in Saint Petersburg, the Russian
Slavist A. I. Sobolevskij delivered a report entitled:
Južno-slavjanskoe vlijanie na russkuju pis'mennost' v XIV -
XV vekax[1]. Some sixty years later, in September, 1958, another famous Russian scholar, a literary historian, medie-
valist and philologist, D. S. Lixačev, delivered to the
Fourth International Congress of Slavists in Moscow a report
entitled Nekotorye zadači izučenija vtorogo južnoslavjanskogo vlijanija v Rossii[2]. These two papers stand alone in
the history of Slavistics, since no other works on the
subject, before or after them, can approach them in scope
and seriousness. Sobolevskij's work "in certain respects

---

1. This report was soon afterward published as
a separate brochure, Južno-slavjanskoe vlijanie na russkuju
pis'mennost' v XIV - XV vekax. Reč', čitannaja na godičnom
akte Arxeologičeskogo instituta 8 maja 1894 goda prof. A.
I. Sobolevskim,
        Nine years later the text was incorporated (with
new bibliographical materials on the subject) as Chapter
One of Sobolevskij's book, Perevodnaja literatura Moskovskoj
Rusi XIV - XVII vekov (Bibliografičeskie materialy), St.
Petersburg, 1903, p. 1-37.

2. D. S. Lixačev, Nekotorye zadači izučenija
vtorogo južnoslavjanskogo vlijanija v Rossii, Issledovanija
po slavjanskomu literaturovedeniju i fol'kloristike
(Doklady Sovetskix učenyx na IV Meždunarodnom s"ezde
slavistov), Moscow, 1960, p. 95-151.

merely stated this influence, rather than studied it"[3].

Lixačev summarized the extant knowledge about changes in the Russian culture of the late 14th and entire 15th centuries, and attempted to explain these changes in terms of the influence of the two Balkan Slavic high cultures of the 14th century - the Bulgarian and the Serbian.

1.1.1. In comparing the reports of Sobolevskij and Lixačev, one remarks how little factual information on the subject of linguistic change in the Russian language was gained by Slavists over the sixty years separating them. Lixačev's final conclusions take the form of four broadly-defined tasks set for future Slavists:

> First, to study the extent of the South Slavic influence, its depth of penetration in different cultural areas.
> Second, to study the ideological content of that intellectual movement which we have tentatively identified as the Byzanto-Slavic Pre-Renaissance.
> Third, to study precisely that style which was connected with the second South Slavic influence.
> Fourth, to conduct textological analyses of literary works translated and brought to Russia. The textological study of 14th and 15th century literary monuments and their copies will shed light on the route of concrete penetration into Russia, of South Slavic and Byzantine influence, on the degree and character of artistic re-working; it will assist in the study of the origin of particular literary borrowings in style, contents, etc. [4].

As far as the structural changes in the language

---

3. D. S. Lixačev, op. cit., p. 96.

4. D. S. Lixačev, op. cit., p. 150.

of late 14th- and 15th-century Muscovite Russia are concerned, the scholar of today must still rely mainly on observations made earlier by Sobolevskij:

a) a comparison of the Russian manuscripts of the
first half of the 14th century with those of the middle of
the 15th century reveals a significant difference with respect to the language[5];

b) the language of the Russian manuscripts of the
middle of the 15th century reflects particular features of
the Middle Bulgarian literary language[6];

c) between the middle of the 14th and the middle
of the 15th century, the Russian language and literature
came under the very strong influence of the South Slavic
languages and literatures, and in the end became completely
submerged by them[7].

It is interesting to note that all Russian authors, discussing the problem of the overall cultural influence in 14th- and 15th-century Russia, refer to this as the
South Slavic influence, and still emphasize the leading
role of the Middle Bulgarian literary language. So far, no
one has been able to distinguish clearly where the Bulgarian element ends and the Serbian begins, or vice versa.
The reasons for this lie in the historical development of

---

5. A. I. Sobolevskij, op. cit., p. 1.

6. A. I. Sobolevskij, op. cit., p. 6.

7. A. I. Sobolevskij, ibid.

the Bulgarian and Serbian languages. The history of the literary languages of these two Balkan Slavic states is closely related to that of the two nations, involving the complex relationships between nationality and nation-state organization, and between regional dialects and literary languages, as well as the mutual influence of the Serbian and Bulgarian cultures of the 14th century.

1.1.2. The enormous territorial expansion of the Bulgarian state in the 13th century, during the reign of the Tərnovo king Ioan Asén II (1218-1241)[8] did not immediately bring about the flowering of Bulgarian literature[9]. The Bulgarian culture reached the peak of its development in the time of Bulgaria's greatest territorial losses, during the reign of the Tərnovo king Ioan Alexandər (1331-1371)[10]. But the cultural expansion in Tərnovo had its roots in the enlarged empire of the 13th-century Bulgarian kings, who gave vast wealth to the Church and the monasteries all over their newly-acquired territories. The only surviving evidence from the time of King Ioan Asén II of such heavy in-

---

8. V. Zlatarski, Istorija na bəlgarskata dəržava prez srednite vekove, III, Sofia, 1940, p. 323-324.
I. Dujčev, Car Ivan-Asen II, Sofia, 1941, p. 1-53.
, Prinosi kəm istorijata na Ivan-Asenja II, SpBAN, LXVI, 1943, v. 3, p. 168-169.

9. P. Dinekov, Literaturnijat život prez XIII v., Istorija na bəlgarskata literatura, I, Sofia, 1963, p. 254.

10. Ju. Trifonov, Despot Ivan-Aleksandər i položenieto na Bəlgarija sled Velbəždkata bitka, SpBAN, XLIII, 1930, p. 61-91.

vestments in the cultural and spiritual life of Bulgaria is the Church of the Forty Holy Martyrs in Tərnovo. But, as can be seen from their gramoty, later kings, especially those of the 14th century, gave most generously to the Church and its institutions[11].

The two centuries (11th - 12th) of Byzantine secular administration in the Balkan peninsula deprived the Slavic culture of any sponsorship from the central authorities. Then, in the 13th century, when Bulgaria expanded again under the Second Empire to encompass almost the entire peninsula, Bulgarians and Serbians worked together in the monasteries and other centers of culture to reshape the Slavic literature and literary language. A similar unity appeared later, in the rise of the Serbian culture of the late 14th and early 15th centuries: from the battle of Velbəžd (today's Kjustendil) on June 28, 1330, to the fatal defeat by the Turks at Černomen (near Adrianopolis) on September 26, 1371, half of the Bulgarian lands were part of the Serbian kingdom of Stefan Dečanski, his son Stefan

---

11. An example of such generosity to the Church is the "Virgino Gramota" of King Konstantin Asěn (before 1277) to the monastery of St. George Gorgos. For details, see:
G. A. Il'inskij, Gramoty bolgarskix carej, Moscow, 1911 (photoreprint: London, 1970), pp. 7-8, 14-21.
G. Balasčev, Səštinski li e xrisovulət na car Konstantin Tix (1258-1277)?, Minalo, II, Sofia, v. 5-6, 1911, p. 178-179.
P. Petrov, Kəm vəprosa za avtentičnostta na Virginskata gramota i dostovernostta na sədəržaštite se v neja svedenija, GSU Fil.-ist. fak., v. I, 2, Sofia, 1958, p. 171-175.

Dušan (1331-1351) and their heirs[12]. In the centers of
learning and literary production of King Dušan's Serbia,
both Bulgarians and Serbians must have taken almost equal
part. The favorable treatment of Bulgarian scholars in
Serbia must have been assured after 1332 by the presence in
the palace of a queen of Bulgarian royal origin - King
Dušan's wife Elena was the sister of the Tərnovo king, Ioan
Aleksandər[13]. Of how little importance were national
differences among the Balkan peoples of the second half of
the 14th century, may be judged from an example in the
Vatican copy of the Manasses Chronicle:

> During the reign of this King Constantine
> [Constantine IV of Byzantium, 668-685], the
> Bulgarians crossed the Danube and, after defeating
> the Greeks, took from them the land where they are
> still living today. Earlier, the name of this
> land was Moesia. But because they were multiply
> numerous (sic!), they filled not only (the land
> on) this side of the Danube, but also (the land)
> all the way to Drač [today's Dures] and even
> further down, for the Wallachians, Serbians and
> the rest are all one and the same[14].

While there must have been distinct structural
differences between the spoken language of the Bulgarians

---

12. I. Dujčev, Bolgarskie licevye rukopisi XIV
veka, Bolgarskaja miniatjura XIV veka (M. V. Ščepkina, ed.),
Moscow, 1963, p. 8.

13. Bəlgarska Akademija na Naukite, Istorija na
Bəlgarija, v. I, Sofia, 1961, p. 223.

14. I. Dujčev, ed., Letopista na Konstantin
Manasi, Sofia, 1963, p. 249.

and that of the Serbians[15], the differences in the two literary languages are mostly reflected in the orthography (due to different phonological systems and to different schools and traditions), while the differences in the grammar are very small. The above statement may seem unexpected, since such a belief is not shared by those Slavists who work in the field of Bulgarian historical grammar. But these scholars have never offered any explanation for the most curious development in the nominal-declension system of Middle Bulgarian: on the one hand, the entire nominal declension moved rapidly toward analytism (a three-case system of nominative, accusative and dative) - a process first observed in the Classical OCS texts, and completely demonstrated in the gramoty of the 15th century[16]; on the other hand, all Middle Bulgarian texts give

---

15. The Serbian writer of Bulgarian origin, Konstantin Kostenečki, refers to two distinct languages, the Serbian and the Bulgarian, in his treatise On the Letters. See:

V. Jagić, Codex Slovenicus Rerum Grammaticarum (photoreprint), Munich, 1968, p. 203.

16. I. Duridanov, Pɘtjat na bɘlgarskija ezik ot sintetizɘm kɘm analitizɘm, BɘlgEz, VII, 1957, 1, p. 5-8.
_____, Kɘm problemata za razvoja na bɘlgarskija ezik ot sintetizɘm kɘm analitizɘm, GSUFil.fak., v. LI, 1, 1955, p. 87-272.

K. Mirčev, Po vɘprosa za naj-rannite primeri na analitičen datelen padež v bɘlgarskite pametnici, Ezikovedski izsledvanija v čest na akademik Stefan Mladenov, Sofia, 1957, p. 37-46.

S. B. Bernštejn, Razyskanija v oblasti bolgarskoj istoričeskoj dialektologii, v. I, Moscow-Leningrad, 1948, 368 pp.

E. V. Češko, Istorija bolgarskogo sklonenija, Moscow, 1970, 319 pp.

numerous examples of "new" case endings for the "dying" (or already "dead") cases, strikingly reflecting the actual historical development of the nominal flexion of the Serbo-Croatian language. These two processes are not mutually exclusive: the disappearance of certain grammatical categories in the living Bulgarian dialects helped determine the great influence of those same categories where they existed, in the neighboring living Serbian dialects. It is only regrettable that, apparently, no serious studies on the mutual influence of Serbian and Bulgarian have ever been conducted.

So far, it is almost impossible to use lexical items as diagnostic forms in determining the national origin of certain South Slavic texts. The fact that a word in a 14th-century writing is registered today only in a dictionary of modern Bulgarian dialects does not prove tha the word does not exist in some unrecorded Serbo-Croatian dialect of today, nor does it prove that this word has always existed in Bulgarian or that it never existed elsewhere. The picture is further obscured by the existence of a wide belt of transitional Bulgaro-Serbian dialects: in modern South Slavic dialectology, the assignment of a certain dialect to either the Serbian or the Bulgarian language is made on the basis of extralinguistic and disputable linguistic factors -- the national identity of the dialect's speakers. It is quite reasonable to

believe that a similar situation has always obtained in the
Balkans, although the belt of transitional dialects may have
had different geographic distributions at different times.
We do not reject a priori the necessity of searching for a
large number of words which can be useful in determining
the Bulgarian or Serbian provenance of a medieval text; at
the present moment, however, such a list of diagnostic words
does not exist, and its compilation will be possible only
after the publication of complete dictionaries of Old and
Middle Bulgarian and Old Serbian, and after a thorough investigation of the lexical wealth of the South Slavic dialects of today. Until then, any effort in this direction
should be extremely cautious, and the results only tentative[17].

The problem of the syntactic differences between
Old Serbian and Middle Bulgarian is still an area untouched
by Slavists. However, certain syntactic "Balkanisms" in the
Bulgarian linguistic area, such as the "double object", the
replacement of the infinitive by "да-constructions", the
use of хотѣти for affirmative future and of не имѣти for
negative future, etc., could be successfully used as diagnostic features, provided they found their way into the

---

17. At the end of the last century, A. I.
Sobolevskij prepared a short list of words, showing the
national origins of Church Slavic texts. See:
    A. I. Sobolevskij, Russkie zaimstvovannye slova
(Litografirovannyj kurs), St. Petersburg, 1891, 401 pp.
    Since then, this list has been widely used by
textologists as a reliable set of diagnostic words (cf. 2.4.
and 2.4.1.).

literary language[18]. The time of first penetration of such features into the Bulgarian literary language is considered to be much later than it actually was (see our discussion in 4.4.2.)

Practically, it is impossible to decide the Bulgarian or Serbian origin of a literary work of the period 11th - 14th centuries when certain phonetic, orthographic, lexical and syntactic features of both languages are present in the copies. In such cases, it seems that the best a researcher can do is to identify the manuscript as of mixed Bulgaro-Serbian recension. The number of such manuscripts in libraries and museums all over the world is substantial[19]. An interesting example of how difficult it is to decide the national origin of a text, is the history of the study of the Eremitical Homilies by Isaak the Syrian. In the description of the 16th-century Russian copy of these Homilies[20] (Sinod. # 131), Gorskij and Nevostruev used for comparison a Serbian copy of the late 14th century (with

---

18. K. Mirčev, Za xronologijata na osnovnite balkanizmi v bəlgarskija ezik, BəlgEz, XVI, 1966, 4, p. 281-293.

19. In a letter to me, Mr. Manjo Stojanov of the Sofia National Library "Kiril i Metodij" stated that that library alone has 45 large manuscripts of mixed Bulgaro-Serbian recension.

20. A. V. Gorskij, K. Nevostruev, Opisanie slavjanskix rukopisej Moskovskoj Sinodal'noj biblioteki, II, 2, Moscow, 1859, p. 156-177. See also:
A. N. Popov, Opisanie rukopisej i katalog knig cerkovnoj pečati biblioteki A. I. Xludova, Moscow, 1872, p. 80-89.

corrections and additions from the early 15th century),

which had been brought to Russia from Mt. Athos by A. N.

Murav'ev. Since the Serbian copy was the oldest of the re-

vised texts known at that time, the two textologists wrote:

> The Athos manuscript represents the transla-
> tion of the <u>Homilies</u> by Blessed Isaak the Syrian
> in its <u>original shape</u>; as shown by the later
> additions in the margins, the new word order and
> the changes in the language itself, the original
> translation was later edited. But even after the
> editorial work, traces of the Serbian origin of
> the translation are preserved in the copies kept
> in the Synod Library[21].

Next in time was the description of a Serbian

copy of the 14th-15th century, made by L. Stojanović[22],

kept in the National Library in Beograd as # 423. Since

this copy was textologically very close to the Mt. Athos

copy, determined by Gorskij and Nevostruev to be an origi-

nal Serbian translation, L. Stojanović simply repeated their

findings. In 1905, A. I. Jacimirskij discovered, in the

library of the Rumanian monastery of Niamţu, a Middle

Bulgarian copy of the same edition of this work, without a

trace of Serbian influence[23]. This manuscript was assigned

by Jacimirskij to the 14th century, although he was not

---

21. A. V. Gorskij, K. Nevostruev, <u>op. cit.</u>,
p. 174.

22. L. Stojanović, <u>Katalog Narodne biblioteke
u Beogradu. Rukopisi i stare štampane knjige</u>, IV, Beograd,
1903, p. 139-146.

23. A. I. Jacimirskij, Slavjanskie i russkie
rukopisi rumynskix bibliotek, <u>SbORJaS</u>, v. 79, 1905, p. 721-
723.

able to determine whether or not it was older than the Serbian copies.

The Bulgarian National Library has recently received from the Archeological Museum in Sofia, a Middle Bulgarian recension of the same text, written on paper, dating from the period 1297-1311 [24]. This is the oldest copy of the same edition known so far, and in the archaic shape of the letters and absolute Bulgarian character of the language, shows itself to be a copy from a much older Bulgarian original[25].

1.2. It is widely accepted, however, that the Middle Bulgarian language played the main role in the re-shaping of the Russian literary language of the 15th century[26]. The best of the 14th-century Bulgarian books which were deposited in the Balkan monasteries or taken to Russia soon after the fall of Tǝrnovo to the Turks (in the summer of 1393)[27] were written in a language which was easily accepted in Moscow as a sample of the correct Church Slavic,

---

24. M. Stojanov, Xr. Kodov, Opis na slavjanskite rǝkopisi v Sofijskata narodna biblioteka, III, Sofia, 1964, p. 182-190.

25. M. Stojanov, Xr. Kodov, op. cit., pp. 182, 189.

26. A. I. Sobolevskij, Perevodnaja literatura Moskovskoj Rusi XIV - XVII vekov, St. Petersburg, 1903, p.6. D. S. Lixačev, op.cit., p. 106.

27. Bǝlgarska Akademija na Naukite, Istorija na Bǝlgarija, v. 1, Sofia, 1961 (2nd edition), p. 244.

and which, as such, served the Russians as a model for the purification and revision of their own older books. The linguistic reforms in Bulgaria (early 14th century) and in Serbia and Russia (late 14th - 15th centuries) were, by and large, movements towards normalization of the literary languages of these countries. In each country the process yielded different practical results; the normative rules gradually established in Serbia and Russia had to accomodate the new features of Middle Bulgarian to their own very strong literary traditions. Still, the reforms in Serbia and Russia followed the same principles as those applied in the revision of the Middle Bulgarian literary language. Sobolevskij generalizes these principles as follows[28]:

a) to separate the literary language from the spoken dialects;

b) to bring the literary language closer to that of the oldest monuments - Old Church Slavic;

c) to establish an orthography which would not reflect the phonological system of the particular national language, whenever this system conflicted with that of Old Church Slavic;

d) to introduce the contemporary Byzantine script and some writing conventions applicable to Slavic - the use of superscripts, abbreviations, stress markings, etc.;

e) to imitate as closely as possible the syn-

---

28. A. I. Sobolevskij, op.cit., p. 3-4.

tactic structure of Byzantine Greek, its rules of word-formation, and the style of the time of the Paleologues.

1.2.1. According to Sobolevskij, the most striking difference between the Russian texts of the first half of the 14th century and those of the end of the 14th and of the entire 15th centuries, is in the script. While the manuscripts of the mid-14th century are written in uncial script. (ustav) or in the old semiuncial (staršij poluustav) typical for Russian, almost all of the manuscripts of the 15th century are written in the new semiuncial (mladšij poluustav) borrowed from the 14th-century Bulgarian and Serbian texts[29]. V. N. Ščepkin studied in greater detail the problem of the South Slavic influence on the Russian script, and reached the same conclusion[30]. Later, M. N. Speranskij was able to determine not only the South Slavic influence on the Russian script, but also the independent Russian borrowing of a new style of handwriting directly from the Byzantine school - the Greek minuscule script[31]. Speranskij's contribution to the problem of this abrupt change in the Russian script[32], with no transitional styles intervening, is of great importance, for it illustrates the

---

29. A. I. Sobolevskij, op. cit., p. 1.

30. V. N. Ščepkin, Učebnik russkoj paleografii, Moscow, 1920, p. 55-58.

31. M. N. Speranskij, "Grečeskoe" i "ligaturnoe" pis'mo v russkix rukopisjax XV-XVI vekov, Byzantinoslavica, IV, 1932, p.58-64.

32. D. S. Lixačev, op. cit., p. 97.

search by the Russians of that time for innovation in their culture and literary production, even to the external form of the letters of the alphabet.

But not all contemporary scholars recognize the importance of the second South Slavic influence on the 15th-century Russian script. A typical representative of a certain group of Soviet scholars, who try to minimize any foreign influence over Russia, is L. V. Čerepnin[33]. His attitude toward the second South Slavic influence in the development of the Russian scripts is best demonstrated by his classification of Russian paleography from the beginning of the 12th century to the end of the 15th into one unified period[34]. His explanations of the appearance of the new semiuncial and of the cursive script (skoropis') are the following:

> A number of new phenomena are observed in the Russian literature of the 12th - 15th centuries. More and more, the writing acquires practical application and a businesslike character. In connection with this, new types of script — the semiuncial (approximately from the 14th century) and the cursive (from the 15th century) spread and become dominant .... The ornamentation of the manuscripts also undergoes an endless evolution of artistic styles. All the above-mentioned phenomena were connected with the wider dissemination of literature, with the greater demands for books, with the appearance of scribes who worked not only on order but also for the

---

33. L. V. Čerepnin, _Russkaja paleografija_, Moscow, 1956, pp. 190, 213-215.
N. S. Čaev, L. V. Čerepnin, _Russkaja paleografija_, Moscow, 1946, p. 75.

34. L. V. Čerepnin, _op. cit._, p. 175-280.

market[35].

When a Marxist historian makes such blunders
as: a) to talk about the 12th - 15th centuries when he
means the late 14th and the 15th centuries; b) to apply the
term "evolution" to the abrupt transition from teratological
(monstrous) illuminations to those of purely geometrical
type[36]; and c) even to invent a "free market" of supply and
demand for manuscripts in 15th-century Russia, he must feel
sure that he can offer with impunity any argument, provided
it avoids any allusion to a second South Slavic influence.

1.3. The South Slavic influence on Russian manuscript illumination is well documented[37], but which of the
Bulgarian and Serbian manuscripts influenced the Russian
style, and precisely in what features, remains an insuf-
ficiently studied problem[38]. E. F. Karskij has emphasized
the heavy dependence of the Russian art of ornamenting manuscripts on the Old and Middle Bulgarian tradition. The
latter was itself either a reflection of the Byzantine art
of the 9th-11th and again of the 13th-14th centuries, or of

---

35. L. V. Čerepnin, op. cit., p. 190-191.

36. D. S. Lixačev, ibid.

37. A. I. Sobolevskij, op. cit., p. 2-3.
D. S. Lixačev, ibid.
V. N. Ščepkin, ibid.

38. The most comprehensive study so far on the
Bulgarian art of illumination is:
M. V. Ščepkina, ed., Bolgarskaja miniatura XIV
veka, Moscow, 1963.

certain Western trends, such as the teratological style, which flourished in the Balkans in the 12th-13th centuries and was still alive in Russia (in Novgorod) even in the 15th[39]. The miniature paintings on some Middle Bulgarian manuscripts may have influenced the later history of the Russian art of miniatures, which declined at the end of the Kievan period but was again well developed from the 15th century onward[40]. Such an influence could only have occurred when Russian painters visited the Balkan or Moldavian monasteries which had Bulgarian books, for the few Bulgarian books with rich illuminations were brought to Russia, if at all, only centuries later[41].

According to some specialists, there were two Bulgarian schools of manuscript illumination: the Popular School and the Palace (Tɘrnovo) school[42]. Such an aprioristic division, although seemingly correct, does not reflect the facts. The primitively illuminated Psalter of 1337 should, according to its style, belong to the Popular School,

---

39. E. F. Karskij, Slavjanskaja kirillovskaja paleografija, Leningrad, 1928, p. 135-157.

40. E. F. Karskij, op. cit., p. 137-139.

41. S. Belokurov, Arsenij Suxanov, v. I, Moscow, 1891, p. 408.

42. N. Mavrodinov, Starobɘlgarskata živopis, Sofia, 1946, p. 153.
B. Filov, Starobɘlgarskata živopis prez XIII i XIV vek, BɘlgIstBibl, III, 1930, 1, p. 87-89.
I. Dujčev, Bolgarskie licevye rukopisi XIV veka, Bolgarskaja miniatjura XIV veka (M. V. Ščepkina, ed.), Moscow, 1963, p. 10.

although it bears an inscription from which one learns that
it was especially made for the Tərnovo king Ioan Aleksandər[4]
On the other hand, the beautiful illuminations in the Exegesis of the Four Gospels[44], made early in 1337 in the provincial town of Anchialo on the Black Sea (today's Pomorie),
should be assigned to the Popular School, since they were
not painted in the capital, Tərnovo; yet they are very clos
in style to the best of the King's own illuminated books.
An examination of the Popular School manuscripts[45]

---

43. B. Conev, Slavjanski rəkopisi na Bəlgarskata
akademija, SbBan, VI, 1916, p. 4-13.

44. The Middle Bulgarian text is a translation
from the Exegesis by Theophylactus, Archbishop of Oxrid
(11th - 12th centuries). It is bound inside a Greek antho-
logy (284 leaflets), currently kept in the Leningrad State
Public Library "Saltykov-Ščedrin" as # Greč-235. For more
information see:
I. Dujčev, Iz starata bəlgarska knižnina, Sofia,
1944 (2nd ed.), pp. xxxiii, 281, 419.

45. Acts of the Apostles (from Oxrid) of the 12th
century. See:
S. M. Kul'bakin, Oxridskaja rukopis' Apostola
konca XII veka, Sofia, 1907, p. vi-vii.

The Four Gospels by the priest Dobrejšo, from
around the year 1221. See:
B. Conev, Dobrejšovoto četveroevangelie, Sofia,
1906, 264 + vi pp.

The Bologna Psalter, from between 1218 and 1241.
See:
I. Dujčev, ed., Bolonski psaltir (photographic
reproduction of the manuscript), Sofia, 1968, 530 pp.

The Radomir's Psalter of the 13th century. See:
V. Zaxariev, Ornamentalnata ukrasa na Radomiro-
vija psaltir ot bibliotekata na Zografskija manastir,
Rodina, II, 1939, 2, p. 154-158.

(with the exception of the above-mentioned Exegesis of the Gospels) shows that all of them belong to earlier times (12th - 13th centuries) and exhibit the teratological style of illumination. This group of manuscripts cannot have influenced the Russian art of the late 14th and 15th centuries, for the Russian teratological style was by that time dying out. All illuminated Bulgarian manuscripts of the 14th century belong to a new school, which had severed all ties with the teratological style of the previous centuries. Whether a manuscript was made for the King in the capital, or for a provincial archbishop, must have had little relation to its artistic merits. The style of the era was unified, reflecting contemporary Byzantine style, and all that counted was the talent, taste and experience of the artist. The only reasonable explanation of why the King's Psalter of 1337 is not "characteristic" of the "Tərnovo School"[46] is that the illuminator was a person of limited artistic abilities.

1.3.1. The very few extant illuminated Bulgarian manuscripts from the 14th century are fully representative of the artistic taste of the time. As for the limited number of surviving manuscripts, it is impossible to judge whether all the illuminations existing in the 14th century are known today, and if not, what percentage the remnants

---

46. I. Dujčev, Bolgarskie licevye rukopisi XIV veka, Bolgarskaja miniatjura XIV veka (M. V. Ščepkina, ed.), Moscow, 1963, p. 11.

represent of the total number of illuminated manuscripts which once existed.

The most remarkable of all Middle Bulgarian illuminated manuscripts is the British Museum's Four Gospels of King Ioan Aleksandər[47], which has 365 miniature paintings[48]. Although most of the miniatures are copies from an older Byzantine gospel book, there are a few original portraits: of the Bulgarian king Ioan Aleksandər, his wife Theodora, his sons Ioan Asěn and Ioan Šišman, his daughters Keraca, Desislava and Kera Themar, and his son-in-law Konstantin, husband of Kera Themar[49].

Another exclusive example of Bulgarian illuminated manuscripts, although almost unknown, is the Tomić Psalter, kept in the State Historical Museum in Moscow, # Muz.2752[50].

---

47. We will discuss in detail this manuscript in the next chapters of the dissertation. For more information on the illuminations of the manuscript, see Chapter Three.

48. Ivan Dujčev gives the incorrect number of 352 miniatures in his article Bolgarskie licevye rukopisi XIV veka, p. 12. Most likely, he was misled by a misprint in the existing literature quoted in his bibliographical footnotes. I have a full microfilm copy of the manuscript, and counted 365 separate miniatures.

49. See the British Museum manuscript # 39627 (Parham Collection, MS XLV), pp. 2b, 3, 5b.

50. The only available description until recently of the miniatures in this manuscript is in a very hard-to-find book:
V. N. Ščepkin, Bolgarskij ornament epoxi Ioanna Aleksandra, Sbornik statej po slavjanovedeniju, posvjaščennyx prof. M. S. Drinovu, Kharkov, 1904, p. 153-158.

This manuscript was found in today's Macedonia by the Serbian philologist S. N. Tomić, who sent it to Moscow in September, 1902[51].

The best-known and most-studied Bulgarian illuminations are those of the famous Vatican copy of the Manasses Chronicle[52]. It has 69 miniature paintings; 18 of them illustrate Bulgaro-Byzantine relations, and four — relations among Russians, Bulgarians and Byzantines[53]. We can be almost certain that the Vatican's illuminated Manasses Chronicle had no influence on Russian art. The whereabouts of the book after the fall of Tərnovo (1393) until its first inventarization in the Vatican Library (1481) is unknown. But most likely, it was taken westward to Croatia or the Dalmatian coast, where two persons, writing in Latin[54]

51. AN SSSR, Dokumenty k istorii slavjanovedenija v Rossii (1850-1912), Moscow-Leningrad, 1948, pp. 181, 183, 213, 218.

52. The manuscript was photo-reproduced by the Bulgarian Academy of Sciences:
I. Dujčev, ed., Letopista na Konstantin Manasi, Sofia, 1963, 415 pp.
Unfortunately, the photoreproduction is in black and white, thus contributing little to the study of its artistic features.
For bibliographic information on the studies of the miniatures and text of the Chronicle (until 1963), see the preface by I. Dujčev, op. cit., p. v - xxxvi.

53. I. Dujčev, Miniatjurite na Manasievata letopis, Sofia, 1962,138 pp.

54. I. Dujčev, Latinskite nadpisi po Vatikanskija prepis na Manasievata Xronika, Izvestija na Bəlg. arx. institut, VIII, 1934, p. 369-378.
_____, Letopista na Konstantin Manasi, Sofia, 1963, pp. xii - xiii, 412-415.

strongly colored by Italian, explained on each page the content of the text and identity of the personages shown in the
miniatures. In Croatia the manuscript formed part of the
library of the bishop of Modros, Nikola Katarski, although
it is not known when he acquired it. Together with some
other books belonging to the bishop, the Manasses Chronicle
was given to the Vatican Library sometime between the years
1475 and 1481[55]. But the Middle Bulgarian translation of
the Manasses Chronicle was well known in Russia through a
Serbian copy. In a passage on Roman history, both the Tale
of the Founding of Moscow[56] and the so-called Chronograph
(First Version)[57] contain the mysterious "Russian" word
spelled ентинарий (in the former) and енътинирие (in the
latter). Credit is due the Soviet scholar M. A. Salmina
for first establishing that this word was a wrong translatior
due to misreading, of a phrase from the Greek original of
the Manasses Chronicle[58]. The corresponding Greek ἐν
Τυρρηνοῖς was written, in one of the Slavic copies, as
one word, ентинарий or енътинирие, instead of the correct

_____

55. I. Dujčev, op. cit., p. xiii.

56. M. N. Tixomirov, Skazanie o načale Moskvy,
IZ, v, 32, Moscow, 1950, p. 233.

57. Pamjatniki starinnoj russkoj literatury,
v. XXII, 1, St. Petersburg, 1911, p. 227.

58. M. A. Salmina, "Entinarij" v "Povesti o
začale Moskvy", TODRL, v. XV, Moscow-Leningrad, 1958,
p. 362-363.

*въ тирины̊. Salmina found a 17th-century Serbian copy
of the <u>Manasses Chronicle</u>[59] which must have been copied
from the same original as the above-mentioned <u>Chronograph</u>
(First Version). The Serbian copy from Novgorod has
the spelling ентинирие, and the <u>Chronograph</u> — енътинирие.
From the <u>Chronograph</u> to the <u>Tale</u> <u>of</u> <u>the</u> <u>Founding</u> <u>of</u> <u>Moscow</u>,
the word was changed into ентинары̊. I. Dujčev[60] traced
the story to the very end. The Bulgarian translator of the
Chronicle failed to understand the phrase ἐν Τυρρηνοῖς as
consisting of two words, and rendered it as е̊нтирѝние: е̊же
оувѣдѣвъ е̊нтирѝние. искоусныи знамениюмъ съмотритель, ре҇ч.
нàко градъ съ̊й глава многымъ ҄зыкѡмъ бѫдетъ...[61] (When
<u>Entirinie</u>, the experienced seer of signs, learned about it,
he said that this city will be head of many nations...").
The correct translation would have been: "When an experienced seer of signs in (the city of) <u>Tyrrenois</u> learned
about it, he said ...". All three[62] known Middle Bulgarian

---

59. The manuscript # 1437 of the former library
of the Novgorod Cathedral Church of St. Sophia, currently
kept in the State Public Library in Leningrad.

60. I. Dujčev, Odna citata iz Manassievoj
Xroniki v srednebolgarskom perevode, <u>TODRL</u>,v. XVI, Moscow -
Leningrad, 1960, p. 647-649.

61. This quotation is from the photo-edition of
the Vatican copy:
I. Dujčev, ed., <u>Letopista</u> <u>na</u> <u>Konstantin</u> <u>Manasi</u>,
Sofia, 1963, p. 138.

62. I. Bogdan, <u>Cronica</u> <u>lui</u> <u>Constantin</u> <u>Manasses</u>.
<u>Traducere</u> <u>mediobulgară</u> <u>făcută</u> <u>pe</u> <u>la</u> <u>1350</u>. <u>Text</u> <u>şi</u> <u>glosar</u> <u>de</u>
<u>Ioan</u> <u>Bogdan</u>. <u>Cu</u> <u>prefaţa</u> <u>de</u> <u>prof</u>. <u>I</u>. <u>Bianu</u>, <u>Bucureşti</u>, <u>1922</u>,
p. 73.

texts of the Manasses Chronicle repeat the same mistake (ентириние) in the original from which they were copied. In an unknown copy dating somewhere between the 14th-century Bulgarian copies and the time of the First Version of the Russian Chronograph, a scribe misspelled ентириние into ентинирие. This unknown copy must have been the source of both the Russian Chronograph (енътинирие) and the Serbian Manasses Chronicle in the copy from Novgorod (ентинирие); the spelling then became ентинарий in the Tale of the Founding of Moscow.

This excursus was necessary in order to clarify two points: first, in how complex a fashion the Bulgarian literature and language influenced those of 15th-century Russia (often through Serbian mediation); second, that it was not the beautifully illuminated Vatican copy of the Manasses Chronicle (for it contains the un-metathesized form ентириние) which was used as a prototype for the Russian Chronograph, but an unknown copy, containing the metathesized form ентинирие from which both the Chronograph and the Serbian Manasses Chronicle from Novgorod were copied.

Another little-known illuminated 14th-century Bulgarian text is the Exegesis of the Four Gospels (cf. 1.3 and fn. 44), written in May of 1337 by the monk Metodij Gemist for the Archbishop of Anchialo[63].

---

63. I. Dujčev, Bolgarskie licevye rukopisi XIV veka, Bolgarskaja miniatjura XIV veka (M. V. Ščepkina, ed.), Moscow, 1963, p. 15-16.

The last of the 14th-century illuminations is
King Ioan Aleksandər's Psalter of 1337 (also known as Sof-
ijski Pesnivec)[64]. Bulgarian art historians consider the
artistic merits of the illumination in the Psalter far below those of the other 14th-century manuscripts (cf. fn. 46).

1.3.2. A very important aspect of the Middle Bulgarian influence on the art of manuscript ornamentation in
15th-century Russia is the characterization of uniquely Bulgarian features in the style of the above-described 14th-
century manuscripts. In this respect, I. Dujčev writes:

> In addition, it is necessary to state that, while
> the Popular School still preserves relative
> originality, the official Tərnovo School reflects
> a strong Byzantine influence[65].

As has been stated above the so-called Popular
School was actually that of the Bulgarian decorative art of
the 13th century. Its originality was a relative one, the
style differing from that of its Byzantine counterpart because of the temporary severance of Bulgaria's ties with
Eastern Orthodox culture. As is known, from 1199/1200 to
1235 the official Bulgarian Church accepted the spiritual
leadership of the Pope of Rome[66]. Even after 1235, the ties

---

64. A. S. Arxangel'skij, Bolgarskij "Pesnivec"
1337 goda. Poxvala i otryvok psaltyrnogo teksta, Izv.ORJaS,
II, 1897, 3, p. 786-794.

65. I. Dujčev. op. cit., p. 10.

66. Bəlgarska Akademija na Naukite, Istorija na
Bəlgarija, I, Sofia, 1961 (2nd edition), pp. 175, 184.

of Bulgaria with the Nicaean Patriarchate were weak, since Constantinople was retained by the Crusaders (Third Crusade) until the year 1261[67]. The non-Byzantine features of the 13th-century Bulgarian ornamental style definitely represent a Catholic influence. The very teratological style was a western influence in Bulgaria. This style originated in the Catholic tradition, or more precisely, it corresponds to the early (7th-century) Roman Barbarian style. It flourished in the South Slavic area (13th century) and was further developed in Russia (end of 13th - 14th centuries)[68]. A definite proof of the Catholic influence in it is the controversial tonsure (shaved top of the head) in the self-portrait of the priest Dobrejšo in a miniature of his Four Gospels (cf. fn. 45). The Russian art historian S. M. Dimitrievič has suggested that in the picture there was not a tonsure, but a head covering of some kind, perhaps a sort of priest's hat[69]

If one writes of strong Byzantine influence on the official Tərnovo School of the 14th century, the reader may

_____

67. Bəlgarska Akademija na Naukite, op. cit., p. 207.

68. E. F. Karskij, Slavjanskaja kirillovskaja paleografija, Leningrad, 1928, p. 148.

69. S. M. Dimitrievič, Est' li tonsury na golovax svjatitelej v starom vostočno-pravoslavnom ikonopisanii? Izvestija na Bəlgarskija arxeologičeski institut, X, 1936, p. 113-128.
Of course, Priest Dobrejšo must have had a tonsure since he was a Catholic priest, not an Eastern-Orthodox one; the painting was made in about the year 1221, and the Bulgarian Church was under the Pope from 1199/1200 to 1235 (cf. fn. 66).

expect to find reference to those stylistic elements which remained uninfluenced. Such references, however, are never made by Bulgarian art historians. Further, a few obscure facts may shed copious light on the problem of the very existence of an artistic school in Tarnovo, as well as on the national character of the illuminations.

The scribe of the Vatican copy of the <u>Manasses Chronicle</u> did not originally plan to have miniatures in the book. He marked the lines for future writing on all leaflets except three which were added later: 145, 178 and 183. When the lines had already been made, something caused the scribe to change his mind, and the miniatures were painted over the marked parallel lines. Through the centuries, the paint has chipped from the scored lines, which are clearly seen in the photostatic edition[70]. The answer does not seem to be very complicated: it may be surmised that when the scribe prepared his pages for writing, there was no artist present, and no illuminations were planned. But when the scribe reached the middle of page 14 (the back page of the seventh leaflet), a talented painter appeared and the first miniature was painted. Then, the next miniatures followed: after four pages, then after one, then after another four, etc. The initial leaflet has the images of Jesus Christ and the chronicler Manasses, as well as a

---

70. These lines are on pp. 1, 3, 4, 14, 19 etc. of the black-and-white photo-publication of 1963.

realistic full-length portrait of King Ioan Aleksandər. The King's portrait here very much resembles that in the British Museum's Four Gospels; we can expect them to be good likenesses, because, since both books were made for the personal library of the King, the royal portraits in them must have been drawn from life.

If the scribe Symon who wrote the texts of both the Manasses Chronicle and the Four Gospels for the King did indeed live in Tərnovo or in one of the nearby monasteries, the painters who illuminated the two manuscripts (from their styles, it is obvious that there was a different artist for each of the two) did not necessarily live in the same place — this is especially true for the illuminator of the Manasses Chronicle. Thus, considerable doubt is cast on the very existence of any set "Tərnovo School" of manuscript illumination.

The illuminations of the Tomić Psalter (cf. fn. 50 reveal significant details as to both the nationality of its artist and the existence of an artistic school in Tərnovo. V. N. Ščepkin has emphasized the Byzantine character of the illuminations: "The head-pieces (of the manuscript), beautifully executed, represent the Byzantine style of the 13th-14th centuries, which had returned to the brilliant traditions of the 10th century"[71]. Additional, linguistic evidence confirms the non-Bulgarian nationality of the artist.

---

71. V. N. Ščepkin, op. cit., p. 154.

While the text was written in Middle Bulgarian by the monk
Symon (the handwriting is identical with that of the British
Museum's Four Gospels and the Athos Služebnik[72]), the illuminations were made by an artist who did not know Bulgarian, but was able to read the Greek instructions in the lower or upper margins of the pages on which he was supposed
to draw the miniatures[73]. There are still traces of such
cursive Greek instructions on many pages. A typical example,
almost completely preserved, is on the back page of the 22nd
leaflet. In translation it reads:[74] "Put David here, standing and holding a book, looking at the sky, and on the op-

---

72. This Služebnik, incorrectly dated to the
13th - 14th centuries, is kept in the State Public Library
in Leningrad, Pogodin Collection # 37. A photocopy of leaflets 44 and 66 (the back side) is available in:
    E. F. Karskij, op. cit., p. 406-407.
    In addition to the name of the scribe on leaflet

44 (помѣнѝте гр҇ѣшнаг҃ѡ симеѡна),   which appears also in
the British Museum's Four Gospels, and the general shape of
the letters and type of spelling conventions (which might,
however, merely indicate a calligraphic school), the cursive
script of the Greek word ἀμήν   is absolutely identical to
that of the same word on p. 125 in the photo-publication of
the Manasses Chronicle; the ligature ℞ (for -тр-) has a
very individual shape - and element of personal handwriting
in the wavy line at the top of the letter т (~); here and
there at the end of a line the letter a is written cursive-
ly, with the final hook leaning downward: ℊ, etc. These features of a very individual handwriting are definite evidence
on which to attribute a number of Bulgarian manuscripts
from the middle and late 14th century, most of them written
for the King, to one person - Symon the Monk.

73. V. N. Ščepkin, op. cit., p. 218.

74. The full (or partially reconstructed) Greek
instructions and their Russian translations are given in:
    I. Dujčev, op. cit., p. 17-19.

posite side — the sky with rays streaming down from it". The miniature on this page represents exactly such a scene.

The presence of a written instruction in Greek raises the following two questions: first, if the painter was a Bulgarian, why should the Bulgarian scribe have given him instructions in Greek; second, if the painter and the scribe lived at the same place, why should the scribe have damaged his beautiful manuscript with unnecessary Greek inscriptions, when he could have given the painter very detailed oral instructions in some language common to both of them. It would seem that the only reasonable answer to these questions is that the artist did not understand Bulgarian, either in spoken or in written form, and that he lived somewhere quite distant from the place of writing. Under these circumstances, it would have been more convenient to send the book to him with written instructions in a language he was able to read and understand. Yet, this is no proof that the painter was of Greek origin; the spelling mistakes and the wrong stresses in Greek inscriptions over some of th miniatures[75] may indeed show that he was not of Greek nation ality. But the Greek Orthodox community of the 14th century was a multinational one. Since artistic ability is not con- fined to a particular national group, one cannot say any- thing more definite about the nationality of this painter than that: a) he was not a Bulgarian; and b) he was perhaps

75. I. Dujčev, op. cit., p. 19.

not Greek either (if it can be proven that his spelling and stress errors must have been made by a non-Greek).

It has been observed for two of the above-described 14th-century illuminated Bulgarian manuscripts, that the painter either arrived unexpectedly at the place where the manuscript was already being written (<u>Manasses Chronicle</u>) or received the book to be illustrated after the text had been written (<u>Tomić Psalter</u>). If these texts were written in the city of Tərnovo or in the surrounding monasteries, we definitely have no right to speak of a "Tərnovo School" of illumination. If the place of writing was the library of an Athos monastery (a possibility which should not be excluded) we have even less right to do so.

1.3.3. On the material evidence existing today, it has not been proven that there was in the 14th century a particular Bulgarian national style of manuscript illumination. And yet, one cannot exclude the possibility that some of the above-discussed illuminations may have contributed to the changes in the 15th-century Russian art of illumination. As long as the history of each individual manuscript after the destruction of the Bulgarian state is scarcely known, no firm conclusion in this direction can be drawn. One might guess that the most likely places for Russian artists to have seen these illuminations would have been the Athos monasteries (for the <u>Tomić Psalter</u> and the <u>Exegesis</u> of the Gospels), if indeed they were there in the late 14th and throughout the 15th centuries. But science has no data on this. Most influential would have been the illuminations of the Four Gospels of King Ioan Aleksandər, which was kept in Moldavia and Wallachia until 1688-1714, when it was presented to the monastery of SS. Peter and Paul on Mt. Athos[76]

1.4. Most students of medieval Russian literature note the drastic changes in style brought about in Russia by the second South Slavic influence. But in general, they have too critical an attitude towards the new style, imposing modern criteria of artistic achievement on a still medieval literature. Common are characterizations of the new style as one of "artificial literary devices"[77], and "rhetorically grandiloquent and declamatory panegyrics"[78], and of the language of the literary works as "impossibly convoluted full of verbal conceits"[79]. D. S. Lixačev is one of the very few literary historians to place the stylistic studies on 14th-century South Slavic and 15th-century Russian literature in their correct historical perspective, especially emphasizing the dependence of the style on the "particular

76. B. Conev, Istorija na bəlgarskij ezik, v. 1, Sofia, 1940, p. 196-198.

77. V. O. Ključevskij, Drevnerusskie žitija svjatyx kak istoričeskij istočnik, Moscow, 1871, p. 79.

78. N. K. Gudzij, Istorija drevnej russkoj literatury, Moscow, 1945 (3rd edition), p. 225.

79. M. N. Speranskij, Istorija drevnej russkoj literatury. Moskovskij period, Moscow, 1921 (3rd edition), p. 101.

artistic method in the literature"[80] of the time. The usual explanation of the peculiarities of the new style, is
that they arose out of the triumph and pride felt by the
South Slavic writers at the rise and successes of their respective states — and subsequently by Russian writers at
the advances of the Muscovite kingdom. Lixačev's criticism
of this historically unmotivated view is most cogent:

> A feeling by itself, no matter how strong, without
> ties to a philosophy, could not alone have deter-
> mined all peculiarities of their style; moreover,
> the very solemnity of the style of the time is
> quite questionable... this style is too dynamic,
> too saturated with the authors' lyrical digressions
> and expressions of dissatisfaction, to have been
> solemn or predetermined for the glorification of
> the state.[81].

1.4.1. The new style of the South Slavic literature is best exemplified by original works and translations
of the Hesychasts, along with new translations of the earlier
writers whom they recommended[82]. But even if the new style
spread only to the "high" literature of medieval Russia[83],
it was typical of all literary genres (including gramoty) in
14th-century Bulgaria (cf. below). The claim of Soviet lit-

---

80. D. S. Lixačev, Nekotorye zadači izučenija
vtorogo južnoslavjanskogo vlijanija v Rossii, Issledovanija
po slavjanskomu literaturovedeniju i fol'kloristike, Moscow,
1960, p. 128.

81. D. S. Lixačev, op. cit., p. 116.

82. D. S. Lixačev, op. cit., p. 133-134.
A. I. Sobolevskij, Perevodnaja literatura Moskovskoj Rusi XIV - XVII vekov, St. Petersburg, 1903, p. 15-24.

83. D. S. Lixačev, op. cit., p. 117.

erary historians (including Lixačev) that this style "a-
chieved its highest development precisely in Russia"[84],
where it was later referred to as the "weaving of words"
(pletenie sloves), is of doubtful validity. But it is definitely incorrect to state that "the connection between the
reform (of Euthymius)... and the new style of 'weaving of
words', characteristic for the 14th-15th centuries, is beyo
doubt"[85]. Here is a typical counter-example, from the 14th
century Bulgarian literary language, to the assertion of
Soviet scholars that the new South Slavic style:

    a) was confined to the "high" literature;

    b) reflected the "thirst for abstraction, the
striving to render the world abstract and to destroy its
concreteness and substantiality"[86];

    c) was created by the "reform" of the Bulgarian
Patriarch Euthymius (which supposedly took place between th
years 1371 and 1375 — cf. 2.6).

    What follows is the first sentence of a gramota
(Golden Bull) by the Bulgarian king Ioan Aleksandər (of a
genre where one does not expect to find "high style"), to t
Zograph Monastery on Mount Athos[87]. It was written in the

---

84. D. S. Lixačev, op. cit., p. 142.

85. D. S. Lixačev, op. cit., p. 114.

86. D. S. Lixačev, op. cit., p. 117.

87. G. A. Il'inskij, Gramoty bolgarskix carej,
Moscow, 1911 (photoreprint: London, 1970), p. 21-23.

year 1342 (30 years before the supposed reform of Euthymius), in the same general style as another Bulgarian gramota from before the year 1277[88]. As is apparent from the full English translation of this overextended sentence, all peculiar features of the Russian style of "weaving of words" are present here, although there is little evidence of a "striving... to destroy the concreteness and substantiality" of the world:

> This, then, was the wish of God the Father and of Our Lord Jesus Christ, by the intercession of our real and true, most immaculate and most blessed Lady and Mother of God, that there should be on the holy Mount of Athos a haven for the salvation of every Christian — and most of all, Orthodox — soul which should eagerly seek refuge there; even for this reason many righteous kings and devout princes and venerable hermits erected with loving labor holy houses, great and marvelous, and decorated and enriched them in every way: with precious stones and pearls and gold and silver,with possessions and much other property, movable and immovable, that those being and residing in those most noble and godly houses should have an abundance and plenitude, so that they might sing and praise the one God, glorified in the Trinity, and His most immaculate and universally praised Mother, and also that they might mention in prayer the Orthodox, Christ-loving and eternally remembered kings and other blessed donors, and every Christian nation, for the builders who are found in that holy place are not only of one nation, or of two, but because there is a common salvation in it for those who seek it, a common place has been given those who endowed it, and houses are to be found from every Orthodox nation and people, first and outstanding among them the Greeks and Bulgarians, then the Serbians, Russians, and Iberians, each of

---

88. This is the undated gramota (Golden Bull or chrysobull) of the Tərnovo King Konstantin Asěn Tix (1257-1277), to the Monastery of St. George Gorgos, published by: G. A. Il'inskij, op. cit., p. 14-21. See also fn. 11.

them having remembrance according to his labors,
and even more, his zeal.
(For the full Middle Bulgarian original, see
Appendix One.)

In the space of one sentence, the Middle Bulgarian
author of this _gramota_ uses such figures and tropes as:

     a) Synonyms: сѫщимъ и̑ прѣбыва́ѫщиимъ; быти въ
довѡ́льство и̑ изобі́лие; и има́н'ми и̑ инѣми правдами многыми;
сѫщыѫ и̑ истиньныѫ... бг҃ородителницѫ.

     b) Words expressing concepts in a relationship
of genus and species: и̑ православныѫ и̑ хрї́столюбивыѫ цр҃ѧ;
въсѣкои дш҃и хрї́стиан'стѣи паче же православнѣй.

     c) Words which, although not synonyms, when used
in a string all allude to a concept embracing all of them:
и̑ оукрасї́шѫ и̑ ѡ̑бѡгатишѫ въсѣко; поѫ́щихъ и̑ славѧ́щихъ;
вл҃чцѫ и̑ бг҃ородителницѫ.

     d) Epithets expressed by compound adjectives:
цр҃ие блг҃очестивии. и̑ бг҃олюбивии вельмѫ́же. и̑ прѣподобнии
инѡ́ци.

     e) Series of epithets, usually in gradation,
expressed by compound adjectives: православныѫ и̑ хрї́сто-
любивыѫ и̑ приснопамѧтныѫ цр҃ѧ; прѣчистыѫ и̑ прѣблг҃ословеныѫ
... бг҃ородителницѫ.

     f) Apposition, expressed by short adjectives, to
substantives with a long-adjective modifier: дѡмовы ст҃ыѫ
велики и̑ дивны.

     g) Paraphrase: дѡмовы ст҃ыѫ = monasteries.

h) Antithesis: не ѿ є̓дïного рѡда тъчих̛ и́ли ѿ
двою...

i) Lexical anaphora: нх̛ понеже о̓бьщее спс̄ение въ
немъ є̓ст' и́скахщиимъ ю̈. о̓б'ще бѿ бъıстъ и́ мѣсто благоволь-
ствоухщиимъ.

None of the above-mentioned tropes were new to
medieval Bulgarian writers. The first detailed translation
of an article on stylistics by Choiroboscus was included in
King Symeon's Almanac (Izbornik Svjatoslava). What was new
for the 14th century, in comparison with the 9th to 11th
century, was the heavy use of tropes in the texts. This was
not an original South Slavic feature, but merely reflected
the style of the medieval Byzantine literature. Even the
style of the Bulgarian and Serbian gramoty, with their for-
mulae, shows them to be simply "copies from analogical
works of Byzantine diplomacy"[89].

1.4.2. The difficult question arises, why did the
early Church Slavic (or particularly - the Old Bulgarian)
literature not reflect the Byzantine style contemporary to
it? I. P. Eremin offers the most convincing explanation, in
his report to the Fifth International Congress of Slavists

---

89. G. A. Il'inskij, op. cit., p. 88.

90. I. P. Eremin, O vizantijskom vlijanii v
bolgarskoj i drevnerusskoj literaturax IX - XII vv., Slavjanskie literatury (Doklady sovetskoj delegacii. V Meždunarodnyj s"ezd slavistov), Moscow, 1963, p. 5 - 13.

in Sofia, 1963[90]. Comparing the Byzantine literature, especially of the 11th - 12th centuries, with that of Kiev in the same period, Eremin notes the huge production and the increasing volume of secular works in Byzantium, which "has no trace in ancient Russia of that time"[91]. Eremin is basically right in stating:

> Even a cursory overview of the translated litera-
> ture (of the 9th - 12th centuries) demonstrates
> that the Bulgarian and Russian bookmen of this
> time, in the selection of materials for transla-
> tion, showed preference to authors from the 4th -
> 6th centuries, the classical writers of church
> literature[92].

Eremin emphasized that the early Slavic translator had first to retrace the development of Byzantine liter-ature before they could undertake the task of translating their Greek contemporaries, writers of a later stage, whose style was more difficult for the newly-baptized Slavs to comprehend[93]. D. S. Lixačev's criticism of this view[94] is quite vague, and unsupported by evidence. His objection that the Slavic translators could not have been aware of the chronological development of Christian literature[95] can be

---

91. I. P. Eremin, op. cit., p. 5-6.

92. I. P. Eremin, op. cit., p. 8.

93. I. P. Eremin, ibid.

94. D. S. Lixačev, Drevneslavjanskie literatury kak sistema, Slavjanskie literatury (VI Meždunarodnyj s"ezd slavistov. Doklady sovetskoj delegacii), Moscow, 1968, p. 15-19.

95. D. S. Lixačev, op. cit., p. 17.

neither sustained nor refuted; however, it overlooks the possibility that the Byzantine teachers of the early Slavic Christians took an active part in the selection of books and establishment of priorities for translation.

Only by accepting Eremin's explanation of the stages through which Slavic Christian literature had to pass in order to reach the level of its Greek contemporary, can one understand the great delay in stylistic innovation in medieval Slavic literature. The style of early Christian literature was determined by its content: the message, not the form, was of paramount importance. Byzantine Greek literature of the 9th - 14th centuries had essentially different goals: to dwell on the now-familiar biblical and historical tales, elaborating the form of the narrative while preserving the content unchanged. Variety and detail served the interest of generality, not particularization: objects were described by enumerating their immanent properties; actions and states, by listing their nuances in order of increasing or decreasing intensity. This view is borne out by observations[96] on the interrela-

---

96. All quotations given here are from the Manasses Chronicle - from the photoreproduction of the Vatican copy:
    I. Dujčev, ed., Letopista na Konstantin Manasi, Sofia, 1963, 415 pp.
    The page numbers indicated here are those of the manuscript, not of the book. All quotations are compared with the texts of the Tulcea and Moscow copies of the Chronicle, published by I. Bogdan (op. cit.). However, Bogdan's references to the Vatican copy are often inaccurate, thus casting some doubt on his readings of the other texts which he uses.

tion of content and form in the Manasses Chronicle.

The Chronicle begins with the biblical story of the creation, which must have been well known to all Christians in 12th-century Byzantium. But the author uses this obligatory part of any medieval world history to reveal his poetic abilities. While Genesis I.16 simply says[97]:

> And God made two great lights; the greater light to rule the day, and the lesser light to rule the night; he made the stars also;

in the Vatican copy of the Manasses Chronicle this episode is told in 51 lines[98] and includes the Greek names for the planets. At the end[99], the author expresses his exaltation at the fruit of God's labors:

> Even such a flowery colorfulness adorned the sky. Even such a many-faced and joyful, fair - faced beauty fitted the heavenly countenance, and made the sky a new-planted garden. Its gardener (was) God; like fruit trees and shoots and multifarious flowers were the starry lights. Then when the sun began to shine and shone forth, and when the beauty of the heavens and the goodness of the day appeared, they for the first time submitted to the command of the Creator, and the fourth day, bowing down, ended. And thus was accomplished everything concerning the stars, and the sun-star ruling the day, was made. And the lunar brow illumined the night.
> (For the full Middle Bulgarian text, see Appendix Two).

---

97. Since this quotation is for illustrative purposes only, it is taken from the Holy Bible (King James Version), London, 1949, p. 7.

98. The story begins on the last line of p. 4b (wrongly bound after page 3), continues on p. 3, 3b and ends on line 4 of p. 5.

99. cf. p. 3b (line 12-23) and p. 5 (line 1-4).

It would seem harsh and unjust to describe the style of the above passage as "convoluted", "pompous" or even "solemnly rhetorical". What we deal with here is poetic style, a tenuous concept, since people of every place and time tend to have their own interpretations of it.

Novelty of content and richness of form appear to be inversely proportional in the <u>Manasses Chronicle</u>. Comparative studies of the relationship between density of information and density of stylistic devices in chapters from Roman history (relatively unknown in Byzantium) and Byzantine history (much better known in the country) are most revealing. Here (in English translation) is a typical passage from the <u>Manasses Chronicle</u> on Roman history:[100]

> <u>Tarquinius' reign, who was the fifth king in Rome after Romulus</u>: Then reigned Tarquinius, fifth after Romulus: who took the kingdom which in no way belonged to him, for it was proper for the sons of King Marcius to reign.
> <u>Tullius' reign</u>: Then reigned Tullius, the son-in-law of Tarquinius, who from childhood, as they say, and from the first age, was called Servius, for he was born of a Slave woman; "Servius" is interpreted as "slave" by the Romans. This (king) united his daughter in marriage with the son of the King, Lucius Tarquinius. Because of their common counsel and murderous intents, he, poor one, was deprived of both life and power, and by common agreement he was called Superbus; so they call, in their speech, "the proud one".
> (For the full Middle Bulgarian text, see Appendix Three.)

While this style could hardly be called impoverished, the straightforward narrative contributes to a better

---

100. cf. p. 67b (line 6-15) and p. 68 (line 1-8).

understanding and remembering of events; it strikingly resembles in its simplicity the style of the Hamartolos Chronicle (9th century). In sharp contrast is the following passage from the Manasses Chronicle[101], representative in style of the entire section on Byzantine history:

> The reign of Basil the Macedonian: This (king) soon expelled Photius from the Church and gave the seat to Ignatius. When he wanted to give wealth to the people and found the gold-keeping houses, which earlier had contained multitudes of wealth, and saw them all empty and having nothing (within) he grieved, mourned, saddened, was downhearted, and could do nothing himself, he could find no (solution) anywhere. For a king without many rich possessions is like an eagle, most ancient and most old, having neither feathers, claws nor beak. This was why Basil saddened and mourned, since King Michael had spent all, giving it away to entertainers, together with his companions in play and feasting.
> (For the full Middle Bulgarian text, see Appendix Four.)

1.4.3. The new style typical of South Slavic literature fully reflects the Byzantine style dominant after the firm establishment of Christianity. It is so far impossible to date the penetration of features of this style into South Slavic literature, because of inadequate dating of the translations. The Chronicle of Constantine Manasses, for example (born in the first half of the 12th century, died 1187) is believed to have been translated in Bulgaria between 1335 and 1340[102]. But the extremely correct

---

101. cf. p. 163b (line 7-12) and p. 164 (line 1-13).

102. Ju. Trifonov, Beležki kəm srednobəlgarskija prevod na Manasievata xronika, Izvestija na Bəlgarskija arxeologičeski institut, II (1923-24), p. 159.

usage of the cases, even where two words in grammatical
agreement are remote from each other within the sentence,
suggests that the date of the Bulgarian translation was in
fact considerably earlier[103].

The Bulgarian translation of the <u>Manasses</u> <u>Chroni-</u>
<u>cle</u> exemplifies superbly the features of this Byzantine
style, which later became known as that of the second South
Slavic influence in Russia. The discussion which follows is
based on the <u>Manasses</u> <u>Chronicle</u>, because it represents the
12th-century Byzantine style (antedating by some two centuries the works of the Hesychasts, by which it can thus
safely be considered uninfluenced), and because, belonging
to a historical genre, it is outside the realm of hagiography
(to which some Soviet scholars limit the domain of this
style, cf. 1.4.1.).

1.4.3.1. The author of the <u>Manasses</u> <u>Chronicle</u>
exploits the richness of his lexicon, and the translator is
obliged to do likewise, insofar as his language permits. He
apparently follows firmly-established tradition in calquing
from the Byzantine Greek. A variety of lexical devices are
used:

a) Synonyms in the strict sense are not much used,
but they do appear, either in parallel phrases or together
as modifiers of one word: й смѣриши льва и тигрѣ. оукротиши.

---

103. See also I. Dujčev's preface to the photo-
edition of the Vatican copy of the <u>Manasses</u> <u>Chronicle</u> (<u>op.</u>
<u>cit.</u>, p. vi-vii).

(p. 8b) - 'and you will quiet the lion, and make quiet the
tiger'; й оу́мѫчи <u>троудными</u> й <u>тѫшкыми</u> дѣланми. (p. 10b) -
'and he made (them) suffer with difficult and heavy labors';
дрѣво... <u>блг̅овонно</u>... и <u>сладкоѧ́ханно</u> (p. 6) - 'tree...good-
odored...and sweet-smelling'; говѧда <u>крѣмѧщи</u>. конѧ
<u>питаѧ́щин</u> й воловы роснаа пажитъ. (p. 4b) - 'the dewy
meadow, feeding cattle, feeding horses and oxen'; й вьсѣ
потопаахѫ глѫбокотѫчными дъжды, й въ водахъ и́здыхаахѫ й
лютѣ <u>помираахѫ</u>, и водами <u>своѧ</u> ‖ <u>дш̅ѫ</u> издаваахѫ. (p. 12b-13)
'and all were drowned by "deep-large" rains, and expired in
the waters, and bitterly died, and because of the waters,
gave up their souls'; вьсѣ въ коупѣ <u>сълиашѫ</u> <u>сѧ</u> й <u>смѣсишѫ</u>
<u>сѧ</u> вьсѣ. (p. 12b) - '(they) all together merged and mixed';
ня́ко же оу́бѡ <u>ви́дѣ</u> е̇го й <u>ȣ́зрѣ</u> (p. 18b) - 'but when he saw
him and saw (him)'.

    b) Most frequently employed are words referring
to concepts of which one is a more general case of the other
ѿ вьсѣхъ оу́ѡ̀ <u>насыщайта</u> <u>сѧ</u> й ѿ вьсѣхъ <u>питаита</u> <u>сѧ</u>.   (p.
9) - 'from all of them eat your fill, and from all feed
yourselves'; я́доста ѡ̀ба ѿ <u>плода</u>, й причѧстиста сѧ <u>овощию̇</u>:
(p. 10) - 'They both ate of the fruit and partook of the
fruit'; яко ѡ́дежда бисриемь ѡбнизана и златотъканаа <u>риза</u>.
(p. 3) - 'like a garment sewn with pearls and a robe woven
in gold'; <u>злотворивыѧ</u> й <u>нечьстивыѧ</u> тъщааше сѧ оу́цѣломѫдрѣти
(p. 12) - 'he tried to make chaste the evil-doing and dis-
honorable ones'; <u>боготворити</u> начѧтъ й <u>чьсти</u> стихї́ѧ. (p. 12)
- '(he) began to deify and to honor the elements'.

c) Very commonly used, also, are strings of words
denoting close but not identical concepts. The words in such
a string delimit jointly one, more general, concept, for
which there is often no corresponding word: ни веслъ и҆мѣѧ,
ни кръмилъ, ни вѣтрилъ. (p. 13) - 'having neither oars, nor
rudders, nor sails'; и҆ на ничьсо же ѡ҆злобившааго е҆го ни
о҆скръбивша, възлоǁжити мышлѣаше длани о҆бииствныѧ. (p. 11-11b)
- 'and on (him who) had in no way provoked him or offended
him, he thought to lay murderous hands'; рѣкы же ѡ҆нꙑ гласѡ҆мъ
и҆ ѕꙗзыкѡмъ си҆рскыимъ нарицаѧт сѧ: фисѡ҆нъ, и҆ геѡ҆нъ; (p. 7) -
'Those rivers are called in the Syrian voice and tongue
Pison and Gihon'; е҆лико же чѧстина ѡ҆врьзааше сѧ листвию,
вьсиаваахꙗ шипкомь доброты. и҆ криномь съвтѣше сѧ бѣлость.
(p. 6b) - 'As soon as the fullness of the foliage had opened
itself, the beauties of the brier roses shone forth and the
whiteness of the lily shone'; кронъ модрѣше сѧ ꙗ҆ко
а҆кинθовъ зракъ· ꙗ҆ко кринъ бѣлѣаше сѧ зевсь· а҆р же ꙗ҆ко
ѡ҆гнь· ꙗ҆ко шипокъ чрьвленыи, сл҃нце сиаше, ꙗ҆ко бѣлоцвѣтнаа
а҆галида, съвтѣше сѧ денница· ꙗ҆ко цвѣтъ чрьмнозрачныи е҆рмие
бльщаше сѧ· наркисъ добролиствень, ꙗ҆влѣаше сѧ лоуна· (p. 3b)
- 'Cronos gleamed pale like the image of a hyacinth; like a
lily Zeus gleamed white; Aries (was) like fire; like a red
brier rose the Sun shone; like a white-blossomed cowslip
shone the Morning Star; like a red-showing flower Hermes
blazed; like a good-leaved narcissus appeared the Moon';
злато же ѡ҆но нескврьнно, и҆ съвтѧше сѧ и҆ бльщꙗще. (p. 7) -
'For that gold is pure, and shining and gleaming'.

Sometimes, however, the more general concept is represented by a separate word, the string of close words serving to concretize the concept: тигръ же нисходѧ ꙗко стрѣла съ <u>шоумомъ</u>· й <u>клопоты</u> творѧ й <u>роуаниа</u> тѧшкаа, вь селѣхъ сѫщиихъ прѣмо земи а̑сирїистѣи течеть. (p. 7b) - 'The Tigris, descending like an arrow with noise, and making gurglings and heavy rumblings, flows in the fields opposite the Assyrian land'.

In a few cases, this device is brought to the point of virtuosity: (таковое̑ же селение красно насадивъ и напльнивъ дрѣвесь) създа й ч҃лка вьседѣлателными дланма· о̑̃ <u>прѣстныѧ</u> й <u>бренныѧ</u> й <u>каломь</u> съмѣшеныѧ тѧготы·(p. 7b) - 'He also created Man, by his all-doing hands, from earthy and clayey material mixed into mud.' The interplay of words and concepts in this sentence is complex. Clay (брение) and earth (прѣсть) have a species/genus relationship, since clay is earth but not all earth is clay; since any earth can be turned into mud by adding water, mud is a different state (not a different species) of earth.

Occasionally, almost all the words in one clause bear to those in another clause the relation of general to specific: тогда звѣзднѫж нб҃о добрѫтѫж просвѣти сѧ· ꙗко о̑дежда <u>бисриемь</u> <u>ѡбнизана</u> и златотъканаа риза· й ꙗко <u>тъканица</u> <u>оу̑крашенаа</u> <u>синаѭщиимъ</u> <u>камениемъ</u>: (p. 3) - 'Then the heaven shone forth with starry beauty, like a garment sewn with pearls and a robe woven in gold, and like a fabric embellished with shining gems.'

d) Paraphrase is extensively used: коснѫ же сѧ сего реброу, спѧщоу. зиждитель и̇ вьзѧть е̇. (p. 9) - 'The Creator (God) touched the rib of this sleeping one (Adam) and took it'; старыи и̇ злосъмрътныи ро̑доуначѧлникъ, (p. 10b) - 'the old and mortal ancestor of the race (Adam)'; и поставль е̇демсцѣи̇ добротѣ пръвожителѣ, ѿ всѣхъ и̇сти о̇вощїи повелѣ дрѣвныхъ• кь садоу же разоу́мномоу ни рѫкоу приложити• (p. 8) - 'And having put the two first inhabit- ants (Adam and Eve) in the beauty of Eden, He commanded them to eat of the fruits of all the trees; but not even to reach out a hand to the tree of knowledge'; ѿ земноро́днаа и̇ е̇дема сего пръвожителѣ• (p. 9) - 'O, earth-born and first inhabitants of this Eden (Adam and Eve)'; разоумѣ же сиѧ̇ насадитель добросадныхъ дрѣвесъ, (p. 10b) - 'The Planter of "good-fruit-tree" trees (God) understood these things'; и̇ на... е̇го... вьзло‖жити мышлѣаше длани о̇бииствныѧ. (p. 11 - 11b) - 'And he...thought to lay murderous hands on (to kill) him.'

e) Tautology appears in several forms. The sim- plest is the repetition of the verb as the corresponding verbal noun: аще бѡ сего тъкмо̑ вькоусита, падение падета великѡ. (p. 9b) - 'For if you even taste this, you will (both) fall a great fall.'

When a certain word is repeated in the same form, an emotional effect is being sought: вь сихъ оу̇бѡ оу̇спѣ а̇дамъ, нѫ горкымъ съномъ. съномъ, начѧтькъмъ низврьженню и вьсегоубителныѧ враждꙑ• (p. 9) - 'And soon Adam fell asleep,

but with a bitter sleep, a sleep (which was) the beginning
of (his) down-casting and of all-destroying emnity'; видѣ
же ѡна плодъ, и бѣше плодъ красенъ: радостенъ бѣ видѣниемь·
и добръ вь снѣдъ· (p. 9b) - 'She saw the fruit, and the
fruit was beautiful; it was gladdening to the sight and good
to be eaten'.

When the same verb is repeated, it is in
two different forms: раздѣлѣѫ раздѣлилъ ѥстъ сиждителъ
дръжаⅡвѫ твоѫ· (p. 21-21b) - 'dividing, the Creator has
divided your realm'.

It would seem that this was such an expected
device that it even occasioned an error by the scribe of the
Vatican copy: despite the resulting grammatical disagree-
ments, he interpreted the verb помазааше as показааше,
under the influence of the first verb in the sentence,
показа: показа сего Ⅱ сатана, и прѣльстнѫѧ чашѫ показааше
[=помазааше] оуслаждаѫщимь медомь прѣльстнымъ. (p. 9b) -
'Satan showed (her) this, and showed [=spread] the cup of
temptation with tempting, sweetening honey.'

The same verbal root can be repeated in the same
form (e.g. in the aorist), but with prefixes which make the
respective meanings very different: и покры вьсѧ вьрхы
глѫбокодолныихъ горъ· съкры же лице земное, и покры нивиа·
(p. 12b) - 'and (the rain) covered all the peaks of the
deep-glenned mountains, and hid the earth's face and covered
the fields'; чрѣвооугодникъ мѫжъ и пищолюбивъ· блѫдникъ и
женолюбивъ· иже ꙗко женѫ сътворивъ себе и съ женами

затворивъ· пишаше лице свое й почрънѣаше вѣждѫ своѫ. (p. 18)
- 'a gourmand and a food-loving man, a rake and woman-loving,
who having made himself like a woman and locked himself in
with the women, painted his face and blackened his eyebrows'.

A frequently-used device is the repetition of a
root in simple and compound words in the same sentence:
сладкосрѣдныимъ й сладкыимъ желаниемь каплѧще. (p. 9b) -
'dripping with sweet-hearted and sweet desire'.

A more complex instance of this type is the use of
a simple root with prefix and its repetition in a compound
but unprefixed root: въсѣ съвръшеноплодна, й прѣсъвръшена
вьсѣ. (p. 4b) - 'everything giving perfect fruit, and everything most perfect'; зефиръ тиходыхателныи подыховааше ѿ
вьсѫдоу, (p. 6b) - 'the soft-breathing Zephyr breathed
(lightly) from all directions'.

For greater variety, the repeated element can
occupy any position within the compound root: тогда прѫвѣе
начѧтъ свѣтити нощь лоуннꙑи бѣлосвѣтлꙑи й свѣтоносныи крѫгъ·
скороѡбьходныи· й вьсесвѣтлꙑи, и многозрачныи, й съвръшеныи.
(p.3) - 'Then first began to light the night the white -
lighted and light-bearing lunar orb, fast-circling and all -
lighted, and much-luminous, and perfect.'

In a very few instances, when the language allows
the use of synonymous roots in compound-derivation, the
translator may employ a combination of tautology and pleo-
nasm. One observes in the text of the <u>Manasses</u> <u>Chronicle</u>
a considerable frequency of use of <u>добро</u>- for Greek εὐ-,

where the older monuments use exclusively благо-; as yet I
have not been able to date the beginning of this trend.
Occasionally one may find a sentence containing tautological
compound words, some with добро- and some with благо-:
дъши бѣ оу цр҃ѣ ми҃скаго а̇стиагѣ доброѡ̇бразна и̇ доброличн҃а̇.
благозрачна и̇ благолѣпнѣиши. (p. 21b) - 'The Median king
Astiag had a daughter fair of image and fair of face, good
of appearance and most goodly-beautiful.'

f) Neologism is intimately connected with the
very process of translation from a language with a long literary tradition such as Byzantine Greek into a lexically les
stable, younger literary language such as Middle Bulgarian.
Before a thorough lexicographic study has been made of all
Old and Middle Bulgarian texts, one can not with certainty
identify a particular word as a neologism, nor as a borrowin
from another Slavic language. Yet, certain compounds used i
the Manasses Chronicle seem nonce words, derived to fit an
unusual context. It may be presumed, until evidence is
found to the contrary, that they were never used before or
since. Such for example, are: птищоноѕі̇и за́ѧци (p. 5b) -
'bird-footed (=fleet-footed) hares' and йастрѧби соуроѡвоѩди
(p. 5b) - 'raw(-flesh)-eating hawks'.

The adjective свиножителна (neut. acc. pl.) is
used to describe the actions of a degenerate king: нѧ глѧ҃т.
йако о̇слышавше ближнии е̇го халдее̇о̇· свиножителна вьсѣчьскыи
сѧща и̇ скотна а̇сирï̇искаго цр҃ѣ· плѧсаниа любѧ́ща и̇ и́гры, и̇ жи-
вѧща йако женѫ̇... нападошѫ. (p. 19) - 'But they say that the

Chaldees close to him, on hearing of the swinish-living and
bestial (acts) of the Assyrian king, who loved dances and
games and who lived like a woman, attacked (him)'.

The substantive своеплеменникъ, however, is most
likely substituted for the existing съплеменникъ to indicate
the unique status of Moses as a father of the Jewish people:
нѫ и бж҃твныи мѡѵси житие ѡ̈стави· многѫ ѡ̈ себѣ ѡ̈ставль
жалость своеплеменникѡмъ. (p. 31b) - 'but even the godly
Moses departed from life, leaving much sorrow in his own
tribesmen'.

1.4.3.2. Many tropes are used in Middle Bulgarian
literature, but there is a certain hierarchy in their
frequency. Only those tropes which are most used will be
discussed here, and in the order of their frequency.

a) Adjectival epithets occur with almost every
substantive. The frequency of adverbial epithets is so low
as to be negligible. Although it is true that most of the
epithets refer to intrinsic, often characteristic properties
of the objects denoted by the modified substantives, some of
the epithets are very unusual and specific: ꙗкы корабникъ
неѡ̈боуреванъ вьнѫтрърⷰдоу плавааше. (p. 13) - 'inside, like
a boatman who has never seen a storm, (Noah) floated'.

The epithets denoting intrinsic, characteristic
properties are in most instances compound adjectives; if not
compound, they tend to be prefixed (прѣпьстрїи). They
generally have two root components connected by epenthetic
-о-, but they may have as many as three: росѡкапльными

цвѣтовы и многоразличными добрωзрачии. (зефиръ... подыховааше.(p. 6b) - (the Zephyr...breathed lightly) with the dew
sprinkled blossoms and multifarious lovely sights'; й дрѣво
вьсѣко прозѫбааше· доброплодно т.амо· блговонно· добросѣнⷱ-
нолиствно· добровѣтьвно· й сладкоѫханно(p. 6) - 'And every
good-fruited tree sprang up there: good-odored, with good
shady leaves, good-branched and sweet-smelling.'

      A peculiar type, very productive and thus charac-
teristic of this new style in Slavic literature, consists of
compound adjectives whose second root is that of a substantive denoting an inseparable quality or body part (compare
CSR: девушка с голубыми глазами → голубоглазая девушка,
in the absence of *девушка с глазами or *глазая девушка).
In contemporary Bulgarian, such an adjective as грѐзнообк,
although not listed in the dictionaries, is a possible formation. The adjective окѐт is listed in all dictionaries,
with the meaning 'having good eyes' or 'watchful'; there are
no examples of such adjectives in the Manasses Chronicle,
which may indicate that they were not valued as literary
epithets. Here are some typical examples of compound adjectives used as epithets: тогда й sвѣрие на земи ꙗвишѫ сѧ
страшнии· львове чѧстогривии· медвѣди· пардоси· тигри· козы
стрѣмозѫбыѧ· птищоносїи заѫци· й пси острозѫбии· й тврѣдо-
прѣсыи ѐлефантинъ· й вьсѣка птица· й вьсѣко пльзаѫщее,
ѐлико вь вѡдахъ живетъ, й ѐлико вь мори; й въ горахъ въ
коупѣ елико. (p. 5b) - 'Then fearsome beasts appeared on
the earth: thick-maned lions, bears, leopards, tigers,

hungry-toothed goats, bird-footed (=fleet-footed) hares and
sharp-toothed dogs, the hard-chested elephant, and every
bird, and every crawling thing — whether it lives in the
waters, whether in the seas, whether together in the mountains'; приводѣше са лвь зинаѫщь, юнцемь гоубитель· мед-
вѣди грозноѡци, й прѣпьстрїи пардоси· елене пьстрокожнии, й
частоѡпахыа лисица· елефандинъ тврѣдочелыи· опаⅡшиа клата,
и юнецъ роговы биѫи.   (p. 8) - 'There were brought
(to Adam) the gaping lion, destroyer of calves, ugly-eyed
bears and most spotted leopards, spotty-skinned deer and
thick-tailed foxes, the firm-browed elephant — wagging his
tail, and the calf butting with his horns.'

     b) Metaphor is an intrinsic feature of the new
style which was brought to Russia in the 14th century. It
was not then a new feature in Slavic literature — the language of the <u>Psalter</u> and of the <u>Codex Suprasliensis</u> offers
abundant examples of it — but in the newer texts this device is extended to many other genres, including the chronicle. Some of the metaphors seem to be fresh and poetic for
their time: авимелехъ же видѣвъ а весь плѣненъ быⷭ еа.
(p. 16b) - 'and Abimelech, having seen her (Sarah) was completely captivated by her'; others are suspiciously frequent,
suggesting that they had already become cliches: егда же
оубѡ испи камвисъ съмртнаа чашх, (p. 25b) - 'as soon as
Cambyses had drunk the cup of death'.

     Here are examples of various metaphors from the
<u>Manasses</u> <u>Chronicle</u>, frequently combined with other tropes

and figures: ꙗко да бѫдѫтъ сѣмѧ и ѡживление рѡдоу своемоу. (p. 12b) - 'so that they (the animals) may be the seed and revival of their own kind'; брата своего ѿдастъ съмртныимъ нѣдрѡмъ. (p. 11b) - 'to give his brother over to the bowels of death'; пожѫтъ начинанїа своего соуемѫдриа. (p. 20) - 'he harvested the deeds of his vain-thinking'; и въ вьнѧтрьнѣа ѥмоу вьнзи весь ножь. и съмрътиѧ напои и ꙗдомь погыбѣлнымъ, (p. 19) - 'and he thrust the whole knife into his entrails, and made him drink of death and mortal poison'; враждннѫ бо пещь клокощѫщѫ имѣше въ себѣ. (p. 11b) - 'For he had within himself a crackling oven of hate'; и ѹбѡ съсѫдъ своемоу злокьзньствоу, зьмиа злоносааго и стрьптиваго ѡбрѣтаеть. (p. 9b) - 'And thus (Satan) finds a vessel for his evil intents — an evil-bearing and obstinate serpent'; аще ми сѧ ѿ сего съхранита, избѣгнета жѫла съмртнаго· и пространьство наслѣдита живота бесконечнаго. (p. 9b) - 'If you two of mine keep yourselves from that, you will escape the sting of death and inherit the vastness of endless life'; и поживе вь благыихъ, и насыти сѧ хлѣба въ сытость, и ѿ зѫбовъ гладныихъ пагоубныихъ избѣже. (p. 29) - 'and he lived among the rich and always had plenty of bread, and escaped the fatal teeth of hunger'; сице живѣше слабѣ, сице оуклонил сѧ бѣ. дондеже въ ровъ себе погыбелныи низведе. и погоуби съ собоѫ и црство. (p. 18b) - 'thus he lived badly, and thus he deviated (from the Law), until he led himself down into the pit of destruction and, together with himself, lost the kingdom'.

c) Personification, like metaphor, is not new to Slavic literature, but is new to the style of the chronicle genre. Here are a few examples: пакы земно лице невидимо бы[стъ]. (p. 13) - 'the face of the earth was still invisible'; лоунное же брьвно просвѣщааше нощь.(p. 5) - 'The brow of the Moon illumined the night'; и ꙗко пра͞х плавааше на водныихъ плещохъ. (p. 13) - 'and like light dust it floated on the shoulders of the water'; зинѫти на нихъ земи молѣста сѧ ширѡкыими оусты. (p. 10b) - 'They begged the earth to yawn on them with its broad mouth.'

d) Simile is also very common in this style, but one example here will suffice: въселѣетъ въ едемъ"стѣмь добросаднѣмь селѣ· ꙗко же вь чрьтосѣ бисеръ дроугы [=драгы?] и вь мирѣ миръ. (p. 8) - 'He set (Adam) in the good(-fruit)-treed field of Eden, like another (?= a costly) pearl in a palace and (like) peace in the world.'

e) Metonymy: и трапезами тльстыми гостѣше ихъ. (p. 21) - 'and with fat tables he feasted them'.

f) Synecdoche: и вавулѡнскѫѧ покори жестокѫѧ выѧ· и мидѣстѣи сътвори дани даати крѣпости. (p. 21b) - 'and he humbled the stiff Babylonian neck, and made it give tribute to the Median power'.

1.4.3.3. Stylistic figures increase the expressiveness of the prose. Still, one syntactic device for today's prose is considered a stylistic figure is, for the medieval Slavic literary languages, entirely neutral: the joining of several successive clauses by the conjunction и.

a) Rhetorical question, exclamation, and lyrical digression are figures by means of which the medieval author expressed his conventionalized attitude toward his story. They do not increase in frequency from the older to the newer period: и̇ что многословити· ѿгна и̇хъ ѿ тѫдоу, и̇ оу̇мѫчи троудными и̇ тѧшкыми дѣланми. (p. 10b) - 'And why be verbose? He chased them from there and made them suffer with difficult and heavy labors'; се же и̇ дръзнѫ сътворити, ѡ̑ле безчл̑чнаго разума· и̇ оу̇ставъ не оу̇стыдѣв сѧ и̇хъ же боѫт сѧ и̇ звѣрие, брата своего ѿдастъ съмртнымь нѣдрѡмъ. (p. 11b) - 'And this he dared to do, woe to inhuman judgment, having no shame of the commandments — even the beasts fear them — to give his brother over to the bowels of death.'

b) Gradation may be of increasing or decreasing intensity. An example of each, in that order, follows: и̇ ѩже ѿ си҇ ни мала не боаше сѧ напасти· лютаа бо и̇ лѫкаваа и злотовориваа злоба, е̑диначе не въселила сѧ бѣ вь ср҇це е̑гω. (p. 8b) - 'And he did not fear in the least the threat of them, for the fierce and cunning and evildoing evil, however, had not yet settled in his heart'; и̇ блѧднивъ бѣ и̇ любодѣивъ, и̇ слабъ и̇ же́нхаръ. (p. 18) - 'and he was lecherous and adulterous and weak; and a girlwatcher'.

c) Antithesis can be combined with other figures, as, for example, gradation: и̇ врѣтоградъ добрѡдрѣвенъ бѣ на саждааше· не мотыками раскопавь ни рылми· ни разоравъ добротѫ прѣкрасныѧ земѧ· ни же дланьми насадителными, нѫ

- 56 -

словомъ є̓динѣмъ. (p. 6) - 'And God planted a good-treed orchard — not digging with hoes, nor with planting-sticks,
nor plowing the goodness of the most beautiful earth, nor
either with his planter's hands — but by the Word alone.'

In a few cases, a lexical antithesis can encompass
not simply two words expressing opposing concepts, but two
complete antonymous clauses: и̓ величааше сѧ б҃ъ, а̓ мѡисіи
въспѣвааше сѧ. и̓ <u>свѣтъ</u> <u>въсиавааше</u> є̓врєѡмъ веселиа. є́гиптѣны
же <u>тъма</u> <u>помрачааше</u>. (p. 31) - 'and God was glorified and
Moses was hymned, and the light of the gladness of the Jews
began to shine, and darkness obscured the Egyptians'.

A very interesting and original example is found
in the following phrase, where the height of mountain
peaks is described in terms of the depths of their valleys:
<u>върхы</u> <u>глѫбокодолныихъ</u> <u>горъ</u>. (p. 12b) - 'the peaks of the
deep-glenned mountains'.

d) The use of a semantically "empty" verb with
the verbal noun, instead of the related verb itself, in-
creases in frequency in the new style. This device was most
likely used to introduce additional modifiers, especially
ones indicating the effect of the action on its object,
which sometimes could not be expressed by adverbs: и̓ о̓у́бѡ
старыи и̓ злосъмрътныи ро̓доуначѧлникъ, и̓згнание ѿ тѫдоу
<u>лютое</u> <u>полоучивъ</u>, ‖ въсели сѧ прѣмо пи̓шномоу се́лоу. (p. 10b-
11) - 'And thus the old and "ill-mortal" ancestor of the
race, having received a bitter banishment from there, settled across from a flourishing field'; или̓ да ц҃рѣ о̓у́биетъ и̓

наслѣдитъ и̑ власть и̑ женѫ самѫѧ, и̑ли на о̑у̑сѣчение съмрът-
ное самъ ѿведенъ бѫдетъ.   (p. 24b) - 'either he will kill
the king and inherit both (his) power and (his) very wife, o
he himself will be led away to the deadly cutting-off'.

   1.4.4. The new style of Middle Bulgarian literature reflects the dominant style of the contemporary
Byzantine literature. Its characterization as a "new style"
is purely conventional, in relation to the styles of the Old
Bulgarian and of the Old Russian literature of the Kievan
Period[104]. As has been illustrated by the examples above,
none of the stylistic devices utilized in the newer literature were in principle new to the Old Slavic literatures.
But they were employed more heavily than ever before, by com
bining several tropes and figures within one, usually very
long, sentence. Medieval Christian philosophy did not
insist on strict separation of word and concept, but dwelt
on the magic strength of the word and thus encouraged the
writer to explore fully the combinatory possibilities of the
words in the language. In this respect D. S. Lixačev writes

> If one is to speak only about the style of "word -
> weaving", one should note the extremely positive
> role this style played in the art of words, in the

---

   104. It has been impossible, so far, to date most
of the translations made in Bulgaria during the period 12th-
14th centuries. A great part of those translations is known
from much later Russian copies. In addition, Russian and
Soviet philologists of this century are unwilling (or unable
to see the Bulgarian features in the late Russian copies,
which they then label as Russian translations. Even such
scrupulous Slavists as Durnovo have failed to perceive the
underlying Bulgarian features of some works (cf. 2.4.2.).

development of rich and various forms of artistic expressiveness, in the enrichment of the Russian literary language[105].

Lixačev's characterization of the style of the Middle Bulgarian literature in connection with the Second South Slavic influence on Russian literature, is the most correct and complete so far[106], with the exception of two points: a) this style was not limited only to the hagiographic genre, but spread to all genres of newly-created literary works; and b) even though fully exploited by the Hesychasts, it was not created by them, nor were their writings the best samples of it. The importation of this style into Russia had absolutely nothing to do with any "reform" by the Bulgarian Patriarch Euthymius (the question of the existence of such a reform will be discussed in 2.3, 3.2 and 3.3). This style is dominant in the Middle Bulgarian literature of the entire 14th century, and most likely of the 13th century too.

---

105. D. S. Lixačev, Nekotorye zadači izučenija vtorogo južnoslavjanskogo vlijanija v Rossii, Issledovanija po slavjanskomu literaturovedeniju i fol'kloristike (Doklady sovetskix učenyx na IV Meždunarodnom s"ezde slavistov), Moscow, 1960, p. 149.

106. D. S. Lixačev, op. cit., p. 107-128.

Chapter Two

THE IMPORTATION OF THE MIDDLE BULGARIAN LITERARY LANGUAGE
TO RUSSIA

2.1. Although, since the time of A. I. Sobolevskij's paper on the second South Slavic influence on Russian
the impact of the Middle Bulgarian language is a generally
accepted fact, the most detailed description of the
spheres of Bulgarian influence on Russian remains that of
Sobolevskij himself. He devotes only one page in his
article to the spheres of influence of the Middle Bulgarian
literary language[107] on Russian, describing some of the
features of the Middle Bulgarian literary language which
penetrated into the Russian literary language of the late
14th and entire 15th centuries.

2.1.1. The following new features, according to
Sobolevskij[108], penetrated into the Russian orthography:

   a)   the letter ѫ was reintroduced;

   b)   after a letter for a vowel, the letter a is

---

107. The term "Middle Bulgarian literary language
is not used by Sobolevskij. He uses the term Middle Bulgarian language (op. cit., p. 6). In connection with the Bulgarian influence on Russian, Sobolevskij uses such terms as:
Bulgarisms (op. cit., pp. 4,11 - fn. 4), Middle Bulgarian
manuscripts (op. cit., p. 6), Bulgarian colony in Constantinople (op. cit., p. 10) and Bulgarians on Athos (op. cit.,
p. 11).

108. A. I. Sobolevskij, op. cit., p. 3, and
also p. 1-2 for the shape of the letters.

written instead of ꙗ (своа, добраа, спасенїа);

  c) the letter ь appears at the end of a word instead of ъ, while the letter ъ appears inside a word instead of the letters ь or е;

  d) words formerly written верхъ, торгъ, etc., are instead written връхъ, тръгъ, etc.

  e) the letters θ, ѵ, -гг- (instead of -нг-, as in а҇ггелъ) are used more correctly (according to the Byzantine spelling).

  f) consonantal clusters are given a new spelling, according to the Byzantine pronunciation of that day: -мб- instead of -мп- (олѵмбъ); -нд- instead of -нт- (андонїи);

  g) some letters and letter combinations take on a new shape, e.g.: the digraph -оу- or the ligature ѹ ("uk") is consistently used for /u/; the special letter ѵ ("ižica"), different from the letter у in the combination оу, is used for /i/, generally representing ѵ in the spelling of Greek words; the letter ъɪ is always replaced by ꙑ with the first element the same as the letter "front jer" - ь; the letter ѕ is introduced not only as a numeral (previously expressed also by ҄), but in the spelling of some words (no examples are given).

  Sobolevskij's review of the orthographic changes is incomplete. He omits the reintroduction of the letter ѡ in both Greek names and Slavic words, of the letter ꙩ ("o очnoe") in Slavic words, of the letter ї (written with two dots), used mostly before a vowel or at the end of

- 61 -

a line, the reintroduction of the letter Ѱ for -пс- and of

Ѯ for -кс- in Greek names, the far more frequent use of

stress and other superscripts, and the complete absence of

the ligatures ꙛ and ꙝ [109].

2.1.2. As far as concerns the influence of the

phonological system of the Middle Bulgarian language (its

expression by the orthography) and its influence on the

Russian spelling system, Sobolevskij's remarks are far from

satisfactory. Besides the general effort to avoid Russisms,

he notes only the following peculiarities:

a) increased use of жд instead of ж, and of щ

instead of ч for the respective outcomes of *dj and *tj;

b) use of the letter ѣ instead of ꙗ. In the

older Russian writings, ѣ was used instead of e — an in-

fluence of the Galicio-Volhynian dialect;

c) interchanging of the letter ꙗ with ю, and

of ѧ with ѫ respectively, as a result of the Bulgarian

orthography. In addition, ꙗ continued to be interchanged

with ѧ in the Old Russian tradition, while the newly rein-

troduced ѫ alternated with ю (since the ligature ꙝ was

not used in late Middle Bulgarian) and with оу, as a con-

sequence of Russian phonology.

Sobolevskij, unfortunately, does not study the

orthography as a system of rules, and therefore he does not

examine the evolution in the system or the general direc-

109. E. F. Karskij, <u>Slavjanskaja kirillovskaja</u>
<u>paleografija</u>, Leningrad, 1928, pp. 172-173, 181-210.

tion of this evolution — toward more phonological or more morphemic spelling. Nor does he speculate on the reasons for introducing changes in the Russian orthography — was it merely a foreign influence, or was it a necessary part of reorganizing the Russian orthographic system and creating a new national literary language?

2.1.3. Most unsatisfactory are Sobolevskij's remarks on the influence of the grammatical system of the Middle Bulgarian literary language on Russian. Here are those few features which Sobolevskij notices:

a)   new forms in -ije for nom. sing. of Greek masculine names (василїе);

b)   extension of the suffix -ov- in the plural paradigm of the old -*u- stems (сыновомъ, сыновѣхъ);

c)   new endings for genitive of the numerals (трїехъ, пятихъ, десятихъ instead of the older три, пять, десять).

In addition, Sobolevskij lists a few lexico-grammatical changes:

a)   introduction of the preposition прѣзъ for чрезъ;

b)   introduction of new possessive adjectives еговъ, тоговъ for его, того;

c)   introduction of the newer Bulgarian form цѣфту for the older 1st sg. цвѣту.

The source of dissatisfaction is not the inadequacy of Sobolevskij's description of the features of the

Middle Bulgarian literary language which influenced the Russian literary language of the late 14th and entire 15th centuries. Sobolevskij's 14-page article was meant only as an introduction to a bibliographic study[110]. The real problem is that Sobolevskij's modest enumeration of some features of the Middle Bulgarian language has been virtually the only correct, even somewhat systematized list, known in Russian and Soviet literature for the greater part of our century[111] The three well-known historical grammars of the Bulgarian

---

110. The subtitle of Sobolevskij's book is Biblio grafičeskie materialy, and the emphasis in the chapter on the Russian literature containing new South Slavic translations is on listing the relevant manuscripts (p. 15-37).

111. A Slavist might use the obsolete works:
P. A. Lavrov, Obzor zvukovyx i formal'nyx osoben nostej bolgarskogo jazyka, Moscow, 1893, 109 pp.
S. M. Kul'bakin, Materialy dlja xarakteristiki srednebolgarskogo jazyka, v. 1, Bojanskoe Evangelie XII - XIII veka, IzvORJaS, IV, 3, p.800-868.
The excellent study of the Middle Bulgarian language of the Bologna Psalter by V. N. Ščepkin limits its interest to features expressed only in this 13th-century manuscript, and thus cannot be used as a manual of all diagnostic features of the whole Bulgarian literary language. See:

V. N. Ščepkin, Bolonskaja psaltyr'. S priloženiem semi fototipij i vos'mi cinkografii, Issledovanija po russkomu jazyku, II, 4, St. Petersburg, 1906.
In recent times, however, the literature has been tremendously enriched by the work of the Soviet Slavist E.V. Češko. See:
E. V. Češko, Istorija bolgarskogo sklonenija, Moscow, 1970, 319 pp.

language[112] give exhaustive information (although with an old-fashioned approach) on the changes that occurred in the Bulgarian language throughout the centuries. But they are not written with the special aim of comparing the development of the Bulgarian literary language with that of the literary languages of the other Slavic nations, and thus do not systematize the specific Middle Bulgarian diagnostic features. All three historical grammars of the Bulgarian language (cf. fn. 112) fail to examine the orthographic systems applied in the Middle Bulgarian manuscripts, or to see development there. All three authors on numerous occasions state that the Bulgarian literary language is a "dead language" and thus close their eyes to the changes in this language and its slow development towards a more and more normalized system at all levels of the grammar and in the orthography; their main concern is actually to follow and study the appearance of "mistakes" from the living Bulgarian dialects. Their approach was justified by the general aim of their studies — to explain the creation of the present - day Bulgarian language and to date the major changes that took place in its history. Because of this specific goal, the historians of the Bulgarian language overlook the his-

---

112. St. Mladenov, Geschichte der bulgarischen Sprache, Berlin - Leipzig, 1929, xiv + 354 pp.
    B. Conev, Istorija na bəlgarskij ezik, Sofia, I, 1919, x + 529 pp.; II, 1934, xvi +560 pp.; III, 1937, vi + 505 pp.
    K. Mirčev, Istoričeska gramatika na bəlgarskija ezik, Sofia, 1963 (2nd edition), 274 pp.

tory of the literary language in Bulgaria from the 9th to the 14th century.

2.2. The Middle Bulgarian literary language was introduced in Russia through the revised editions of the oldest Slavic religious literature in translation, newer translations of the more recent Byzantine literature, Middle Bulgarian versions of Old Bulgarian literature (for example, the treatise On the Letters by Černorizec Xrabər) and the works of some Bulgarian writers of the 12th - 14th centuries. Among the revised religious texts, Sobolevskij includes the Four Gospels, the Apostles (Acts and Epistles), the Psalter, and a long list of translations from the Old Testament, of the Church Fathers, and of Byzantine writers from the 6th - 14th centuries, including the Hesychasts, and the works of a few Bulgarian writers[113].

2.3. In explaining the ways in which Middle Bulgarian literature was introduced in Russia, Sobolevskij is extremely cautious: he places the copying done by Russians from the South Slavic originals mainly on Mt. Athos and in Constantinople and its surrounding monasteries[114], and carefully gives credit to the two Bulgarian church leaders in Muscovite Russia and Russian Lithuania, Kiprian and Grigorij Camblak, respectively[115].

---

113. A. I. Sobolevskij, op. cit., pp. 4-5, 15-37

114. A. I. Sobolevskij, op. cit., pp. 6-11, 24 - 26, 31-34.

115. A. I. Sobolevskij, op. cit., p. 12.

2.3.1. But in most of the other Russian and
Soviet writings on the subject, the second South Slavic influence is attributed mainly to the fall of Bulgaria under
Turkish domination (1293-1396) and the influx of "Bulgarian
refugees" to Russia. This belief about the mechanism of the
second South Slavic influence in Russia (and especially —
that of the Middle Bulgarian language and literature) is
exemplified in a recent typical statement by a Soviet scholar:

> Both Serbia and Bulgaria, which literarily on
> the eve of their destruction were at the zenith of
> their might, were swallowed in a short time by the
> Turkish aggressors and ceased to exist as indepen-
> dent state unions. This was exactly the time when
> the mass emigration of the Southern Slavs began,
> in which first of all fled, of course, people of
> the intellectual and generally creative vocations,
> since under the conditions of the Turkish occupa-
> tion their activity in their own country became
> unthinkable...[116].

> ...Main centers of Russian-South Slavic com-
> munication, besides the cities of North-Western
> and North-Eastern Russia, were Athos and Constan-
> tinople. At the end of the 14th century the flow
> of South Slavic refugees to Russia went almost
> wholly through intermediate points, such as the
> Slavic monasteries of Athos and Constantinople...[117].

> ...How can one envision the concrete sources
> of the second South Slavic influence in the illumi-
> nations and graphics of the Russian manuscripts?
> Beyond doubt, a very important role was played by
> those South Slavic scribes and artists who immigra-
> ted to Russia and took up permanent residence in
> the Russian cities and monasteries. In this respect

---

116. G. I. Vzdornov, Rol' slavjanskix monastyrskix masterskix pis'ma Konstantinopolja i Afona v razvitii
knigopisanija i xudožestvennogo oformlenija russkix rukopisej
na rubeže XIV - XV vv., Literaturnye svjazi drevnix slavjan
(Trudy ODRL, v. XXIII), Leningrad, 1968, p. 171.

117. G. I. Vzdornov, op. cit., p. 172.

one could hardly argue that <u>the most representa-</u>
<u>tive personality</u> is the <u>Metropolitan Kiprian</u>[118].
(All italics are mine. I. T.)

These statements must be seriously criticized as
antihistorical in all points; it is regrettable that a
philologist should write with such inadequate research in a
field which is outside his specialty. The grave historic
mistakes in it about Bulgaria will be enumerated since
some appear in similar formulations by other Slavists[119].

a)   On the eve of its destruction by the Turks,
Bulgaria was far from being at the "zenith of (its) might".
Here are the more important developments in this regard:

The Bulgarian state, after reaching the peak of
its political power under King Ioan Asěn II (1218-1241)[120],
declined, and was even temporarily conquered by the Tatars
(1298-1300)[121]. While the Bulgarian Tərnovo kingdom was

---

118. G. I. Vzdornov, <u>op. cit.</u>, p. 173.

119. See, for instance:
L. A. Dmitriev, Rol' i značenie mitropolita
Kipriana v istorii drevnerusskoj literatury (k russko-
bolgarskim literaturnym svjazjam XIV - XV vv.), <u>Trudy</u> <u>ODRL</u>,
XIX, Moscow-Leningrad, 1963, p. 210-216.
V. Mošin, O periodizacii russko-južnoslavjanskix
literaturnyx svjazej X - XV vekov, <u>Trudy</u> <u>ODRL</u>, XIX, Moscow -
Leningrad, 1963, p. 103-105.
L. V. Čerepnin, <u>Russkaja</u> <u>paleografija</u>, Moscow,
1956, p. 213.
V. A. Desnickij, ed., <u>Istorija</u> <u>russkoj</u> <u>litera-</u>
<u>tury</u>, v. I, 1, Moscow, 1941, p. 127.

120. Bəlgarska Akademija na Naukite, <u>Istorija</u> <u>na</u>
<u>Bəlgarija</u>, v. 1, Sofia, 1961 (2nd edition), p. 181-185.

121. Bəlgarska Akademija na Naukite, <u>op. cit.</u>,
p. 218.

able to unite some lands north of the Danube — southern Bessarabia to the Dnestr River (1300)[122] and part of Thrace along the Black Sea coast (1307)[123]—the northwestern region of Bulgaria around Vidin became an independent kingdom[124]. Bulgaria was temporarily united (1323 to around 1345)[125] by the Vidin king Mixail Šišman. After its defeat by the Serbian armies of King Stefan Uroš III (Dečanski) in 1330 near Velbəžd (today's Kjustendil), Bulgaria lost most of its southwestern lands to Serbia[126]. In the early 1340's Balik, a local ruler between the Black Sea and the lower reaches of the Danube, seceded from the Tərnovo kingdom. His son Dobrotica expanded the new country southward at the expense of Tərnovo: this land was later called Dobrudža[127]. In the late 1340's the Tərnovo king Ioan Aleksandər divided his country in two and gave the western part (the Vidin kingdom) to his son Ioan Sracimir, retaining for himself only the regions around the city of Tərnovo[128]. Thus it becomes clear that almost 50 years before the fall of Tərnovo, part of Bulgaria was divided into three kingdoms (Tərnovo, Vidin,

---

122. op. cit., p. 219.

123. ibid.

124. ibid.

125. op. cit., pp. 221, 228.

126. op. cit., p. 222.

127. op. cit., p. 228.

128. ibid.

Dobrudža) while the remaining southwestern parts of the former (13th-century) empire either were under the Serbian
kings (between 1330 and 1355) or had become independent
regions (after the death of Stefan Dušan in 1355), under local rulers like Vəlkašin and his son Marko (Prilep, Skopje
and Prizren), Ioan Ugleša (around Serres and Drama), Ioan
and Konstantin, sons of Despot Dejan (Velbəžd, Zletovo,
Kratovo, Kumanovo and Štip), Xlapen (Ver, Kostur and Voden)
Andrej Gropa (Oxrid) and Bogdan (Strumica)[129].

b) The Turkish conquest of the Balkan peninsula
was a long historical process, taking approximately a century; the conquest of Bulgaria alone lasted about four decades. Here are the most important events in the fall of the
Bulgarian states and regions:

In 1352 the Turks captured the fortress of Tsimpe
on Gallipoli, and thus firmly set foot on the Balkan peninsula[130];

In 1361 the Turkish capital was transferred to
Europe, to the city of Didimotike, and thus the Turks expres
sed their intention to conquer the neighboring states[131];

In 1362 they captured the city of Adrianopolis[132]

---

129. op. cit., p. 229.
D. Angelov, Agrarnite otnošenija v Severna i
Sredna Makedonija prez XIV v., Sofia, 1958, p. 9-15.

130. AN SSSR, Istorija Vizantii, v. 3, Moscow,
1967, p. 158.

131. op. cit., p. 162-163.

132. op. cit., p. 163.

and two years later - the Bulgarian cities of Plovdiv and Beroe (Stara Zagora)[133]. But in 1364 King Ioan Aleksandər joined forces with the Turks: they attacked the Greek city of Mesembria and captured Anchialo[134]. Meanwhile, the Turks resettled large populations from Asia Minor in the recently conquered Bulgarian territory.

Two independent rulers in the southwestern regions of Bulgaria, Vəlkašin of Prilep and Ioan Ugleša of Serres, decided to attack the Turks. They entered the region, at that time called Macedonia (today's Thrace), and met the Turks near the city Adrianopolis, by the village of Černomen on the Marica River[135]. Most of the Bulgarian fighters, including the two leaders Vəlkašin and Ugleša, died there in the failure of the last serious active resistance by the Bulgarians. The Turks captured the fortified cities of Ixtiman and Samokov, most of today's Macedonia and the entire Rhodopa Mountains[136]. Especially heroic was the defense of

---

133. Bəlgarska Akademija na Naukite, _Istorija na Bəlgarija_, v. 1, Sofia, 1961, p. 229.

134. _ibid._

135. _op. cit._, p. 242; see also the account of this event in the contemporary chronographic note by the monk Isaja in:
D. Radojčić, _Antologija stare srpske književnosti_ Beograd, 1960, pp. 99, 325.
The original text by Monk Isaja can also be found in:
B. Angelov, _Iz starata bəlgarska, ruska i srəbska literatura_, v. 2, Sofia, 1967, p. 148-161.

136. Bəlgarska Akademija na Naukite, _Istorija na Bəlgarija_, v. 1, Sofia, 1961 (2nd edition), p. 242.

the city of Monastir (Bitola)[137].

But not all Balkan feudal rulers resisted the
Turks. Many local leaders joined them, thus preserving
their own privileged position and saving their cities and
the lives and freedom of their people. The most famous
rulers of southwest Bulgaria who submitted to the Turks in
the invasion of 1371 were Ioan Dragaš and Konstantin of
Velbəžd, as well as Marko of Prilep, the son of Vəlkašin
who died at Černomen[138]. The Tərnovo king Ioan Šišman also
became a vassal of the Turkish sultan Murad, and gave him
as a wife his sister Kera Themar (between 1371 and 1382)[139].

In 1382 Sofia fell[140], and in 1386, with the fall
of Niš (later only temporarily regained by the Serbians),
the Turks approached the principality of Vidin and separated
the Bulgarian from the Serbian lands[141]. In 1387 the Bosnia
and Serbian troops defeated the Turks at Pločnik. However,

---

137. D. Angelov, Turskoto zavoevanie i borbata
na balkanskite narodi protiv našestvenicite, Istoričeski
pregled, IX, 1954, 4, p. 382.

138. AN SSSR, Istorija Jugoslavii, Moscow, 1963,
p. 123.

139. Bəlgarska Akademija na Naukite, Istorija
na Bəlgarija, v. 1, Sofia, 1961 (2nd edition), p. 243.

140. ibid.

141. AN SSSR, Istorija Jugoslavii, Moscow, 1963,
p. 109.

the Tərnovo king[142] and the ruler of Dobrudža, Dobrotica[143], failed to raise and send armies to the aid of the Serbians and Bosnians, as they had promised.

After Pločnik (1387) the Turks reorganized their forces and increased their pressure on Bulgaria. In 1388 the Turkish army captured the important fortresses of the cities of Oveč (Provadija), Šumen and Madara, and unsuccessfully attacked Varna, which was part of Dobrotica's kingdom[144]. By that time the Turks either possessed or controlled most of northern Bulgaria.

On June 15, 1389, at Kosovo Pole, the Turks defeated the combined Bosnian-Serbian armies led by the Serbian prince Lazar, who was captured and killed in revenge for the death of the Turkish sultan Murad[145].

Tərnovo fell in the summer of 1393, after three months' siege, and soon afterward the Danubian city of Nikopol, where the Tərnovo king Ioan Šišman was captured. The fate of the king is unknown, but this marked the end of the Tərnovo kingdom[146]. In 1396 the city of Vidin was taken by

---

142. Bəlgarska Akademija na Naukite, _Istorija na Bəlgarija_, v. 1, Sofia, 1961 (2nd edition), p. 243.

143. Şt. Pascu, ed., and others, _Istoria Medie a României_, v.1, Bucharest, 1966, p. 166.

144. Bəlgarska Akademija na Naukite, _Istorija na Bəlgarija_, v. 1, Sofia, 1961 (2nd edition), p. 233

145. AN SSSR, _Istorija Jugoslavii_, Moscow, 1963, p. 110.

146. Bəlgarska Akademija na Naukite, _Istorija na Bəlgarija_, v. 1, Sofia, 1961 (2nd edition), p. 144-145.

the Turks[147], and this date is considered the final one for the existence of the Second Bulgarian Kingdom.

However, in 1388-1389 the Wallachian king Mircea, who already controlled the former kingdom of Dobrotica and had added to his title "Despot of the land of Dobrotica and lord of Drəstər" lost his first battle with the Turks and became their vassal[148]. He sought the help of Moldavia, Poland and Hungary in his fight against them[149], but after his death in 1418 his descendents continued to be vassals of the Sultan.

After Kosovo Pole (1389) the Serbian despot Stefan Lazarević also became a vassal of the Turks. The Serbians were even obliged to send troops to Ankara to help the Turks in their battle with Tamerlane (1402). Stefan Lazarević was involved in complicated diplomatic games with Hungary, Constantinople and different parties within the Turkish ruling groups[150]. During his reign (1389-1427), Serbia was described by Western travellers as a <u>prosperous country</u>[151]. Serbia was finally conquered by the Turks during the reign of Despot Đorđe Branković in 1459, six years after the fall

147. <u>op. cit.</u>, p. 245.

148. Şt. Pascu, ed., and others, <u>Istoria Medie a României</u>, v. 1, Bucharest, 1966, p. 167.

149. <u>op. cit.</u>, p. 168-173.

150. AN SSSR, <u>Istorija Jugoslavii</u>, Moscow, 1963, p. 111.

151. <u>ibid.</u>

of Constantinople[152].

This lengthy, although very sketchy, review of the main events in the destruction of the Bulgarian states and their neighbors, reveals that the struggle for southeastern Europe was a long and complicated one. It lasted through several generations, and was not always clearly defined as a struggle of Christians against Moslems, Europeans against Turks. The Balkan nations obviously had accepted the Turkish presence in their lands as a fact, and were trying to do "business as usual", very often not foreseeing the tragic historical consequences.

In the light of the real, highly complex historical events in the Balkans during the century between the Turkish conquest of Gallipoli (1352) and the final battle of the Serbian army at Smederevo (1459), the statements by the Soviet scholar Vzdornov (similar to those of other poorly - informed philologists) that Serbia and Bulgaria "were swallowed in a short time", and that "this was exactly the time when the mass emigration of Southern Slavs (to Russia) began", is remarkably naive. For one thing, the assumption of any such mass emigration to Russia is unsupported by a single fact. For another, one may ask when, actually, was the time when this "emigration" began: after the fall of the Rhodopa Mountains or the fall of Monastir (Bitola), after the

---

152. op. cit., p. 114.
AN SSSR, Istorija Vizantii, v. 3, Moscow, 1967, p. 190-198.

fall of Niš or the fall of Tərnovo, after the fall of Vidin or the fall of Beograd? Obviously, some people were running from the Turks (cf. the testimony of Monk Isaja of Serres, fn. 135). But why should they have gone all the way to Moscow or Novgorod when they could have gone to the next principality, the next town, the next monastery in their own land, or to neighboring Serbia, or to Wallachia or Moldavia, which had flourishing Slavic-language cultures throughout the 15th century? The Russian scholars' misunderstanding of the historical events connected with the Turkish conquest of the Balkans, and their invention of the myth of a "mass migration" of Southern Slavs to Russia, can perhaps be sought in the traditional concept of the mechanism of the second South Slavic influence, which entered 19th-century literature of the problem when there was little real information available on the subject. And yet, Sobolevskij never mentions the word "refugee, emigrant", while Lixačev uses it in quotation marks[153].

c) The statement that "under the conditions of the Turkish occupation, their (the "emigrants'") activity in their own country became unthinkable" cannot be taken seriously. The author seems unaware that it was precisely under the Turkish occupation that Konstantin Kostenečki went to a Bulgarian monastery to pursue his studies, or that the great activity of Russian copyists in the monasteries of Athos

153. D. S. Lixačev, op. cit., p. 149.

(which is the topic of his article!) was conducted under the Turkish occupation. Besides, this author has hardly asked himself the question, how did the Russian scribes from Moscow and Novgorod reach Mount Athos if not by being permitted to cross the Turkish-occupied territories. And where did the hundreds of 15th-century Bulgarian manuscripts come from, if all intellectual and cultural activity by the Balkan Christians had become "unthinkable"? The early Turkish administration of the South Slavic lands undoubtedly brought much suffering to some people; it definitely had a negative influence on the cultural and religious life of the Christian nations there, but it was not as severe as the Soviet scholars tend to portray it.

d) Yet the greatest error in all this mass of uncorroborated "information" is the statement that "in this respect (i.e., as concerns emigrants who took up permanent residence in Russia)...the most representative personality is the Metropolitan Kiprian." Kiprian was never an "emigrant"; he reached Moscow as the confirmed Metropolitan in the late spring of 1389, four years before the fall of Tərnovo[154]. However, his first, unsuccessful stay as Metropolitan of Moscow was even earlier — from May 23, 1381 to sometime after October 7, 1382[155].

---

154. E. Golubinskij, *Istorija russkoj cerkvi*, v. 2, 1, Moscow, 1900 (photoedition: The Hague, 1969), p. 300.

155, *op. cit.*, p. 249-251.

Nor was Camblak an "emigrant" or "refugee" to Kiev
and Russian Lithuania: he was officially invited from Moldavia by Prince Vytautas (or Vitovt) (Cf. our discussion on
the contribution of these two Bulgarians, in 2.3.2 and 2.3.3

e) Still, one must distinguish strictly the concepts behind the two Russian words выходец and эмигрант.
The former[156] is defined as "a new settler who has come from
another country" or "one who has moved up from another social group"; there is no implication that the person was a
refugee. In the totality of the concept expressed by
the priority is on the decision by the person to change his
place of residence or his social group for the better. Such
a person is fully integrated into his new society. On the
other hand, эмигрант[157] implies, in any case, a refugee,
who has either been expelled from his own country or fled
from it, legally or illegally, and then found some means of
existence elsewhere. Such a person has never fully integrated into the new society, but has stayed on as a resident
foreigner.

---

156. S. I. Ožegov, <u>Slovar' russkogo jazyka</u>,
Moscow, 1960 (4th edition), p. 119.
    The full definition in Russian is : Вы́ходец, -дца,
м. 1. Пришелец, переселенец из другой страны. 2. Тот, кто
перешел из одной социальной среды в другую (устар.)

157. <u>op. cit</u>, p. 892.
    The full definition in Russian is: Эмигра́нт, -а,
м. Человек, к-рый находится в эмиграции; where Эмиграция,
-и, ж. 1. Вынужденное или добровольное переселение из своего отечества в другую страну по политическим, экономическим
или иным причинам. 2. Перебывание в другой стране после та-
кого переселения. 3. <u>собир.</u> Эмигранты.

In the Russian-English dictionary these two Russian words
are translated, respectively, as "being of a certain nationality by birth, being of a certain extraction" (for выходец)[158]and as "emigrant; emigre; exile" (for эмигрант)[159].
The word эмигрант can also be translated as "refugee" (cf.
"refugee - 1) беженец;   2) эмигрант [160]).

It becomes clear that the Russian term эмигрант
always implies in its complexity a refugee, a person who is a
stranger in the new land, who stays somehow out of society,
etc., while выходец only stresses that he was foreign-born.
A. I. Sobolevskij very correctly called Kiprian, Camblak and
Paxomij Logofet "južno-slavjanskie vyxodcy"[161], thus saying
nothing about their reasons for settling in Russia, and emphasizing their integration into the Russian society. Evidence for the fact that he had become truly Russian is the
spiritual testament of Metropolitan Kiprian to the Russian
clergy, in which he speaks as one Russian to others[162].

158. See the translations and examples in:
      A. I. Smirnickij, Russko-anglijskij slovar',
Moscow, 1969 (8th edition), p. 116.

159. op. cit., p. 719.

160. V. K. Mjuller, Anglo-russkij slovar',
Moscow, 1960 (7th edition), p. 827.

161. A. I. Sobolevskij, op. cit., p. 12.

162. This testament can be found in the chapter
for September 16, 6915:
      VIII letopisnyj sbornik, imenuemyj Patriaršeju ili
Nikonovskoju letopis'ju, Polnoe sobranie russkix letopisej,
v. XI, St. Petersburg, 1897 (photoedition: Moscow, 1965),
p. 195-196.

History gives no indication that Bulgarian (or Serbian) scribes became _refugees_ _to_ _Russia_ as a result of the Turkish conquest. The reason lies in the peculiar status of a scribe or writer in 14th - 15th-century Bulgaria or Serbia: his craft was not his main vocation. Translating, compiling and copying books was not a secular profession but a "soul-saving" activity, performed by monks and priests. While we do not know who worked in the Balkan kings' chancelleries of that time, the heavy Church Slavic language of the existing _gramoty_ of the Bulgarian and Serbian kings definitely speaks for the hypothesis that the people who wrote them were the same people who wrote the "holy" books. Even after the Turkish conquest, the Balkan monasteries remained centers of literary activity. In my opinion, any claim that Bulgarian and Serbian scribes became "refugees" to Russia is arbitrary and antihistorical, since it has never been supported by any evidence - not by names mentioned in historical documents, or by the existence of books, written _in_ _Russia_ by South Slavic scribes other than Kiprian, Camblak and Paxomij (who can in no way be called refugees).

The problem of the South Slavic and Greek craftsmen in 14th - 15th-century Russia is a very different one. There is some historical evidence for the presence of such masters in Russian towns and monasteries. For instance, the _Nikon_ _Chronicle_ mentions (under the year 6912) that «лазарь чернец сербинъ, иже новопришелъ изъ сербскїа земли» built

a clock in the courtyard of the Muscovite grand prince, behind the Church of the Annunciation[163]. In a different version of the same story[164] it is said that his (Lazar's) price
was over 150 rubles. This statement, although ambiguous,
would more likely suggest that Lazar charged the prince over
150 rubles, rather than that he was ransomed (from the
Turks?) for this sum; the latter, however is not an impossible explanation. I. Zabelin has found evidence in the Russian chronicles[165] that a Roman (римлянинъ could have meant
either 'from Rome; or 'Roman Catholic') master Boris, in
1346, in Moscow, cast three large and two smaller church
bells. Zabelin notes that the name Boris is unusual for an
Italian, and suggests that he was of South Slavic origin[166].

Additional information and bibliographic reference
on the problem of the works of Greek and Serbian craftsmen
and artists in Russian cities, churches and monasteries can
be found in D. S. Lixačev's article[167]. However, in all of
the existing works quoted by Lixačev, the participation of
foreign-born craftsmen in the building and ornamentation of

---

163. op. cit., p. 190.

164. Simeonovskaja letopis'. Polnoe sobranie
russkix letopisej (Izdannoe po vysočajšemu poveleniju
Imperatorskoj Arxeografičeskoju komissieju; A. E. Presnjakov,
ed.), XVIII, St. Petersburg, 1913, p. 95.

165. op. cit., p. 95.

166. I. Zabelin, Istorija goroda Moskvy, I,
Moscow, 1902, p. 86.

167. D. S. Lixačev, op. cit., p. 99-106.

Russian churches has been explained primarily by the need
for experienced masters in the expanded construction pro-
grams in Russia after it had regained its independence from
the Tatars. (Compare, for example, the above-mentioned
"Roman Boris", who cast the bells in Moscow in 1346, six
years before the Turks set foot on the Balkan peninsula.)

2.3.2. For 25 years, Kiprian's activities at the
end of the 14th and the very beginning of the 15th centuries
were connected with the Muscovite Russian Church and the revision of its literature and language. Thus Kiprian became
the most influential Bulgarian in the process of reshaping
the Russian culture of that time. In contemporary works on
the history of Russian literature, his Bulgarian nationality
is established beyond doubt[168]. But for almost a century
there was a dispute in the literature about Kiprian's national origin. The oldest information on the subject is a short
reference in Stepennaja kniga (16th century) and in the Nik-
onian compilation of the Russian Chronicle (also 16th century). In both sources it is said that Kiprian was Serbian
by birth (родомъ сербинъ)[169]. The next data are given by

_____

168. J. Ivanov, Bəlgarskoto knižovno vlijanie v
Rusija pri mitropolit Kiprian (1375-1406), IzvIBL, VI,
Sofia, 1958, p. 25-79.

169. Kniga Stepennaja carskogo rodoslovija, Polnoe sobranie russkix letopisej, XXI, 2, St. Petersburg,
1913, p. 441.

VIII letopisnyj sbornik, imenuemyj Patriaršeju
ili Nikonovskoju letopis'ju, Polnoe sobranie russkix letopisej, v. XI, St. Petersburg, 1897 (photoedition: Moscow,
1965), p. 194.

Nil Kurljatev in 1552, in a preface to a copy of the translation of the __Psalter__ by Maksim Grek. In praising the new translation, Nil Kurljatev compares it with the similar one by Kiprian. Since this is the first recorded negative attitude toward Kiprian (and toward the second South Slavic influence on Russian), the quote should be given in full[170]:

> But Metropolitan Kiprian did not understand much Greek, neither did he sufficiently know our language. While we speak in our language clearly and loudly, they speak with snuffling, and their words do not resemble ours in writing. But he thought he had corrected the Psalms according to our language, while he had put more nonsense into them, and in their discourses and words he wrote entirely in Serbian. Even today many among us spend their time writing books, but because of their lack of sense they write entirely in Serbian ... Whenever, according to our language, there should be а, according to Serbian, it is ѣ or ѧ; where, according to our language, it is ю, in Serbian it is ѧ; in our language — ȣ, but in Serbian — ѧ; for us it is ы; in Serbian — и. Our words like не заме(д)ли in Serbian, or equally in Bulgarian, will be не замȣди; in our language it is кóсно- or ме(д)ленноѧзыченъ, or гȣгни(в), but in Serbian it is мȣдноѧзы́че(н); or other words unclear to us бохма, васнь, реснотивïе, цѣщи, ашȣтъ, and many more similar ones which we do not understand, some Serbian, some Bulgarian. A year's time would not be enough for us to tell about these matters.
> (The Russian Church Slavic text is given in Appendix Five.)

A number of highly-respected authorities have repeated the 16th-century "testimonies" to the Serbian origin

---

170. Arximandrit Amfiloxij, Čto vnes Sv. Kiprian, mitropolit Kievskij i vseja Rossii, a potom Moskovskij i vseja Rossii, iz svoego rodnogo narečija i iz perevodov ego vremeni v naši bogoslužebnye knigi?, __Trudy Tret'ego Arxeologičeskogo s"ezda v Rossii, byvšego v Kieve v avguste 1874 g.__, II, Kiev, 1878, p. 231-232.

of Kiprian. Among them are P. M. Stroev, Archbishop Makarij, E. Kałużniacki, and, in more recent times, V. I. Ščepkin and M. N. Tixomirov[171]. Another group of equally serious scholars have maintained that Kiprian was of Bulgarian origin, mainly by doubting the authenticity of the 16th-century evidence. Among them are E. Golubinskij, N. M. Glubokovskij, A. I. Jacimirskij, and most recently, L. A. Dmitriev[172].

First, A. I. Sobolevskij accepted Kiprian's Bulgarian origin[173], but seven years later, in the revised edition[174] of

---

171. Bibliologičeskij slovar' i černovye k nemu materialy P. M. Stroeva (a posthumous edition, A. F. Byčkov, ed.), Sbornik ORJaS, XXIX, 4, St. Petersburg, 1882 (photoedition: Nendeln, Liechtenstein, 1966), p. 165.
    Arxiepiskop Makarij, Istorija russkoj cerkvi, V, 2, St. Petersburg, 1866, pp. 183, 213.
    Em. Kałużniacki, Werke des Patriarchen von Bulgarien Euthymius, Vienna, 1901, p. v.
    V. I. Ščepkin, Učebnik russkoj paleografii, Moscow, 1920, p. 116.
    M.N. Tixomirov, Istoričeskie svjazi russkogo naroda s južnymi slavjanami, Slavjanskij sbornik, Moscow, 1947, p. 177.

172. E. Golubinskij, Istorija russkoj cerkvi, II 1, Moscow, 1900 (photoedition: The Hague, 1969), p. 297.
    N. M. Glubokovskij, Sv. Kiprian, mitropolit vseja Rossii, kak pisatel', Čtenija v Obščestve ljubitelej duxovnogo prosveščenija, 1, January 1892, p. 358-424.
    A. I. Jacimirskij, Grigorij Camblak, St. Petersburg, 1904, p. 20-21.
    L. A. Dmitriev, Rol' i značenie mitropolita Kipriana v istorii drevnerusskoj literatury (K russko-bolgarskim literaturnym svjazjam XIV -XV vv.), Trudy ODRL, XIX, Moscow - Leningrad, p. 216.

173. A. I. Sobolevskij, Južno-slavjanskoe vlijanie na russkuju pis'mennost' v XIV - XV vekax..., St. Petersburg, 1894, p. 14.

174. A. I. Sobolevskij, Perevodnaja literatura Moskovskoj Rusi XIV - XVII vekov (Bibliografičeskie materialy), St. Petersburg, 1903, p. 12.

his article, he called Kiprian "half-Greek, half-Bulgarian".

The Bulgarian literary historian J. Ivanov, in an unfinished study, published 11 years after his death[175], proves beyond doubt the Bulgarian origin of the Russian Metropolitan Kiprian. Ivanov dismissed Sobolevskij's allegation that Kiprian was half Greek, quoting a letter by Patriarch Matthew of Constantinople to Kiprian (1400), in which Kiprian is said to be "attached to the Greeks" and a "friend of theirs"[176]; if he had been even part Greek, the Patriarch would surely have reminded him of it. The thorough analysis of Camblak's eulogy for Kiprian, as well as the language and the spelling of all texts positively identified as Kiprian's autographs, made by J. Ivanov, speak for his Bulgarian — not Serbian — origin[177].

2.3.2.1. The original writings of Kiprian, positively identified today, are negligible in number. In addition to his spiritual testament to the Russian clergy (cf. fn. 162), Kiprian also wrote a new version of the Vita of St. Peter, sometime between the years 1397 and 1404[178]. Basically, Kiprian used the biographical facts in the older

---

175. J. Ivanov, Bəlgarskoto knižovno vlijanie v Rusija pri mitropolit Kiprian, Izvestija IBL, VI, 1958, p. 25-79.

176. op. cit., p. 35.

177. op. cit., p. 35-75.

178. K. Kuev, Kiprian, Istorija na bəlgarskata literatura, 1, Sofia, 1963, p. 310-313.

vita by Proxor, but added new information: he names the
native place of St. Peter as Volhynia, mentions the desire
of the Volhynian prince to have his own metropolitan, and
remarks on the economic and political situation in Volhynia[179]. The style of his vita is new for Russia, very different from that of the older version by Proxor, which was
strictly representative of the 14th-century South Slavic
literature. The vita by Kiprian, in general, departs from
the Balkan hagiographic tradition (followed, for instance,
by the works of Euthymius) in that it gives abundant historically true facts from the life of the saint. Kiprian utilizes the Vita of St. Peter to affirm the future historic
role of Moscow, and of the Muscovite grand princes, in the
unification of Russia[180].

2.3.2.2. In the Soviet libraries there are three
original autographs by Kiprian and a 14th - 15th-century
Russian copy from a Služebnik translated by him. Before
Jordan Ivanov's article on Kiprian (cf. fn. 175), it was
believed that all these represented new translations from
Greek, done by Kiprian partly in the Balkan monasteries
and partly in Russia[181]. In his study, Ivanov proves these

179. op. cit., p. 311.

180. B. St. Angelov, ed., Žitie na mitropolit
Petər ot Kiprijan, Iz starata bəlgarska, ruska i srəbska
literatura, I, Sofia, 1958, p. 159-176.

181. J. Ivanov, Bəlgarskoto knižovno vlijanie pr
mitropolit Kiprian, IzvIBL, VI, Sofia, 1958, p. 38.

"translations" (with the exception of the Služebnik) to be
another myth. For instance, in the postscript of his copy
of the Lestvica ("Ladder") by John of Sinai (Climacos),
Kiprian wrote: "In the year 1387, on April 24, these writings were completed in the Monastery of John Stoudites, by
the humble Metropolitan of Kiev and All Russia, Kiprian":

в лѣ͗т᷍ ҂ѕ.ѿ.ч.е. а͗прилїа .кд: съвръшиша᷍с сїѧ книгы в стꙋ-
дїискои ѡ͗бітѣли кипрїаноᷟ͞ смѣренны́мъ митрополи́тоᷟ͞ кыев-
скымъ и͗ все ᷋ рѡсїѧ:[182]

This has wrongly been interpreted as an indication
that Kiprian was the translator. J. Ivanov compares Kiprian's copy of the same Lestvica, kept in the Museum of the
Rila Monastery, # 3/10. Here are short parallel passages
from both texts, taken from Ivanov's study[183] as the best
illustration of Kiprian's ability scrupulously to copy the
religious texts (clearly, both copies are from another
original).

Rila Lestvica	Kiprian's Lestvica
ѡ͗ безпристрасти. сло᷍в ҃в:	о безпристра́стїи сло́во ҃в.
и͗же и́стинож Г҃а възлю́бивыи.	І͗же и́стинноѧ Г҃а възлюбивы. и́же
и͗же и́стинож бѫдѫщаго цр҃᷍твїа	и́стинноѧ бѫдѫщаго цр҃᷍твїа
полочи́ти възыскавы. и́же въ и́с-	полочи́ти възыскавы. иже въ ис-

182. op. cit., p. 48.

183. op. cit., p. 49.

тинѫ болѣзнь о свои съгрѣ- тинѫ болѣзнь о свои съгрѣ-
шени имѣѫ. йже въ йстинѫ шенихъ имѣѧи. иже въ истинѫ
пáмѧ мѫченїа стѧжавы и сѫда памѧ мѫченїа стѧжáвыи сѫди
вѣчнаго. йже въ йстинѫ стра вѣчнаго. иже въ йстинѫ стра
о своѐмъ исходѣ въспрїѐмыи, о своемъ исходѣ въсприемыи,
ктомѹ не възлюбитъ. ктомѹ ктомѹ не възлюбитъ, ктóмѹ
нѐ попечет сѧ или поскръбитъ. не попечé сѧ или поскръбитъ.
ни о имѣни. ни о стѧжанихъ. ни о имѣни. ни о стѧжанихъ.
ни о родителе. ни о слáвѣ ни о родителехъ.ни о славѣ
житѐйстѣи. ни о дрѹѕѣ. ни житéистѣи. ни о дрѹѕѣ. ни
о братїи. ни о чьсóм же зем- о братїи. ни о чьсом же зем-
ныи въсѣко. нѫ всѐ свое ныхъ всѣко нѫ все свое
съдръжáнїе...   съдръжанїе...

Today, Kiprian's <u>Lestvica</u> is kept in the Lenin
State Library of the USSR in Moscow, # ф. I73, Фунд., I52.
The manuscript has been studied often[184].

Another copy by Kiprian is a 426-leaflet manu-
script containing the <u>Works</u> of Dionysius Areopagites with
a commentary. Today it is kept in the Lenin State Library
of the USSR in Moscow, # Ф. I73, Фунд., I44 [185].According

---

184. For a detailed bibliography of paleographic,
textological and theological studies on this manuscript,see:
   G. I. Vzdornov, Rol' slavjanskix monastyrskix
masterskix pis'ma..., <u>Literaturnye svjazi drevnix slavjan</u>
(<u>Trudy</u> <u>ODRL</u>, v. XXIII), Leningrad, 1968, p. 189.

   185. L. A. Dmitriev, Rol' i značenie mitropolita
Kipriana v istorii drevnerusskoj literatury (k russko-
bolgarskim literaturnym svjazjam XIV - XV vv.), <u>Trudy</u> <u>ODRL</u>,
XIX, Moscow-Leningrad, 1963, p. 223-224.

to P. M. Stroev, this manuscript is an "autograph translation" (собственноручный перевод) by Metropolitan Kiprian[186]. Actually, Kiprian copied the new Middle Bulgarian translation of 1371 by Father Isaja of Serres[187]. P. Stroev's wrong assignment of the translation is probably owing to the fact that Kiprian did not copy Isaja's preface (or, in some late manuscripts, postscript) to the translation, in which he tells of the defeat of Ugleša and Vəlkašin in 1371 near the village of Černomen (cf. fn. 135). Isaja explains that when he had reached "the evening of his sunny day" — that is, his '70's — and had learned "a little of the Greek language, enough to be able to understand its riches and the hardship of translation from that (language) into our language"[188], Metropolitan Theodosius of the city of Serres asked him to translate the Works of Dionysius Areopagites[189].

Very indicative for the Bulgarian origin of Kiprian, and for his thorough knowledge of the available revised copies of the religious writings in Bulgaria, is his copy of the Psalter (the one that was so sharply criticized for its

---

186. P. M. Stroev, Bibliologičeskij slovar' i černovye k nemu materialy, Sbornik ORJaS, XXIX (4), St. Petersburg, 1882 (photoedition: Nendeln, Liechtenstein, 1966), p. 168.

187. J. Ivanov, op. cit., p. 51-52.

188. The Slavic text is known from a 15th-century Russian copy (the Rumjancev manuscript), published for the first time by B. Angelov (p. 157-161). See:
B. St. Angelov, Iz starata bəlgarska, ruska i srəbska literatura, II, Sofia, 1967, p. 157.

189. B. St. Angelov, op. cit., p. 158.

"Serbian" features by Nil Kurljatev in 1552; cf. fn. 170).
Ivanov has found that Kiprian copied his text very precisely
from the Psalter of King Ioan Aleksandər of 1337[190]. In addition, Kiprian included short passages praising the Bulgarian saints Petka (Paraskeva), Ioan Rilski, Ilarion
Mǝglenski, Kiril Filosof and Ioakim[191]. Kiprian's copy of
the Psalter is presently kept in the Lenin State Library of
the USSR in Moscow, # ф. I73, Фунд., I42 [192].

2.3.2.3. Kiprian's work in introducing into Russia the revised Middle Bulgarian editions of the 14th-cen-
tury religious literature has another aspect. In the fall
of 1382, after October 7, when Kiprian was expelled from Mos
cow by Prince Dmitrij (Donskoj), he went back to the Monastery of John Stoudites, taking with him Afanasij Vysockij, th
famous abbot of the Vysockij Monastery near the city of Ser-
puxov[193]. The two friends stayed there together until
Kiprian returned to Russia as the acknowledged Metropolitan
of Kiev (and later of Moscow). But even before being expelled from Russia in 1382, Kiprian must have begun his long
friendship with Afanasij Vysockij, and must have told him
about the revised editions available in the Balkan monasteries, since in 1381 the abbot Afanasij especially sent the

---

190. J. Ivanov, op. cit., p. 38-45.

191. op. cit., p. 45-47.

192. L. A. Dmitriev, op. cit., p. 224-225.

193. J. Ivanov, op. cit., p. 27.

novice Vun'ko to the Zograph Monastery to copy the <u>Pandects</u>
of Nikon Černogorec. The first 210 leaflets were copied by
Vun'ko and were brought back to the Vysockij Monastery before August 10, 1382, when Abbot Afanasij added 18 more
leaflets in his own handwriting, with items from the <u>Pater-</u>
<u>ikon</u> and the <u>Instruction to Monks</u>[194]. From the note by
Vun'ko (front of leaflet 1) it is not clear exactly where
the copy was made. But J. Ivanov implies that it was copied
in the Zograph Monastery on Mt. Athos, from a Middle Bulgarian manuscript sent to this monastery as a present by the
Tərnovo Patriarch Theodosius[195]. From the description of
Vun'ko's copy, given by Gorskij and Nevostruev[196], it becomes obvious that Vun'ko used a Bulgarian original. Although he does not use the letter ѫ (which is a significant
indication that the second South Slavic influence did not
begin in the orthography), his use of ꙗ and ѧ (for the
correct Russian ю) reflects the so-called Middle Bulgarian
confusion of the nasal vowels (cf. требуꙗ on p. 81 for the
1st person singular, which should be требую; творѧ on p.
92 for the correct творю). In addition, Vun'ko copies in
the margins the Bulgarian glosses to some Greek words: ко-
риды . древѧнъіи <u>вошькъі</u> именуютсѧ (p. 53b), хиновоскиӧ

---

194. A. Gorskij, K. Nevostruev, <u>Opisanie slav-</u>
<u>janskix rukopisej Moskovskoj sinodal'noj biblioteki,</u> II, 3,
Moscow, 1862, p. 10.

195. J. Ivanov, <u>ibid.</u>

196. A. Gorskij, K. Nevostruev, <u>op. cit.,</u> p.10-11.

и́менует сѧ по болгарьскому ꙗзыку гуска̃ паша (p. 94b), etc

2.3.2.4. The only known original translation from Greek made by Kiprian while in Russia is the Služebnik, translated in 1397. The original has been lost, but a Russian copy is kept today in the State Historical Museum in Moscow, # Син. 601[197]. From the note on p. 132b one learns the name of the Russian copyist — Ilarij — who testifies on p. 72 that this Služebnik "was copied from the Greek book into Russian by the hand of the humble Kiprian, Metropolitan of Kiev and All Russia"[198].

A note in Manuscript # 7 from the Cathedral Church of the Assumption (Успенский Собор) from 1403, says that the Russian land now "shines more than the dawn of the sun because of his (Kiprian's) revision of the books and teachings"[199].

2.3.2.5. Kiprian's revision of the books in Russia, thus, proceeded in three different ways:

a) He brought with him his own copies from the revised Middle Bulgarian editions of religious books (the Psalter, the Lestvica of John Climacos, and the Works of Dionysius Areopagites) already in existence;

b) While residing in Moscow as the Russian metro-

---

197. G. I. Vzdornov, op. cit., p. 174.

198. A. Gorskij, K. Nevostruev, Opisanie slavjanskix rukopisej Moskovskoj sinodal'noj biblioteki, III, 1, Moscow, 1869, p. 11-12.

199. A. I. Sobolevskij, op. cit., p. 12-13 (fn. 3 on p. 12).

the Turks in 1393, because of the legendary character of his description of the events. I. Dujčev has found the proto-type of Camblak's text both in the Old Testament and in the works of many Byzantine writers[207]. By the end of the 14th century, Camblak was an abbot in the Dečanski Monastery in Serbia, and in 1402 (or 1403) he was preaching in the Cathe-dral Church of St. John the Baptist in the Moldavian capital, Suceava[208]. On his way to Moscow in 1406 to visit his uncle, the metropolitan Kiprian, he learned of the latter's death[209] and swiftly returned to Constantinople as a pretender to the vacant Moscow See[210].

With the increase of hostilities between the Mus-covite and the Russian-Lithuanian principalities after Kipri-an's death, the Lithuanian Grand Prince Vitovt (Vytautas) in 1414 selected Camblak as Metropolitan of Russian Lithuania, and sent him to Constantinople for the appointment and bles-sings of the Patriarch[211]. The Patriarch, who was already dependent on the financial support of the Muscovite prince in the war against the Turks, and who had even arranged the

---

207. I. Dujčev, Legendarnyj motiv u Grigorija Camblaka, Slavia XXI, 1952-53, p. 345-349.

208. V. Velčev, op. cit., p. 327-328.

209. The text of Camblak's eulogy of Kiprian says, "and we...were trying to reach your land in order to see the pastor who was guarding his flock" when the arrow of the news of his death touched Camblak's heart. See:
B. St. Angelov, ed., op. cit., p. 181.

210. V. Velčev, op. cit., p. 328.

211. E. Golubinskij, op. cit., pp. 374, 377.

marriage of the 10-year-old daughter of that prince (Vasilij Dmitrievič) to the equally young son of the Emperor in Constantinople, refused to create a separate Lithuanian Church with Camblak as its metropolitan[212]. As a result, Vitovt asked the bishops of Lithuania to elect Camblak metropolitan according to an old church practice. Thus on November 15, 1415 the bishops formally consecrated Grigorij Camblak as Metropolitan of "Kiev, of Galicia and of All Russia', with his seat in Vilna[213]. After he was anathematized by the Patriarch of Constantinople and the Metropolitan of Moscow, Camblak turned to the Pope of Rome. Between 1414 and 1418, Camblak,leading an imposing delegation of about 300 Lithuanian clergymen and nobles[214], took an active part in the Council of Constance, which under the Roman Pope John XXII ended the Great Schism in 1417. Camblak died in 1420[215].

We know nothing about Camblak's work in Russian Lithuania on the revision of the Church books and their language, because of the negative attitude of Russian officialdom towards this fruitful and talented writer and religious leader. Research on this aspect of his work can be conducted even today only in the Soviet museums and archives, where it has not been pursued up to now. Camblak

---

212. op. cit., pp. 367, 377.

213. op. cit., pp. 378, 384.

214. V. Velčev, op. cit., p. 328.

215. L. Stojanović, Stari srpski zapisi i natpisi, Beograd, 1905, # 495.

committed great "sins" against Moscow by actively supporting the struggle of the Ukrainians and Belorussians
for cultural and political independence in the years when
Moscow's aggressive unification policy towards the neighboring cities and states had just begun. That he is still being punished for them is unfortunate, since Grigorij Camblak
must have played an important and integral part in the
history of the Ukrainian and Belorussian languages and culture. One can only surmise that Camblak had a similar influence in Russian Lithuania to that of Kiprian in Moscow:
features of the Church Slavic language used in Russian Lithuania before "South-West Russia" became attached to Moscow
in the 17th century point in this direction. His activities
also may have triggered the changes in the literary language
which later influenced Muscovite Russian, sometimes referred
to as the "third South Slavic influence" (Shevelov). In the
absence of serious studies of Grigorij Camblak's activities
in Vilna between 1414 and 1420 related to the revision of the
literary language and of the religious texts, anything said
in this connection must remain speculative.

2.3.4. A critical examination of all the well-
established facts about the penetration of South Slavic (and
particularly Bulgarian) books into Russia in the 14th and
15th centuries indicates that the most important factor was
the copying of texts in the Balkans. This process started
in the 13th century, but reached its highest point at the
end of the 14th and the beginning of the 15th centuries.

- 97 -

Persons like Kiprian and Camblak must have done much to accelerate the process, but did not cause it. Nor was the
Turkish conquest of the Balkan Slavic countries the direct
cause of the second South Slavic influence.

2.3.4.1. The earliest record of the Russian demand for new Church Slavic translations, previously made in
Bulgaria, is from 1262 (or 1270 — texts disagree), when the
metropolitan of Kiev, Kiril III (approximately 1242-1281)
ordered a copy of the Kormčaja kniga (Nomokanon)[216]. The
letter of the Kievan metropolitan, asking for this book, has
not yet been found, but the answer of the Bulgarian despot
of Russian origin, Jakov Svjatislav, to Kiril III has been
known to Slavists since 1842[217]. All known Russian copies
of Jakov Svjatislav's letter   include a note by the chief
Bulgarian copyist Ioan Dragoslav; both letter and note give
interesting information on the cultural relations between

---

216. B. St. Angelov, Pismo na Jakov Svetoslav
do Ruskija mitropolit Kiril III, Iz starata bəlgarska, ruska
i srəbska literatura, II, Sofia, 1967, p. 139.
        V. N. Zlatarski, Istorija na bəlgarskata dəržava
III, Sofia, 1940, pp. 322-323, 456-457, 499-519.

217. A. Vostokov, Opisanie russkix i slovenskix
rukopisej Rumjancovskogo muzeuma, St. Petersburg, 1842, #
CCXXXII, p. 290-291.
        Vostokov began the practice of calling this Bul-
garian feudal lord of Russian extraction Jakov Svjatoslav,
although his name is spelled (in the genitive) as нива
свѧтїславѧ   in MS # 232, and ιакова свѧтислава   MS # 233
(both manuscripts studied by him). In all other copies the
name is written (in the genitive) as свѧтислава (cf. the
Kievan MS in B. St. Angelov, op. cit., p. 143). The form
Svjatoslav is an arbitrary Russism, and should be avoided.

Russia and Bulgaria in the second half of the 13th century.[218]

The Russian metropolitan asked Jakov Svjatislav to sponsor the copying of the Nomokanon (known in Bulgaria as Zonara). Jakov Svjatislav states in his letter that he has asked the Patriarch of Tərnovo for permission to copy this book, in memory of his parents and for the good of his own soul. He reminds the metropolitan that "by no means should this Zonara be re-copied, because it is accepted that there should be only one Zonara in the cathedral church of each kingdom, as the holy fathers had commanded and passed this commandment

---

218. The oldest Russian copies of this Kormčaja are from the 13th century: Sofijskaja (Novgorodskaja) kormčaja (of 1282) and Rjazanskaja kormčaja (or 1284); but they do not include Jakov Svjatislav's letter. See:
    A. I. Sobolevskij, Osobennosti russkix perevodov domongol'skogo perioda, Sbornik ORJaS, 88, 3, St. Petersburg, 1910, p. 162-177.
    The letter is included in several later copies of the Kormčaja kniga:
    a) The oldest copy is in the 15th-century Kormčaja # 375 of the manuscript collection of the former Kiev Seminary (leaflets 144-145), presently kept in the Central Scientific Library of the Ukrainian Academy of Sciences in Kiev, # Дух. акад., Но.375, published in:
    B. St. Angelov, op. cit., p. 142-144;
    b) A 16th-century Kormčaja, published by A. Vostokov in 1842 (cf. fn. 217);
    c) A 16th-century Kormčaja, kept in the Lenin State Library in Moscow, # CCXXIII (leaflet 85), published in:
    B. St. Angelov, op. cit. , p. 145-147;
    d) A 16th-century Kormčaja, kept in the Lenin State Library in Moscow, # CCXXXIV, unpublished;
    e) A Kormčaja dated 1552, a manuscript of the former Petersburg Seminary (I was not able to discover its present location), published by Sreznevskij. See:
    I. I. Sreznevskij, Obozrenie drevnix russkix spiskov Kormčej knigi, Sbornik ORJaS, 65, 1899, p. 60-61.

on to us"[219]. Ioan Dragoslav, who in his own words was "not

that good a scribe"[220] and two other scribes divided the

text into three parts and copied it in 50 days, beginning on

November 10 and finishing on January 7.

A. I. Sobolevskij tried to prove that, actually,

this translation was originally made by a Russian on Mount

Athos, and then taken to Bulgaria[221]. He reached this con-

clusion while studying the language of the 13th-century

Serbian Ilovačka krmčica (1262), whose translation has been

traditionally assigned to St. Savva. The text shows indis-

putable Russisms. In the orthography, for example: a is

frequently used for ѧ (быша); pleophony occurs in a few

instances (черѣнь for чрѣнь), and ж is often found in

place of the traditional So. Slavic -жд- (from *dj). The

rest of the orthographic features listed by Sobolevskij are

not diagnostically Russian (for instance, confusion of the

letters ѣ and е could also be either Serbian or dialectal

Bulgarian). Among the lexical Russisms only руга and вьрст

(for поприще) seem convincing, while others, like пожарь,

---

219. The quotation is an English translation
from the 15th-century Kiev copy, published in:
B. St. Angelov, op. cit., p. 143.

220. This is expressed by a very typical syntactic Bulgarism, preserved in all three Russian copies published by Angelov: понеже не бѣх до тамо писець (cf.
B. St. Angelov, op. cit., pp. 143, 145).

221. A. I. Sobolevskij, Materialy i izsledovanija v oblasti slavjanskoj filologii i arxeologii,
Sbornik ORJaS, 88, 3, St. Petersburg, 1910, p. 178-180.

сѣно (сухая трава)   are still known in all of the Bulgarian dialects and in many Serbian dialects. Sobolevskij
admits that words like свѣнь, свѣнѣ [=кромѣ], прѣзъ
[=черезъ], село [=поле], перпира, срѣдьць   (the early
Bulgarian name of the city of Sofia, in Greek Σαρδικἠ)   are
typical South Slavisms, but maintains that "they do not add
coloring to the text"[222]. He further maintains: "As regards the data quoted, we may conclude that the translation
(sic) of this edition of the Kormčaja came from the pen of
a Russian"[223].

　　　　Sobolevskij's conclusion, however, is incorrect;
it does not explain why none of the rest of the Serbian
krmčice have even a trace of the heavy Russian orthographic
and sporadic lexical features of the Ilovačka krmčica. And
Sobolevskij's understanding of the penetration of Russian
phonological and orthographic features is unacceptable for
a non-Russian. While the Russian spelling with жд represented the higher, literary norm of Church Slavic, the spelling with ж reflected the native phonology. Such an alternative spelling would have been possible only in Russia,
where both вижду and вижу were meaningful words (perhaps
representing different styles). For a South Slavic scribe,
a form like вижу would have been unexpected and considered
incorrect; he would have sought to avoid it as a dialectism,

---

222. op. cit., p. 179.

223. op. cit., p. 180.

correcting it where it occurred. This can be shown by examination of the types of Russisms in the 14th-century Bulgarian _Four_ _Gospels_ text, copied from a Russian original which was published by B. Conev[224]. With respect to the phonology and orthography, the Bulgarian scribe did not spo (and thus re-copied) forms confusing ф with θ (фома, Iосиθ), and ѫ with оу (тѫжити, ѫже for оуже); but the latter feature is not a diagnostic Russism, for it reflects the development of the nasal vowel in both Bulgarian and Serbian dialects. Within one word, the only occurrence for each, -оло- stands in place of -ла- and -ч- for -шт- (толочи for тлашти). Again, ч for шт could as well be a West Bulgarian feature as a Russian one. The scribe in a few instances uses typically Russian interpretations of the Church Slavic imperfect tense forms, with final -тъ, -ть (молѣшетъ, хоулахѫть) and the sole certain Russism — семь for седмь [225]. If one compares these types of Rus- sisms (acceptable to the Bulgarian scribe of the Four Gospe] with the abundant number of orthographic Russisms in Ilo- vačka krmčica (many of them being of types inadmissible by a South Slavic scribe, since they represent neither a dia- lect he might have known nor his literary norm), there is only one possible conclusion — the Ilovačka krmčica is a

---

224. B. Conev, ed., _Vračansko_ _evangelie_ (Bəlgarski starini, IV), Sofia, 1914, 236 + x pp.

225. _op._ _cit._, p. 6-7.

copy made by a Russian monk, perhaps well known on Mt. Athos for his calligraphic abilities.

M. N. Speranskij showed some doubt about the lexical Russisms in the 13th-century South Slavic text, calling them "not glaring" (не яркие) [226]. And still, he agreed with Sobolevskij that the Serbian Ilovačka krmčica (1262) was copied from a Russian original. But he also stated that "the Russian Rjazanskaja kormčaja of 1284, which overlaps textually with the Ilovačka krmčica swarms (кишит) with Bulgarisms, or better, Middle-Bulgarisms"[227]. This appears to mean that Speranskij agreed with Sobolevskij that there are some Russian features in this particular Serbian copy; he explained this by the presence of Russian monks on Mount Athos when the Serbian St. Savva was there (1218-1219)[228].

However, Speranskij did not even suggest that the earliest translation of the Nomokanon, which was copied in Tərnovo for Metropolitan Kiril, was made by Russians. That is why it is so strikingly unexpected to find in M. N. Tixomirov (who cites only this one article by Speranskij, first published in 1921) a statement like the following: "The Metropolitan of a devastated Russia asked for a manu-

---

226. M. N. Speranskij, K istorii vzaimno-otnošenij russkoj i jugoslavjanskix literatur (Russkie pamjatniki pis'mennosti na juge slavjanstva), Iz istorii russko-slavjanskix literaturnyx svjazej, Moscow, 1960, p. 31.

227. ibid.

228. op. cit., p. 31-33.

script from far-away Bulgaria, which had suffered relatively little from the Tatar pogroms. It is no less
significant, that the Kormčaja which was sent to him, as has
been proven now (sic) was not from a South Slavic, but originally from a Russian translation"[229]. The Bulgarian schol
ar I. Snegarov suggests that the Middle Bulgarian translation was made on Mt. Athos at the end of the 12th or the
beginning of the 13th century[230].

The history of the early 13th-century copy from
a Middle Bulgarian translation of the Nomokanon, made in
Tərnovo for the Kievan Metropolitan, reveals two important
aspects of the second South Slavic influence in Russia:

a) While new Slavic translations from Greek appeared in the Balkans, Russian literature had slowed
down significantly because of the Tatar political domination; but the Russians either were aware of the existence of
particular new books, or were making inquiries. (Since
Kiril's letter to Jakov Svjatislav has not been found, both
possibilities exist);

b) For the Russians it was more convenient to
order a copy of an already existing Middle Bulgarian translation than to duplicate the work of translating the mater-

---

229. M. N. Tixomirov, Istoričeskie svjazi
russkogo naroda s južnymi slavjanami, Slavjanskij sbornik,
Moscow, 1947, p. 167.

230. I. Snegarov, Duxovno-kulturni vrəzki
meždu Bəlgarija i Rusija prez srednite vekove (X - XV v.),
Sofia, 1950, p. 50-54.

ial over again. In this particular case, the fact that
Jakov Svjatislav paid for the manuscript (повеленїемь же и
по цѣнѣ великаг гⷣна ѧкова свѧтислава деспота болгар-
скаго)[231] may also indicate the financial difficulties
faced by the Kievan Church in the 13th century.

2.3.4.2. The Russian **Four Gospels** of 1355,
copied in Constantinople, reveal another facet of the complex phenomenon of the second South Slavic influence. This
revised edition of the New Testament was traditionally attributed to the hand of the Russian metropolitan St. Aleksij
(1354-1378)[232]. Until the Revolution, the manuscript was
kept in the Čudov Monastery of the Kremlin in Moscow, but
it has since been lost[233]. There are two photoeditions of
the manuscript, however, and thus this interesting document
is not completely lost to historians of the Russian language[234]. The text of this manuscript is extremely correct

---

231. B. St. Angelov, op. cit., p. 143.

232. Sobolevskij believes that St. Aleksij's
authorship is purely a legend. See:
A. I. Sobolevskij, Perevodnaja literatura
Moskovskoj Rusi XIV - XVII vekov, St. Petersburg, 1903,
p. 29.

233. G. I. Vzdornov, op. cit., p. 186.

234. Novyj zavet gospoda našego Iisusa Xrista,
pisannyj rukoju svjatitelja Aleksija mitropolita, sfoto-
grafirovannyj v 8-m' dnej v načale avgusta 1887 g. foto-
grafom Aleksandrom Andreevičem Bagnerovskim pod nepo-
sredstvennym nabljudeniem danilovskogo arximandrita Amfi-
loxija (photoedition).
Novyj zavet gospoda našego Iisusa Xrista. Trud
svjatitelja Aleksija, mitropolita moskovskogo i vseja Rusi.
Fototipičeskoe izdanie Leontija, mitropolita moskovskogo,
Moscow, 1892.

in comparison with other Russian <u>Four Gospels</u> texts of the
mid-14th century[235]; the entire text must have been thoroughly compared with the Greek original and corrected according to it. It generally follows the Russian 14th-cen-
tury version of the New Testament, but sentences from the
12th-century Bulgarian <u>Exegesis of the Gospel</u> by Theophylaktes have replaced the traditional Russian ones here
and there, although in these passages some Bulgarian words
have been replaced by Russian equivalents (верста for
поприще, <u>погостъ</u> for вьси,etc.)[236]. The orthography
of the manuscript is of particular interest: while new
letters from the Greek alphabet are boldly introduced (ὄ,
υ, ω and ∞, increased used of ï), along with many
Greek ligatures and all types of Greek stress marks, there
is a complete absence of Middle Bulgarian orthographic fea-
tures (ѫ; <u>рь</u>, <u>ль</u> for <u>ор</u>, <u>ер</u> and <u>ол</u>, and — in Slavic
words only — <u>a</u> for the Russian ꙗ after vowels)[237].

When the orthographic features of this early and
independent Russian revised edition of the <u>Four Gospels</u> are
compared with those of Vun'ko's copy (1382) from a Middle
Bulgarian text (cf. 2.3.2.3.), it is apparent that the Rus-

---

235. G. Voskresenskij, Xarakterističeskie
<u>čerty</u> <u>četyrex</u> <u>redakcii</u> <u>slavjanskogo</u> <u>perevoda</u> <u>Evangelija</u> <u>ot</u>
<u>Marka</u> <u>po</u> <u>sto</u> <u>dvenadcati</u> <u>rukopisjam</u> <u>Evangelija</u> <u>XI</u> - <u>XVI</u> <u>vv.</u>,
Moscow, 1896, pp. 48-54, 258-291.

236. A. I. Sobolevskij, <u>op. cit.</u>, p. 29.

237. M. Korneeva-Petoulan, K istorii russkogo
jazyka, Osobennosti pis'ma i jazyka moskovskix vladyk XIV
v., <u>Slavia</u>, XV, 1937, 1, p. 1-23.

sian orthographic traditions — Muscovite and Novgorodian—
still hold their own against the Middle Bulgarian orthography, while the spirit of the South Slavic revision of the
holy books, and even the somewhat different language of the
new South Slavic translations, are freely accepted by the
Russian bookmen. By the early 15th century, however, the
Middle Bulgarian orthography had completely triumphed in the
works of the Russian copiers and writers. The Russian scribe
Evsevij-Efrem, working in a Constantinople monastery, introduced into his copy of the Lestvica (1420-1421) not only the
letters from his Middle Bulgarian prototype but also the confusion of the letters ⱥ and ⱬ (cf. пр҃отыⱥ вл҃чицⱥ на́шⱥ
бц҃ⱬ)[238].

The drastic change in Russian orthography at the
end of the 14th century, and especially in the early 15th
century, is very hard to explain. It would have been quite
possible for the Russians, while using South Slavic revised
texts of older translations or of new translations, to copy
them and send them to Russia, following all the rules of the
established local Russian orthographies (as did Vun'ko), or
to innovate the Russian alphabet only by introducing the contemporary Greek shapes and variety of letters, ligatures and
superscripts (as did Evsevij-Efrem). But as we know, this

---

238. See the photoreproduction of Evsevij-Efrem's
postscript to Lestvica (leaflet 324 b) in:
    G. I. Vzdornov, op. cit., Illustration 2 (between
pp. 176 and 177).

practice was followed only temporarily and in isolated cases. It seems that the answers can be sought only in the totality of factors which finally determined the new trend, the importation of certain Middle Bulgarian orthographic features into Russian writing:

a) The Russian spiritual leaders of Bulgarian origin, Kiprian and Camblak, must have insisted with all th weight of their authority that the Middle Bulgarian spellin system was closer to that used in the oldest Church Slavic books, while the Russian system had deviated, reflecting phonological features of the spoken Russian language. Such an argument would have been difficult to oppose because there were older Russian manuscripts from the Kievan period which had been only marginally russified;

b) At the end of the 14th century there were var ious Russian orthographic and literary schools, created as a result of the feudal fragmentation of the country, the Tatar domination and the lack of an authoritative center of culture. In the new tendencies toward national unification (expressed in the expansion of both Russian Lithuania and Muscovite Russia) the need arose for a national graphic system, purged of features based on the phonology of partic ular Russian dialects. Although we do not have explicit testimony to such a need in the Russian historical sources, it may still be inferred by analogy with the similar situation in the South Slavic countries in the 13th and early 14th centuries, which called forth the newer Bulgarian and

Serbian orthographic systems. It must be pointed out, however, that Russia had two options: either to develop its own supradialectal orthographic system by searching for models in the oldest Russian Church Slavic literature, or to borrow an already established orthography which very much resembled that of the oldest Church Slavic texts and still did not come into irreconcilable conflict with the Russian concept of the Church Slavic language. In this respect, both the Serbian and the Bulgarian orthographic systems were borrowed from, but the influence of the Bulgarian system was definitely predominant[239];

    c) The role of the Balkan monasteries as rich repositories of Bulgarian and Serbian Church Slavic books is of tremendous importance. Russian monks who lived in these monasteries for many years must have been impressed by the language, orthography and artistic merits of the South Slavic books there, and from long exposure must have come to accept all their features as superior. We should not for a moment forget that both Bulgarian and Serbian books were written in a language which was first of all Church Slavic;[240]

---

239. M. N. Speranskij, K istorii vzaimootnošenij russkoj i jugoslavjanskix literatur (Russkie pamjatniki pis'mennosti na juge slavjanstva), Iz istorii russko-slav-janskix literaturnyx svjazej, Moscow, 1960, p. 13-14.

240. In this respect the term "Middle Bulgarian literary language" is unfortunate and misleading, since it overemphasizes the national characteristics of the language (cf. our discussion from Chapter Three to the end of this dissertation).

supranational, and in which certain national features were of only secondary importance.

The combination of these three major factors must have caused the rapid change in the Russian language and literature under the influence of their South Slavic counterparts, which took place around the year 1400. But while the reasons for the choice of the Bulgarian (and partially the Serbian) versions of Church Slavic as models for imitation are not entirely clear, the place where this cultural transfer occurred was, beyond doubt, not Russia, but the international communities of the Balkan monasteries, and specifically those in Constantinople and on Mount Athos. Not only did Russian monks go to these monasteries on pilgrimage, but many of them remained as members for short or long periods, and performed much fruitful work in transferring the accumulated Church Slavic literature from the Balkan monasteries to the main cultural centers of Russia.

An illustrative example is the activity of the Russian scribe and monk, Evsevij-Efrem (cf. fn. 238). His first copy, from a known Middle Bulgarian antecedent which was also completely influenced by the Bulgarian orthography, is from the year 1420[241], made in the Constantinople Monas-

---

241. The manuscript is dated by the water-marks on the paper. See:
N. P. Lixačev, Paleografičeskoe značenie bumažnyx vodjanyx znakov, II, St. Petersburg, 1899, pp. 58, 267.

tery of Our Lady of Perivlepti; it is a **Mineja** for November-May. The present location of the manuscript by Evsevij-Efrem is unknown[242], but another Russian copy made from Evsevij's manuscript in 1432-1433 (Lenin State Library of the USSR in Moscow, # Ф. 304, Но. 669)has Russian orthography[243]. Between Dec. 7, 1420 and March 18, 1421, in the same Constantinople monastery, Evsevij-Efrem copied the **Lestvica**, now kept in the Lenin State Library in Moscow, # Ф. ІІЗ, Волокол, 462 (cf. fn. 228). There are three known 15th-century Russian copies from this manuscript by Evsevij-Efrem[244]. Two years later, on Dec. 10, 1423, the monk Evsevij-Efrem began another copy of the same book in the same monastery, but after completing leaflet 64 he apparently moved to Mt. Athos, where in the Vatopedi Monastery another Russian scribe, Mitrofan, finished the copying (leaflets 65 through 329). But as can be concluded from the handwriting, it was Evsevij - Efrem who wrote the short postscript on p. 329, from which we learn that the manuscript was finished on March 15,

---

242. G. I. Vzdornov, op.cit., p. 193. See also: A. I. Sobolevskij, op. cit., p. 25, point 8.

243. A. I. Sobolevskij, ibid.

244. G. I. Vzdornov, op. cit., p. 193-194.

1424[245]. It is kept today in the State Historical Museum in Moscow, # Усп. I8 - бум.

The last information on the literary activities of Evsevij-Efrem in a Balkan monastery is from a Sbornik of eremitic homilies, copied by him in 1425, translated especially for him by the Serbian monk Iakov Dobropisec. The translation and copying were done in the Monastery of St. Paul on Mt. Athos. The original copy by Evsevij-Efrem is lost, but two other Russian copies made from it by other scribes, in 1431 and in the second half of the 15th century, are known, as are many others from later times[246].

We have an idea, although only an incomplete one, of what kinds of literature were copied or, in a few cases,

245. G. I. Istomin, Opis' knig biblioteki Moskovskogo Uspenskogo sobora, Čtenija v Obščestve istorii i drevnostej rossijskix pri Moskovskom Universitete, Moscow, 1895, 3, # 18.
A. I. Sobolevskij, ed., Novyj sbornik paleografičeskix snimkov s russkix rukopisej XI - XVIII vv., St. Petersburg, 1906, Tables 22, 23.
A. I. Sobolevskij, Slavjano-russkaja paleografija S 20 paleografičeskimi snimkami, St. Petersburg, 1908 (2nd edition), Table 8.
I. F. Kolesnikov, ed., Sbornik snimkov s russkogo pis'ma XI - XVIII vv., I, Moscow, 1913 (2nd edition), Table 15.
G. I. Vzdornov, op. cit., p. 194-195.

246. P. Stroev, Bibliologičeskij slovar'..., p. 121-122.
Ilarij i Arsenij, ieromonaxi, Opisanie slavjanskix rukopisej biblioteki Svjato-Troickoj Sergievoj lavry, I, Moscow, 1878, # 175; III, Moscow, 1879, # 756.
T. B. Uxova, Katalog miniatjur, ornamenta i gravjur sobranij Troice-Sergievoj lavry i Moskovskoj duxovnoj akademii, Zapiski Otdela rukopisej (GB SSSR im. V. I. Lenina 22, Moscow, 1960, pp. 104-105, 145.
G. I. Vzdornov, op. cit., p. 195-196.

especially translated, by Russian monks in the Balkan monasteries. According to the preliminary count by Sobolevskij, at the turn of the 14th/15th century the Russian literature was enriched by not less than 56 major literary works previously unknown or almost unknown in Russia[247]. Since the oldest Russian copy has not been found for each of them, it is impossible to state that all, without exception, were copied in the Balkan monasteries by Russian scribes. However, the relatively small number of available Russian copies of these works from the late 14th and early 15th centuries contain notes by the scribes definitely stating that the copies were made in the monasteries of Constantinople or Mt. Athos (cf. below). These were the two unique locations on the Balkan peninsula where such an activity is known to have taken place; this can be explained by the fame of those monasteries situated in Constantinople and on Athos in their capacity as international cultural centers. G. I. Vzdornov, in his recent study on the role played by those monasteries in the development of the Russian literature, has noticed an interesting phenomenon: the literary production in Constantinople was mostly directed toward Moscow and its monasteries, while the literary production on Athos had as its final destination Novgorod and Tver'[248]. This can be explained by the increased connections between the Patri-

---

247. A. I. Sobolevskij, op. cit., p. 15-37.

248. G. I. Vzdornov, op. cit., p. 180-181.

archate in Constantinople and the Metropolitans in Moscow, as well as the desire of the Greek Patriarch to involve Muscovite Russia in the struggle against the Turks (cf. 2.3.3.).

But as Vzdornov notes, this difference in origin between the new Muscovite books and those of Novgorod and Tver' did not place Moscow in any advantageous position, because there was no basic difference whatsoever between the South Slavic originals kept in Constantinople and those of Mt. Athos[249].

Vzdornov lists after his study 17 new books definitely copied in these monasteries at the end of the 14th and in the first half of the 15th centuries and taken to Russia. Two of them, the New Testament (of 1355) and the Aprakos (of 1383), are practically uninfluenced by the language or spelling of the South Slavic revised editions of the Gospel text[250]. Another two from this list are Middle Bulgarian books, copied in these monasteries and taken to Russia: Kiprian's Lestvica (cf. 2.3.2.2.)[251] and an Aprakos (undated bought by the Russian monk Afanasij in 1430 at the Mount Athos Monastery of Pantokrator, for a monastery in Tver'[252]. Of the total number of 17 books studied by Vzdornov, all of

---

249. G. I. Vzdornov, op. cit., p. 181.

250. G. I. Vzdornov, op. cit., pp. 176, 186-188.

251. G. I. Vzdornov, op. cit., pp. 173-174, 189.

252. P. Stroev, Bibliologičeskij slovar'..., p. 27.
V. N. Ščepkin, Učebnik russkoj paleografii, Moscow, 1920, p. 35.
G. I. Vzdornov, op. cit., pp. 180, 196-197.

which were made in Constantinople or on Mt. Athos, 12 were made by Russian scribes from either Middle Bulgarian or Serbian manuscripts (the latter with strong Middle Bulgarian features)[253], and another, the Sbornik (of 1425), was translated especially on the order of Evsevij-Efrem by the Serbian monk Iakov Dobropisec (cf. fn. 246). All of these manuscripts were unknown in Russia before being copied for Russia in the Balkans[254]. Although this ratio does not have statistical value, being founded on only 17 manuscripts out of a total possibly numbering in the hundreds, it is still indicative of the predominance of Middle Bulgarian features even when transmitted through Serbian copies.

2.4. Establishing the national origin of the translator of a certain literary work is not an easy task. The Middle Bulgarian features in the language of the immediate Russian copies, discussed above, are readily apparent, mainly because the Russian scribes who lived in the Balkan monasteries regarded their prototypes with considerable respect; having been heavily exposed to the lexicon and grammar of the Middle Bulgarian language (whose authority as a model of Church Slavic they had accepted), they did not find

---

253. G. I. Vzdornov, op. cit. p. 181-182.

254. See the list of most of these manuscripts in: A. I. Sobolevskij, op. cit., pp. 24-26, 31-32. G. I. Vzdornov gives an exhaustive bibliography of the available studies on these Russian manuscripts. However, his bibliographic references are full of mistakes, which unfortunately sharply decreases the value of his otherwise impressive research. See: G. I. Vzdornov, op. cit., p. 189-198.

it necessary to russify the language of the books they copied. But with each successive copy of these works, the most
striking features of Middle Bulgarian were gradually
eliminated. The mere use of the new Russian orthography,
reshaped under the second South Slavic influence, does
not in itself indicate that the prototype of a certain
copy was of South Slavic origin, but rather shows the
spelling habits of the scribe. A most striking example
of the gradual russification of a Middle Bulgarian text is
the evolutionary development of Černorizec Xrabər's treatise
On the Letters[255]. Of the 73 copies of the text (all of
which can be related textually to one Middle Bulgarian proto
type), 63 are Russian[256]. By the 17th century, however,
the Russian texts are so perfectly russified at all levels
of the language, that it would be virtually impossible from
a linguistic point of view to identify the prototypes of all
Russian copies as Middle Bulgarian, if the transitional copies with steadily decreasing numbers of Bulgarisms (or the
Middle Bulgarian copies themselves) were unknown today[257].
It seems that textual identification of an Old Russian copy

---

255. K. Kuev, ed., Černorizec Xrabər, Sofia,
1967, 454 pp.

256. K. Kuev, ed., op. cit., p. 165.

257. Compare, for instance, the language of the
Kostroma copy, which has no traces of the diagnostic peculiarities of the Middle Bulgarian prototype (cf. K. Kuev, ed.
op. cit., p. 355-359). But it adds references from Russian
history, and the phrase: стꙑи ко(н)стянти(н) ѳилосоѳъ... и
меѳо(д) братъ его. состависта азбѹку грамоты рѹ(с)скꙗ.
(p. 358).

from the Kievan period (11th and early 12th centuries) as an original Russian translation or as a Russian copy from an Old Bulgarian or, perhaps, West Slavic text, is easier than textual identification of a 16th-century Russian copy of a Middle Bulgarian, Serbian or original Russian translation (cf. below).

2.4.1. In his discussion on criteria for the national origin of a certain translation, known only in Russian copies beginning with the pre-Mongol period, Sobolevskij definitely rejects the orthographic, phonological and even morphological features of the language in a certain copy as diagnostic[258]. From his personal experience, he concluded that the only possible basis for determining national origin is the presence of lexical items whose exclusive national character can be identified beyond any doubt[259]. This conclusion has two serious weaknesses: in the first place, it is not that easy to make a list of exclusively language-specific words. In the study quoted, Sobolevskij offers three groups of lexical items, exclusively Russian[260]:

a) Names of objects and of the surrounding reality, officers, weights and measures, vessels, clothing. Even in the carefully-selected words he lists in this group,

---

258. A. I. Sobolevskij, Materialy i izsledo-vanija v oblasti slavjanskoj filologii i arxeologii. Osoben-nosti russkix perevodov domongol'skogo perioda, Sbornik ORJaS, 88, 3, St. Petersburg, 1910, p. 162-163.

259. A. I. Sobolevskij, ibid.

260, A. I. Sobolevskij, op. cit., p. 162-166.

one can spot кожух, which is by no means exclusively Russian since it is known all over the Balkan Slavic dialects (as well as in West Slavic).

    b) Borrowings from non-Slavic tongues into Russian.

    c) Names of countries, states, nations known mainly to the Russians.

    The idea of compiling such a list is admirable, but the practical results are of little value. The very conservative list offered by Sobolevskij in this particular paper consists of only a few dozen words, yet includes such obvious misfits as кожухъ, сѣно, думати [=советоваться], which can as well be Bulgarian or Serbian as Russian. But a like effort becomes a disaster in Istrin's own account of his publication of the <u>Hamartolos Chronicle</u>[261]. Here he lists as absolutely diagnostic Russian words, items such as бо-лѣсть, быль, дроужина, корста, ловъ, наговорити, намлъвити, неговорливъ, недѣлꙗ [=седмица], одвериѥ, пополошитися, пристроити, слонꙗтися, сълъба, съмълвитися, сѣни, чинъ[262]. Of these, сѣни is attested in the oldest Gospel texts (cf. the glossary to <u>Mar.</u>), while all the rest are widespread in modern Bulgarian dialects. (I have not checked the other words from Istrin's list with available dictionaries of those modern Bulgarian dialects unknown to me, nor of dia-

---

    261. V. M. Istrin, Xronika Georgija Amartola v drevnem slavjano-russkom perevode, <u>Slavia</u>, II, 1923, 2/3, p. 460-467.

    262. V. M. Istrin, <u>op. cit.</u>, p. 463-465.

ects of the other Slavic languages.) As has already been
iscussed, preliminary lists like Istrin's have little sci-
ntific value because they are not based on thorough examin-
tion of the lexical wealth of all the Slavic dialects (the
equisite data collection will hardly be accomplished in our
eneration). Such a list, even when it can be made, will
epresent only modern Slavic dialects; it could not take
nto account the steady lexical loss in the languages, nor
he lexical innovations reaching them from the surrounding
ialects and literary languages.

The second weakness of Sobolevskij's reliance upon
exical items as a criterion for the nationality of a Slavic
translator lies in the minimal number of words that are
eally terminological for only one Slavic country. Since
ne deals with established terms (e.g. the Russian вьрста as
a measure of distance, погостъ for a small unfortified
settlement), one can understand why the Russian copyist,
as long as he understood the meaning of the original terms
in his prototype (in this case, поприще and вьси),
would automatically replace them with their Russian equivalents so as to make the content clear to his Russian readers.
As has been pointed out, such a replacement was made by the
scribe who revised the Russian Four Gospels in Constantinople in 1355, using in part the Middle Bulgarian work by
Theophylaktes (cf. 2.3.4.2.). In my opinion, similar lexical
replacements were made in the Old Russian Pčela, generally
believed to be a Russian original translation. As long as

the scribe understood the meanings of the South Slavic
terms, he replaced them with their Russian counterparts.
But when he came to the word *мжжьца he left it with only
slightly altered shape (моужика). The publisher, who did
not understand it either, put a question mark after it[263].
The word мъже́ц in Contemporary Standard Bulgarian and some
dialects, with further dialectal variants ма́жец, мо́жец,
му́жец means 'uvula'; the Russian equivalent is язычо́к.
Here we face the absence of a general Slavic word for an insignificant anatomical term; the isogloss *mǫzьcь vs.*języ-
čьkъ could be very old, perhaps reflecting semantic influences of the different substrata in Bulgaria and Russia.

    2.4.2. If, as Sobolevskij states, orthographical,
phonological and morphological features are unreliable
criteria for establishing the national origin of a Slavic
translation of the earlier period, and if the lexical items
are so far not very reliable either, each of these is even
less trustworthy in the later periods, when certain national traditions and local schools in the Slavic literary languages were well established and the replacement of striking foreign dialectal features by domestic traditional grammatical norms and lexical terms should be expected in a
greater degree than before. Throughout its entire history

    263, Чювьство сластьною предѣлъ имѣеть до
моужика (?) и до гортани, прешедъше же предѣлъ, нѣ разнь-
ства надомоꙁмоу, но вса равна ѣствоу на гнои премѣнꙗющи.
This quotation is from:
    V. Semenov, Drevnjaja russkaja Pčela, Sbornik
ORJaS, 54, 4, St. Petersburg, 1893 (photoedition: Nendeln,
Liechtenstein, 1966), p. 247-248.

Church Slavic was by function an international language and thus the number of local features in it was consciously kept to a minimum. The international monasteries in Constantinople and on Mt. Athos, where most of the Russian copying of South Slavic texts took place, was an excellent location, for example, for learning the meanings of local Bulgarian and Serbian words which were then and there replaced by Russian words, either dialectal or national.

One should not exclude another possibility: Russian copies from South Slavic prototypes could have been revised later in Russia by comparison with the Greek texts, and certain typically Russian features introduced at that point. Such seems to have been the situation with the "Russian" translation of Akir the Wise (Povest' ob Akire Premudrom)[264]. N. Durnovo, studying the lexical differences between the 16th-century Russian copy # 46 of the Soloveckij Monastery (Solov.) and the 16th-century Serbian copy # 828 of the Beograd Library (Bgrd.), noted that certain Russian words, presumably hard for the Serbian copyists to understand, are completely missing from the Serbian version, and states that "all copies of the (Serbian) first redaction have their origin in a Russian copy"[265]. In this particular

---

264. My study of the Russian and Serbian copies, representing two different versions of the translation, is based on Durnovo's publication:
N. Durnovo, K istorii povesti ob Akire, Materialy i izsledovanija po starinnoj literature, I, Moscow, 1915, 131 pp.

265. N. Durnovo, op. cit., p. 131.

study he is careful not to join fully A. I. Sobolevskij and
A. D. Grigor'ev in their identification of the Russian copies as original Russian translations. Although he calls
their opinion "very probable", he does not accept that it
has been "completely proven"[266]. Durnovo's mistakes in ide
tifying the Serbian copy as from a Russian prototype can be
explained by his absolute reliance upon tentative considera
tions of the national character of lexical items and by his
disregard of all other features in the language. In addition he cites the lexical differences one-sidedly. He list
бебромъ, хоудобы, боголишивоу, синьць, небылое дѣло, ореве,
etc. as Russian words missing from the Serbian copies, and
adds that коноплянъ портъ and порты свѣтлы are completely
absent from some Serbian copies, while in others they are
replaced by конопно предено and новие ризи, respectively[26]
But he fails to note typical South Slavic words like гиздав
('handsome, well-groomed'), срѣщати ('to meet'), строувати
('to destroy, waste'), etc., which are not present in the
Russian texts. Here are the parallel phrases: не коупи
раба гіздава ни крадлива (Bgrd., p. 38)[268]vs. не кѹпи раб
величава ни рабѹ величавѹ (Solov., p. 22); аще те кто
срѣщеть й рѣеть к' тебѣ (Bgrd., p. 38) vs. аще к'то
оѹсрѣтъ възмолви к' тебѣ (Solov., p. 22); не строуваи

---

266. N. Durnovo, ibid.

267. N. Durnovo, op. cit., p. 130-131.

268. The page numbers quoted here refer to
Durnovo's publication.

именїа моюего (Bgrd., p. 39) vs. не порти скота моего
(Solov., p. 27). It is an impossible task to try to establish the priority of the South Slavic or the Russian lexical
variants without taking into consideration other linguistic
evidence.

In addition to the overwhelming Church Slavic vo-
cabulary of both texts (most of the words used in Akir the
Wise are found in the New Testament, the Manasses Chronicle
(including the Tale of Troy), the Serbian (Bgrd.) and the
Russian (Solov.) copies contain striking Bulgarisms which
Durnovo was unable to identify as such. In 1915, when he
published his study, little was known to students of
comparative Slavic linguistics about the structural
peculiarities shared by the modern Bulgarian dialects, or
about the historical development of Bulgarian, especially
as a participant in the common processes within the
Balkan convergence area. For example, in Bgrd. there
are forms of the "double object", a Balkan feature rare
but characteristic for middle Bulgarian: в'са ти прошенїа
испльне и͞х (p. 37 'I will fulfill them all your demands');
наоучи͞х юего сестрїичика своюего ана͞на сїи͞х
(p. 39 'I taught him the son of my sister, Anadan, these
things'); of the genitive singular masculine in -e instead
of -a (caused by the usual Serbian rendering of etymological
jat', applied to the Middle Bulgarian ending — especially
common with foreign words — which was written ѣ, representing phonological /ja/ or /a/ after a soft consonant): м͞ца

мар̄θе (p. 39); instead of the usual Serbian conjunction
нь, the form ноу twice (pp. 41, 42), this being another
diagnostic Middle Bulgarian word — (cf. 4.3.5.4.). These
and other less exclusive features of the Serbian copy (Bgrd.
definitely indicate a Middle Bulgarian prototype rather
than a Russian one.

The Middle Bulgarian features of the Russian copy
(Solov.) are as arresting as those of the Serbian one, with
two cases of "double object": с͞но̏ оу̏ богата мѫжа. с͞нъ
з'мию с͡н̈ѣлъ. ю е͡с. и и оу̏бога мѫжа с͞нъ з'мию с͡нѣлъ
(p. 21 'Son, the son of a rich man ate her the snake, and
the son of a poor man ate a snake'); и а̇зъ тѧ оу̏дрѣ̄х'
тѧ. и̇ и̇справих' тѧ — the second тѧ, however, could be
merely a copying error by the Russian scribe — (p. 30 'I yo
preserved you and fixed (helped) you'). Other Bulgarisms
are: не͞гли (p. 25, for не же ли); бор'зо (p. 27 'fast');
брачнины (p. 25 'fancy clothes'); пер'сть (p. 26 'earth')
вретитище (sic) for the correct вретище (p. 31 '(poor) garment made of hemp'); ͡Ѡсоудо̏ instead of ͡Ѡсюдо̏ (p. 32),
reflecting the Middle Bulgarian change of the adverbials
сѣмо > само, сѫ̇доу > сѫ̇доу (cf. 4.3.4.5.); locative after
a verb of motion[269]: е̇ди̏ в' домо̏ ͡Ѡц̃а своего (p. 31); consistent use of the verb имѣти to express forms of the futur

---

269. A detailed discussion on this peculiarity of
the Bulgarian texts can be found in:
I. Duridanov, Kəm problemata za razvoja na bəlgarskija ezik ot sintetizəm kəm analitizəm, Godišnik SU, LI,
1955, 3, p. 185-191.

negative: не има̂^м поустити тѧ ни пожалоую тѧ (p. 36), etc.,
which could, however, be a reflection of the Greek original
if indeed the translation was made from Greek rather than
from a Semitic language. In addition to these various diagnostic Bulgarian features, one must consider the peculiar
correctness (from the point of view of the Bulgarian language) in the use of the past tenses, even in cases involving
difficult tense agreements[270]. But while different tenses
were used correctly in their proper places, the wrong personal endings indicate that the scribe did not actually understand the meaning of the forms he copied and reinterpreted:
тъ̏ оўпо^Пбих’ сѧ (for оўпо^Пби сѧ) мц҃ю (p. 33); тъ̏ оўпо^Пбих’
сѧ (for оўпо^Пби сѧ) цвѣт̆ дн҃вномо̆   (p. 33), etc. Still,
there are new, Middle Bulgarian verbal forms, like the newer
Middle Bulgarian aorist form of the verb жити: на̇ко дро̆^жбою
живѧховѣ [=живѣховѣ] въ многы дн҃и .   (p. 30). All of
these features, if studied in their totality, give sufficient evidence that the prototype of the Russian Solov. copy
was a Middle Bulgarian text. Of course, there are Russisms
in this text too (for instance жем’чюго̆, p. 35), but
this is, after all, a Russian copy, dated approximately

---

270. My personal experience with Russian students
as an instructor of Bulgarian as a second language in the
Institute for Foreign Students in Sofia (1963-to 1964) has
convinced me that the category of past tenses and, particularly, the agreement of different past tenses in Modern Bulgarian (which principally is no different from that in
Church Slavic: cf. K. Mirčev, Istoričeska gramatika..., pp.
185-186, 191-213), is beyond the intuition of a native
Russian.

300 years after the Bulgarian translation was made[271].

On the other hand, according to Istrin[272], the rendering of the Greek -μβ- as -мб- in the Slavic texts is a Russian feature. He mentions this peculiarity in connection with the Russian copies of Akir the Wise (it actually appears there only in the name а̂мбекамъ or а̂мбакоу̑мъ) but Durnovo is skeptical about the translation from Greek and rather suggests translation from a Semitic language[273]. The form with -мб-is, indeed, strange for a South Slavic translation from Greek, where one might expect either -вв- or -мв-[274], and may also be considered a late Russism.

The most surprising fact about Durnovo's inadequately motivated conclusions on the origin of the Serbian and Russian versions of Akir the Wise is that, although he himself did not categorically identify the Russian version as an original Russian translation (cf. fn. 266),it is commonly accepted in the literature[275] that Durnovo "proved"

---

271. Durnovo agrees with Grigor'ev and Sobolevskij that the translation was made before or at the beginning of the 13th century. See:
N. Durnovo, op. cit., p. 128-129.

272. V. M. Istrin, op. cit., p. 461.

273. N. Durnovo, op. cit., p. 102-103.

274. N. Durnovo, op. cit., p. 100-102.

275. See, for example:
V. M. Istrin, ibid.
V. N. Peretc, K istorii teksta Povesti ob Akire Premudrom, Izvestija ORJaS, 21, 1916, 1, p. 3-6.
N. A. Meščerskij, Iskusstvo perevoda Kievskoj Rusi, Trudy ODRL, 15, Moscow-Leningrad, 1958, p. 58.

nationality of the original translator. There are, however,
scholars who still doubt the East Slavic origin of the
translation[276].

2.4.3. The problem of incorrect identification of
the national origin of translations in the Church Slavic
literature is a serious one, since not all Russian and Soviet
scholars are as scrupulous as Durnovo (whose only fault was
unawareness of certain definite Middle Bulgarian features).
Because of wrongly identified translations, the extent of the
second South Slavic (and particularly Middle Bulgarian) influence on the Russian language is unclear. One must emphasize that what we know today about medieval (Church) Slavic
literature, original and translated, is only some fragments
of the fantastic wealth of this literature kept in libraries
and museums all over the world. According to the incomplete data collected by N. K. Nikol'skij and his students,
in Russian libraries and museums alone there are about
1560 different works translated from the Greek[277].   In
addition to this huge number of Greek and non-Russian

---

276. D. Čiževskij, Comparative History of Slavic
Literatures, Baltimore, 1971, pp. 31, 36.
          While Čiževskij questions the national origin of
Akir the Wise, Bulgarian literary historians are unanimous
in considering it an early Middle Bulgarian translation. I
am not, however, aware of any studies by linguists, Bulgarian or of other nationality, which would definitely prove
the Middle Bulgarian character of the translation.

277. V. F. Pokrovskaja, Kartoteka akademika N.
K. Nikol'skogo, Trudy Biblioteki Akademii nauk SSSR, 1,
Moscow-Leningrad, 1948, p. 142-150.

Slavic titles, there are about 11,580 different works by known and unknown Russian writers[278]. All these figures re resent works in manuscripts dated from the 11th through 18t centuries. Nikol'skij's data, assembled before 1904 and only for the major Russian centers, show that these are represented by between 80,000 and 100,000 separate manuscripts, containing between 1,200,000 to 2,000,000 copies of the above-listed individual works[279]. Of course, these figures are obsolete, since in the last 60 years or so many additional manuscripts have been discovered in Rus- sia and preserved for eventual study by the major Soviet institutions[280].

In the light of such figures one feels very humbl attempting to rediscover past trends in inter-Slavic cult- ural transfer and to examine their manifestations. The study of a few selected Russian manuscripts from the period of the so-called second South Slavic influence might produc conclusions of limited validity with respect to the rest of the Russian literature — translated, imported or original of the same period. One can only trust the judgment of seri ous and very knowledgeable workers in the field, such as Sobolevskij and Lixačev, who having examined hundreds or

---

278. V. F. Pokrovskaja, ibid.

279. V. N. Peretc, K voprosu o racional'nom opisanii drevnix rukopisej, Tver', 1905, p. 3.

280. D. S. Lixačev, Tekstologija, p. 97-102.

thousands of the manuscripts kept in Russia, concluded that
there was a change in the entire Russian literary production
at the end of the 14th - beginning of the 15th centuries,
and that this change was caused by a second wave of South
Slavic (especially Middle Bulgarian) influence.

ON THE SO-CALLED REVISION OF THE MIDDLE BULGARIAN
LANGUAGE AND LITERATURE

3.1. The term "Middle Bulgarian" is applied both to the literary language of Bulgaria, and to the spoken Slavic dialects in that country, during the 12th, 13th and 14th centuries[281]. This term is an unfortunate one, since it implies the existence of a language very different from OCS (or Old Bulgarian). This was clearly singled out by N. van Wijk in his comparison of the relationships between, on the one hand, OCS and its Russian, Serbian and Croatian recensions, and, on the other hand, OCS and Middle Bulgarian: "The relations between the Middle Bulgarian language and the Old Bulgarian language are very different, because here are present only different periods in the development of the same language" (italics mine, I. T.)[282]. By and large the difference between the language of a 13th-century copy from an OCS text and that of the oldest known OCS texts is often insignificant, appearing mainly in the phonology and spelling. Such is the case with the Tərnovsko Evangelie

---

281. K. Mirčev, Istoričeska gramatika na bəlgarskija ezik, Sofia, 1963 (2nd edition), pp. 8, 12-20, 30-32, 52-56.

282. N. van Wijk, Istorija staroslavjanskogo jazyka (translated from German), Moscow, 1957, p. 37.

(1273), kept in Zagreb[283]. The usual striking peculiarity of the Middle Bulgarian language, the redistribution of the letters for the nasal vowels (compared to the situation in OCS), sometimes has limited manifestation, as for example in the 12th-century Dobromirovo Evangelie, Grigorovič Parimejnik, Bologna Psalter[284], etc. Even a cursory glance at the newer 12th-century copies of the OCS texts causes a serious doubt as to the wisdom of calling their language (separated by about 300 years from the time of the translations) by a different name from the language of the 11th-century "classical" texts, separated from the time of the translations by about 200 years. In addition, there is the mere theoretical chance that a "Middle" Bulgarian copy could have been made directly from a 9th-century prototype and thus, except in the phonology, would better reflect the morphological and syntactic structure, as well as the lexicon, of the OCS language of

---

283. M. Valjavec, Trnovsko tetrajevanđelije XIII vieka, Starine, XX, Zagreb, 1888, p. 157-241; Starine, XXI, Zagreb, 1889, p. 1-68.

284. For a short review of the peculiarities of these manuscripts, see:
K. Mirčev, op. cit., p. 12-13.
For lengthy discussions on the peculiarities of two of these manuscripts, as well as for their texts, see:
V. Jagić, Evangelium Dobromiri; ein altmacedonisches Denkmal der kirchenslavischen Sprache des XII. Jahrhunderts, Vienna, v. 1, 1898, 138 + ii pp.; v. 2, 1899, 140 +iii pp.
V. N. Ščepkin, Bolonskaja psaltyr'. S priloženiem semi fototipij i vos'mi cinkografij, Issledovanija po russkomu jazyku, II, 4, St. Petersburg, 1906.
V. Jagić, Slověn'skaja psal"tyr'. Psalterium Bononiense, St. Petersburg, 1907.
I. Dujčev, ed., Bolonski psaltir (photopublication of the manuscript), Sofia, 1968, 530 pp.

- 131 -

the 9th century, while an 11th-century glagolitic text might have been copied from other 11th-century prototypes and thus have more grammatical and lexical innovations. It is a well-established fact that in the 12th century some Bulgarian copyists made use of old glagolitic manuscripts, and even used the glagolitic letters marginally in their own writings (such as, for instance, the linguistically very archaic Šafarikov triod)[285].

The term "Middle Bulgarian language" is justified only when applied to the Slavic dialects of the population which called itself Bulgarian. From the sporadic new grammatical forms penetrating into the literature as "mistakes" one can judge that serious structural changes had occurred in the dialects, the spoken Bulgarian language (as a totality of all its dialects) having moved towards analytism. In this respect, Bulgarian gradually diverged from the rest of the Slavic languages, participating in common processes with the non-Slavic languages of the area — Albanian, Rumanian and some dialects of Greek. This development is known as the Balkanization of the Bulgarian language (referring to its changes within the Balkan convergence area)[286], but the earliest penetration of Balkan features into the Bulgarian literary language are already to be seen in most of the glagol-

---

285. K. Mirčev, op. cit., p. 13.

286. The Balkan features of the Middle Bulgarian language, with basic bibliography on the Balkan convergence phenomenon, will be discussed in Chapter Four.

itic texts of the 11th century[287]. In this respect, the

---

287. The earliest occurrence of the Balkan "double object" has been found by me in Mar. (11th century). I have found the same feature in the 11th - 12th-century Russian copy of Sinajskij paterik. These examples will be given (and discussed) in 4.4.2.
Other Balkan processes, like the development of the post-positive article, replacement of the infinitive by да -clauses, non-distinction of direction and location with the verbs of motion (as part of the reduction of the cases to three: subjective, objective and dative), establishment of the dative possessive, expression of affirmative future by a combination of хотѣти + verb and of negative future by не имѣти + verb, are studied in detail by many Slavists and Balkanologists. Among the most important are:
M. Małecki, Zagadnienia sporne lingwistyki bał-kańskiej, Zbirka odgovora na pitanja 1 (III Međunarodni kongres slavista), Beograd, 1939, p. 216-217.
J. Kurz, K otázce členu v jazycích slovanských se zvláštním zřetelem k staroslověnštině, Byzantinoslavica 7, 1937-1938, p. 212-340; 8, 1939-1946, p. 172-288.
K. H. Meyer, Altkirchenslavische Studien II. Das Supinum. Eine syntaktische Untersuchung, Schriften der Königsberger Gelehrten Gesellschaft 18. Jahr., geisteswis. Kl., 3, Halle, 1944, p. 284-285.
K. Mirčev, Koga vəznikva člennata forma v bəlgar-skija ezik, BəlgEz, 3, 1953, p. 45-50.
Z. Gołąb, Funkcja syntaktyczna partykuły da w językach pd.-słowiańskich (bułgarskim, macedońskim i serbo - chorwackim), Biuletyn polskiego Towarzystwa językoznawczego, XIII, Cracow, 1954, p. 67-92.
K. Horálek, K otázce staroslověnského infinitivu, Posta Fr. Trávníčkovi a F. Wollmanovi, Brno, 1948, p. 159 - 165.
_____, Evangeliáře a čtveroevangelia, Prague, 1954, p. 159-176.
I. Duridanov, Kəm problemata za razvoja na bəl-garskija ezik ot sintetizəm kəm analitizəm, Godišnik SU, 51 Sofia, 1955, p. 85-272 (Photoreprint, Sofia, 1956).
_____, Za načenkite na analitizma v bəl-garskija ezik, Rocznik slawistyczny, 20, 1958, p. 16-26.
H. Birnbaum, Untersuchungen zu den Zukunftsum-schreibungen mit dem Infinitiv im Altkirchenslavischen, Stockholm, 1958, pp. 25-26, 213-232, 253-260, 276.
_____, Balkanslavisch und Südslavisch, Zeitschrift für Balkanologie, III, 1965, 1-2, pp. 31-38, 61-62.
J. Sedláček, Sintaksis staroslavjanskogo jazyka v svete balkanistiki, Slavia, XXXII, 1963, 3, p. 385-394.
A. Minčeva, Razvoj na datelnija pritežatelen padež v bəlgarskija ezik, Sofia, 1964, 175 pp.

Bulgarian literature of the 12th - 14th centuries does not reflect the beginning, but only the continuation of structural changes in the language which had started earlier. Although we have indirect evidence (the Wallachian and Moldavian gramoty written in Bulgarian dialects)[288] that by the mid-15th century most of the features of the Modern Bulgarian language were completely established, the language of Church Slavic literature in Bulgarian even at that time was extremely conservative. In this connection, K. Mirčev writes:

> Unfortunately, we must emphasize, that we do not known of literary monuments from the most important epoch, when the decisive turn of the Bulgarian language from synthetism towards analytism took place, which might reflect better the language of the people. Almost all monuments connected with this epoch have a Church character and strictly follow tradition, and give no place at all to the peculiarities of the popular language[289].

Another serious weakness of designating the Bulgarian literary language of the 12th - 14th centuries as Middle Bulgarian, while calling that from the 15th century onward New Bulgarian, is that it virtually excludes from the history of the Bulgarian literary language the entire traditional Church Slavic literature created after the 14th century. The Bulgarian, Serbian, Wallacho-Moldavian and

---

288. S. B. Bernštejn, Razyskanija v oblasti bolgarskoj istoričeskoj dialektologii, 1, Moscow-Leningrad 1948, 370 pp.

289. K. Mirčev, Istoričeska gramatika..., p. 144.

Russian Church Slavic texts were diligently copied in Bulgaria all the way to the mid-19th century, at the end paralleling the creation and development of the modern Bulgarian literary language.

While "Middle Bulgarian" is the appropriate term for the Bulgarian dialects between the 11th and the end of the 14th centuries[290], it has little if any justification when applied to the literary language. The time between the 12th and the 14th centuries is only a period in the history of the literary language in Bulgaria. And although the flow of Russian Church Slavic books in the mid-18th century seriously reshaped the Church Slavic language in Bulgaria[291], some Middle Bulgarian texts were still being copied later. An example will suffice to illustrate this point: the 16th-century Tulcea copy of the Manasses Chronicle reflects a more archaic language than the mid-14th-century

---

290. The beginning of this period is connected with the destruction of the independent Bulgarian state of Samuil (1018), which turned the country into a Byzantine province, and the waves of mass invasions by Turkic populations into Bulgarian territory (in the 1030's, 1048, 1064 and the last two decades of the 11th century). See:
    Belgarska Akademija na Naukite, Istorija na Belgarija, I, Sofia, 1961 (2nd edition), pp. 146-149, 155-156.
    The end of the period is connected with the final Turkish conquest of Bulgaria (1396). The Turks virtually destroyed the Bulgarian nation as it had existed until their advent, through mass relocation of the population of the Balkan territories and Asia Minor, as well as through intensive Turkish colonization of Bulgaria.

291. K. Mirčev, op. cit., p. 85.

Moscow copy of the same text, made by the priest Filip[292].

In this study, the term "Middle Bulgarian literary language" is used because of the already-established tradition in historical studies of the Bulgarian language, but with the explicit reservation that it simply refers to a period in the development of the Church Slavic language in Bulgaria. For the practical purpose of the present study — the impact of this language on the Russian literary language of the end of the 14th - beginning of the 15th centuries — developments in the Church Slavic of Bulgaria after the Turkish conquest are of no interest.

The Middle Bulgarian literary language (until 1396) is a version of Old Church Slavic (in this context it is therefore also appropriate to speak of the Old Bulgarian literary language) which reflects only certain features of the spoken Bulgarian dialects of the 12th - 14th centuries. Nevertheless, these dialectal features are present in varying degree in all texts and are very useful diagnostic tools in determining the national origin of a certain translation or original Slavic literary work. Inasmuch as the search for these features is essential, one must outline the territorial boundaries of the Bulgarian dialects spoken at that time.

---

292. I. Bogdan published the Tulcea copy, comparing it with both the Vatican and the Moscow copies. The numerous spelling and grammatical variants from the Moscow copy, given by Bogdan, demonstrate the more conservative character of the Tulcea copy. Cf.:
I. Bogdan, Cronica lui Constantin Manasses..., p. 3-222.

3.1.1. Today the northern boundary of the Bulgarian dialects is the Danube River, but this cannot be projected backward to the period of the Bulgarian language under consideration in this study. The most exhaustive investigation of the Bulgarian dialects north of the Danube was conducted by S. B. Bernštejn on the extremely rich linguistic material of the Wallachian and Moldavian gramoty (before 1508)[293]. But Rumanian scholars have, with very few exceptions (e.g. I. Bogdan) always had a strongly negative attitude towards any suggestion that large masses of Bulgarians in Wallachia and Moldavia could, through assimilation, have been among the "ancestors" of the modern Rumanian and Moldavian nations. Here is a curious item from the end of the last century, recounted by Bernštejn:

> Some most precious Slavic gramoty from the
> city of Brashov came into the hands of the Ruman-
> ian historian Tocilescu, who was unable to read
> them. The Rumanian historian did not know the
> language in which most of the Rumanian monuments
> up to the 17th century were written. One can
> hardly imagine a Polish historian who would not
> know Latin! But everything Slavic caused the
> Rumanian historians and philologists such emotions
> as did not allow any objective studies. In the
> well-known work on the history of the Rumanian
> language and literature by Prof. A. Densusieanu,
> one reads: "One of the most unhappy coincidences
> for the language, the culture and even for the

---

293. S. B. Bernštejn, Razyskanija..., 370 pp.
More recent papers, contributing to Bernštejn's study with additional data and observations, are:
O. Stojkovič, Srednobəlgarski morfologičeski osobenosti v ezika na vlaxo-bəlgarskite gramoti (XIV - XV v.), BəlgEz, XIV, 1964, 2-3, p. 149-159.
A. Stančeva-Daskalova, Za njakoi dialektni osobenosti vəv vlaxo-bəlgarskite gramoti, BəlgEz, XVI, 1966, 6, p. 556-563.

substance of the Rumanian element was the contact
of the Rumanians with Slavs and the introduction[294]
of the Slavic language in the Church and state"

In the mid-14th century there certainly was a
Slavic Church in Wallachia, and in 1370 both of the Metropolitan sees in Wallachia were under the control of the
Slavic archbishop of Oxrid[295]. But the number of Wallacho -
Moldavian gramoty written in 15th-century Bulgarian dialects
reaches a few thousand (there are twice as many Moldavian
gramoty as Wallachian)[296].

In his serious examination of the contradictory
theories in Rumanian historiography from before World War
II, in their relationship to historic facts known to contemporary science but only partially used by those Rumanian
scholars who disregarded the Slavic background of the Rumanian nation[297], Bernštejn comes to the following conclusion:

> Thus, the Slavic population of Wallachia (and
> also Moldavia) is more ancient than the population

---

294. S. B. Bernštejn, op. cit., p. 44.
But the situation today is different. Contemporary Rumanian scholars acknowledge the participation of the
Slavic (Bulgarian) ethnic element in the formation of their
nation and the importance of the Church Slavic culture in
the history of the country. For basic reference to such
major Rumanian works, see the bibliographical notes in:
Şt. Pascu, ed., and others, Istorija Medie a
României, v. 1, Bucharest, 1966, p. 111-112.

295. Acta Partriarchatus Constantinopolitani, II,
p. 230. This work was unaccessible to me, and the reference
is from: S. B. Bernštejn, op. cit., p. 57.

296. S. B. Bernštejn, op. cit., p. 67.

297. S. B. Bernštejn, op. cit., p. 80-127.

which carried the Roman linguistic tradition. The intensive interrelations between them began from the 13th century. As a result of this process, a new language with multiple Slavic and Romance elements was created on the Wallachian territory. The Slavic tribes of Wallachia belonged to a group of tribes which is known under the name Bulgarian. This is confirmed by the analysis of the language of the Slavic gramoty, and above all, of the Serbian elements in it[298].

The following three phrases will suffice to demonstrate the nature of the language of the Wallachian gramoty of the 15th century: купил тия овни летоска – 'he bought these rams last summer';а вие да га оставите да отиде дома си – 'you should let him go home'; наидете един кон велик и хубав –'find a big and handsome horse'[299]. These phrases, which could be from a modern Bulgarian dialect, show beyond any doubt that the persons who wrote them were native Bulgarians, and not Wallachians who had learned the Church Slavic literary language. Nothing like them is registered in the territory of today's Bulgaria until the mid-16th century; thus foreigners could not have learned such a language from books.

But the presence of native Bulgarians on Wallachian and Moldavian territory in the period under study (12th-14th centuries) is related to the characterization of the literary, Church Slavic language known as Middle Bulgarian. Books, known today, written in Church Slavic, might well

---

298. S. B. Bernštejn, op. cit., p. 127.

299. S. B. Bernštejn, op. cit., p. 78.

have been written in Wallachia or Moldavia and still have had all the peculiarly Middle Bulgarian features.

3.1.2. The southern boundaries of the Bulgarian linguistic area are unclear. In the mid-16th century, the easternmost point of this boundary appears to have been immediately north of Adrianopolis. A German traveller of 1553-1555 testifies: "From Adrianopolis begins Bulgaria. In all the villages they speak the Bulgarian language"[300]. Such evidence, however, is too late to be absolutely reliable for the earlier period. There is earlier historical evidence (14th century) of Bulgarians' living in today's Greece but it is not clear whether they were minority groups within Greek settlements, or residents of scattered Bulgarian villages on Greek territory. From the archives (in the Italian language) belonging to the Cretan notary Manoli Bresciano, who documented the slave trade in the city of Candia, one learns that on Sept. 14, 1382 "a slave Maria, Bulgarian by nationality, from the township of Livadia" (in Epirus) was sold for 115 perpers[301]. On Dec. 5, 1382 another slave was sold, "Mixail, Bulgarian by birth, from the region of Thessalonike, from the village called Phylokarna"[302]. While

300. Fr. Babinger, ed., Hans Dernschwamms Tagebuch einer Reise nach Konstantinopel u. Kleinasien (1553-5), Munich-Leipzig, 1923, p. 245-246.

301. I. Sakəzov, Novootkriti dokumenti ot kraja na XIV v. za bəlgari ot Makedonija, prodavani kato robi, Makedonski pregled, VII, 1932, 2-3, p. 23-62 (entry # 63).

302. I. Sakəzov, op. cit., entry # 85.

Bulgarian settlements (or neighborhoods in Greek towns and villages) on Greek territory might have penetrated far to the south, a considerable number of Greeks lived on the territory of the Bulgarian kingdom, especially on the Black Sea coast and in the larger Bulgarian cities. This was always used by the Bulgarian kings to justify their claim to the title "King of all Bulgarians and Greeks".

3.1.3. The north-west boundary of the Bulgarian dialects in the past has been disputed between some Serbian and Bulgarian linguists. A. Belić seriously claimed the modern West Bulgarian dialects as Serbian, part of the Prizren-Timok dialect group[303]. As far as the Prizren-Timok dialects on Serbian territory are concerned, he suggested them to be "fundamentally Serbian dialects"[304], which borrowed certain Bulgarian features in the 17th - 18th centuries[305]. But there is historic evidence which seems absolutely to contradict such a theory. At the end of March,

---

303. A. Belić, Dialektologičeskaja karta serbskogo jazyka, Stat'i po slavjanovedeniju, II, St. Petersburg, 1906, p. 58-59.
   Serious Yugoslav dialectologists today do not repeat Belić's erroneous statements. Cf.:
   P. Ivić, Die serbokroatischen Dialekte. Ihre Struktur und Entwicklung, Hague, 1958, p. 93-95.
   For further Yugoslav bibliography on this problem see:
   P. Ivić, op. cit., p. 47-48.
   _____, Dijalektologija srpskohrvatskog jezika. Uvod i štokavsko narečije, Novi Sad, 1956, p. 124-129.

304. A. Belić, O srpskim ili hrvatskim dijalektima, Beograd, 1908, p. 100.

305. A. Belić, op. cit., p. 102-103.

1433, the French nobleman Bertrandon de la Broquière crossed the Morava River west of Niš. He wrote:

> Et vins en une ville que l'on nomme Corsebech [Kruševac] et furent X journées depuis Adrenopoly. Ceste dite ville est à un mile près de la rivyere de la Morave qui vient de Bossene et est une grosse rivyere qui depart la Vulgairie et la Rascie ou Servie, qui est une mesme chose[306].

The same statement: the River Morava separates Bulgaria from Serbia (which at that time can only be geographic and ethnic — not political — terms) is repeated two centuries later, in 1671, by the Englishman John Burbury (Gent.) in his account of a journey from Vienna to Constantinople:

> From Jogada, on a fine and strong wooden Bridge, we passed the River Morava, which separates Servia ‖ Servia (sic) from Bulgaria. The next place was Baraizin, then Pellacderesi and afterwards Aleschinti, where in a little Brook, an on the Grass thereabout, we saw many Tortoises..[30]

---

306. Ch. Schefer, ed., Le voyage d'outremer de Bertrandon de la Broquière, premier écuyer tranchant et conseiller de Philippe le Bon, Duc de Bourgogne, Paris, 1892, p. 205.

307. J. Burbury, A Relation of a Journey of the Right Honourable My Lord Henry Howard, (From London to Vienna, and thence to Constantinople; In the Company of his Excellency Count Lesley, Knight of the Order of the Golden Fleece, Councellour of State to his Imperial Majesty, etc., And Extraordinary Ambassadour from Leopoldus Emperour of Germany to the Grand Signior, Sultan Mahomet Han the Forth. Written by John Burbury Gent.), London, 1671, p. 124-125.

I would like to express my special gratitude to the staff of the William Andrews Clark Memorial Library in Los Angeles, who were able to direct me to this source of information and to provide the original edition of this extremely rare miniature book of 1671.

3.1.3.1. Both testimonies are reliable with respect to correct ethnic identification of the territories,
because neither Bertrandon de la Broquière nor John Burbury
shows any special sympathy with the Bulgarians, which might
have prompted them to "locate" the ethnic boundary farther
to the west. The literature on the status of the Torlak
dialects since Belić does not give a precise nor universally accepted explanation of their origin. Their Balkan
(and Bulgarian) features have been explained by early (9th-
13th century) Bulgarian influence[308],by the early influence

---

308. A. Marguliés believes that the Torlak dialects were bulgarized over the period 9th - 13th centuries,
since their territory was successively within the domain of
the Bulgarian kings of the First Empire (Boris, Symeon and
Samuil) and of the Second (Asenid) Empire. See:
A. Marguliés, Historische Grundlagen der südslavischen Sprachgliederung, Archiv für slavische Philologie,XL, 1926, 3-4, p. 203-208.
There is historic evidence that around the year
680 the Protobulgarians resettled the seven Moesian Slavic
tribes (which were the Slavic element in the future Bulgarian nation north of the Balkan Mountains) westward around
the rivers Timok and Morava, with the task of guarding the
newly-formed Bulgaro-Slavic federation from the Avars on
the north-west. Two of the original seven Slavic tribes
(from the later Bulgarian group) received their names from
the new territory - Timočane and Moravjane. See:
Bəlgarska Akademija na Naukite, Istorija na Bəlgarija, I, Sofia, 1961 (2nd edition), p. 60-61.
V. Zlatarski, Istorija na bəlgarskata dəržava
prez srednite vekove, I, 1, Sofia, 1918, pp. 142-143. 146.
K. Mirčev, op. cit., p. 42.
If it could be proven that there were in the 6th-
7th centuries tribes of the Serbo-Croatian Slavic group already settled in the Prizren-Timok area, one might in a
certain sense place the start of their "Bulgarization"
even earlier than does Marguliés. Undeniably, the dialects
of the area were involved in the Balkan convergence processes, parallel with the Slavic dialects of present-day
Bulgaria and Macedonia.
However,on the basis of available historical evi-

of the Romance substratum[309], and according to the most recent theories, by independent (from Bulgarian) participation
in the Balkan convergence phenomena, in which no other Serbo-Croatian dialects took part[310]. One can only agree with
the theoretical premise of some contemporary linguists, that
whatever forces affected the historical development of the
Torlak dialects are of little relevance to the _present_ position of these dialects, within the Serbo-Croatian language
and within the Balkan convergence area[311].

---

dence, it seems that the creation of the transitional Bulgarian-Serbian dialects was a much more complicated phenomenon than a simple "Bulgarization" as a result of political
domination. It is possible (althoughI could find no reference to this in Serbian history) that the penetration
of Slavs into the Timok-Prizren area came simultaneously,
from the end of the 7th century on, in two directions:
westward from Bulgaria and north-eastward from Serbia, and
thus that the dialects there had from the beginning a transitional character. This area must have been quite sparsely
populated even in the 11th century, since it was there that
the Byzantine authorities chose to settle the defeated Pe-
chenegs, sometime after 1048. See:
        V. Vasil'evskij, Vizantija i Pečenegi, Žurnal
Ministerstva Narodnogo Prosveščenija, 164, 1872, II, p. 116-
165, 243-332.

        309. N. van Wijk, Taalkundige en historiese ge-
gebens betreffende de oudste betrekkingen tussen Serven en
Bulgaren, Mededelingen der Koninklijke Nederlandse Akademie
van Wetenschappen, Afd. Letterkunde, 55, A, 3, Amsterdam,
1923, p. 55-76.

        310. P. Ivić, Dijalektologija srpskohrvatskog
jezika..., p. 108-129. More recently, P. Ivić does not
classify the Torlak dialects as part of the Štokavian group,
but rather as an independent group among the Serbo-Croatian
dialects, on an equal footing with the Štokavian and Čaka-
vian groups. See:
        P. Ivić, O klasifikaciji srpskohrvatskih dija-
lekata, Književnost i jezik, X, 1963, 1, p. 27-28.

        311. H. Birnbaum, On Typology, Affinity, and
Balkan Linguistics, Zbornik za filologiju i lingvistiku, IX,
Novi Sad, 1966, pp. 27, 30.

3.1.3.2. There is no question at all that today the people in eastern Serbia (with the exception of the officially recognized Bulgarian minority in the area around Dimitrovgrad and Pirot) think of themselves as Serbians and call their dialects Serbian. But this is not a sufficient reason to project that national consciousness back some 600 – 900 years into the past. Yugoslav linguists (both Serbian and Macedonian) appear not to be aware of the extremely complex situation in the undisputedly Bulgarian dialects[312]: whenever they speak of isoglosses between the South Slavic dialects, they quote as Bulgarian features only those features shared by the Bulgarian literary language[313], which is built on the grammatical structure of two numerically insignificant dialects of the central Balkan Mountains[314]. As a result, the "Serbian" dialectal isoglosses are projected eastward into the territory of the modern Bulgarian state over an area where approximately three out of the eight million Bulgarians live[315].

---

312. In addition to St. Stojkov's Bəlgarska dialektologija, one can find numerous monographs on the peculiarities of dialects, published in the series 'Bəlgarska dialektologija'; they best reveal the tremendous difficulties in singling out a definite number of "Bulgarian features".

313. P. Ivić, Die serbokroatischen Dialekte..., p. 35-41.

314. St. Stojkov, Literaturen ezik i dialekti, Izvestija na Instituta za bəlgarski ezik, II, 1952, p. 129-171.

315. P. Ivić, op. cit., fig. 1 (p. 31), fig. 2 (p. 32), fn. 2 (p. 39-40).

The problem of the north-western boundary of the Bulgarian dialects in the 11th - 14th centuries is not solved at all. It can be solved only in a spirit of co-operation between South Slavic linguists (which seems to be still far in the future) and on the basis of two major principles: first, the national identification and belonging of a certain Slavic population in medieval times has no bearing on the ethnic and political borders between the Balkan Slavic states of today, and vice versa; second, in the national identification of the dialects of two neighboring Slavic peoples, allowance should definitely be made for a belt of transitional dialects which include features of both languages (this has not been done yet, either in Bulgarian or in Yugoslav dialectology, which is itself a very strange "Balkan" phenomenon).

3.1.3.3. Transitional dialects between the Serbian and Bulgarian languages exist and must have existed from the very formation of Bulgarian and Serbian as two different Slavic languages. Without such an understanding, Slavists would search in vain for the "Bosnian" dialectal origin of the Codex Marianus on the sole grounds of the realization of *Q as [u] when all other typically Bulgarian (including Balkan) features are present in the language of that manuscript[316]. Without accepting the existence of suc

---

316. V. Jagić, ed., Codex Marianus Glagoliticus (photoedition), Graz, 1960, p. 410.
V. Jagić explains the confusion of the letters ᚕ

transitional dialects in South Slavic dialectology, one is
unable to explain many phonetic peculiarities in the literature of the Bulgarian kingdom of Vidin (14th century)[317].

An examination of some 14th - 16th century manuscripts written in Western Bulgaria, gives abundant evidence that in
some of the dialects on this territory the etymological *Q
yielded [u], which is not true for most of these dialects
today. Evidence for the mid-14th century is the literary
production in Vidin; for the 16th century the best illustration is the impressive literary activity of Vladislav Grama-

---

and oy by the influence of the spoken language of the scribe
(Serbian or Croatian), while the representation of ъ as o
and of ь as e (with no single occurrence of the Serbo-Croatian a for either of them) he explains as the result of "a
conventionalized pronunciation of these sounds on non-nation-
al grounds" (V. Jagić, op. cit., p. 427-428).

317. A very interesting document (although the
sole surviving sample) from the 14th-century Vidin language is the gramota of King Ioan Sracimir, written between 1363 and 1396 . It reveals many phonetic features
of the modern transitional dialects between Bulgarian and
Serbian: *Q > [u] - (порѫчали); preposition and prefix
*vъ > [u] - (ȣ гра(д); на (instead of азъ) for the pro-
noun of the first person singular; but no vocalization
of ъ/ь into a. See:
            G. A. Il'inskij, Gramoty bolgarskix carej,
p. 30.
            Similar phonetic, morphological and lexical
peculiarities, indicating a north-west Bulgarian dialectal
basis (transitional to Serbian), are shared by the Sbornik of Vitae of female saints (of 1360), kept in the University library of Ghent; as well as by the writings of the
Vidin metropolitan Ioasaf Bdinski.
See:
            I. Martynov, Bdinskij sbornik 1360 g., ruko-
pis' Gentskoj biblioteki, Pamjatniki drevnej pis'mennosti
i iskusstva, XIV, St. Petersburg, 1882.
            E. Kałużniacki, Aus der panegyrischen Literatur
der Südslaven, Vienna, 1901, p. 97-115.

tik[318]. Unfortunately, most of these works have received little attention from historians of the Bulgarian language[319].

3.1.4. The south-western boundary of the Bulgarian dialects[320] of the 13th - 14th centuries was in today's eastern and south-eastern Albania. According to Seliščev, the earliest contacts between the Slavic and Albanian popu-

---

318. There are four extant manuscripts originally written by Vladislav Gramatik in 1456, 1469, 1473 and 1479, totalling 4300 pages and including 260 works by about 50 Byzantine and Bulgarian writers. His language, although reflecting Serbian phonetic features, also reflects Bulgarian morphological and syntactic features. Most of Vladislav's writing activities took place in the West Bulgarian Rila Monastery, which would indicate that his language was fully accepted by his contemporaries as adequate Church Slavic.
For a very comprehensive bibliography and samples of Vladislav Gramatik's writings, see:
G. Dančev, Vladislav Gramatik — knižovnik i pisatel, Sofia, 1969, 147 pp.

319. The only study (and a marginal one) of the peculiarities of the language of Vladislav Gramatik is in connection with textological considerations. See:
G. Dančev, Rilskata povest na Vladislav Gramatik i sporovete okolo dvete i redakcii, Trudove na VPI "Bratja Kiril i Metodij", Veliko Tərnovo, III, Sofia, 1966, 1, p. 49-88.
The linguistic peculiarities of the works of Vladislav Gramatik, as well as of the remnants of the literary production of the Vidin kingdom of the 14th century, have been outside the interest of Bulgarian linguists. K. Mirčev does not include any of those works (cf. fn. 316, 317) in his review of important works in Middle Bulgarian literature (op. cit., p. 17-23). He mentions the development of *ǫ to /u/ in the north - western dialects, without referring to manuscripts in which it was reflected (op. cit., p. 103).

320. The south-western Bulgarian dialects of the 12th - 14th centuries (also referred to as the Macedonian (Slavic) dialects) will be discussed in 3.1.5.

lations on the territory of modern Albania began in the 6th
- 7th centuries. A. V. Desnickaja identifies the modern
Albanian dialects which were influenced most heavily by
the Macedono-Bulgarian population in the area, as the following five: Central Geg, Southern Geg, a transitional
belt south of the River Shkumbin, Northern Tosk and Southern
Tosk[321]. The problem of the interrelationship of Bulgarian
and Albanian dialects, not only in Albania but on the
entire Bulgarian (and present-day Macedonian) territory,
is very complex; but beyond any doubt the Albanians (or
their Thraco-Illyrian ancestors) played a very important
role in the processes of mutual influence that took place
in the Balkan convergence area[322]. The problem of Alban-

---

321. A. M. Seliščev, Slavjanskoe naselenie
v Albanii, Sofia, 1931, p. 7-35.
    A. V. Desnickaja, Slavjanskie zaimstvovanija
v albanskom jazyke, Doklady sovetskoj delegacii na V
Meždunarodnom s"ezde slavistov, Moscow , 1963, p. 27.
    A. V. Desnickaja, Slavjano-albanskie jazyko-
vye otnošenija i albanskaja dialektologija, Slavjanskoe
jazykoznanie (VI Meždunarodnyj s"ezd slavistov), Moscow,
1968, p. 136.
    A. Desnickaja cites a number of pertinent ar-
ticles by Albanian linguists, but since they are all in
Albanian I was unable to make use of them. However, her
report on the problem of the Albanization of an older
Bulgarian population is well documented by lexical evidence, both from the Albanian dialects and from the literary language (cf. op. cit., p. 120-147).
    M. Camaj, Zur Entwicklung der Nasalvokale der
slavischen Lehnwörter im Albanischen, in: Die Kultur
Südosteuropas, ihre Geschichte und ihre Ausdruksformen,
Wiesbaden, 1964, p. 18-25.

322. Z. Gołąb, Conditionalis typu bałkańskiego w językach południowosłowiańskich ze szczególnym
uwzględnieniem macedońskiego, Wroclaw-Cracow-Warsaw, 1964,
p. 172-174.
    E. Çabej, Ältere Stufen des Albanischen im

- 149 -

ian participation at least in the copying of the Middle

Bulgarian literature, before the time of their conversion

to the Moslem religion, has never been considered in the

history of the Bulgarian language. Yet, the type of mis-

takes in some Middle Bulgarian manuscripts raises serious

doubts as to the Slavic origin of the copyist. One such

manuscript is the Aprakos Apostle of the 13th century (kept

in the Sofia National Library "Kiril i Metodij", under #

880)[323]. The scribe of this Apostle writes: нарицаемое

добраа [=добро(ю)] пристанище   (p. 54 a)[324]; "vocalizes

jers" in a strange fashion: тогода (p. 12b), тькомо

(p. 21 b), кото (p. 22 a), or inserts jers in most unex-

pected places: зьнамение   (p. 20 b, 14 a), вьзвратисьтасх

(p. 30 b), сьлишати and иськаше   (both on p. 37 b); confuse

Lichte der Nachbarsprachen, Zeitschrift für Balkanologie,
II, 1964, p. 6-32.
        V. Polák, Die Beziehungen des Albanischen zu
den europäischen Substratsprachen mit Rücksicht auf die
balkanische Situation, in: Die Kultur Südosteuropas,
ihre Geschichte und ihre Ausdrucksformen, Wiesbaden,
1964, p. 207-217.

        323. M. Stojanov, Xr. Kodov, Opis na slavjan-
skite rəkopisi v Sofijskata Narodna biblioteka, III,
Sofia, 1964, p. 52-53.
        See also the Ph.D. dissertation of K. Steinke,
in which the author studies the language of this manuscript, but does not mention the possibility of a copyist of non-Slavic origin. This factor would have addi-
tionally complicated the already complex picture of the
disintegration of the Bulgarian nominal declension:
        K. Steinke, Studien über den Verfall der
bulgarischen Deklination (Slavistische Beiträge, 29),
Munich, 1968, 133 pp.

        324. K. Steinke, op. cit., p. 54.

both ŏ and ь for etymological *ǫ : сѣдъ (p. 22 a), мьжи (p. 20 b), vs. рекѫтъ (p. 83 b); inexplicably uses the letter ѥ: слишитѥ (p. 8 a), рѥкоста (p. 42 b), сѥго (p. 49 a); confuses the letters оу and оі (spelled reversed, as in many 13th-century Bulgarian manuscripts): нашемоі (p. 8 a), разоімоі (p. 69 a), etc., vs. лоудьстии, лѭдемь (both on p. 12 b), etc.[325]. Some of the spelling mistakes might indicate a certain pattern (as, for instance, non - distinction of [l] and [l,] or [m] and [m,], prothetic iotation of initial /u/, etc., but the examples quoted, for illustration only, by M. Stojanov and Xr. Kodov are too few to draw conclusions from.

It might be an interesting task for specialists in the non-Slavic Balkan languages to examine the types of mistakes and to try to relate them to a specific Balkan phonological system.

3.1.5. The geographic distribution of the dialects of Middle Bulgarian is connected with a relatively new problem in Slavistics — the existence of a "Middle Macedonian" language. A. Vaillant was the first to write quite seriously about the "Old Macedonian" language, created by Kliment of Oxrid as a language distinct from the Old Bulgarian language in Preslav; he even goes further, claiming that "when the center of the Bulgarian (sic) state moved

---

325. M. Stojanov, Xr. Kodov, op. cit., p. 53.

to Oxrid, the Old Macedonian language took over"[326]. Approximately 20 years before Vaillant, in 1931, N. van Wijk wrote in relation to the two schools (Eastern and Western) in the Old Bulgarian language:

> One, however, should not oppose the East and the West to each other, because there were many various interrelations and mutual influences between them, while there were no sharp distinctions among the various dialects. For certain texts, it is difficult to say of what origin they are: Eastern or Western[327].

B. Koneski, in his Istorija na makedonskiot jazik, does not use such terms as "Old Macedonian", "Middle Macedonian", "New Macedonian"[328]. However, he first suggests that "the language of the Macedonian Slavs", after the second half of the 9th century, "like the Bulgarian language and, in a lesser degree, the South-East Serbian dialects, underwent many radical structural changes under the influence of the Balkan linguistic milieu"[329]. But the term

---

326. A. Vaillant, Manuel du vieux slave, Paris, 1948. This quotation is from the Russian edition of the book:
A. Vajan, Rukovodstvo po staroslavjanskomu jazyku, Moscow, 1952, p. 17-18.
For detailed analysis of this theory of Vaillant's see:
D. Ivanova-Mirčeva, Starobəlgarski, staroslavjanski i srednobəlgarska redakcija na staroslavjanski (In: Konstantin-Kiril Filosof), Sofia, 1969, p. 45-62.

327. N. Van-Vejk, Istorija staroslavjanskogo jazyka (the Russian translation), Moscow, 1957, p. 31.

328. B. Koneski, Istorija na makedonskiot jazik, Skopje-Beograd, 1965, 203 pp.

329. B. Koneski, op. cit., p. 7.

"Macedonian language" soon appears in a statement about its

"immediate contact with the neighboring South Slavic

languages - Bulgarian and Serbian"[330], and the mechanism

of these "contacts" is spelled out:

> The temporary close contact with the Bulgar-
> ian (respectively, Serbian) language was yet,
> naturally, in medieval times dependent on
> which of the created state centers - the Bulgar-
> ian or the Serbian - in different periods a-
> chieved power in Macedonia[331].

If one compares the changes in the "Macedonian"

language from the mid-9th century to modern times, as de-

scribed by B. Koneski in his historical grammar, one will

find them identical with the changes in the Bulgarian lan-

uage during the same period, as described by K. Mirčev[332].

Most of the specific features of the Macedonian dialects,

not attested in medieval writings, exist in modern

Bulgarian dialects too, as can be seen from the description

by St. Stojkov in his short university textbook on the con-

temporary Bulgarian dialects (Stojkov did not study

any Slavic dialect on Yugoslavian territory)[333].

---

330. B. Koneski, op. cit., p. 8-9.

331. B. Koneski, op. cit., p. 9.

332. For a detailed comparison of Koneski's historical grammar (1965) and Mirčev's Istoričeska gramatika na
bəlgarskija ezik, 1958, 1963 (2nd edition), see:

P. Penkova, P. Ilčev, K voprosu o makedonskom
jazyke i ego istorii, Balkansko ezikoznanie, XII, Sofia,
1967, p. 5-37.

333. St. Stojkov, Bəlgarska dialektologija,

For the entire period from the 9th through the 19th centuries, B. Koneski, in his search for national identity, boldly introduces such terms as "Macedonia" (as a national territory coinciding with the geographical area called Macedonia today), "Macedonians" (as a separate Slavic nation), "Macedonian language" (spoken by this nation and having its own literary form, different from that of the neighboring Bulgarian literary language) as if they were self-evident and undisputed in history and slavistics. He makes no effort to justify them, either by offering serious linguistic considerations (such as a list of grammatical features present exclusively in the Macedonian writings and dialects but absent from their Bulgarian counterparts) or by citing any historical records, testifying to the reality of his terms in all the periods to which he applies them. This is just as well, because they are unjustifiable.

3.1.5.1. To begin with, the geographic region called Macedonia in medieval times (9th - 15th centuries) was located between the city of Adrianopolis on the east, the city of Philipopolis (Plovdiv) on the west, and the Aegean coast at the mouth of the Marica River on the south. The western boundary of the medieval geographic region of Macedonia lay approximately where the eastern boundary of today's region of Macedonia lies[334]. After the Turkish

---

Sofia, 1968 (2nd edition), 296 pp. + maps.

334. The Byzantine historian Leo Grammaticus (10th - 11th century) describes how the Bulgarian khan Krum in 813 captured Adrianopolis and took as prisoners 12,000

conquest in the mid-15th century, the geographic region of Macedonia shifted westward: with Plovdiv as an administrative center, it included Thessalonike, Skopje and Vardar. Yet today's western Macedonia was called Illyria[335].

3.1.5.2. Then the question is, if today's Macedonia was not even called Macedonia until the middle of the 15th century, how could there have been a Macedonian nation and a Macedonian language there? The answer is, that there were not. In the period 9th - 19th centuries the ethnic

---

Macedonians, who later returned to their country, Macedonia. See:
Leonis Grammatici Chronographia, Bonn, 1842, pp. 208, 231, 233; in the same work this author states that the Byzantine emperor Basil I (867-886) was born "in Macedonia, in a village near Adrianopolis" (op. cit., p. 228). The 11th-century Byzantine historian Michael Psellus writes that the Emperor's second cousin Leo "lived in Adrianopolis and was imbued with Macedonian haughtiness". See:
E. Renault, ed., Michel Psellos, Chronographie ou histoire d'un siècle de Byzance (976-1077), II, Paris, 1928, p. 14. Further in his discourse on the events of 1047, the chronicler writes that the rebels "reached Macedonia, seized Adrianopolis as a fortress and immediately set to work" (op. cit., p. 17).
Compare also the historical testimony of the Slavic monk Isaja (1371) on the defeat of Vəlkašin and Ugleša at Černomen, near Adrianopolis, in Macedonia (cf. 2.3.1.b and fn. 135).

335. The Byzantine historian Leonicus Chalcocondyles (15th century) writes that the Turkish ruler Bayazid (1389-1402) signed a peace treaty with the princes in Macedonia, settled Skopje, then penetrated into Illyria and even sent troops to the land of the Albanians. See:
Leonici Chalcocondylae De Rebus Turcicis, Bonn, 1843, p. 60.
The French nobleman Bertrandon de la Broquière reports that soon after March 12, 1433, "je arrivay à Philipopoly [= Plovdiv] qui est le chief de Macedoine et est ceste dicte ville en ceste belle plaine sur ladite rivyere de la Maresche...". (Cf. Ch. Scheffer, ed., op. cit., p. 200).

name of the Slavic people living in today's Macedonia was

Bulgarian, and the language they spoke was called Bulgarian

also[336]. One of the earliest books in a contemporary Bulgar

---

336. The earliest historic record is from the
7th century, when the Protobulgarian chieftains Maurus and
Kuber settled their tribe among the Slavs in the valley of
Bitolja. See:
Miracula Sancti Demetrii, Grəcki izvori za bəlgar-
skata istorija, III, Sofia, p. 158.
In the 10th century, St. Kliment, the creator of
the Oxrid School, is called "Bulgarian Bishop of Oxrid".
See:
H. Delehaye, Synaxarium Ecclesiae Constantino-
politanae, Brussels, 1902, col. 255-256.
In 1019-1020 the Byzantine emperor Basil II
("Bulgaroctonus") issued charters with regulations for the
conquered western Bulgarian kingdom of Samuil. In the First
Charter (1019) it is written that "the Byzantine state expanded and the state of the Bulgarians passed into yoke
with it". See:
J. Ivanov, Bəlgarski starini iz Makedonija,
Sofia, 1931 (2nd edition), p. 547.
Theophylactus, the 11th -12th century Greek bishop of Oxrid, in his numerous letters calls the local in-
habitants Bulgarians, and the language spoken by them —
Bulgarian. See:
Simeon Mitropolit, Pismata na Teofilakt Oxridski,
prevel ot grəcki Mitropolit Simeon, SbBan, XXVII, Sofia,
1931, pp. 18, 71, 72, 128, 181. This same Theophylactus
wrote the Vita of St. Kliment of Oxrid, in which he calls
him the Bulgarian Bishop; the people of Kliment's see (the
same as his own) he calls Bulgarians, and their language,
Bulgarian. See:
Al. Milev, Grəckite žitija na Kliment Oxridski,
Sofia, 1966, pp. 79, 81, 129, 133, 135.
In a letter of June 3oth, 1502, the Dubrovnik mer-
chants Vladislav de Sorgo and Luca de Bona report to the
hospital administration of Dubrovnik that the plague "began
to appear in many places in Skopje, penetrating chiefly in
small places, and affected good people in the homes of Bulgarians and in the homes of Turks...". The letter is published in Italian in Diversa notarie, v. 81, p. 138-139; it
is quoted here from the English translation in:
Bulgarian Academy of Sciences, Documents and Materials on the History of the Bulgarian People, Sofia, 1969
p. 63.

In the Zograph Pomenik (Dead-Roll) from 1527 to
1728, the names of the deceased from today's Macedonia, with

ian dialect from Macedonia was published in 1814 in Budapest
under the following title: По́вѣсть ра́ди стра́шнаго и втора́-
гѡ прише́ствїѧ хрїсто́ва со́бранна̧ ѿ разли́чныхъ сти́хъ писа́нї-
ѧхъ, и̇ преведе́нна на просте́йшїи ѧзы́къ болга́рскїй, по́льзова-
нїѧ ра́ди просте́ишыхъ чл҃вѣ́кѡвъ и̇ некни́жнихъ. Списанна̧ ѿ
Хаджи̇ І́ѡакі́ма да́скала и̇ преведе́сѧ на ту́пъ потща́нїемъ госпо-
дара ку́ръ Хаджи̇ Пе́ца ѿ Щип, и̇ куръ Хаджи̇ Ста́нко ѿ Кра́тово,
и ку́ръ Дими́трїи̇ Фїлі́пповичъ ѿ Е̇гри̇ Дере́ Пала́нка за дꙋше́в-
ное и̇́хъ спасенїе. Настоѧ́тель бы́сть Дими́трїи Іѡа́нновичъ
Зѻзѻ́ра ѿ Се́чища. Въ Бѻдинѣ градѣ, писмены кра́левї Все-
ꙋчи́лища Оꙋнга́рскагѡ, 1814. (Italics mine, I. T.) [337].

A significant testimony on the Bulgarian national
identity of the people in today's Greek and Yugoslav Macedonia in 1850-1860 is given by the Bosnian folklorist Stefan Verković [338]. In his preface he writes:

> But I called these songs Bulgarian rather
> than Slavic, because if one were to ask today a
> Macedonian Slav: "What are you?", he would an-
> swer at once: "I am a Bulgarian, and I call my
> language Bulgarian..." [339].

---

indication of their town or village, are listed on pages entitled пефлагонїа (Bitolja) бл̌гарска земла or бл̌гар'ска
земла, гра́дъ би́толıа. See the publication of this list in:
     J. Ivanov, Bəlgarski starini iz Makedonija,
Sofia, 1908, pp. 281, 284-287.

     337. The complete title is taken from the photo-
reproduction of the front page of the original publication
in:
     J. Ivanov, op. cit., p. 258.

     338. St. Verković, Narodne pesme makedonski
bugara. Knjiga prva. Ženske pesme, Beograd, 1860, 337 pp.

     339. The original text is as follows: «Но я самь
ове песме назвао бугарскима, а не словенскима, збогъ

Volumes could be written on the Bulgarian national consciousness of the Slavic population in today's Macedonia until the end of the last century. The conditions for the creation of a new, Macedonian nation — and later, of a Macedonian literary language — were generated by the intervention of the European powers after the liberation of all Bulgaria from the Turkish yoke in 1878; the European powers keeping their commitment to Turkey, returned Macedonia for 34 more years to Turkish colonial administration. This is when the histories, as well as the languages, of the Bulgarians and the Macedonians really separated.

3.1.5.3. Today the existence of a new Macedonian nation on the territory of Yugoslavia is a fact which cannot be disputed[340]. Nor can one dispute the existence of a young Macedonian literary language, as artificial a creation as the Bulgarian literary language is. But this does

---

тога, ѥр данасъ кадъ бы когодъ македонскогъ Словенина запитао: што си ты? съ места бы му одговоріо: я самь Болгаринъ, а свои ѥзыкъ зову болгарскимъ...» The quotation is from: St. Verković, op. cit., p. xiii.

340. This cannot be claimed for the people who live in Bulgarian Macedonia, since they took part in all the modern history of the Bulgarian nation as equal participants. It is true that in 1947 many of the inhabitants of western Bulgaria were forced by the Communist authorities in Bulgaria to declare themselves Macedonians by nationality, as a first step toward the formation of the Balkan Federation planned by Tito and G. Dimitrov. (The latter, by the way, although born in Greek Macedonia, never thought of himself as Macedonian rather than Bulgarian in origin.) In that year the government authorities in Sofia came a few times to our house, unsuccessfully pressing us to change our nationality to Macedonian because my father's side of the family came from Prilep.

not entitle anyone to project the facts of today backward into history. Such projections are not naiveté, but intentional falsification of historical fact. B. Koneski, while solemnly discussing the "contact" of the "Macedonian" language with the "neighboring Bulgarian", slips, quoting examples demonstrating the development of the "Macedonian" comparative degree of adjectives from the Tərnovo copy of the <u>Manasses</u> <u>Chronicle</u>[341]. In his study of a 16th-century Bulgarian dialect from the village of Bogorsko, district of Kostur (in today's Greece), represented in a brief Bulgarian-Greek dictionary written with Greek letters[342], A. Vaillant writes about the author of the dictionary: "C'était un Grec curieux du <u>slave</u> <u>macédonien</u>", (italics mine, I. T.)[343]. In fact, however, the author was curious not about "Macedonian Slavic", as claimed by Vaillant, but about Bulgarian, for he entitled his dictionary: "Beginning. <u>Bulgarian</u> <u>words</u> and their correspondence in the popular (Greek) language" (italics mine, I. T.)[344]. The dialect of

---

341. B. Koneski, <u>op. cit.</u>, p. 120.

342. G. Gianelli, A. Vaillant, <u>Un</u> <u>lexique</u> <u>macédonien du</u> XVIe <u>siècle</u>, Paris, 1958, 69 pp.

343. A. Vaillant, in his study on the grammar, published together with the 16th-century dictionary (G. Gianelli, A. Vaillant, <u>op. cit.</u>, p. 46).

344. The front page with this title is given in photoreproduction between pp. 44 and 45 of the French publication. In addition, the title is printed in Greek (with reconstructions) on p. 23. However, this is the only Greek sentence in the entire book which has not been translated into French! Here is the Greek title from the photoreproduction of the original: ἀρ[χη] ἐν βουλγαρίοις ῥιμάτον,

the village of Bogorsko was extinct before the creation of the Macedonian nation[345]; the dialect was Bulgarian, and its study is part of Bulgarian historical dialectology.

One is hardly convinced by Vaillant's assertion that: "Ce macédonien du XVI siècle est très semblable au macédonien moderne,"[346] especially when one sees the features which he adduces to prove his point. Here are a few of them: *ě̃ > [ja] (vjáter, vjáždi); systematic preservation of initial *x (xljáb-o); *tj > [št] (nóštvi , ovóštje) and *dj > [žd] (vjáždi). While it is true that all of these features exist in modern Macedonian dialects, it is also true that they are among the most frequently cited characteristic features of Bulgarian[347], and that as such they have been selectively purged from the Macedonian literary language.

3.1.5.4. The term "Middle Macedonian" was first used by the Macedonian linguist R. Ugrinova, but with no definition of its chronological boundaries, nor of the geographic area in which it was written[348]. The basic charac-

εἰς κινῆ γλῶτα ἐρχομένη:

345. Bl. Šklifov, Edin trud vərxu "makedonskata" leksika ot XVI v., BəlgEz, XVII, 1967, 4, p. 380-381.

346. A. Vaillant, in his study on the grammar, published together with the 16th-century dictionary (G. Gianelli, A. Vaillant, op. cit., p. 45).

347. P. Ivić, Die serbokroatischen Dialekte, pp. 36, 38.

348. R. Ugrinova, Spomenici na staromakedonska-ta pismenost, Slovenska pismenost — 1050-godišnina na Kliment Oxridski, Oxrid, 1966, p. 65.

eristic of the manuscripts singled out by Ugrinova as Middle Macedonian is the vocalization of ъ > о and ь > е, which, since it even today exists in some of the Rupski dialects of south-eastern Bulgaria, is rather to be considered a South Bulgarian feature. Other characteristic features of the language she calls "Middle Macedonian" are the use of the letters ѕ and ꙃ; the confusion in the use of the letters ѫ and ѧ; the use of е and нѣ for the third person singular, affirmative and negative respectively, of the verb 'to be'; the use of the grammatical ending -ме for the first person plural of the present tense; the sporadic use of the post-positive article; and the wrong usage of grammatical cases, indicating the existence, in the dialects, of a generalized objective case[349]. Reading Ugrinova's article, one is saddened by the total ignorance of the history of the Bulgarian language, as well as of the present situation in its dialects, on the part of an author who has made it her specialty to investigate the history of one of the former dialectal subgroups of Bulgarian. By contrast, B. Koneski in his historical grammar scrupulously lists many (though not all) of those developments in Bulgaria which coincided with those in Macedonia, and does not use the term "Middle Macedonian" at all.

3.2.   It is accepted in Slavic philology

---

349.   See also the criticism on Ugrinova's article by D. Ivanova-Mirčeva:
D. Ivanova-Mirčeva, op. cit., p. 61-62.

and in the historical studies of the Bulgarian language
that the texts from the classical Church Slavic period in
Bulgaria were revised during the second half of the 14th
century. The credit for this revision is universally attributed to the Bulgarian Patriarch of the last quarter of
the 14th century — Euthymius of Tərnovo.

A typical expression of this opinion is given by
K. S. Mirčev (rendered here in English translation)[350]:

> It must be emphasized that the Middle Bulgarian
> literature was deprived of graphic unity by the
> unfavorable conditions under which it developed,
> the greater difference between the literary and
> the spoken language giving rise to large discrep-
> ancies or errors even in the liturgical books.
> Departure from the norms of a given epoch was
> possible at all levels. This encouraged Patriarch
> Euthymius, in the second half of the 14th century,
> to undertake his reforms, whose main goal was to
> establish order and homogeneity in the spelling
> of Middle Bulgarian monuments and to canonize a
> number of dead linguistic norms; meanwhile, there
> was a conscious resistance to any innovation in
> the literary language and to its rapprochement
> with the spoken language. Thus, for example,
> Euthymius, this "great artist of Slavic letters"
> as his pupils called him, severely criticized the
> omission of the epenthetic -l- in the texts.
> Concerning the use of the nasal vowels and jers,
> he recommended the following: at the beginning of
> a word one should write only ѫ (e.g. ѫзыкъ, in-
> stead of the OBulg. ιѧзыкъ), the back jers
> whould be written only in the middle of a word
> and in prepositions, while the front jer should
> be written only at word end (for example: влъкъ,
> вънь, връхь); wherever two nasal vowels
> follow each other, one should first write ѫ,
> then ѧ (for instance: добрѫѧ instead of the
> OBulg. добрѫιѫ). In general, the reforms of
> the Bulgarian Patriarch aimed to preserve fully
> the archaic aspect of the literary language

---

350. K. Mirčev, Istoričeska gramatika...,
p. 54-55.

which had really become an artificial and dead
language.

This is a typical statement of the role attributed
to Patriarch Euthymius in the archaization and stan-
dardization of the Bulgarian literary language. The tradition which assigns this important role to Euthymius goes
back as far as the early 15th c., when two prominent
writers, Grigorij Camblak and Konstantin Kostenečki,
testified to the merits of Euthymius.

3.2.1. The first, and more reliable, of them
is the Slavic writer and religious leader <u>Grigorij</u>
<u>Camblak</u> (1360's to 1420). In his Vita of Patriarch
Euthymius he writes about Euthymius' activities after the
year 1371 at the monastery of the Holy Trinity near Tərnovo
(before his becoming Patriarch in 1375)[351]:

> What were his activities? The translation of the
> liturgical books from Greek into Bulgarian. And
> nobody who hears me say this should think that
> I shrink from the truth, because the Bulgarian
> books are very old due to their many years of
> existence, and because they have been in exis-
> tence since the Christianization of the people,
> and even because it was those books, which this
> man, who reached all the way to our days, great
> amongst the saints, had studied. This is what I
> know, and there is no other truth. But be it
> because the first translators did not know
> fluently the language and the dogma of the Greeks,
> be it because they used an unpolished language,
> their books differed in words and meaning from
> the Greek books and were rough and unharmonious
> in respect to expression. They were believed
> to be exact only because they were called holy
> books. They concealed many mistakes and dis-

---

351. Bəlgarska Akademija na Naukite, <u>Istorija</u>
<u>na Bəlgarija</u>, 1, Sofia, 1961 (2nd edition), p. 236.

agreed with the true dogmas. That is why many heresies originated from them. After destroying all old books, this new legislator, carrying the new ones in his working hands, descended from the mountain of his erudition and surrendered to the Church a true heavenly treasure, like scripture written by God, and all of it new, all exact, agreeing with the Gospel, not deviating from the dogma..."[352]

3.2.2. In this testimony one must try to separate the usual legendary exaggeration in the Vitae, from the facts. First of all, Camblak does not mention the New Testament as one of the books Euthymius translated; on the contrary, Euthymius tried to bring the other books into accord with its text. That he destroyed the old books must be doubted. At that time Euthymius possessed no particular power within the Church hierarchy; he was a very prominent monk, with some connections with the Palace and the Patriarch, but was still not in a position to decide which books could be "destroyed". The only books which he might have surrendered to the authorities would have been those already forbidden by the Church, and listed in the numerous indices of heretical books. Even if he had been able to suggest to the authorities the destruction of a few liturgical books on account of their gross deviations from orthodox dogma, these must have been the books of that one particular monastery and thus of no importance amid the bulk of distorted copies available even today in great

---

352. P. Dinekov, Evtimij Tərnovski, in: Istorija na Bəlgarskata literatura, 1, Sofia, 1962, p. 287-288.

numbers in the Bulgarian and Yugoslav museums and libraries.

Grigorij Camblak is definite in dating the literary reform of Euthymius: it took place in the monastery of the Holy Trinity between the years 1371 and 1375, before Euthymius became Patriarch. We must question the freedom of even a prominent monk to promulgate such a significant reform. Within the social conventions of the epoch, the only freedom a particular person could have had would have been one of choice among different already-existing norms and schools.

3.2.3. The second of the earliest historical allusions to Euthymius'literary activities is by the Serbian writer of Bulgarian origin, Konstantin Kostenečki, who mentions a few times the name of Euthymius in his treatise On the Letters, written before 1418 in the Serbian state of Despot Stefan Lazarević[353]. The treatise is known in two versions: the full, preserved only in one 15th-century copy[354], and the abbreviated, known in numerous Serbian, Bulgarian, Russian and Wallacho-Moldavian copies from after the 16th century.

The entire problem of the existence of a "testi-

---

353. K. Kujew, Konstantyn Kostenecki w literaturze bułgarskiej i serbskiej, Cracow, 1950, p. 11-30.

354. The full version is published by V. Jagić in his Razsuždenija stariny o cerkovno-slavjanskom jazyke, 1, St. Petersburg, 1885-1895. I used the German photoedition of Jagić's work, which has a different order of the articles and a different pagination:
V. Jagić, ed., Codex Slovenicus Rerum Grammaticarum (Slavische Propylaen, 25), Munich, 1968, 782 pp.

mony" by Konstantin Kostenečki about a revision of the books and the language in Bulgaria by Euthymius, is connected with Jagić's interpretation of what K. Kostenečki really wrote. Here is how Jagić states it:

Konstantin considers Euthymius of Bulgaria the highest authority on different problems of Slavic literature. He talks of him as "a great artist of the Slavic letters", calls him the light of those (Bulgarian) countries "all the way to the Marica River, and the Scythian lands, and in Zagora". Obviously he was not personally acquainted with Euthymius, did not consider himself his immediate student, but as a student of one of his students — named Andronik from the Romanian regions — he bowed before the glory of the Tərnovo Patriarch. And this teacher of his, according to his testimony, belonged to that number of outstanding persons, who knew well the Slavic literature and maintained in it the traditions of the old Tərnovo school. According to Konstantin's opinion, in his own time there were very few such knowledgeable people: "the lights of the letters faded out from the Marica to Thessalonike and Beograd". Even in the Tərnovo countries the Slavic literature was about to decline, but "the King and the Patriarch" elevated it again. As the King one must understand either Ioan Šišman alone, the closest contemporary of Euthymius, or together with him also his ancestor, Ioan Aleksandər; the Patriarch, of course is Euthymius himself. Unfortunately, Konstantin does not touch all of the activities and merits of Euthymius, but only by allusions gives us to understand that Euthymius had influenced considerably that side of Slavic literature which was dearest of all to our author, i.e., he contributed to the stabilization of certain orthographic norms. Since, in the main, only this problem interested Konstantin, he tells in relation to Euthymius, that the latter did not have time (не успел) to formulate precisely his graphic system, that he did not leave behind any spelling manual, where he would have stated his theory: «не потщася списати утверждение симъ». According to Konstantin's words, which are not altogether understandable, Euthymius was satisfied with some kind of «изъявленїя». It is hard to

- 166 -

define what was the nature of these «изъявленїя»
— whether they were his orders or practical regulations[355].

This very long quotation from Jagić was necessary
in order to see the different stages of the evolution in the
understanding of Konstantin Kostenečki's "testimony"
on Euthymius' reform. In an article on K. Kostenečki, the
Bulgarian literary historian K. Kuev writes:

> If Despot Stefan Lazarević wills it, Konstan-
> tin is ready to write such a manual, as will
> have as a basis the spelling of Cyril and Metho-
> dius as well as the orthographo-linguistic re-
> form of Euthymius....
> His grammatical treatise ... gives such an
> array of information (редица сведения) about
> the reform of Euthymius as cannot be found any-
> where else (italics mine, I. T.)[356].

In Lixačev, this line of thought goes even further:

> In order to establish the essence of the
> second South Slavic influence in Russia, it
> would be of great importance to clarify the
> philosophical sense of the literary reform of
> Euthymius, which penetrated into Russia: a reform
> of the literary language, orthography and graph-
> ics.... We can only partially judge the sense
> of Euthymius' reform from a single work by a stu-
> dent of one of his students, Konstantin the Philo-
> sopher Kostenečki (italics mine, I. T.)[357]

---

355. V. Jagić, ed., op. cit., p. 81-82.

356. K. Kuev, Konstantin Kostenečki, in: Istorija na balgarskata literatura, 1, Sofia, 1963, pp. 317,
324-325.

357. D. S. Lixačev, Nekotorye zadači ..., (1960),
p. 107.

The most "advanced" stage of the evolution in the interpretation of Konstantin Kostenečki's testimony on Euthymius is represented by Mirčev's statement already quoted (cf. 3.2.; fn. 350), where even individual points of his supposed spelling reform are listed.

Konstantin Kostenečki's testimony on Euthymius has been interpreted in the literature to a degree which has already made it unrecognizable in the interpretations. Here is exactly what Konstantin himself wrote:

> And still, this artist is imperfect, because I did not reach that great artist of Slavic letters, and as I would say, the father of Tərnovo Kyr Euthymius, who truly appeared, and who is still today, like a light for those lands from the river called Marica even to the Scythian lands and Zagore. But I will give a warm portrait with a godly love which will fill even the non-gifted. To this man, marvelous in his words, a certain Andronik from the Romanian (=east Thracian) regions was a student for a while; and when he was our teacher in writing, he explained thus: no matter how heavy and strong the things you build on firm ground (which is, at the beginning of learning), they will stay there. And only he who will teach the children these things in this way at the beginning is perfect in the letters and in his philosophy (въ мнѡгыи(х) рас'соуж(д)éнии(х)). Having explained this, I will now speak boldly: that the lights of literature faded away, beginning from the Marica, all the way to Salonike and Beograd, with the exception of a few, and those who can still be found are from the Tərnovo lands or taught by such....
> In the same way the letters were destroyed in the Tərnovo lands, but the King and the Patriarch enlightened (the people), and behold, how much go they did by this, and not only then and in their own region, but their plantings and foundation remain forever, and even until now enlighten the surrounding kingdoms. If this is not so, let him who has an objection tell me about it.
> And Kyr Euthymius was the most artistic one in these lands, although many others appeared who

were very prominent in the word of the teachings
and fear of the Lord, but not on the basis of the
letters, as he was. But even he did not make an
effort to write down an affirmation of this, such
as one can find in the Greek writings, or even
some sort of partial exposition. For he who
rules, has no fear of anything, and whatever he
orders, happens; thus he, having taught precisely, or having laid down the fundamentals of
learning, uprooted evil and no one stood against
him, while this poor slave, in the grip of fear
... cannot in this way...[358].

As one can see, Konstantin Kostenečki does not

even mention the word "reform" in his original writing.

His statement can be broken down into several points:

a) Konstantin studied with Andronik, who was for

a while a pupil of Euthymius. From Andronik, Konstantin

learned that a perfect teacher of the language (as well as

a superb thinker) is one who teaches properly from the be-

ginning. Such a perfect teacher was the father of Tərnovo,

Euthymius, whose level Konstantin Kostenečki has not yet

reached (since he has not formulated for his students the

fundamentals of learning; this becomes evident from his

further exposition in the treatise, where he tries to set

them forth).

b) The few in the Balkans (after the death of

Euthymius?) who are still competent in the Slavic writings

are either from Bulgaria or have been taught by teachers

from Bulgaria. In this way Konstantin emphasizes the worth

---

358. V. Jagić, ed., op. cit., p. 102-103.

of his own credentials, although he suspects that someone might argue with him.

c) The Balkan Slavic literature has faded away (with few exceptions, among whom Konstantin himself must be numbered) in the same way as, long ago, it had been destroyed in the Tərnovo lands, but the King and the Patriarch enlightened the people. Jagić's translation of this passage is unacceptable; he writes that "the Slavic literature was about to decline"(пришла было в упадок), while in the original it is said пи́смена та́ко погы́бла была̀ со́уть. The Church Slavic (and especially, Bulgarian) pluperfect can by no means be translated as Jagić does here. Its main function as a tense is to indicate action which had occurred long ago, and whose results were visible in the past, to which the author refers in the aorist. The pluperfect has the same relation to the aorist as the perfect has to the present tense[359]. Konstantin Kostenečki here uses a rare form of the pluperfect — the conjugated verb 'to be' in the present tense plus the l-participle of the verb 'to be', plus the l-participle of the lexical verb, instead of the more usual form бѣшѧ погы́бла. But the same formation of the pluperfect is observed by

---

359. K. Mirčev, op. cit., p. 199.
Cf. also the discussion and numerous examples of agreement of the past tenses throughout the history of the Bulgarian language, in:
I. K. Bunina, Istorija glagol'nyx vremen v bolgarskom jazyke, Moscow, 1970, p. 88-97.

S. B. Bernštejn in Wallachian gramoty from the 15th century: смо били послали [360]. It existed as a variant formation for the pluperfect until it came to be utilized to express the category of reported speech in the pluperfect. But Mirčev, for instance, believes that reported speech is a new category in Bulgarian (though he does not date it), introduced under Osman Turkish influence[361].

There was indeed a time when Church Slavic literature had been destroyed in Bulgaria: this was the time of the Byzantine administration of the country, from the fall of Samuil's kingdom in the 11th century to the creation of the Second Bulgarian Empire in the late 12th century[362]. Konstantin Kostenečki does not know the names of the King and Patriarch who reintroduced the Church Slavic language in the service; otherwise he would have given them.

There is no positive record in Bulgarian history of when the Church Slavic liturgy was reintroduced in the

---

360. S. B. Bernštejn, Razyskanija v oblasti bolgarskoj istoričeskoj dialektologii, 1, Moscow-Leningrad, 1948, p. 214.

361. K. Mirčev, op. cit., p. 208-210.

362. The desperate position of Bulgarian Church Slavic literature under the Byzantine domination is reflected in the so-called "Second Apology of the Bulgarian Book", whose oldest copy dates from the 13th century. Cf.:
    N. Dragova, Vtorata apologija na bəlgarskata kniga i nejnite izvory, in: Konstantin-Kiril Filosof, Sofia, 1969, p. 315-347.

Church, but it could hardly have been before 1235, when
the Bulgarian Patriarchate was reinstated; from 1199 until
that year the Bulgarian Church of the early Second Empire
had been under the Church of Rome, which insisted on the
Latin liturgy (cf. fn. 66). The continuation (after 1211)
of the Synodikon of King Boril includes the story of the
reinstatement of the Bulgarian Patriarchate:

> Іѡаннь асѣнь цр҃ь велиікыи и бла
> гочьстивыи сн҃ъ стараго асѣнѣ
> цр҃ѣ. иже многꙗ любовь имѣꙗ.
> къ бо҃у. прославивь и просвѣти[въ]
> блъгарское цр(с)тво. паче всѣх'
> цреи блъгарскыихь бывшіих'
> прѣжде его...
>   ... и въсꙗ
> ст҃ыꙗ и бж(с)твныꙗ цр҃квы,
> мнѡгыми дарми ѿдаривь...
> и свободꙗ чистꙗ на нихь ѿбыꙗ
> вивь. и въсѣкь сщеннничьскыи
> чинь...
>   ... ѿбно
> вивь патрїаршьство блъгар'ск(а)
> го цр(с)тва. тѣмже оубо ѿбновле
> ніе сиіце бы(с)[363].

The year 1235 is the earliest possible time when
both the King and the Patriarch could have "enlightened the
people". But it is possible, too, that Konstantin Kostenečki is referring to an earlier time, when the King, together
with the Bishop of Tərnovo, partially reinstated the Church
Slavic books (although not in the liturgy).

Konstantin Kostenečki definitely did not have in

---

363. M. G. Popruženko, Sinodik carja Borila
(Bəlgarski starini, VIII), Sofia, 1928, p. 82-84.

mind King Ioan Šišman, King Ioan Aleksandər or Patriarch
Euthymius as these enlighteners of the people. We know
(and he must have known too) that during Ioan Aleksandər's
time (1331-1371) the Bulgarian Church Slavic literature
was in its second "Golden Age"[364], while Konstantin talks
of a time when "the letters were destroyed in Tərnovo".

Jagić's identification of Euthymius with the Patriarch-en-
lightener was quite unmotivated, yet because of his great
authority as a linguist (but hardly as a historian) this
interpretation started travelling from book to book as an
"established" fact.

d) In the last point of Konstantin Kostenečki's
testimony, the only one that says anything concrete about
the activities of Euthymius, the author hardly alludes to
a reform by the Tərnovo Patriarch. The phrase нѣ нє въ
писмене ѡснованїа (with misused cases) can be interpreted
either as 'not on the basis of the letters' or as 'not on
the basis of the literature', since the word писмена in
Middle Bulgarian has the same ambiguity as the Greek gram-
mata (cf. English letters). The second interpretation is
the more likely, however, in the light of the introductory
phrase: "And Kyr Euthymius was the most artistic one
(хѹдѡжнѣйшїи) in these lands". Konstantin Kostenečki
speaks of Euthymius' ability as a teacher rather than as a

---

364. I. Dujčev, K. Kuev, Bəlgarskata literatura
prez XIV v., in: Istorija na bəlgarskata literatura, 1,
Sofia, 1963, p. 267-284.

reformer. But he emphasizes that Euthymius, as Patriarch, had the power (which he himself did not have) "to lay down the fundamentals of learning". As far as Euthymius' prominence in the field of letters is concerned, Konstantin states plainly that "he did not make the effort" (and not не успел, as Jagić interpreted it) to leave even a partial instruction to future generations.

3.2.4. There was no spelling reform carried out by the 14th-century Bulgarian Patriarch, Euthymius of Tərnovo. His "orthographic" and "grammatical" reform of the Bulgarian literary language is one of those 19th-century myths, created in the literature at a time when very little was yet known about the entire epoch. Undoubtedly, Patriarch Euthymius was a prominent Bulgarian religious writer, translator and leader. We know many of his original writings and some of his translations (or revised editions of older translations) from Greek[365]. But there is considerable evidence that the Church Slavic language in Bulgaria had acquired a normalized orthography, grammar and lexicon long before Euthymius became patriarch, as will be shown.

---

365. E. Kałužniacki, Werke des Patriarchen von Bulgarien Euthymius, Vienna, 1901, cxxiii + 450 pp.
      P. A. Syrku, K istorii ispravlenija knig v Bolgarii. II. Liturgičeskie trudy patriarxa Evtimija Ternovskogo, St. Petersburg, 1890, xcvii + 231 pp.
      _____, Evtimija patriarxa Ternovskogo služba prepodobnoj carice Teofane, St. Petersburg, 1900, 2 + xxvii + 15 pp.
      V. Ćorović, Poslanica bugarskog patrijarha Jevtimija Tismenskomu arhimandritu Nikodimu, Južnoslovenski filolog, XII, 1932-1934.

3.2.4.1. In the year 1370 Euthymius, not yet the
Patriarch, translated from Greek some liturgies, rites and
prayers, which he included in a book later known as the
Služebnik of Patriarch Euthymius of Tərnovo[366]. Within
the liturgies were short quotations from the Four Gospels
which, most likely, Euthymius had translated afresh together
with the rest of the texts. It would be fruitful to compare the language of Euthymius' translation of these short
New Testament passages with the language of a previously -
existing Middle Bulgarian edition of the Four Gospels. A
highly suitable text is that of King Ioan Aleksandər's Four
Gospels of 1355-1356 (which will henceforth be referred to
as IAG)[367]. IAG was selected for comparison with Euthymius'
translation for two reasons: first, IAG was a new, revised
edition, made for the King of Tərnovo, and thus must be one

366. This manuscript is kept today in the library
of the Zograph Monastery on Mt. Athos, as MS # 1. In 1890
it was published by the Russian Slavist P. Syrku. Cf.:
        P. Syrku, K istorii ispravlenija knig v Bolgarii.
II. Liturgičeskie trudy patriarxa Evtimija Ternovskogo, St.
Petersburg, 1890, p. 1-109.
        Someone wrote, with Arabic numerals, "lěto 1370"
on the first page of the manuscript; Syrku, a recognized
authority, accepted this date as correct (p. xiii).

367. The manuscript is kept today in the British
Museum under the number 39627 (Parham Collection, MS XLV).
Detailed information on the history of the manuscript and
of the translation, ordered by King Ioan Aleksandər of
Tərnovo, along with a discussion of the grammatical, lexi-
cal and orthographic peculiarities of the text, can be
found in the present study under 3.4. and in Chapter 4.
See also:
        R. Scholvin, Einleitung in das Johann-Alexander -
Evangelium, Archiv für slavische Philologie, 7, Berlin,
1884, pp. 1-56, 161-221.

of the best examples, for its time, of a Church Slavic language so correct as to be fit for a king; second, the
scribe in his postscript dates the translation and copying
of the manuscript to 1355-1356, which indicates that the
language and the orthographic system employed in it are 15
years older than those of Euthymius' translation of 1370;
thus the norms of IAG were the ideal of between 15 and 20
years before the time Euthymius supposedly introduced his
reform (cf. 3.2.1. and 3.2.2.).

EUTHYMIUS[368]   IAG[369]

е҆ѵ̑ ѿ І꙰ѡ. (V, I - 4)	
в' врѣ̑м ѡ̑н. възы́де І꙰ѵ᷍ въ	възыде І꙰с᷍ въ Іе́р᷍лмъ.
Іе́р᷍лмъ. е᷍ же въ Іе́р᷍лмѣ᷍ на	е᷍стъ же въ Іе́р᷍лмѣ оу̑ ѿвча
ѿвчи́ кѫпѣли. ꙗ́же гл҃е(тсѧ) е᷍в-	кѫпѣли нꙗ̑же нари́цает сѧ е᷍в-
ре́искы виѳезда᷍. пѧ̑т притвѡ́ръ	ре́искыи виѳезда᷍. пѧ́ть при-
и́мѫщи. въ не́и сълѣ̑жаше мно̑-	творъ и́мѫщи. въ тѣ́хъ сълежа⸱
ство мнѡ́го бѡ́лѧщі̑и̑. слѣ́пыи̑.	ше мно́жьство болѧщихъ.слѣпы
хрѡ́мы̑. соу́хы̑. ча̑щи̑ движе́-	хромы. соухы. ча́щихъ възмѧ-
нїа воды. а̑гг҃лъ бо бж҃і҇и по	щение водѣ. а̑гг҃лъ бо гн҃ь.по
въсѣ вре́мена съхѡ̑ж̑да̑аше въ	всѣ лѣта съхож̑да̑аше въ
кѫпѣль, и̑ възмѧ̑щааше вѡ́дѫ. и̑	кѫпѣль.и̑ възмѧ́щааше водѫ. и̑
и̑же оу̑бо пръвѣ̑е вълѣзь по	и̑же пръвѣ̑е вълазѣ̑аше по

---

368. P. Syrku, op. cit., p. 99-100.

369. The quotation is from a microfilm of the
IAG original, kept in the British Museum (cf. fn. 367),
p. 224-224 b.

змѫщени <u>воды</u> з҃рⷣа́въ бꙑваа—	възмѫщени <u>водѣ</u>. здравъ бꙑваа—
ꙗцѣⷨ же недѫго҃ⷨ одрѣ—	ше. ꙗцѣⷨ же недѫгомъ о́дрⷤъ—
ⷨ бꙑвааше +	жимъ бꙑвааше.

At first glance, the differences in the two texts
eem to be significant: they involve the use of different
rammatical forms, often where the two forms had been in
ree alternation even in OCS (possessive genitive and pos-
essive dative); choice of different prepositions expressing
ocation (на vs. оу); alternative use of the past active
articiple or a past tense of the verb (dependent on
nother verb conjugated in the past tense, within the same
ompound sentence); and also grammatical agreement with
ifferent lexical items. Examples are:

ъ і҆ер҃сⷧмѣ҃ⷯ — въ і҆ер҃сⷧмѣ

ъ не́и [=кѫпѣли] — въ тѣхъ [=пѧть притворъ]

а́ѫщиⷯ движе́нїа — чаѫщихъ възмѫщение

движе́нїа воды — възмѫщение водѣ

ьлѣзь — вълазѣаше

о възмѫ́щени воды — по възмѫщени водѣ

а ѿвчи кѫ́пѣли — оу҆ ѿвчѧ кѫ́пѣли

In these two short parallel passages, the two
translators use different Slavic words to render the Greek
text. But the lexical differences are less numerous than
the grammatical; they represent either full synonyms (б҃жіи
~ г҃нь), or, in some instances, may reflect lexical differ-

ences in the Greek originals (cf. the numerous examples of Greek lexical differences in the texts of the New Testament quoted by V. Jagić in the footnotes of his publication of the **Codex Marianus**):

гл҃е(тсѧ) - нарищает сѧ

мнѡ҇ство мнѡ́го бѡлѧщі҄и҇ – множьство болѧщихъ

бж҃їи - гн҃ь

врѣмена - лѣта

оу҄бо - ——

In addition to these grammatical and lexical differences, one observes in IAG a case of disagreement in apposition, found sporadically throughout the Middle Bulgarian literary monuments including the original writings of Patriarch Euthymius (cf. his **Vita of St. Ioan Rilski**). In the text quoted above, the grammatically correct syntagma is found in Euthymius: бѡлѧщі҄и҇. слѣпыи҇. хрѡмы҇. соу҄хы҇. IAG has the incorrect apposition: болѧщихъ. слѣпы. хромы. соухы.

The more closely one compares parallel passages from Euthymius' translation and IAG, the better one comes to understand that, no matter how different their wording may appear, they actually represent the same literary language, allowing the same kinds of alternative lexical and grammatical forms, and applying the same orthographic principles:

еѵⷢлїе ѿ лоуⷦ: (X, I6 - 2I)	
реⷱ гⷤь своимь оученикѡⷨ.	
слоша҇и ваⷵ мене слоушаеⷮ.	слоушаѧ васъ, мене слоушаетъ.
	и̑ слꙋша҇и мене, слоушаеть
и̑ ѿмета҇и сѧ	послаⷡшааго мѧ. и̑ ѿмета҇и сѧ
васъ, мене сѧ ѿмѣтаеⷮ. а̀	васъ, мене сѧ ѿметаетъ. а̀
ѿметаѧ сѧ мене, ѿметает сѧ	ѿмета҇и сѧ мене, ѿметает сѧ
послаⷡшаго мѧ. възвратишꙗⷢ	послаⷡшааго мѧ. възвратишꙗ
.о̃. съ радостиѫ	же сѧ седмь десѧть съ ра[до]-
гла҇ще. г҃и, и̑ бѣси пови-	стиѧ гла҇ще. г҃и и̑ бѣси пови-
ноуꙗⷮ сѧ на́мь о и̑мени твоемь	ноуꙗⷮ сѧ намь о̑ и̑мени твоемъ.
реⷱ же и̑мъ, видѣ҇ꙁ сатанꙗ	реⷱ же имъ і̑с҃. видѣхъ сатанѫ
ꙗ̑ко млъні҇ꙗ съ нб҃съ падша.	ꙗ̑ко млъні҇а съ нб҃се падша:
сё да҇ вамь вла҇ꙵ настѫпати	сё дахъ вамъ власть настѫпати
на зъмі҇ꙗ и̑ скорпі҇ꙗ.	на зьмиꙗ, и̑ на скорпиꙗ.
и̑ на въсѧ си́лѫ враж҇і҇ꙗ. и̑	и̑ на всѧ силꙗ вражиꙗ. и
ничто же ваⷵ не врѣди҇ꙵ.	ничто же васъ не врѣдитъ.
Ѻбаче ѡ̑ семь не раⷣуите сѧ ꙗ̑-	Ѻбаче ѿⷵ семъ не радоуите сѧ.
ко доуси вамь повиноуꙗⷮ᾽ сѧ	
раⷣуите же сѧ ꙗ̑ко и̑мена ва-	раⷣу́йте же сѧ, ꙗ̑ко и̑мена ва-
ша написана сѫтъ на нб҃се҇ꙵ.	ша написана сѫтъ на нб҃сехъ.
въ тъ̈ ча҇ꙵ възраⷣува сѧ	въ тъ̈ часъ възрадова сѧ

---

370. P. Syrku, <u>op. cit.</u>, p. 103.

371. From the manuscript of IAG, p. 169-169 b.

дхомь І̄с и ре꙯ч. исповѣдоуѧ
ти сѧ ѻ̂꙯че г̄и нбси и земли.
ꙗ̇ко оу̇таилъ е̇си сиа ѿ прѣмѫд-
ры꙯х̇ и разоумны꙯х̇. и ѿкрылъ
е̇си младенцемь. е̇и ѻ̂꙯че. ꙗ̇ко
тако бы꙯с блговоленїе прѣ꙯д
тобѫ: +

дхомь І̄с, и ре꙯ч. и̇сповѣдаѧ
сѧ тебѣ ѻ̂꙯че. г̄и нбси и земл
ꙗ̇ко оу̇таи̇ль еси се̇; ѿ мѫд-
рыхъ и̇ разоумныхъ. и ѿкрылъ
е̇си младенцемь. е̇и ѻ̂꙯че ꙗ̇ко
тако бы꙯с благоволение прѣ꙯д
тобѫ.

The same sort of oscillations in the spelling of
certain words are found in both texts. The ѭ of OCS is
represented by ѧ or ѫ (in free alternation). Euthymius
has млънїѫ and даѧ, while IAG has млънїѧ and исповѣдаѧ сѧ
(cf. млъниѭ, даѭ and исповѣдаѭ in Mar.). Both author
use in free alternation (although in different sentences)
the long and short forms of the nominative singular masculine of the active participles. Euthymius has слоушаѫи,
ѿметаѫи сѧ, but also ѿметаѫ сѧ. IAG has слꙋшаѫи, ѿметаѫи
сѧ, but also слоушаѫ.

In one respect, the orthography of IAG is more
consistent (and hence more regulated) than that of Euthymius: while Euthymius uses both spellings — мене сѧ
ѿметае꙯т and ѿметает сѧ, alternating ѣ and e in the same
word form, the scribe of IAG is consistent in the use of
the letter e in all forms of this verb in the passage quoted (for oscillations in other prefixed forms, cf. 4.3.4.11

There is hardly anything in Euthymius' translation which would make his language, as a whole, stand out

as "more correct" Church Slavic than the language of IAG.

While the scribe of IAG uses the correct OCS forms (spelled according to the Middle Bulgarian conventions) възрадова сѧ, йсповѣдаѧ сѧ, Euthymius uses newer, Middle Bulgarian dialectal forms such as възраⷫ҇ува сѧ (influenced by the present tense), исповѣдоуѧ ти сѧ(the classical Gospel texts have only исповѣдаѩ or исповѣмь (cf. the glossary and the variants cited in the footnotes of Mar.). This comparison of two passages from Euthymius and from an older Middle Bulgarian revised text should serve to show that Euthymius had no **different** (much less, **better**) grammatical and orthographic system to offer as a "reform" of the Middle Bulgarian literary language.

3.2.4.2. Against any possibility that Euthymius initiated a spelling and linguistic reform in the Church Slavic language in Bulgaria is the evidence of the **Psalter** of Kiprian[372]. Until 1958, it was believed that the text of this **Psalter** was an original translation from Greek (or a revised copy from an older translation), done by Kiprian

372. Cf. our discussion in 2.3.2.2.; for more details on Kiprian's manuscript, kept today in the Lenin State Library of the USSR in Moscow, # ф. I37, Фунд. I42, see:
    Arximandrit Amfiloxij, Čto vnes svjatoj Kiprian ..., Kiev, 1878, p. 238-241.
    I. Mansvetov, **Mitropolit Kiprian v ego liturgičeskoj dejatel'nosti**, Moscow, 1882, p. 66-100.
    J. Ivanov, Bəlgarskoto vlijanie v Rusija pri mitropolit Kiprian, **Izvestija IBL**, VI, Sofia, 1958, p. 37-47.
    G. I. Vzdornov, Rol' slavjanskix monastyrskix masterskix pis'ma..., **Literaturnye svjazi drevnix slavjan** (**Trudy ODRL**,v. XXIII), Leningrad, 1968, p. 173-174.

himself; but J. Ivanov proved that Kiprian simply copied
his Psalter from the Psalter of King Ioan Aleksandər (of
1337) or, which is less likely, from some unknown
copy of the King's Psalter. Here, for illustration, are
two very short parallel passages from the King's Psalter
and from Kiprian's[373].

KING'S PSALTER	KIPRIAN'S PSALTER
блаженъ мѫжь ѝже не ѝдѐ на	блаженъ мѫжь ѝже не ѝде на
съвѣтъ нечьстивыихъ. й на пѫ-	съвѣтъ нечьстивыхъ. й на пѫ-
ти грѣшныхъ не ста. и на сѣ-	ти грѣшныхъ не ста. й на сѣ-
далїщи гоубителъ не сѣде. нѫ	далищи гѹбитель не сѣде. нѫ
въ законѣ гни волѣ его, ѝ въ	въ законѣ г͡ни волѣ его. ѝ въ
законѣ его пооучит сѧ дьнъ ѝ	законѣ его по͞учит сѧ день ѝ
нощъ. ѝ бѫдетъ ꙗко дрѣво	нощь. ѝ бѫдеть ꙗко древо
сажденоѐ при їсходищихъ во-	сажденно при исходищи во͡д.
дамъ. ѐже плодъ своѝ дастъ	ѝже пло͡д свои да͡с
въ врѣмѧ своѐ. ѝ листъ его	въ врѣмѧ свое. ѝ листъ его
не ѿпадетъ.	не ѿпаде͡т.

The differences in the two texts are very few
and extremely insignificant; without exception, they represent permissible alternative spellings and grammatical
forms in the Middle Bulgarian Church Slavic of the 14th and
15th centuries — both before and after Euthymius. If

---

373. These passages are taken from the lengthy
comparison made by J. Ivanov in his article:
J. Ivanov, op. cit., p. 38.

there had been a reform initiated and carried out in the years 1371-1375 by Euthymius, the Russian Metropolitan Kiprian, who is supposed to have been one of his most ardent followers, would not have taken to Russia in 1379 a Psalter copied from a "pre-reform" original dated positively to 1337. Some 40 years would have elapsed from the writing of King Ioan Aleksandǝr's Psalter to the alleged reform of Euthymius.

The reform of the religious writings in Bulgaria was a process, not the doing of a single person. It started at the very dawn of the literature: each new copy of a manuscript was either an improvement or a corruption compared with its original, depending on the knowledge of the copyist and the facilities of the library where he worked. Many scribes took part in this process, and it is impossible to list the names of the most decisive and influential of them. Almost the entire list of spelling reforms — rules and suggestions — ascribed by K. S. Mirčev to Euthymius, can be traced back to the beginning of the 14th century. These spelling rules, with the sole exception of that for the distribution of the two jer letters, and with some fluctuation in the treatment of the nasal vowel in word initial position, were consistently employed in many earlier manuscripts. One of these is the Vatican copy of the Manasses Chronicle, written for the Bulgarian king sometime after 1355-56 but before 1371 (though incorrectly identified in the literature as dating from 1345)[374].

3.3. In the existing literature on the second
South Slavic influence in the Russian culture and language,
the "reform" of the Tərnovo Patriarch Euthymius is closely
connected with the philosophy of the Hesychasts — Byzantine and Slavic. D. S. Lixačev links the Hesychasts' pre-
occupation with the word to their "reforming" activities:
"To recognize a phenomenon means to express it by a word,

---

374. The date 1345 was established by the
literary historian Jurdan Trifonov in his article "Beležki
kəm srednobəlgarskija prevod na Manasievata letopis", in
Izvestija na Bəlgarskija Arxeologičeski Institut, II,
1923-24, p. 137-173. It has been accepted by other
scholars, recently by Ivan Dujčev in his preface to the
publication Letopista na Konstantin Manasi, Sofia, 1963. p.
xxxv. Dujčev's reasoning is the following: "If we accept
that the Moscow copy of the Chronicle was made in the last
three months of 1344 and not earlier than the spring of
1345, we can presume with great probability that King Ivan
Alexandər's copy, which has traces of editorial changes,
was copied and ornamented with miniatures at approximately
the same time — most likely, at the end of the spring or
during the summer of 1345."
    However, neither author takes into consideration
these very important data: page 2 of the Vatican copy is
ornamented with a scene from the funeral of the King's son
Ioan Asěn, with an inscription above it: "The souls of the
righteous are in the Lord's hands. The powers of heaven
opened the heavenly gates to receive the soul of King Ioan
Asěn, son of the Great King Ioan Aleksandər, being carried
by angels." The original text reads as follows: дш҃ѧ правед-
ны(х) въ рѫцѣ гн҃и. н҃бснаа врат(а) й силы н҃бсны ѡ(т)врѣзош(ѫ
приѫти дш҃ѫ носимѫѧ а҃г҃гломъ Іѡана асѣнѣ цр҃ѣ. сн҃а великаг(о)
Іѡа. алеѯандра цр҃ѣ.
    But the Four Gospels, written in 1355-56, **contain
on** page 3, in the rightmost corner, a full-length portrait
of that same Ioan Asěn, which could only indicate that he
was still living at that time, with the inscription: "King
Ioan Asěn, son of the King" - Іѡ. а҃сѣ(н) цр҃ь. сн҃ъ. цр҃евъ.
Therefore, the date 1345 is incorrect. The earliest that
the Vatican copy of the Chronicle could have been written
would be sometime after 1355-56.

to name it. Here is the source of their intolerant attitude toward any kind of errors, toward variants in the copies, toward corruptions in the translations. Here is the
source of their exclusive attachment to literal translations"[375]. In the Church Slavic literature of the late 14th
and 15th centuries, the religious concepts of Hesychasm
were reflected in the writings of its creator, Gregory
Sinaites, and his Byzantine and Slavic followers: the Pa-
triarchs Callistes and Phylotheus of Constantinople, the
Patriarch Euthymius of Tərnovo, and Camblak[376]. Lixačev,
in his report to the Fourth International Congress of Slavists, gave a new interpretation of the second South Slavic
influence, connecting it with Hesychasm as part of a supranational pre-Renaissance. According to his concept, this
pre-Renaissance, beginning in the second half of the 14th
century, embraced the Slavic cultures in the Balkans and in
Russia, the Byzantine culture on the European continent and
partially also that in Asia Minor, as well as those Christian cultures in the Caucasus[377].

3.3.1. It appears that the effort to call the
revival of the South Slavic literatures in the 14th century,
and of the Russian literature toward the end of that cen-

---

375. D. S. Lixačev, Nekotorye zadači..., p. 113.

376. I. Dujčev, Centry vizantijsko-slavjanskogo
obščenija i sotrudničestva, Trudy ODRL, XIX, Moscow-Leningrad, 1963, p. 127-128.

377. D. S. Lixačev, op. cit., p. 107-150.

tury, a "Renaissance" leads to misuse of the term. Lixačev's interpretation of the new South and East Slavic literary productivity and its relation to the Hesychast movement
is met with reservations by H. Birnbaum:

> Throughout the entire Byzantine period there
> were scholars and writers intimately familiar
> with the classical tradition. Since the role of
> this spiritual heritage in Byzantine intellectual
> history has not yet been fully identified, it may
> be somewhat premature to generalize and even ten-
> tatively to define anything like a "revival of
> classical antiquity" in Byzantium. There was
> never any need for the Byzantines to "discover"
> classical antiquity as something entirely new...
> This, among other things, explains one of the fun-
> damental differences in the history of Byzantine
> civilization as compared to that of Western Eu-
> rope in the late Middle Ages and the Renaissance
> period ...[378]

The concept of Renaissance (and pre-Renaissance)
is primarily connected with the philosophical interpretation
of the Universe and Man's place in it. The first period in
late Byzantine philosophy (until about 1340) is usually
characterized by the feeling of superiority toward Western-
ers on the part of the Byzantine philosophers, as expressed
particularly by Theodoros Metochites[379]. In the early 13th
century some Byzantine writers and philosophers tried to
write in the Attic dialect of the 5th - 4th centuries B. C.
while there appeared in the chronicles the ancient Greek

---

378. H. Birnbaum, Some Aspects of the Slavonic
Renaissance, The Slavonic and East European Review, XLVII,
1969, 108, p. 41.

379. F. Fuchs, Die höheren Schulen von Konstantinopel im Mittelalter, Leipzig-Berlin, 1926, p. 53-54.

names for the months. At the same time philosophers like
Metochites complained that after the ancients nothing new
could be created in philosophy; the educated Byzantine readers were familiar with the ideas of pre-Christian thinkers,
and had only contempt for the pseudo-philosophy of later
times[380]. By mid-13th century Aristotle, once anathematized
by the Church as a pagan, had become, in the eyes of the
Byzantines, something close to a Christian prophet[381]. And
throughout the entire period of late Byzantine philosophy,
the subject of philosophy was intertwined with that of rhet-
oric, never once outstepping the framework set by the ancients; as in ancient times, man continued very close to
the center of the philosophical universe. The continuity
with ancient Greece never ceased in Byzantine philosophy,
although in different times the emphasis was placed on different questions: if in the ancient period a central problem was that of the origin and nature of matter, in the
Byzantine philosophy of the 13th - 15th centuries a central
problem was that of absolute causality in the development
of societies - the problem of regularity and chance[382].

380. R. Guilland, Correspondance de Nicéphore
Grégoras, Paris, 1927, p. 63.

381. F. Schultze, Georgios Gemistos Plethon und
seine reformatischen Bestrebungen, Jena, 1874, p. 12.

382. F. Schultze, op. cit., p. 254-258.
E. Bréhier, Histoire de la philosophie, II,
Paris, 1949, p. 232-261.
H. G. Beck, Theodoros Metochites. Die Krise des
byzantinischen Weltbildes im XIV. Jh., Munich, 1952. p.15-42,

The South Slavic philosophers and religious leaders must have been aware of the developments in Byzantine
philosophy, and especially so in Bulgaria after the break
with the Roman Church in 1235. But from our inadequate
knowledge of medieval Slavic literature in its entirety
(cf. 2.4.3.) we do not today have reason to believe that
the rationalistic and humanistic elements in Byzantine
culture were in the mainstream of South Slavic spiritual
life. What we know of 14th-century South Slavic literature represents, indeed, the opposite trend - mysticism -
especially as reflected in the teachings of Gregory Palamas
and Gregory Sinaites[383]. A telling piece of evidence is

p. 61-198.
    Fr. Masai, Pléthon et la platonisme de Mistra.
Les classiques de l'humanisme, Paris, 1956, p. 161-240.
    I. Ševčenko, Études sur la polémique entre Théo-
dore Métochite et Nicéphore Chumnos. La vie intellectuelle
et politique à Byzance sous les premiers Paléologues,
Brussels, 1962, p. 191-245.
    D. J. Geanakoplos, Byzantine East and Latin
West, New York-Evanston, 1967, p. 124-125.

    383. V. Sl. Kiselkov, Prouki i očerti po staro-
bəlgarska literatura, Sofia, 1956, p. 178-180.
    J. Meyendorff, Introduction à l'étude de Gregoire
Palamas, Paris, 1959, pp. 25-32, 55-58.
    H.-G. Beck, Humanismus und Palamismus, Actes du
XII-e Congrès International d'Études byzantines, I, Beograd,
1963, p. 78.
    I. Dujčev, Centry ..., p. 127-128.
    I. Dujčev, K. Kuev, Bəlgarskata literatura prez
XIV vek, in: Istorija na bəlgarskata literatura, 1, Sofia,
1963, p. 270-275.

p. 170.   S. Vryonis, Byzantium and Europe, London, 1967,

    G. M. Proxorov, Isixazm i obščestvennaja mysl' v
vostočnoj Evrope, in: Literaturnye svjazi drevnix slavjan,
Trudy ODRL, XXIII, Leningrad, 1968, p. 86-108.

the anathema of 1351, pronounced by both the Byzantine and
the Bulgarian Church on the leaders of the reformist, pro -
Western movement in the Balkans: Barlaam, Akintynos and the
priest Proxor: а̇киндина варлаама. и̇ по́па пр꙼ѡхора кидѡнѣ,
и́же паче въсѣхъ е̇ретикъ хоу́лнаа на б҃а и̇зг҃лавши҃ ... и̇ тѣмь
е̇диномѫдръны҃, а̇наѳема: ⨯ 384.

3.3.2.   In connection with the cultural interchange among the Slavic Orthodox nations (and, in a narrow-
er sense, with the second South Slavic influence in Russia)
a new concept has been propagated lately in the history of
Slavic literatures - "Slavia Orthodoxa".   It was first suggested by R. Picchio[385].   Even before formulating his term
"Slavia ortodossa", in his study on the second South Slavic
influence in Russia, R. Picchio writes that "the unity of
the Orthodox Slavic culture throughout the entire Middle
Ages was not based on government or national principles",
and that one thus cannot speak of "the influence of one literature over another; one should rather speak of different
phases of the same process of development"[386].

---

384. M. G. Popruženko, ed., Sinodik carja Borila
(Bəlgarski starini, VIII), Sofia, 1928, p. 95.

385. R. Picchio, Die historisch-philologische
Bedeutung der kirchen-slavischen Tradition, Die Welt der
Slaven, VII, Wiesbaden, 1962, p. 1-27.
_____, A proposito della Slavia orto-
dossa e della comunità linguistica slava ecclesiastica,
Ricerche slavistiche, XI, Rome, 1963, p. 105-127.

386. R. Picchio, Storia della letteratura russa
antica (in the series: Storia delle letterature di tutto il
mondo), Milan, 1959, p. 142.

Such a concept as Slavia Orthodoxa presents three
basic obstacles to a truly unified view of Church Slavic
culture:

a) It excludes from what we know to be Church
Slavic literature the old Moravo-Pannonian literature, the
entire Croatian literature created in Church Slavic, and
both the Bulgarian and the Russian Lithuanian literatures
during their periods of union with the Roman Church. It
disregards the existence of some ties between the literatures of the Catholic Slavic and the Orthodox Slavic nations
(cf. the Vita of St. Václav in Russian literature).

b) It does not take into account that the Church
Slavic literature and language were used by the Wallachian
and Moldavian societies through the end of the 17th century,
and that, perhaps, those Albanians living in the medieval
Bulgarian and Serbian states also used them before their
conversion to the Moslem religion.

c) It fails to see medieval Church Slavic literature as an integral part of the Byzantine one (although
every national literature has its own national peculiarities
But throughout the Middle Ages, the local characteristics of
the national Slavic cultures (including those of their
literatures) are of secondary importance. R. Picchio
is right in stressing the unity of the Slavic national
cultures; but this unity can be understood only within
the framework of the larger, multi-national Byzantine

cultural community, where the Greek literature and language played an undisputably major role[387].

3.3.3. In analyzing the processes in the South Slavic literatures immediately before the beginning of the second South Slavic influence in Russia, an understanding of the role of the Balkan monasteries as centers of international exchange within the Byzantine supra-national communities is of extreme importance. In 1963 I. Dujčev published an interesting paper, with exhaustive bibliography, on the role of the monasteries of Constantinople and Mt. Athos in the process of disseminating Byzantine culture in the Slavic lands, depicting the true international spirit in these monastic communities[388].

---

387. D. S. Lixačev, Drevneslavjanskie literatury kak sistema, Slavjanskie literatury (Doklady sovetskoj delegacii. VI Meždunarodnyj s"ezd slavistov), Moscow, 1968, p. 5-48.

388. I. Dujčev, Centry vizantijsko-slavjanskogo sotrudničestva, Trudy ODRL, XIX, Moscow-Leningrad, 1963, p. 107-129.
See also these previously published important contributions to the problem of the international exchange and cooperation in the Balkan monasteries:
E. Kałużniacki, Aus der panegyrischen Literatur der Südslaven, Vienna, 1901, p. 35.
A. I. Sobolevskij, Južno-slavjanskoe vlijanie na russkuju pis'mennost' v XIV - XV vekax, Perevodnaja literatura Moskovskoj Rusi XIV - XVII vekov, St. Petersburg, 1903, pp. 8-12, 24-34.
G. A. Il'inskij, Značenie Afona v istorii slavjanskoj pis'mennosti, ŽMNP, XI, St. Petersburg, 1908, p. 1-41.
A. Protič, Sveta Gora i bəlgarskoto izkustvo, Bəlgarski pregled, I, Sofia, 1929, 2, p. 249-276.
A. Solovjev, Histoire du monastère russe au Mont Athos, Byzantion, VIII, Brussels, 1933, p. 213-238.
R. Janin, Constantinople byzantine, Paris, 1950, p. 34-46.

And yet, in these international centers too, Greek monks played the leading role in the creation of the Byzantine culture and literature, while the Slavic monasteries and the Slavic monks in the Greek monasteries had as their main task, to follow closely the developments in the Byzantine centers and to translate into Church Slavic whatever seemed to them most important for the enlightenment and salvation of the Slavic reading public. Efforts to magnify the role of the Slavs in the Byzantine religious life and culture[389] have put some scholars in awkward situations. I. Dujčev, for example, in his eagerness to demonstrate the active participation of Bulgarians in Byzantine Church affairs, discovered a Bulgarian on the Patriarch's throne in Constantinople[390]. According to Dujčev, in the second half of the 14th century Ioan Asěn, son of King Ioan Aleksandər of Tərnovo, became a monk on Mt. Athos and, early in the 15th century, was elected Patriarch of Constantinople (1416-1439). The embarrassment arises from another, almost simultaneous publication by Dujčev: in 1962 he published a study on the miniatures of the Vatican copy of the Manas-

---

389. Cf., for instance, the statement by C. Korolevskij, that the Byzantine Church was "incorrectly called Greek", since it was predominantly Slavic:
        C. Korolevskij, Liturgie en langue vivante, in: Orient et Occident, Paris, 1955, pp. 18, 25-26.

390. I. Dujčev, Obrazi na bəlgarin ot XV v. vəv Florencija, Izkustvo, 1, Sofia, 1961, p. 22-24.
        _____, A propos de la biographie de Joseph II patriarche de Constantinople, Revue des études byzantines, XIX, Paris, 1961, p. 333-339.

ses Chronicle with color reproductions of the miniatures; in 1963 he published, in photocopy, the entire Manasses Chronicle with a 34-page preface[391]. Yet he failed to notice the picture and accompanying text for the funeral of Ioan Asěn, who must have died before the book was finished, between 1355 and 1371 - at least 45 years before his supposed elevation to the Patriarchate (cf. fn. 374).

An interesting problem, involving the role of the monasteries on Mt. Athos in the second South Slavic influence in Russia, is the alternation of Bulgarian and Serbian leadership in the Slavic monastic communities during the 13th - 15th centuries. Until the mid-14th century the Bulgarians played the primary role in most of the monasteries, and the majority of the Slavic books of that time are of Bulgarian origin; but from the second half of the 14th century onward, the Serbians became the leading element in the Slavic communities, and the number of manuscripts of purely Serbian or of mixed Bulgarian-Serbian recension sharply increased, until by the early 15th century the Serbians dominated in all spheres of the cultural and religious life of these monasteries[392].

In connection with the literary activity in the

391. I. Dujčev, ed., Miniatjurite na Manasieva-ta letopis, Sofia, 1962, 138 pp.
_____, ed., Letopista na Konstantin Manasi, Sofia, 1963, xxxiv + 415 pp.

392. G. I. Vzdornov, Rol' slavjanskix master-skix pis'ma Konstantinopolja i Afona ..., p. 181-183.

Balkan monasteries before the second South Slavic influence began, it seems that the entire problem of the importance of Hesychasm in creating a new style in the hagiographic genre should be re-examined. A positive step in this direction is the paper by H. Birnbaum, 'Byzantine Tradition Transformed: the Old Serbian Vita' [393]. H. Birnbaum establishes the evolutionary development in the Serbian hagiographic genre from early 13th to early 15th century, and the corresponding Serbian impact on Slavic literature. The insistence on a very special role of the Hesychasts in the evolution of the "new" hagiographic style of 15th-century Russia de facto denies any purely Slavic developments in this genre, since the South Slavic Hesychasts are known to have been primarily followers of their contemporary Byzantine teachers.

3.4. The Church Slavic language of the 14th-century Bulgarian manuscripts, although having specific features which characterize it as Middle Bulgarian, is not the same in all literary monuments. The type of language in different works may, from the limited data available in publications and accessible manuscripts, be broken into three subgroups: a) revised OCS translations of the New Testament Psalter, various Paterika sections of the Old Testament, and books translated during the time of King Symeon; b) new-

---

393. H. Birnbaum, Byzantine Tradition Transformed: the Old Serbian Vita, in: Aspects of the Balkans: Continuity and Change, H. Birnbaum and S. Vryonis, Jr., ed's., Hague: Mouton p. 243 – 284.

r translations of Byzantine (and perhaps other) authors,
ade after the 12th century. Here the most representative
ork is the _Manasses Chronicle_ (translated between the early
3th and mid-14th centuries). In the same group should be
ncluded also the few known original works by Bulgarian
riters, such as the works of Patriarch Euthymius, Grigorij
amblak, etc.; c) works of early secular literature, of
hich so far only one is known - the _Tale of Troy_ (included
n the Vatican copy of the _Manasses Chronicle_).

Samples of the spoken dialects, represented by the
ripiski (notes) of semi-literate scribes in certain
opies, cannot seriously be considered part of the literary
anguage. Even today we do not study the speech of the ig-
orant in contemporary novels as part of our modern literary
anguage, nor do normative grammars of the standard languages
escribe the grammatical structure of such speech. The notes
f the scribes, although yielding most valuable data for
istorical dialectology, are, for the student of the history
f the literary language, mostly indicators of how different
hat language was from the spoken dialects.

The language of the early secular literary works
in Bulgaria, e.g. the _Tale of Troy_, is irrelevant to the
problem of the second South Slavic influence in Russia. The
language, representative not of the spoken dialects but of
the colloquial language of the ruling classes in 14th-cen-
tury Bulgaria, lacks the properties of a supra-national
medium of communication.

The Middle Bulgarian literature which was understandable for the Russians (and thus suitable for copying
by them) was that which followed as closely as possible the
norms of Old Church Slavic.

It is extremely difficult to identify the literary
works which were translated in Bulgaria between the 12th and
the 14th century. Almost all of them are preserved in later
Russian copies; the Russian copyists, beginning with those
who first copied from the Middle Bulgarian prototypes, tried
to replace new Middle Bulgarian grammatical forms, unfamil-
iar to Russian readers, with Russian Church Slavic forms.
The same was done with characteristic Bulgarian or South
Slavic lexical items (cf. 2.3.4.2. and 2.4.).

The most important role in the influence of the
Middle Bulgarian literary language on the Russian literary
language of the late 14th and early 15th centuries, was undoubtedly played by the most frequently used Church books -
the New Testament and the Psalter. The text of the New Testament is the best for studying the developments in the Bul
garian literary language from late 10th - early 11th to mid
14th century in connection with the revising of the books
in Bulgaria. One can best compare the evolution from the
earliest known classical OCS texts (and also the Russian
Ostromir Gospel) towards a well established, artificial but
normalized literary language in mid-14th-century Bulgaria,
by an examination of the peculiarities of the Ioan Aleksandər Gospel (IAG).

3.4.1. The New Testament is the pivotal text of the Christian Church, the one that was most carefully preserved in copying and most scrupulously compared with the Greek originals. And still, as B. Conev notes in his Opis, there are no two single surviving manuscripts whose texts are fully identical[394]. It seems that every scribe tried to improve his own copy, to make it a more truthful translation of the available good Greek originals and to reconcile the translation with the then-existing dogmas of the Orthodox Church.

The most typical example of this process is the new "translation" of the Gospel in the year 1355/56, ordered by the Bulgarian king Ioan Aleksandər (1331-1371). We will give a full translation of the postscript to the manuscript, since this text is not readily available to American scholars:

> Glory to God glorified in the Trinity, to him who
> fulfills every good beginning, which was begun in
> him, and who also gives an end after the begin-
> ning. This life-giving source of new virtue,
> of the sweetest teaching of Christ and of his
> godly witnesses, pupils and apostles, which is
> called the Four Gospels, was written not only with
> external color or gold, or decorated with well-
> spun linen or gems and pearls, but by the
> outpouring from within the Word of God, thus
> fulfilling the secret providence which is in the
> lordly and godly incarnation and miracle-making,
> which he did for us, due to his mercy and
> kindness, even to the Cross and burial and the
> glorious resurrection on the third day and the
> ascension. And who is content to count or to
> narrate in order all the things in it which are

394. B. Conev, ed., Opis na rəkopisite i staro-pečatnite knigi na Narodnata biblioteka v Sofija, Sofia, 1910, p. vii-ix.

a reflection of Christ's deeds, which truly
are like a spring in waterless land, that
whoever drinks from it in his thirst will never
thirst again. Because its stream runs and gives
pleasure to the soul, gives joy to both the heart
and the mind, and it is like a hidden treasure
in the field of the heart.

When the devout and Christ-loving, supreme and
God-ordained King Ioan Aleksandər sought this
(Gospel), lying as it were like a lamp in a dark
place, forgotten and placed aside in carelessness
by the ancient kings, he found it. This Christ-
loving King Ioan Alexandər found it by the will
of the Lord, and after he translated it from the
Greek words into our Slavic language he copied
it and displayed it openly. He wrought it on
the outside with gold plates and decorated it on
the inside by the labor of painters with life-
bringing images of the Lord and His glorious
disciples (painted) in bright colors and gold,
for the strengthening of his kingdom.

Just as the emperor Constantine, great amongst
the saints, and his mother Helene took from the
earth the lifegiving cross of the Lord, thus did
this King with these Four Gospels. Then he
held the scepter of the Bulgarian and Greek
kingdom with his devout, glory-crowned and newly-
enlightened Queen, the Lady Theodora - which
means 'the Lord's Gift' - and with his first-
born and much beloved son King Ioan Šišman, to
the glory of the Creator of all and His evangel-
ists Matthew, Mark, Luke and John. May he,
through their prayers, receive victory from God
over the enemies who fight against him, and (may
he) break their heads under his feet. Amen.

The current year is 6864 (1355/56), indict 9,
and the slave of the Lord my king, who wrote this
book, is called Symon the Monk. (see Appendix Six)

The manuscript, kept today in the British Museum
(cf. fn. 367), is written on fine parchment; it consists of
284 leaves, generally in gatherings of eight, with text on
both sides of each leaf. The average plain page has
from 21 to 33 lines. The manuscript includes 365

miniatures, comprising scenes from the New Testament and portraits of the Bulgarian king and his family. The illustrations from the New Testaments are from the same series as that of the Greek manuscript numbered # 74 in the Bibliothèque Nationale in Paris, described by H. Bordier[395]. The British Museum has prepared a comparison with this manuscript based on the publication by H. Omont: Evangiles avec peintures byzantines du XIe siècle, 2 vol's., 1908[396].

Eight miniatures from Omont's manuscript are not included in the Slavic copy, which is also missing the original page 75 (containing Matthew XXV. 39-46) which might have had a picture of the Last Judgment. On the other hand, the Slavic manuscript contains, at the end of the book of Luke, four miniatures not known in the Greek copy. On page 3 the Slavic manuscript represents the King's family, from left to right: the queen ("Theodora, faithful to Christ our Lord, and newly enlightened queen and sovereign of all Bulgarians and Greeks"), the crown prince ("King Ioan Šišman, son of the Great King Ioan Aleksandər"), the king ("King Ioan Aleksandər, faithful to Christ our Lord, and

---

395. H. Bordier, Peintures et autres ornements dans les MMS grecs de la Bibliothèque Nationale, Paris, 1883, p. 133.

396. For more information on this subject, see:
B. Filov, Die Miniaturen des Ev. Iwan Alexanders in London, Byzantion, IV, 1927-1928, p. 313-319.
                    , Londonskoto evangelie na Ivan Aleksandər i negovite miniatjuri, Spisanie BAN, XXXVIII, Sofia, 1929, p. 1-32.
                    , Les miniatures de l'Evangile du roi Ivan Alexandre à Londres, in: Monumenta Artis Bulgariae, 3, Sofia, 1934.

Sovereign of all Bulgarians and Greeks") and the other
son ("King Ioan Asěn, son of the king"). On page 2b are
portraits (also full-length) of the king's daughters and
son-in-law (from left to right): "Despot Konstantin, son-
in-law of the Great King Ioan Aleksandər; the Despot's
wife Kera Themar, daughter of the King; Keraca, daughter
of the King; Desislava, daughter of the king."

This manuscript had an interesting history in
the last decades of the 14th century. Being hard pressed,
perhaps in the difficult months of the last defense of the
Bulgarian capital against the victorious Turks, or,
possibly, in exile after the fall of Tərnovo (summer 1393)[3]
the Bulgarian royal family deposited their Gospel as
security on a loan. They were never able to repay that
loan, and the Moldavian king Alexander the Good (1402-1432)
paid the money to the lender and became the new owner of th
Gospel. Thus a scribe wrote on page five of the manuscript
"The son of Stefan Voevoda, Ioan Alexander, faithful to
Christ our God, Voevoda and lord of the entire Moldavian
land, bought these Four Gospels, which had been kept as
security; may God forgive his sins and give him eternal lif
and many years of life here (below)"[398] The book was most

---

397. Bəlgarska Akademija na Naukite, _Istorija
na Bəlgarija_, 1, Sofia, 1961 (2nd edition), p. 244.

398. Here follows the original text from p. 5
of the MS in Moldavian Church Slavic of the 15th century:
       ✝ сн҃ь стеф[а](н)а воеводе
       ✝ Iѡа́нь алӗз(а)нд(рь) въ х(с)а ба́ вѣрны вое-

likely kept in Moldavia or Wallachia until the late 17th
or early 18th century, when the Wallachian Voevoda
Konstantin Bankobano (1688-1714) established the monastery
of SS. Peter and Paul on Mt. Athos. In the early 19th century, Sir Robert Curzon received the Gospel as a gift from
the Greek administration of the monastery, in recognition of
his involvement in the Greek liberation movement and of his
financial aid to the monastery. After Lord Curzon's death
(1873), the manuscript was inherited by the British Lord
Zouche[399], and in the 1920's the last private owner of the
manuscript, the widow of Lord Parham, donated it to the
British Museum, where it is preserved today.

This translation was prepared for the King's
library and made available to the reading public. According
to the postscript, the king "found it by the will of the
Lord, and having translated it, he copied it from the Greek
into our Slavic language and displayed it openly." Our
studies of the manuscript will show that the new translation
created virtually a different version of the Four Gospels,
although at first glance the text seems to be very close to
the already-known "classical" and mid-Bulgarian texts[400].

вода й г(с)нь. въсей земли млѣдоускои ѡткоупи сѫ тетро-
ѐѵгль. щò ѐ бы́ль· Ȣ залоге. ѣь да га прости. й да моу дарȢѐ
живо(т) вѣчны й здѐ мно(г)[о]лѣтны живо(т).

399. B. Conev, Istorija na bəlgarskij ezik, 1
Sofia, 1940 (2nd edition), p. 196-197.

400.   There is a rich collection of Middle Bulgarian gospels from the 12th to the 15th century (as well as
from later periods) in the Bulgarian National Library "Kiril
i Metodij" (for bibliography cf. fn. 403).

Since we are dealing with the most sacred of all sacred books of the Christian Church, we may ask ourselves about the role of the official Church authorities in the revision. The Postscript emphasizes the role of the monarch in the translation and mentions the name of the scribe "who wrote this book" - Symon the Monk. This, however, is an ambiguous statement: did Symon merely copy the drafts of the revised edition, or was he the head of a group of translators, or did he translate the book all by himself and then have someone else do the mechanical copying?

A careful examination of other books belonging to King Ioan Aleksandər reveals a striking similarity of handwriting in five famous manuscripts: the Služebnik from Mt. Athos (cf. fn. 72), the Sbornik of 1348[401], the so-called Tomić Psalter (df. fn. 50), the Manasses Chronicle (Vatican

---

401. After the fall of Tərnovo (1393) the Sbornik might have been taken to Moldavia or Wallachia, and sometime between 1649 and 1655, taken to Russia (together with 700 other old Greek and Slavic manuscripts) by the envoy of the Muscovite Patriarch Nikon, Arsenij Suxanov. (See: S. Belokurov, Arsenij Suxanov, v. I, Moscow, 1891, p. 408). In 1863 the book became part of the I.P. Saxarov collection of the Public Library in Petersburg (Leningrad Public Library, Number F.I.376).

A brief discussion on the language can be found in: B.M. Ljapunov, "Neskol'ko zamečanij o jazyke i v osobennosti o slovare bolgarskogo sbornika 1348 g.", Sbornik Miletič, Sofia, 1933, p. 95-107. See also: I.I. Sreznevskij, Svedenija i zametki, XXXVI, p. 43-45; P. Syrku, K istorii ispravlenija knig v Bolgarii v XIV veke, v. I, pt. 1, St. P., 1896, p. 430-432.

Eight pages of the manuscript, precisely those of the treatise On the Letters by Černorizec Xrabər, are given in photoreproduction by K. Kuev in Černorizec Xrabər, Sofia, 1967, p. 421-428.

copy) from the second half of the 14th century, and IAG. Similarities include the shape of the letters, the shape and character of the ligatures and of the superscripts used for abbreviation, as well as the spelling and grammar (cf. fn. 72). Still, a difficulty arises from the fact that the King's Sbornik of 1348 is believed to have been copied by the monk Lavrentij, whose name appears in the postscript to the manuscript. But on close examination the statement in the postscript is seen to be by no means a reference by the copyist to himself. It calls this book the "burden and pain of the most sinful, as is usually said, hermit Lavrentij"[402]. The tone of the postscript is one of praise for the work of Lavrentij; expressions such as "burden and pain" and "most sinful, as is usually said" indicate a reverence toward Lavrentij and his work which could only have been expressed by someone else. The peculiarities of Symon's handwriting are so typically his, that there can be no doubt that it was Symon the Monk who was the King's copyist.

3.4.2. The language of IAG was thoroughly studied in the last century (1884) by the Slavist R. Scholvin (cf. fn. 367), but has been outside the interest of Bulgarian students of the history of their language. Such neglect has doubtless been motivated by the extreme correctness of the language of IAG, which gives little evidence of developments

---

402. The entire postscript is published in: P. Lavrov, Obzor zvukovyx i formal'nyx osoben- nostej bolgarskogo jazyka, Moscow, 1893. p. 13.

in the Bulgarian dialects of the 14th century. For just
that reason, however, this new translation of the text of
the Four Gospels is of extreme importance for the study of
developments in the Bulgarian <u>literary</u> language, especially
in relation to the second South Slavic influence in Russia.
The Russian copyists in the Balkan monasteries must have
been interested only in perfect Church Slavic manuscripts,
whose texts were correct translations from the Greek originals and whose language was a correct Church Slavic, as free
as possible from local features.

Scholvin's study of the language of IAG concen-
trates mainly on the morphological peculiarities, paying
little attention to the phonology and none at all to the
lexical features. And yet, his monograph is an excellent
introduction (as he himself entitles it - 'Einleitung') to
this manuscript.

In my own study of the language of IAG, I have
concentrated on two aspects: first, the orthographic system
followed in the manuscript, and its relationship to the
Church Slavic phonology of 14th-century Bulgaria (and partially to the phonology of the Bulgarian dialects of the
time); second, the systematic lexical changes found in the
text by a comparison with the classical OCS Gospel texts.
In studying the grammatical structure, my findings largely
coincided with Scholvin's, and I will report here only on
those morphological and syntactic innovations which are not
dealt with in Scholvin's monograph.

As far as lexical changes are concerned, I discovered that in more than 1500 cases there was some kind of lexical innovation in comparison with the classical Gospel texts. The results of my study in this respect cannot be fully reported here because of a lack of space; I will summarize in brief the major types of lexical innovations only.

In regard to the orthography of IAG, my presentation will be very detailed: thorough study of the text has convinced me that the literary language of 14th-century Bulgaria in its best instances had strict spelling rules, and by no means represented all features of the Bulgarian dialects of the time; on the contrary, its orthography was much less influenced by the speech of the scribe than was that of the known OCS texts. I hope my findings on the orthographic regularities of this manuscript will convincingly support my contention that the Bulgarian orthography of 1355 did not need a "reform" by the Patriarch of Tərnovo in 1371-1375. Having proved that such a reform was not needed, and having searched in vain for any positive historical evidence that it occurred, we may with some confidence assert that, indeed, it never did.

Chapter Four

SPELLING AND PHONOLOGY, GRAMMATICAL AND LEXICAL INNOVATIONS

IN THE REVISED EDITION OF THE FOUR GOSPELS (IAG)

4.1. All of the existing monographs on Middle Bulgarian manuscripts examine the spelling of the texts and try to relate the spelling mistakes to the phonology of the scribe's dialect. Bulgarian scholars usually assign the manuscripts to certain orthographic schools. Such a tradition was set up by Benjo Conev, and employed by him in his publication of literary monuments in Bəlgarski starini and the first two volumes of his Opis[403]. A detailed outline of the spelliŋg schools can be found in the preface to Vračansko Evangelie[404].

4.1.1. A traditional distinguishing principle in determining the orthographic school is the use of the jers. According to some obvious rules of their use, the schools are divided into those with regulated and those with unregu-

---

403. B. Conev, Opis na rəkopisite i staropečatnite knigi na Narodnata biblioteka v Sofija, I, Sofia, 1910, 555 + xviii pp.
    B. Conev, Opis na slavjanskite rəkopisi v Sofijskata narodna biblioteka, II, Sofia, 1923, 552 + lii pp.
    M. Stojanov, Xr. Kodov, Opis na slavjanskite rəkopisi v Sofijskata narodna biblioteka, III, Sofia, 1964, 497 + xi pp.
    In volume I of his Opis (p. ix), B. Conev simply lists six orthographic schools without elaboration.

404. B. Conev, Vračansko Evangelie (Bəlgarski starini, 4), Sofia, 1914, p. 13-15.

---

lated spelling. B. Conev distinguished four schools with
regulated spelling:

Schools (West Bulgarian) using only one jer:

a) The Oxrid School, using only ъ.

b) The Zletovo School, using only ь.

Schools using two jers:

a) The East Bulgarian (perhaps Tərnovo) Etymological School, which "actually maintained the Old Bulgarian etymological tradition, as much as it could be supported
by the living language"[405].

b) The East Bulgarian (perhaps Tərnovo) Two-jer
School, which implemented "a mechanical, stereotyped
(šablonna) differentiation between ъ and ь, where ъ is used
in such positions (root syllables) where both ъ and ь have
an indefinite sound (təmen zvuk), and ь in all positions
(roots, suffixes, endings) where neither ъ nor ь has any
sound value"[406].

In addition to these four regulated schools,
Benjo Conev establishes the existence of two more unregula-
ted ones:

a) The Oxrid-Zletovo School, using ъ and ь
"without a rule, but with some traces of the West Bulgarian
School"[407].

---

405. op. cit., p, 14.

406. ibid.

407. ibid.

b) A continuation of the old tradition (?) - "those monuments where there are traces of the Eastern (Tərnovo) School"[408].

Such a division of the orthographic schools cannot possibly be accepted today. We do not see any significant distinction among the four schools using both jers. In our opinion, the only reasonable (but hardly essential) division would be into two schools, one using one jer, the other using two.

King Ioan Aleksandər's Gospels use both jers, and since this text was specially written for the Tərnovo king, it should be considered representative of the Tərnovo orthographic school of the second half of the 14th century. However, in order to establish the principles of its spelling, one must study in detail more than just the rules of usage for the jers. We shall try to outline the basic principles of the spelling system, as well as variations of, or deviations from them, and whenever possible to draw some conclusions as to the phonological system of the literary language.

4.1.2. Students of Church Slavic possess a valuable monument of the Slavic alphabet - the treatise on the letters by Černorizec Xrabər (of the 10th or 11th century). The oldest preserved manuscripts[409] are from the

---

408. ibid.

409. K. Kuev, *Černorizec Xrabər*, Sofia, 1967, pp. 166, 187-210.

14th and 15th centuries. This work is of extreme importance
in determining the number and character of the letters in
the mid-14th century, since even the reformer of the Serbian
spelling - Konstantin Kostenečki (15th century) - establishes the number of the letters in the Serbian alphabet as 38,
the very number laid down by Xrabər[410].

The existing copies of Xrabər's article fall into
two groups: those which simply give the number of the
letters in the Slavic alphabet as 38, and those which both
give the number 38 and list the letters. We shall take
into consideration only the four oldest copies with Middle
Bulgarian features: Sava's copy (Bulgarian-Serbian of the
15th century)[411], the Moscow copy (Bulgarian-Russian of the
15th century)[412], the Moldavian copy (Bulgarian of the 16th
century)[413], and the Wrocław copy (Bulgarian-Russian of the
16th century)[414].

Unfortunately, considerations of which alphabet -
glagolitic or cyrillic - the author had in mind, and of
whether the listing of the letters was part of the author's
text, although very interesting in themselves, are outside

---

410. V. Jagić, Codex Slovenicus Rerum Grammaticarum (photo-reprint), Munich, 1968, pp. 111, 204-205.

411. K. Kuev, op. cit., p. 195-197.

412. op. cit., p. 191-194.

413. op. cit., p. 210-214.

414. op. cit., p. 214-217.

the scope of this study[415]. The important fact for us is that Bulgarian writers of the 14th - 15th centuries believed that the Slavic alphabet had 38 letters, and that some of them perhaps compiled their own lists of the complete alphabet. The text of the Moscow copy is obviously unreliable: after stating that 24 of the Slavic letters are taken from Greek, the scribe proceeds to illustrate with 28 letters, some of which are repetitions and some, like х̃лъ (!), pure inventions. The final count comes to 43, although the scribe asserts more than once that the alphabet has 38 letters.

The other three texts are completely identical in their listing of the alphabet. We shall quote the passage from the Moldavian copy (16th century), since this monument contains many archaic features[416]:

«4. - се᷍ж ст᷍ писмена слѡвѣнскаа сᷦце и᷍х по᷍дбае писати и᷑ гла́шати. а᷍. б᷍. в᷍. да᷍ж до а̃[417] и᷑ ѿ си᷍х ст᷍ четы́ре меж᷍ду деса᷍тма по᷍дбна грѣ᷍чскы᷍м писменѡ᷍м. ст᷍ же си᷑. а᷍. в᷍. г᷍. д᷍. е᷍. з᷍. и᷍. ѳ᷍. і᷍. к᷍. л᷍. м᷍. н᷍. ѯ᷍. о᷍. п᷍. р᷍. с᷍. т᷍. у᷍. ф᷍. х᷍. ѱ᷍. ѡ᷍. а҃ четыринадеса᷍т по слѡвѣнскомꙋ ѧзы́коу и᷍ж ст᷍ сïа҃. б᷍. ж᷍. ѕ᷍. ц᷍. ч᷍. ш᷍. щ᷍. ъ᷍. ы᷍. ь᷍. ѣ᷍. ю᷍. ѫ᷍. ѧ᷍.»

_____

415. <u>op. cit.</u>, p. 47-48.

416. <u>op. cit.</u>, pp. 54, 211.

417. In the other two copies the letter is given correctly, as ѫ̃.

In their effort to present an alphabet of exactly
38 letters, the scribes ignore the ligatures <u>ıa</u>, <u>ıe</u>, <u>оу</u> or
<u>ȣ</u> and render the Greek <u>upsilon</u> as <u>y</u> instead of <u>υ</u> (which
also occurs in the classical texts), although all three
manuscripts use these ligatures as well as the <u>upsilon</u> of
the form <u>υ</u>. It is noteworthy, however, that they list the
two jers as two separate letters, and the <u>ш</u> and <u>щ</u> as letters
rather than ligatures. The only conclusion one can draw
from the list is that in the minds of those men <u>y</u> and <u>υ</u>
were only variants of the same letter, <u>upsilon</u>; while the
ligatures represented not letters, but combinations of
letters, and thus, in the Greek tradition, had no place
in the alphabet.

4.1.3. In determining the orthographic system
of a time one must raise the question: what was the relation between the letters and the phonemes or morphonemes
of the literary language? In this respect there are almost
insurmountable difficulties. In the consonantal phonemes
there is no clear indication from the alphabet as to
whether the consonants were paired on the basis of palatalization. One might draw certain conclusions from the distribution of the letters <u>ѣ</u> and <u>ю</u> about the character of
the preceding consonant, but nothing definite can be said
concerning the neutralization of palatalization in consonantal clusters or at word end. The present-day Bulgarian
dialects give contradictory data on the subject, and even
if they were uniform, one could hardly accept their evidence

as relevent to the situation of 400 years ago[418]. On the contrary, one should expect significant differences between phonetic norms of the established literary language in the 14th century and those of the peasant dialects.

4.1.4. The vowels of the literary language pose even more problems than do the consonants. The texts indicate stress only sporadically, hence there is no assurance that stress marks were added by the original scribe and not by a reader some centuries later in a very different region. From the text no conclusions can be drawn concerning the stress alternation, if any, or other prosodic features - the existence or nonexistence of pitch, or of vowel reduction in non-stressed position. One encounters great difficulty in determining the number of vowel phonemes in the language.

4.1.5. The language under study here is an established system by itself; it had already existed for five hundred years and had served different generations, different societies and nations. In addition, it had been sanctioned by the Church as a holy language. On the other hand, we know of no detailed description of its grammatical structure available to the medieval users of the language

---

418. St. Stojkov, Bəlgarska dialektologija, Sofia, 1968 (2nd edition), 296 pp. + maps.
_____, Palatalnite səglasni v bəlgarskija ezik, IzvIBE, I, 1952, p. 5-65.

in question[419]. Their only clue to the grammar must have been the existing copies of the holy books. Thus, we may assume that the better those copies were, the better chance the scribes had to generate an adequate Church Slavic grammar.

The text under consideration - the <u>Four Gospels</u> of King Ioan Aleksandər - represents without any doubt a superb implementation of the 14th-century idea of Church Slavic (and an excellent example of the Middle Bulgarian literary language). If the grammatical properties and stylistic norms of this language could be determined, it would be possible to describe the ideal system of the 14th-century literary language in Bulgaria, and then to establish the changes that had occurred in it over the previous centuries.

The following approach to the spelling is proposed: to postulate a tentative set of morphonemes and to examine their relationship to the letters used to represent them.

4.1.6. In determining the morphonemic status of certain items we must outline a broader theoretical framework. As has already been mentioned, the identifica-

---

419. It was believed in the mid-19th century that the treatise "On the eight parts of speech" was written by John Damascene and translated into OCS by John the Exarch (10th century). V. Jagić rejected this identification of both author and translator, and derived the numerous 17th - 18th-century Russian copies from a much later Serbian translation.

tion of phonemes in Jakobsonian terms[420] in the 14th-cen-
tury Church Slavic used in Bulgaria, is an impossible task.
We must seek a more abstract level of representation for
the underlying segments, since we cannot identify either
the vowel alternations due to stress shifts, or neutralizations in voicing at morpheme boundaries. The real problem is how abstract the representation should be and what
quantitative relationship will obtain between items and
rules. One possible stand, advocated in its extreme by
T. Lightner[421], is to reduce the number of items to the
absolute minimum and to expand the number of rules. Thus,
one must discard as useless to the abstract representation
items such as {ʒ}, {c}, {ž}, {š}, and {č}, as well as the
soft counterparts of the rest of the consonants, since they
are predictable provided the number of vocalic items is
drastically increased. Just this happens in Lightner's
system, where he expands the number of units again (e.g.
tense vs. lax vowel series). Counting the overall number
of items, consonantal and vocalic, one would hardly find a
significant reduction. But as a result one must increase
the number of rules necessary to yield the final phonetic
string. Such a method may be useful in linking derivation

420. R. Jakobson, Remarques sur l'évolution
phonologique du russe comparée à celle des autres langues
slaves, Prague, 1929, 188 pp.
_____, On Slavic Diphthongs Ending
in a Liquid, Word, 8, 1952, p. 2-6.

421. T. M. Lightner, On the Phonology of Old
Church Slavonic Conjugation, IJSLP, X, 1966, p. 1-28.

with flexional morphology, but may also obliterate the morphonemic alternations in the language at a given stage,
since they will simply be listed as consecutive rules for
the terminal phonetic representation. Most objectionable of
all, such an approach completely disregards the conscious
awareness of the users of a language, which is a powerful
force in creating microsystems based on not-so-deep structure analogies. A linguistic description must be able to
account for this factor. If the underlying representation
of польза were {polĭg-}, one could never explain the existence of the adjective полéзный instead of *полéжный.

In this study we follow approximately the system
outlined in M. Halle's Sound Pattern of Russian[422], with
slight modifications. The palatal consonants, anywhere else
but at a morpheme boundary with suffixes or desinences, are
treated as morphonemes, with the exception of {c} and {ʒ}.
When {c} and {ʒ} immediately precede such a morpheme boundary, they are morphonemes, while [č], [ž], [š], [žd] and
[št] are predictable outcomes of the velar consonants and
the dental stops plus jod. The phonetic outcome of the ending {...k-i$_{Nom.pl.masc.}$} is [...c-i], while that of the ending {...k-i$_{Acc.pl.}$} is [...k-i]; this alternation is not
phonologically, but morphologically, motivated. But if the
suffix {-#c-} is represented as {-#k-}, one needs complicated and highly artificial rules not merely to turn {k}

---

422. M. Halle, The Sound Pattern of Russian,
The Hague, 1959, 206 pp.

into [c] throughout the nominal paradigm, but to associate that paradigm with that of the soft declensions.

For the purposes of derivational morphology, only two rules need be introduced:

Rule 1: Before a morpheme boundary which turns hard consonants into soft, {c} > [č] and {ʒ} > [ž].

Rule 2: Before the suffix {-in,-}, which forms substantives denoting female persons, {c} > [k] and {ʒ} >[g.

4.2. The consonantal morphonemes. Most of the consonantal morphonemes are paired by voicing: {b}~{p}; {d}~{t}; {ʒ}~ {c}; {z}~{s}; {ž}~{š}; {g}~{k}. Unpaired are: {č}, {x} and {θ} and the sonorants {m}, {n}, {l}, {r}.

It is likely that {f} was at that time already established as a morphoneme in both the dialects and the literary language, as evidenced by the numerous Greek borrowings containing it. It is clear that the obstruent {f} was paired with the glide {v} in a voicing opposition: власфимиѩ (<u>Mar</u>.) ⟶ власвимиѧ(p. 79). The possible morphonemic status of {θ} in the literary language will be discussed later.

Since the text of IAG has very few new words compared with the known glagolitic texts, we shall omit the problem of the distribution of the consonantal phonemes, which belongs rather to the description of "classical" Church Slavic.

4.2.1. In word-final position, except in prepo-

sitions, the spelling always represents the underlying morphoneme, and no neutralization in voicing is expressed. The
only exception is the word кладѧѕь (Zogr.) → бѣ же тоу́
кладѧцъ їакѡвль. (p. 221, John IV.6). In this case, however, we may be dealing with a reinterpretation of the final
consonant on the model of the suffix $\{-\#c-\}$[423] (see the
parallel studenec ~ kladec): in some modern Bulgarian dialects, as well as in the standard language, the word exists
as kladenec. Nor does the spelling express any neutralization in voicing at the enclitic boundary with бо and же,
although the presence of же as an enclitic makes the use of
a jer optional as a word-end marker: дастъ же прѣдаꙗи ѐго
знамение (p. 127b, Mark XIV.44); І͞с же ставъ прѣдъ
и͞гемѡномъ (p. 80b, Matth. XXVII.11); съвѣ́т же створше
(p. 80b, Matth. XXVII.7); д͞хъ бс бѣдръ, а͗ пльть немощна
(p. 127, Mark XIV.38); свѧзаꙗтъ бо брѣмена тѧжка (p. 66b,
Matth. XXIII.4).

While discussing these problems of consonantal
neutralization in different positions within the word, we
do not necessarily imply that this phenomenon occurred in
all positions discussed. The situation in today's Slavic
dialects, in particular those of Ukrainian and Serbocroatian,

---

423. The marker $\{\#\}$ represents a morphoneme
which will be called in this dissertation "the fleeting
vowel $\{\#\}$". For detailed discussion cf. 4.3.6.

should make us very cautious in our approach to the entire problem. (Since, as will be seen, the spelling rarely reflects neutralization, one may with equal plausibility assert mutually incompatible hypotheses: that neutralization at morpheme boundaries, as a morphonological phenomenon, existed consistently, partially, or not at all, with or without concomitant compensatory lengthening of the preceding vowel.)

4.2.2. The problem of voicing neutralization within a word is more complex. At different types of morpheme boundaries, the spelling represents it differently:

4.2.2.1. No voicing or devoicing occurs at suffix boundaries. A few examples will illustrate:

a) Suffix {-#b-} : татбы. о̑биды. лѫка́вства.

(p. 106, Mark VII.22).

b) Suffix {-#k-}: что а̊зкаа врата и̊ тѣсныи пѫть.

(p. 22b, Matth. VII.14); и̊ о̊стрии вь пѫти гладкыѫ.

(p. 145, Luke III.5); и̊ брѣмѦ мою̊ ле́гкое ю̊стъ: (p. 35b, Matth. XI.30).

c) Suffix {-#c-}: и̊ сътворѦ ва ловца чл҃комь.

(p. 89b, Mark I.17).

d) Suffix {-#č-#n-}: бѣхѫ о̊тѦгчени съномъ.

(p. 166, Luke IX.32); бѣстѣ бо о̊чи и̊хъ о̊тѦгченѣ. (p. 77b, Matth. XXVI.43).

e) Suffix {-#sk-}: кни́жники лю̑с҃кыѦ. (p. 9, Matth. II.4).

f) Suffix {-#stv-}: молите же сѧ да не бѫдеть бѣгъство ваше зимѣ ни вь сѫботѫ. (p. 70b, Matth. XXIV.20); разоумѣв же Ісъ лѫкавьство ихъ. реч. (p. 65, Matth. XXII.18); ѿ множьства рыбъ. (p. 270b, John XXI.6); и множьство много людии. (p. 154, Luke VI.17); Ісухво же рождьство сице бѣ. (p. 8, Matth. I.18). Of the last few cases only бѣгъство offers definite proof that the neutralization was not expressed at this morpheme boundary. There is a strong possibility (cf. details below) that in cases such as множьство and рождьство there was an inserted vowel. (As far as лѫкавьство is concerned, the glide {v} must have been paired in voicing with the obstruent {f}; compare also власвимиѧ, (in 4.2.).

g) The word ковчегъ is always spelled with в although it is hard to imagine that the speakers treated the segment -čeg- as a suffix: вьниде ное вь ковчегъ. (p. 71b, Matth. XXIV.38); вьниде ное въ ковчегъ. (p. 190, Luke XVII.27).

4.2.2.2. At a boundary with grammatical endings, devoicing occurs only before the infinitive ending {-ti}: и абие оубѣди Ісъ оученикы своѫ вьлѣсти въ корабль. (p. 44b, Matth. XIV.22).

But compare the situation before the past active participle ending: и влѣзшоу Ісоу вь корабль. (p. 26, Matth. VIII.23); гѫбѫ же напльнивше оцта на трьсть вьзньзше, придѣшѫ къ оустомь ѥго. (p. 226b, John XIX.29);

и ѡшедше скоро ѿ гроба. (p. 85b, Matth. XXVIII.8).

4.2.2.3. The spelling is very complex at the prefix or preposition boundary. Only prefixes and prepositions ending in a consonant or the fleeting vowel {#} will be treated here. The major distinction in the orthography is made on the basis of the initial morphoneme of the word (or morpheme) following the preposition (or prefix).

I) Prepositions or prefixes before consonants.

a) Preposition or prefix ending in an obstruent stop or the fleeting vowel {#}. No neutralization in voicing is reflected by the spelling (thus the spelling is morphonemic). In almost all cases, making this the rule, the preposition (or prefix) is separated from the following morphemes by a jer, either front or back[424].

{k#}, preposition only: идѫ й приидѫ къ вамъ (p. 254b, John XIV.28); събралъ сѧ кь дверемь (p. 90b, Mark I.33); й съвъпрашаахѫ сѧ дроугъ къ дроугоу (p. 149, Luke IV.36).

{nad#-}, not registered as a prefix in IAG: наⷣ челѣдиѫ своѫ. (p. 178, Luke XII.42).

{pod#-}, both preposition and prefix: събираетъ кокошь птенцѧ своѫ подь крилѣ (p. 69b, Matth. XXIII.37); не ймать где главы подъклонити (p. 25b, Matth. VIII.20).

{pr,ad,#-}, both preposition and prefix: йже

---

424. The problem of the distribution of the jers will be discussed below in relation to more general rules.

- 220 -

оуготовитъ пѫть твои прѣдъ тобоѫ (p. 158, Luke VII.27);
и прѣдьстоѫщимъ реч: (p. 194b, Luke XIX.24).

{ob-}, both preposition and prefix: и бѣ ѻб нощь
въ молитвѣ бжїи (p. 153b, Luke VI.12); обьстоимъ вби
Іерслмъ. (p. 199b, Luke XXI.20); и ѡбьхождааше вессѝ
окрстныѫ оучѧ: (p. 101, Mark VI.6).

In IAG, the spelling of the prefix {ob=} follows
exactly the rules of the classical texts. This spelling
principle was __phonological__ in the 9th century, as well as
__morphonemic__. In IAG (14th century), however, such a spelling as ѡбьхождааше(p. 101) no longer has a phonological
basis. The __Manasses Chronicle__, written by the same scribe
at approximately the same time (cf. 3.4.1., fn. 72) applies
the 14th-century __phonological__ principle, which leads to
such forms as: источникъ... садовнаа ѡптичаше корениа
(__Manas__. __Chron__., p. 7) 'The spring flowed around the tree
roots'; нил же бѣлостроуиныи опходитъ еѳїопїѧ, и тльсто-
браз ныѧ нивы егїпетскыѧ. (__Manas__. __Chron__., p. 7) 'The
white-streamed Nile encompasses Ethiopia and the fertile -
furrowed fields of Egypt.' (cf. fn. 391).

This discrepancy may be explained by the assumption that in his revision of the Gospel texts, the monk
Symon had at his disposal older copies of the Gospels em-
bodying the older spelling tradition. The __Manasses Chroni-__
__cle__, being a recent translation, reflected in its spelling
the contemporary phonological norms. At first glance it

may seem contradictory to state that in the spelling of prefixes ending in obstruent stops or the fleeting vowel {#}, the scribe applied the morphonemic principle - both in IAG and in the Manasses Chronicle - while to {ob=} in the Manasses Chronicle he applied the phonological principle. It should be recalled, however, that the morpheme {ob-} had a very low frequency as a prefix and, as a preposition, existed only in the two fixed phrases ѡ̃бъ онъ полъ 'on the other side' and о̃бъ нощь 'during the night' (see below). It might thus have been difficult for the scribe, while copying the Manasses Chronicle, to recognize the prefix {ob=} in the spelling о̃п- of the Slavic original, so as to re-introduce the morphonemic principle. He faced a similar situation in IAG with the cluster {-zd,#n-} > [zn] in празники (p. 206b) and непразнож (p. 141b), where the morphonemic shape was obscured by the absence of alternations (see below).

Such an assumption is in accord with the evidence of contemporary Bulgarian, which tends to reinterpret the prefix {ob=} as a prefix {o=}, the {b} being understood as the first phoneme of the following lexical morpheme. The verb *ŏb-vlĕk-tī 'to dress, clothe' was reinterpreted as {o=blĕk-}, which then paired with a new derivation {sə=blĕk} 'to undress'; *ŏb-ou-tī 'to put shoes, socks, pants, etc. on', was correspondingly reinterpreted as {o=buj-}, then paired with {sə=buj-} 'to take shoes, socks, pants, etc. off'; *ŏb-vĕs-ĭ-tī became {o=bĕs,-i-}, with subsequent derivations {běs,-i-} 'to hang s.o.', {běs,-i-l-o}'gallows'.

Since the **Manasses** **Chronicle** must have been written after IAG (cf. 3.2.4. and fn. 374), it is most improbable that the scribe should have recognized the morphonemic
shape of {ob=} while revising the New Testament, and then
have failed to recognize the same morphonemic entity a
little later, in his copying of the **Manasses** **Chronicle**. It
must be concluded that in his spelling of this morpheme, the
scribe was guided neither by the **morphonemic** principle nor
by the phonological norm of his time, but by some third
principle. This is the "**traditional**" principle[425], which
is referred to in the Russian grammars as "tradicionnye
napisanija".

The **traditional** principle reflects the phonology
of a much earlier period of the language, and most likely
of a particular dialect, highly-valued in that period. This
so-called "principle" actually has two areas of application:
the spelling of a limited number of words, learned as exceptions (ишѫдиа < [iščṽd,ia] < {j#z=čṽd,-#j-a})[426] and the
verbatim copying of a text considered authoritative.

{ot#-}, both preposition and prefix. In most

---

425. V. V. Vinogradov, ed., *Obzor predloženij po
usoveršenstvovaniju russkoj orfografii*, Moscow, 1965, 450 pp.

426. The symbol Ṽ in morphonemic, phonemic and
phonetic transcription, represents the single nasal-vowel
morpheme of Middle Bulgarian (resulting from the merging
of *ǫ and *ę) and its phonemic and phonetic outcomes. For
further details, cf. 4.3.5.

cases it is spelled as Ѿ. There are a few instances where the prefix alternates with o-; this is also known from the older Slavic texts: cf., e.g., исходѧще отътѫдоу отътрѧсѣте прахъ (Ostr.); исходѧще Ѿтѫдȣ. отрѧсѣте прахъ. (p. 101b, Mark VI.11); ι ошедъ съкры сѧ отъ нихъ (Mar.); Ѡшедъ съкры сѧ Ѿ нихъ. (p. 249b, John XII.36); да не би отъшелъ отъ нихъ (Mar.); да не би ѡше‖лъ Ѿ нихъ (p. 149-150, Luke IV.42).

We can offer a few examples with the preposition (and prefix) въ, although {v} should be treated as a glide paired with {j} rather than as an obstruent[427]: въ тѫ нощь бѫдета двѣ (p. 190b, Luke XVII.34); и вь разбоиникы въпаде (p. 170, Luke X.30); вьстѣ скоро (p. 245b, John XI.29).

   b) Preposition or prefix ending in a voiced continuant obstruent {z}: {j#z-}, {b,oz-} - as both prepositions and prefixes - and {bl,iz-}, {v#z-}, {n,iz-}, {raz-} - only as prefixes. Here the orthographic rules are different depending on the following consonant, although generally neither the prefixes nor the prepositions are separated by jers.

   1) Before voiced stops no changes occur: бѣахѫ же жены из далече зрѧщѫ. (p. 132b, Mark XV.40); нѫ избранныхъ ради ѧже избра (p. 123, Mark XIII.20); иже вь

---

427. In this I follow:
   H. Andersen, The Phonological Status of the Russian "Labial Fricatives", Journal of Linguistics, 5, 1969, p. 121-127.

васъ без грѣха ѥ҃. (p. 235, John VIII.7); да не повелитъ
имъ въ бездн҄ѫ ѝти (p. 162, Luke VIII.31); на възглавници
сп҄ѧ (p. 98, Mark IV.38); раздра сѧ на двоѥ (p. 83b,
Matth. XXVII.51).

2) Before the sonorants {n}, {m}, {l}, and the
glide {v}, these prefixes and prepositions are spelled without change. The phonetic change {z} > [ž] observed in the
older texts, as in ѣж нен҃же (Mar.); ꙇ беж н҃его (Zogr.)
is not found in IAG: и́з неѫ же (p. 133b, Mark XVI.9);
ꙗко не и́знеможетъ (p. 139b, Luke I.37); и́ без него
(p. 213, John I.3); и́ възношааше сѧ на н҃бо (p. 212, Luke
XXIV.51); и́змрѣшѫ бо (p. 11, Matth. II.20); не възмогѫтъ
(p. 188, Luke XVI.26); о҃ни же и́з лиха дивлѣахѫ сѧ.
(p. 114b, Mark X.26); и́ и́злѣзь и́с кораблѣ (p. 45b, Matth.
XIV.29); и́ а҃зъ възлюбих вы (p. 255b, John XV.9); чл҃къ да
не разлѫчаетъ (p. 113b, Mark X.9); изволи сѧ и́ мнѣ
(p. 137, Luke I.3); и безъ врѣтища (p. 203, Luke XXII.35);
прѣходить скозѣ безводнаа мѣста (p. 173, Luke XI.24); и́
възвръгше ри́зы своѫ. (p. 195, Luke XIX.35); ви́дѣ разводѧща
сѧ н҃бса (p. 89, Mark I.10).

3) In IAG there are two coexisting orthographic
principles in the spelling of these prefixes before {r}.
The prefixes {j#z=}, {b,oz=}, and {v#z=} are always spelled
according to the morphonemic principle, which is different
from the situation in the classical texts, where the combination -z=r- phonetically yielded [zdr]. The following

examples are from IAG: <u>изрече</u> (p. 43b, Matth. XIV.7); и
в҃ы <u>без</u> <u>разоума</u> ю̇сте (p. 47, Matth. XV.16); <u>възрадова</u> <u>сѧ</u>
(p. 140, Luke I.47); <u>възрасте</u> (p. 180b, Luke XIII.19);
<u>възрыдаете</u> (p. 157b, Luke VI.25).

However, IAG treats differently the prefix {raz=};
with no exception, when {raz=} precedes a lexical morpheme
beginning with {r}, the spelling indicates the same cluster
[zdr] as in classical Church Slavic: <u>раздроушение</u> (p. 23b,
Matth. VII.27), and p. 156, Luke VI.49); <u>раздрѣшити</u>
(p. 88b, Mark I.7, and p. 180, Luke XIII.16); <u>раздрѣшиши</u>
(p. 50, Matth. XVI.19); <u>раздрѣшите</u> (p. 54b, Matth. XVIII.
18); <u>раздрѣши</u> <u>сѧ</u> (p. 107, Mark VII.35); <u>раздрѣшено</u>
(p. 50, Matth. XVI.19).

This absolute consistency in the different treat-
ments of {raz=} raises the question, whether or not it is
only a spelling rule which is at work here. {raz=} differs
from the other prefixes ending in {z}, in that it never
appears as a preposition. The preposition {v#z}, although
not registered in IAG, definitely existed in the literary
language of the 14th century; even today it is found in the
northeastern Bulgarian dialects. The preposition {v#z},
governing the accusative case, is often used in the Bulgarian <u>gramoty</u>, with the meaning 'around, near' (cf. Russian
возле). Example: й̇ низ рꙑ́лѫ. въ стрꙋ́мѫ й̇ <u>въз</u> стрꙋ́мѫ. до
гѐрманщицѫ. и <u>въз</u> гѐрманщицѫ. до блъга́рина ⁴²⁸.

Most likely the spelling of IAG reflects the phonological norm of its time; the cluster [zdr] was retained (as an archaism) only with the "pure" prefix {raz=}, while it was eliminated for the other prefixes, which occur also as prepositions. This seems to be a result of the following sequence of events: stage one - (classical OCS) both prefixes and prepositions ending in {-z-} before an {r} caused insertion of the dental stop {d}: [zdr]; stage two - (between the 11th and 14th centuries) the prefixes ending in {z} before an {r} still caused the insertion of the dental stop {d}, while at the preposition boundary there was an innovation - no {d} was inserted: *издрече but *без разоума (this is a hypothetical stage); stage three (14th century, IAG) attests to the tendency in the language to treat the prefix boundary and the prepositional boundary in the same fashion; as long as the morpheme is utilized as both prefix and preposition, the rules should be the same: из рѣкы and изрече but раздроушение; stage four - (after 14th century) - here the morpheme {raz=} follows the rules which govern the prepositional boundary, although it itself is never a preposition. This process of morphonemic leveling at the prefix boundary was complete only after the 14th

---

428. G. A. Il'inskij, <u>Gramoty bolgarskix carej</u>, p. 27. The quotation is from the Golden Bull of King Ioan Šišman to the Rila Monastery, dated September 21, 1373.

century.

4) Before the voiceless stops and the unpaired voiceless {x} a regressive neutralization in voicing takes place, which is always reflected by the spelling: и̑с тебе бѡ изыдетъ, во́ждь. (p. 9, Matth. II.6); видѣшѫ смоковницѫ и̑съхшѫ ис корениıа (p. 117b, Mark XI.20); каженици и̑же и̑сказишѫ сѧ (p. 56b, Matth. XIX.12); гла̄ста же и̑сходъ е̑гѡ̑ (p. 166, Luke IX.31); бес порѡка (p. 137b, Luke I.6); и васъ бес печали створимь (p. 86, Matth. XXVIII.14); вьскысошѫ вьсѣ (p. 180b, Luke XIII.21); и не вьсхотѣсте (p. 181, Luke XIII.34); кни́гы распоустныѫ написати (p. 113, Mark X.4); и влькь расхытъть (sic) (p. 242, John X.12).

However, there is one exception to the rule: the prefix {v#z=} is always spelled morphonemically throughout the paradigm of the verb възпити (in IAG, a jer never separates the prefix from the lexical morpheme): възпи къ немоу гла̄щи (p. 47, Matth. XV.22); и̑ възпи́въ народъ начѧть просити (p. 130, Mark XV.8); възпишѫ же вьси гла̄ще (p. 263b, John XVIII.40).

5) Full assimilation in voicing occurs before {s} and {z} at the prefix boundary; the spelling always simplifies the geminated sibilants /z=z/ and /s=s/ as з and с respectively: дѣлаѭщеи безакониıе (p. 23b, Matth. VII.23); и̑ творѧшжѧ безакониıе (p. 42, Matth. XIII.41); и̑ съ беззаконникома причьтенъ бы̑с (p. 131b, Mark XV.28); и̑ и̑сьше а̑бие смоковница (p. 62, Matth. XXI.19); и̑же бѣ

и́сѣче^н въ камени (p. 132b, Mark XV.46); вънъ и́сыплѫтъ ѫ
(p. 183b, Luke XIV.35); и́сѧкнѫ и́сточникъ кръве ѥѫ
(p. 100, Mark V.29); лице оу́бо нбси оу́мѣѥте расѫждати
(p. 49, Matth. XVI.3).

The prefix {v#z=} before {s} and {z} becomes
{v#=}, thus homographous with the prefix {v#=}. Although
its shape has been obliterated by the spelling, the prefix
in the words listed below is most likely {v#z=}; this conclusion rests on that prefix's connotation of upward movement, increasing degree or sudden onset of a state or
action, a connotation not shared by the prefix {v#=} but
present in these examples: възва   (p. 214, John I.15);
възвашѫ   (p. 104, Mark VI.49); възовѫтъ   (p. 182, Luke
XIV.12); възрѣвыи   (p. 17b, Matth. V.28);   възрѧтъ
(p. 267, John XIX.37); въсиꙗ́   (p. 146, Matth. IV.16);
въсмѣѥте сѧ   (p. 154, Luke VI.21);   въстаниѥ   (p. 143b,
Luke II.34);   въставъ   (p. 25, Matth. VIII.14);   въсѣдъ
(p. 61, Matth. XXI.5).

6)   At the preposition boundary before {s}, however, the preposition {j#z} is always spelled without assimilation (with or without the word-end marker jer):   и́
а́бие и́зыде и́зъ сънмища   (p. 90b, Mark I.29);   въстав же
и́з сънмища   (p. 149, Luke IV.38).

7)   The only occurrence of the sequence {z=š}
across a prefix boundary, registered in IAG, is in the stem
{j#z=š#d-}.   On the basis of these limited data it would
appear that the orthographic rules for these prefixes before

a stem beginning in {š}, at the time of the writing of the
manuscript, allowed the application of two alternative principles: the _phonological_, expressing a complete regressive
assimilation (as is the situation in all the glagolitic
texts which I have thoroughly compared with IAG): ишед же
рабъ тѣи (p. 55, Matth. XVIII.28); о͡цъ же ѥго ишедъ
молѣаше и (p. 186, Luke XV.28); and, appearing much more
frequently, the _morphonemic_, which demands the spelling-out
of the prefix (as из-) regardless of the phonological rules
of neutralization in voicing ({z=š} > /s=š/) and assimilation in articulation (/s=š/ > [š] or, quite possibly, [š̄]):
изшедъ і͡с видѣ многъ народъ (p. 44, Matth. XIV.14); въ
единыи же на десѧте ча изьшедь (p. 58b, Matth. XX.6).

Since the original scribe was not entirely consistent in introducing the morphonemic spelling in this instance, someone else, perhaps much later, in some cases inserted -з- or -зь- over the word with phonological spelling.
This is a very indicative fact, illustrating the general
tendency in Church Slavic spelling towards overall establishment of the morphonemic principle in orthography: и
ишедше проповѣдаахѫ (p. 101, Mark VI.12).

8) The text does not have examples of the prepositions {j#z} and {b,oz} before a word beginning with {ž}.
There are only a few examples of the corresponding prefixes
in an analogous position. Here, the orthography usually
expresses dissimilation at the morpheme boundary: иждившоу
же ѥмоу вьсѣ. бы гладь крѣпокъ (p. 184b, Luke XV.14);

нѐгда поносѧть вамь, и̑ и̑жденѫ̄т вы (p. 16, Matth. V.11);
въжделѣшѫ видѣти (p. 40, Matth. XIII.17); въждѫдах сѧ, и
напоисте мѧ (p. 74b, Matth. XXV.35).

Against the only such example, on p. 74b (въждѫдах
сѧ), there are two other examples where the spelling expresses full assimilation of {z} in a very common word: 'to
become thirsty': въжѫждет сѧ пакы (p. 221b, John IV.13);
не въжѫждет сѧ никогда же (p. 229b, John VI.35).

9) Only {j#z=} the prefix and {j#z} the preposition are registered before {c}. In the OCS texts, as can be
seen, for instance, from the glossaries in <u>Mar.</u> and <u>Sav.</u>,
the spelling indicates this type of assimilation of {z} in
the preposition {j#z} in most cases, but shows only a few
instances of assimilation of {z} in the prefix {j#z=}.

In IAG, however, no simplification of the type и̑
цр͡кве is reflected in the spelling of the preposition.
There is some hesitation as to how to spell it - morphonemically, as <u>и̑з</u>, or phonologically, as <u>и̑с</u> (indicating regressive neutralization in voicing): и̑ и̑зьгна и̑з цр͡кве
(p. 217b, John II.15); и̑ и̑зыде <u>и̑с</u> цр͡кве (p. 238b, John
VIII.59); и̑ и̑зшедь и̑і͡с̃ <u>и̑с</u> цр͡кве и̑дѣаше (p. 69b, Matth.
XXIV.1). As a prefix, {j#z=} is spelled in most cases as
<u>и̑с-</u>: гл͡ахѫ же І̑оу̑де́и и̑сцѣлѣвшомоу̑ (p. 224b, John V.10).

There are still, however, a few words where elimi-
nation of {z} before {c} is reflected by the spelling. We
may presume that here the Tərnovo orthographic school simply
accepts the tradition: и̑ трѣбоуѫщихь и̑цѣлѣнї̈а, цѣлѣаше

(p. 164b, Luke IX.11).

    10) At a boundary before {č} the OCS texts usual-
ly employ the ligature щ or the digraph шт in order to reflect more closely the phonological processes which take
place there. In our text this rule is followed in the spelling of only one word - ишѫдина. Compare ишѫдїа ѥхиднова
(p. 37b, Matth. XII.34); ишѫдїа ѥхиднова (p. 145, Luke
III.7). It seems that this word alone was spelled traditionally. It must have become de-etymologized and, for the
writers, completely separated from the word чадо.

    There is a strong indication that whenever the
scribe was able to etymologize, he wrote the prefix as ис-.
On p. 211 he first wrote ишезе, then erased the ш and wrote
сч: и тѣ [ишезе >] исчезе ѿ нею (p. 211, Luke XXIV.31).

    On the other hand, the hesitation between the let-
ters з and с before the voiceless {č} may constitute additional evidence that the phonological process at this boundary actually yielded [šč], which the scribe did not know how
to represent: и бы̄ идѫщемъ имъ изчистишѫ сѧ (p. 189, Luke
XVII.14); вьси исчьтени сѫтъ (p. 175b, Luke XII.7); нако
нѣ прⷪркь безъ чьсти (p. 101, Mark VI.4); и послашѫ и
бесчьстна (p. 119, Mark XII.4); и тѣ бесчѧденъ оумретъ
(p. 197b, Luke X.28); расчитаетъ имѣнїе аще иматъ
(p. 183, Luke XIV.28).

    c) The preposition {s#} and the prefix съ-/с-
The spelling of the preposition as съ (always with a jer)
does not give any information on neutralization in voicing

before voiced obstruents or on other phonological processes which might take place at this boundary: и̂ възрѣвъ ‖ на на̨ съ гнѣвомь (p. 93b-94, Mark III.5); сь силоѭ и̂ славоѭ велиеѧ (p. 71, Matth. XXIV.30); и̂ пришедши въ народѣ съ зади (p. 100, Mark V.27).

The prefix съ-/с- is used in these two alternate forms following specific rules. No neutralization in voicing, assimilation or dissimilation is expressed by the orthography - opposite to what was already observed with the prefixes из-, без-, раз- and въз-. An examination of all forms in the text having the prefix съ-/с- brings conclusive evidence concerning the orthographic rules governing the literary language of the 14th century.

1) Before a morpheme beginning in a voiced obstruent the prefix is always spelled with a jer: се̏ гл҃ахъ вамъ, да не съблазните сѧ (p. 256b, John XVI.1); и̂ събираѭ̈тъ и̂ въ ѡ҃гнь въметаѭ̈тъ, и̂ сьгараѭ̈тъ (p. 255b, John XV.6) съзираахѭ же сѧ междоу собоѭ оӱченици (p. 252, John XIII.22).

2) Before a morpheme beginning in a voiceless stop, the prefix is usually spelled without a jer. The few cases where the prefix is spelled as съ- are either at the end of a line, and thus comply with a general rule on the use of the back jer as a marker of this orthographic boundary (cf. 4.3.6), or they represent remnants of a tradition of always spelling this prefix as съ-: ѿ толи начѧть сказати I҃с оӱченикѡмь своимъ (p. 50, Matth. XVI.21); до скончаниѧ вѣка, а̂ми́нъ + (p. 86b, Matth. XXVIII.20);

по‍добаєть да <u>скончаєт</u> с‍а о҄ мнѣ   (p. 203, Luke XXII.37);

не <u>скрываите</u> себѣ <u>скровиша</u> на земли   (p. 20b, Matth. VI.19);

й звѣздь <u>спадѫть</u> сь н‍бсе   (p. 71, Matth. XXIV.29);   да

<u>спо‍добите</u> с‍а оу҄бѣжати вьсего того   (p. 201, Luke XXI.36);

<u>сьтвори</u> се҄, й҄ <u>створить</u>   (p. 157, Luke VII.8).

The word <u>съкроушѫ</u> (p. 166b) and <u>ськр҄ошит</u> с‍а

(p. 267) are individual exceptions to this new rule.

3)   Before voiceless obstruents other than stops,
the prefix is spelled as <u>съ-</u>/<u>сь-</u>: вьсѣ сиꙗ҄ <u>съхранихъ</u>
(p. 191b, Luke XVIII.21);   й ю҄же оу҄бо б‍ъ ‖ <u>съчеталъ</u> е҄стъ
(p. 113-113b, Mark X.9);   а҄зь е҄смъ хлѣбъ <u>сьшедыи</u> сь н‍бсе
(p. 230, John VI.41).

4)   If the prefix <u>съ-</u> alternates with <u>сѫ-</u> it is
always spelled with a jer, independent of the environment:
сѫпрѫгъ: <u>съпрѫгъ</u> воловныхъ коупихъ пѫть   (p. 182b, Luke
XIV.19);   сѫсѣдъ: <u>съсѣди</u> же й҄же бѣхѫ видѣли е҄го прѣжде
(p. 239, John IX.8).

5)   The prefix is usually spelled without a jer
(as <u>с-</u>) if the following morpheme begins with a sonorant (or
the glide $\{v\}$), immediately followed by a vowel: нѫ о҄собь
<u>свить</u> на е҄диномь мѣстѣ   (p. 268, John XX.7);   й҄ раскопавше
<u>свѣсишѫ</u> ѡ҄дрь   (p. 91b, Mark II.4);   <u>свѫзаноу</u> сѫшоу   (p. 98b
Mark V.4);   никто же не можаеше е҄гѡ <u>свѫзати</u>   (p. 98b, Mark
V.3);   й҄ й҄же на ‖ кровѣ, да не <u>слазить</u> въ домъ   (p. 122b-12
Mark XIII.15);   ѡ‍ѿ <u>сложенїа</u> всего мира   (p. 41b, Matth. XIII
35);   й҄ <u>сломивъ</u>, дааше оу҄ченикомъ своимъ   (p. 165, Luke IX.
16);   <u>смотрите</u> врановъ   (p. 176b, Luke XII.24);   ни с҄мѣ кто

- 234 -

Ѿ дне того, въпросити его (p. 66b, Matth. XXII. 46); и очи

свои смѣжишѫ (p. 40, Matth. XIII.15); ꙗко призрѣ на

смѣрение рабы своѫ (p. 140, Luke I.48); ихъ же крьви пилать

смѣси съ жрьтвами ихъ (p. 179, Luke XIII. 1); абие

срѣте его чл҃къ (p. 98 b, Mark V.2.)

The word свѣдѣтель and its derivatives, which are
registered in a large number of grammatical forms, are never
spelled with съ-: аще свѣдѣтельствоуѫ ѡ мнѣ, свѣдѣтельство
мое нѣ҇ истинно (p. 226, John V.31); вы же есте свѣдѣтеле
симъ (p. 212, Luke XXIV. 48).

In contrast, the word съвѣтъ is always spelled with
a jer. A possible explanation may be the existence of a minimum pair съвѣтъ ('council') vs. свѣтъ ('light, world'):
сꙉи не бѣ присталъ съвѣтѣ и дѣлѣ ихъ (p. 209, Luke XXIII.51).
A further possibility is the attempt to keep the same number
of syllables within the derivational group: съвѣтъ, Ѿвѣтъ,
завѣтъ. This is not a Middle Bulgarian spelling innovation,
however, since the same convention is registered in the
older texts (cf. Supr.).

6) If the prefix precedes two sonorants (or the
glide {v} followed by a sonorant), it is always spelled as
съ-: ꙗко бѫдетъ съврьшение гл҃аным' ‖ еи ѿ г҃а (p. 139 b -
140, Luke I.45); съвлѣкошѫ съ него хламидѫ (p. 82, Matth.
XXVII.31); коеѧ съмрьтиѧ хотѣаше оумрѣти (p. 249 b, John
XII.33).

II) Prepositions and prefixes before vowels.

a) All prepositions ending in a consonant, when they precede a word beginning in a vowel, may be spelled either with a jer (front or back) or without a jer. Thus it seems that the jer was used as an optional marker of thi boundary (see the chapter on the jers): й ѡ̈брѣтше ѐго ѡ̈б онь полъ морѣ (p. 229, John VI.25); йже стоаше ѡ̈бь ӧнь полъ морѣ (p. 228 b, John VI.22). There is never a jer after the preposition {ot#} spelled as the ligature Ѿ (which is the situation in most cases): й ни ёдина же Ѿ нею падеть на земли, безь бг҃а вашего (p. 32, Matth. X.29) гл҃а емоу ѐдинъ Ѿ оӱченикъ ѐго (p. 122, Mark XIII.1).

There is a distinction between the prepositions ѡ̈бъ and ӧ in the language of IAG. The preposition ѡ̈бъ is used only in two idiomatic word combinations: ѡ̈б онь полъ (p. 229) 'on the other side (of a sea, river, lake)' and ѡ̈б нощь 'throughout the night': й бѣ ѡ̈б нощь въ молитвѣ бж҃їи (p. 153 b, Luke VI. 12).

In all other instances before a word beginning in a vowel, only the preposition ӧ is used (the same as in the classical texts): слышавши же ӧ Їс҃ѣ (p. 100, Mark V.27); ӓрхиереи же въпроси Їс҃а ӧ оӱченицѣхъ нёго й ӧ оӱчени его (p. 262, John XVIII.19).

b) Prefixes before non-front vowels ({a}, {o}, {u}) are not separated by jers, nor are any phonetic chang expressed by the orthography. Only a few prefixes are regi stered in this position in IAG, all of them ending in the

voiced continuant {z} : и́зшедшемъ и́мъ ѿ виѳаниѧ, въза́лка
(p. 117, Mark XI.12); нѫ за безѻ̆чьство е̑го (p. 272, Luke
XI.8); хоула. гръдꙑни. безоумиѥ (p. 106 , Mark VII.22);
а́ко възѧсте ключь разоумѣнию. (p. 175, Luke XI.52).

c) Prefixes before morphemes beginning in front
vowels or the glide {j} are spelled according to more complex
rules. The initial glide {j} must be treated together with
the front vowels because of its prothetic character. The
spelling gives abundant evidence of optional jotation before
initial *e. In addition, the *ě reconstructed on
comparative Slavic evidence merged with the sequence *j-ā in
the Bulgarian linguistic area and yielded in initial position {ja} (for details, cf. 4.3.4.).

More complicated is the situation with the initial
nasal vowel. The alphabet possesses only two letters for
the nasal vowel: ѫ and ѧ, which in IAG never have the jotated forms: *ю̈ѫ, *ꙗѧ. The rules of distribution for these
two letters will be discussed in the appropriate section (cf.
4.3.5.). The following rule can be formulated: in word -
initial position and at some prefixal morpheme boundaries,
the nasal vowel is represented by the letter ѫ (on the premise that the nasal vowels merged); the letter ѧ expresses
the same nasal vowel, implying palatalization of the preceding consonant.

Thus, depending on the final consonant of the prefix and the initial vowel of the following morpheme, the
prefixes are spelled in various ways:

1) Prefixes ending in an obstruent stop before initial {i} or {ji} are followed by a jer with the exception of the prefix ѿ-(a few times written от-): прѣдъйдеши бѡ прѣд лицемъ гнимъ (p. 141, Luke I.76); ѡбъидошѫ ѥго Іоудеи глаще ѥмоу (p. 243, John X.24); й ѡбъйдѫт тѧ й ѡбъимѫт тѧ въ сѫдоу (p. 195 b, Luke XIX.43); BUT: й ѿиметь слово (p. 96 b, Mark IV.15); йнѣмъ пѫтемъ ѿидошѫ въ странѫ свож. (p. 10, Matth. II.12).

2) Prefixes ending in voiced continuant obstruent {z} before initial {i} or {ji} are spelled without indicatio of the palatalization of the final {z}, and the initial vowel of the root becomes phonetically [y]. In all examples attested in IAG except one, the fact that the prefixes change the initial vowel of the following morpheme into [y] creates a new morphonemic alternation at this boundary: [i] versus [y]. Here the evidence shows that, for the scribe, the prefixes were not separable entities:ы after the prefix is not a combination of a jer and the letter i, but the 14th - century Bulgarian grapheme jery (never ᑭ): възыгра сѧ младенец. (p. 139 b, Luke I.44); прииде... възыскати й спсти погыбшаго (p. 54, Matth. XVIII.11); възыде въ виѳаниѧ. (p. 117, Mark XI.11); ѿ нѫдоу же изыдохъ (p. 38 b, Matth. XII.44); много й изыщет сѧ ѿ него (p. 178 b, Luke XII.48); й разыдѫт сѧ ѡвцѧ стада (p. 77, Matth. XXVI.31).

The sole exception to this practice, възьищѫтъ, can be regarded as a spelling mistake, caused by the inter-

ruption of the prefix by the end of the line: въ‖зьищѫтъ
вънити и не възмогѫтъ. (p. 180 b, Luke XIII.24).

    3) Prefixes ending in an obstruent stop before
initial {jo} > [e] are followed by a jer (except when the
prefix is written as a ligature). This environment is registered in IAG only with the prefixes ѡбь- and ѿ-, and in
various forms of the verbal stem *-(j)ę-ti: и ѡбьемъ ѥ
рече имъ; (p. 112, Mark IX.36); еда ѡбьемлѧть ѿ тръниꙗ
грозды. (p. 23, Matth. VII.16); ꙗко Гь мои, ѿемлетъ
строѥниѥ домоу ѿ мене. (p. 186 b, Luke XVI.3).

    There are only two examples in the entire IAG
where the morphemes which follow the prefixes begin in {jo}
without graphic expression of the jotation of [e]. The jer
is spelled only after the prefix {ob=}, but not after the
ligature ѿ: ни ѿ кѫпины гроздь ѡбъемлѧть (p. 155 b. Luke
VI.44); и ѿемлѧщаго твоа, не истѧꙁаи (p. 155, Luke VI.30).

    4) Prefixes ending in voiced continuant obstruent
{z} before initial {jo} > [e] are not separated from the
root by jers. The examples from IAG are restricted to the
same verbal stem *-(j)ę-ti and to the prefixes {j#z=} and
{v#z=}. In these words {jo} after the prefix is never expressed by ѥ, but only by the letter е: и въставъ послѣдоу
ими въземь крстъ (p. 114, Mark X.21); ничьсо же не
въземлѣте на пѫть. (p. 164, Luke IX.3); и иземь два
пѣнѧꙁа, дастъ гостыньникоу. (p. 170 b, Luke X.35).

    5) Prefixes ending in an obstruent stop before in-
itial nasal vowel are always followed by a jer (except, as a

general rule, the prefix ⱉ-, due to the ligature). Three
different prefixes are attested in IAG: <u>ѡбъ-</u>, <u>подъ-</u>, and ⱉ-
The verbal stem *(j)ę-ti always begins with the letter ѫ:
й тъма ѥго не <u>ѡбѫтъ</u>. (p. 213, John I.5); нѫ не можете
<u>подьѫти</u> нинѣ (p. 257 b, John XVI.12); ѐгда ⱉѫтъ бѫдеть ⱉ
нихъ женихъ. (p. 152 b, Luke V.35).

      6) Prefixes ending in the voiced continuant {-z}
when followed by a nasal vowel (only the prefixes {v#z=} and
{j#z=} are registered in IAG in this environment) are never
followed by a jer, and the nasal vowel is always spelled as
ѧ : не достоит' тй <u>възѧти</u> ѿдра своѥю(p. 224 b, John V.10)
како хлѣбы не <u>възѧхомъ</u> (p. 49, Matth. XVI.7); <u>възѧшѫ</u>
троупъ ѐго. й положишѫ и въ гробѣ (p. 103, Mark VI.29); й
тогда оѹзриши <u>изѧти</u> сѫчець. (p. 155 b, Luke VI.42); и тогда оѹзриши <u>изѧти</u> сѫчець. (p. 22, Matth. VII.5).

      7) The two prefixes {ob=} and {j#z=}, which fol-
lowed different orthographic rules in the previous examples
are written according to the same rule before initial <u>jat'</u>
(reconstructed from comparative Slavic data). Only derivatives from the stem *ěd- 'to eat' are found with the prefix
{ob=} and {j#z=} in IAG. The derivatives of the verb stem
*-ěxa-ti, registered in the glagolitic Gospels, are consist-
ently replaced in IAG by derivatives of the verb *<u>iti</u>. (In
all modern Bulgarian dialects, as well as the standard language, the verb <u>jáxam/jázdja</u> exists, but only with the meaning 'to ride on horseback or "piggyback"'. It is possible
that this semantic narrowing took place before the 14th cen-

tury, causing the replacement of the stem *-ĕxā-tī in the
sense of 'locomotion by conveyance'.)

The prefix {ob=} is not, except in one case, separated by a jer from the initial vowel of the stem nor is the
morpheme boundary marked by the spelling, in contrast to all
previously described situations. Here are a few examples:
сѐ ѡбѣдь мои оуготсвахъ (p. 64b, Matth. XXII.4); гл҇а
имь І҇с, прїидѣте о҇бѣдоуите (p. 271, John XXI.12); егда же
ѡбѣдовашх. гл҇а сѵмѡноу пе́троу (p. 271b, John XXI.15); ю҇гда
же сн҇ъ твои сѣ҇и, изѣдъ имѣ́ние твое. (p. 186, Luke XV.30).

The one exception to this spelling rule is significant because it follows the general rules of spelling for
the prefix {ob=} before a vowel, as described: a jer should
be written after the prefix, and the initial vowel of the
stem should be spelled as in most cases when in absolute
initial position: ꙗ (for etymological jat'), ѥ, ѫ: да
некогда отѧгчажть ср҇ца ваша обьѩдѣ́нїемь и пиꙗ́нствомъ.
(p. 200b, Luke XXI.34).

The prefixes {s#=} and {v#=} before a morpheme
beginning in a vowel or prothetic jod are realized in their
variants {s#n=} and {v#n=}. The texts of the New Testament
do not offer examples with these prefixes before vowels
other than {jo}, {i}, {ṽ} and etymological jat'. (The
only exception with respect to the realization of {v#=}
as {v#n=} is in the glagolitic Mar.: ι въѣдх ѣджштемъ же
имъ (Luke VIII.23). But the other OCS texts and Ostr. dif-

fer in this passage: against the въѣдѫ of <u>Mar.</u>, <u>Ostr.</u> has
вънидошѧ, while <u>Zogr.</u> has прѣѣдѫ and <u>Assem.</u> - прѣидѫ. IAG
follows <u>Assem.</u>: и̂ <u>прѣидошѫ</u>. и̂ и̂дѫщим же и̂̈мъ,   (p. 161 b,
Luke VIII.23).)

The orthographic rules on this particular boundary
of {s#=} and {v#=} before initial {jo} are very similar to
those for the prefixes ending in {z}: и плата вънѐмша сѧ
не оу̂гаситъ   (p. 36 b, Matth. XII.20);   вънемлѣте ѿ лъжнихъ
пр҄ркъ. (p. 22 b, Matth. VII.15);   ф҆ них же сънемшем сѧ
тъмамъ народа   (p. 175, Luke XII.1);   и̂ сънемь ѥ̑ ѡ̑бвить
пла[ша]ницеѫ.   (p. 209, Luke XXIII.53).

Before initial {i} there is never a jer, but neither does the {i} turn into [y] (as in the case of the prefixes ending in {z}): на̂ко не ѡ̑ хлѣ‖бѣхъ вамь вънимати
рѣх (p. 49 - 49 b, Matth. XVI.11);   съ н҄е̑ди̑нѣмь о̂комь
вънити въ цр҄твие̑ бж҄ие̑   (p. 112 b, Mark IX.47);   и вьниде
ї҃с въ капернаоу̑мъ.   (p. 149, Luke IV.31);   и̂ вънидеть и̂
и̂зыдеть и̂ пажить ѡ̑брѧще҄   (p. 242, John X.9);   и̂ тꙑ̑
капернаоу̑ме. възнесыи сѧ до н҃бсъ. до а̂да сънидеши.
(p. 34 b, Matth. XI.23);   на̂ко сънидохъ съ н҃бсе, да не
творѧ волѧ моѫ   (p. 229 b, John VI.38).

In the numerous examples with the words вьнѧтрь,
вьнѧтрьа̂доу and вьнѧтрьнее, the initial nasal vowel after th
prefix вън- is always spelled as ѧ: и̂ петръ ... и̂де. до
вьнѧтръ въ дворъ архїереѡвъ.   (p. 128, Mark XIV.54);
вьнѧтрьа̂доу же пльни сѫтъ костии мрътвыныхъ. (p. 68 b, Matth
XXIII.27);   и̂ вьнѧтрьнее сътвѡри   (p. 174, Luke XI.40).

The developments in some present-day Bulgarian
dialects indicate that such spelling in IAG actually followed a phonological rule and not just an orthographic convention. In the West Bulgarian dialects this word is
[vnétre] or [unétre], showing an origin *vъn=ętrě rather
than *vъn=ǫtrě. The Standard Bulgarian /vѐtre/ has a different origin - it is a petrified locative *ǫtrě with prothetic *v- before an initial back vowel (compare /vəžě́/
'rope', /və́si/ (arch.) 'mustaches', /və́zel/ 'knot', /və́glen/
'coal', etc.).

Parallel with the prefixes ending in {z}, one
might expect that the prefix сън- too would be followed by
the letter ѧ. However, the only such example in IAG does
not follow such a rule: а̑ще приидеть и̑лиа сънѩти е̑гѡ.
(p. 132, Mark XV.36). This very contradictory, yet isolated
example does not disprove the existence of such a rule,
which would require writing only ѧ after сън-, вън- and all
prefixes ending in {z}. Thus the word сънѩти can be considered a mistake, together with such spellings as пѧть for
пѫть 'road' (cf. 4.3.5.6.).

Etymological jat' is registered in IAG only
after the prefix сън-, and is always spelled as ѣ: и̑деже
пасхѫ съ оу̑ченикы моими сънѣмъ (p. 125 b, Mark XIV.14);
и̑мате ли что сънѣдно зде; (p. 211 b, Luke XXIV.41).

c) The prefix {ob=} before the initial glide {v}
is spelled according to the same rule as in classical OCS:
initial {v} is truncated. If the lexical morpheme has ini-

tial {v} before a vowel, the spelling never separates the
prefix from the truncated morpheme by a jer. Here are a few
minimum pairs: {ob=jṽ-t-ø} > ꙍбъѩтъ (p. 213). BUT:
{ob=v,ṽz-aj-ø} > о̂бѧ̄за: и пристѧпль о̂бѧ̄за строупы ѥго
(p. 170 b, Luke X.34); {ob=id-ṽt-ø} > ꙍбьйдѫт(p. 195 b).
BUT: {ob=v,in-uj-ṽ} > о̂биноуѧ: и̂ не о̂биноуѧ сѧ слово
гла̄аше. (p. 109, Mark VIII.32) and {ob=v,id,-j-ṽ} > ꙍбиждѫ:
дроуже не ꙍ̂биждѫ тебе (p. 59, Matth. XX.13).

    This orthographical, and most likely phonological,
rule applies to all words except the derivatives of the lexical morpheme {v,ij-} 'to wrap'. In all three existing exam
ples in IAG the word обитъ (as spelled in Mar. and Zogr.) is
written ꙍ̂бвить: и̂ сънемь е̂, ꙍ̂бвить въ плашаницѫ.(p. 132 b
Mark XV.46). On page 267 b, the scribe first wrote ꙍ̂биста
but later he, or someone else, put a small letter в over the
line: възѧста же тѣло Ісво. и [ꙍ̂биста>] ꙍ̂б^виста ѥ ри́зами.
(p. 267 b, John XIX.40).

    4.2.2.4. This detailed examination of suffix,
morphological ending and prefix boundaries shows that the
pairing of the consonants according to voicing shown by
neutralizations in voicing, is very little reflected by the
spelling. The only conclusive evidence so far has been demonstrated in two respects: first, the final consonant in
the prefixes ending in the voiced {z} becomes /s/ before
voiceless obstruents (IAG lacks examples only for initial
{s}, {š}, {f}); second, the following pairs are established:

	Voiced Obstruents			Voiceless Obstruents	
{b}	избавити	(p. 210 b)	{p}	распѫдить	(p. 242)
{d}	вьздьхнѫ	(p. 107)	{t}	йстръгнетъ	(p. 137 b)
{ʒ}	no examples in IAG	{c}	исцѣлѣвшомоу	(p. 224 b)
{g}	йзгнании	(p. 114 b)	{k}	вьскысошѫ	(p. 180 b)
----			{č}	расчитаѥть	(p. 183)
----			{x}	исходъ	(p. 166)

4.2.2.5. Although trivial, additional evidence is
needed to prove not only that {b} was a voiced obstruent
and {p} a voiceless one, but also that they were paired
(yielded the same phonetic results in environments demanding
neutralization) in respect to voicing. Such an environment
is provided by the "newly formed" consonantal clusters other
than those at morpheme boundaries, where the orthography expresses only the devoicing of {z}. By "newly formed" in
this context we understand "attested after the period of
classical OCS", that is, after the glagolitic texts of the
10th and 11th centuries. The data are not abundant, but are
consistent and reliable:

{b} ~ {p}: Both Mar. and Zogr. in Luke XXIV.42
have the word бъчелъ. In IAG (p. 211) it is written: ѿни
же дашѫ ѥмоу рыбы печéны чѧсть. й ѿ пчелъ сътъ.

{z} ~ {s}: In addition to the neutralization of
the prefixes and prepositions, the word съде (from the classical texts) in IAG is spelled as зде without exception.

{g} ~ {k}: The OCS texts always spell къде with
voiceless k, usually with a back jer following it. In IAG
this word, like зде, is written with the voiced counterpart

of the initial consonant: где (with no exception).

{v} ~ {f}: The morphoneme {f} must have been firmly established in the language because of the numerous borrowings from Greek. For example, the word фарисеи, used 95 times in different cases, was never written with substitution of some other letter for the initial {f}. No mistakes are made in the spelling of фалéковъ (p. 146 b), фаноуѝлева (p. 143 b), фаресъ (p. 6 b), фарéсовъ (p. 146 b), филипъ (used 21 times in different cases), финикъ (p. 248), Ïѡсифъ (used 24 times in different cases etc., etc. Church Slavic must have had a phonological restriction on the distribution of this phoneme, as of a newly borrowed one, not well established yet. In such cases {f} and {v} are paired, and often в is substituted for {f}. The glagolitic texts know this type of substitution (for example власвимлѣатъ in Mar., Matth. IX.3). Two such spellings of this word are found in IAG: нáко власвимиѧ рéче. (p. 79, Matth. XXVI.65); съгрѣшение й власвимиѧ (p. 95, Mark III.28).

In the other three cases, the substantive is written correctly as власфимиѫ (p. 79; p. 128 b) and власфимиѧ (p. 47); in four other cases it is replaced by хоула (p. 106), хоулѫ (p. 92; p. 151 b) and о хоулѣ (p. 243 b). The verb is always spelled correctly as власфимисоуетъ (p. 27), власфимисаетъ (p. 95 b) and власфимисаѫтъ (p. 95 b), or else replaced by хоулиши (p. 243 b) or похоулитъ (p. 176).

This same restriction on the distribution of {f} still operates in Modern Bulgarian (see [svérə] for сфера, [əsvált] for асфалт, etc.). It is demonstrated in Russian by the name Матвей (from Ματθαῖος).

4.2.2.6. The orthography of IAG reflects another type of pairing of voiced and voiceless continuant obstruents in the environment before the sonorant {m} and before the voiced stop {d}. A Byzantine sigma is represented in Slavic by strict rules as either с or з. When the Byzantine pronunciation of voiceless continuants before the sonorant {m} or the voiced stop {d} as their voiced paired counterparts, did not violate Slavic phonology, they were spelled in IAG as voiced, with very few exceptions. Thus the Greek cluster {sm}, pronounced as [zm]: и о мáтизмѣ (< ἱματισμός) моеи мѣташѫ жрѣбиѫ. (p. 266, John XIX.24); и се катапе- тазма (< καταπέτασμα) цр̃квнаа раздра сѫ (p. 83b, Matth. XXVII.51); смѣшение змирно (< Σμύρνης) и алои (p. 267b, John XIX.39).

But in one instance in IAG this word is spelled with –см–: принесошѫ юмоу дары. злато и ливанъ. и смирнѫ (< Σμύρνα) (p. 10, Matth. II.11).

The phonological rendering of foreign (and in particular Greek) words according to the norms of 14th-century Byzantine Greek is a spelling rule in IAG, insofar as the voicing of a voiceless obstruent continuant before the sonorant {m} does not violate the phonological system of

Slavic. In Byzantine Greek {γ} is paired with {x} in respect to voicing, while in literary Bulgarian of the 14th century {g} is paired with {k} (къде > гдѐ). Still, **Mar.**, **Zogr.** and **Sav.** always spell the Greek word δραχμή as драгма and δίδραχμον as дидрагмъ. Obviously, the scribe of IAG must have found such a spelling, dictated by Greek phonology to be in violation of the phonology of Church Slavic. He writes these words as дрàхмъ (p. 184), драхмѫ (twice on p. 184 b), дидрахма (p. 52 b), and only once with **г** (according to the strong tradition of the Classical texts): оу̊чи-тель вашъ не даѥт ли дидрагма (p. 52b, Matth. XVII.24).

4.2.2.7. The Greek cluster {sd}, pronounced as [zd]: ꙗ̊же нарѝцает сѧ еврѐискыи виѳезда̀ (< Βηθεσδά) (p. 224, John V.2), is spelled phonetically in IAG.

4.2.2.8. The classical OCS texts also include voicing of {s} before {r}, but in most cases offer doublets - words, spelled through application of the principle of transliteration of the Greek words (or Hebrew words which had passed through Greek): есромовъ (< τοῦ 'Εσρόμ)(**Mar.**, Luke III.33), or else according to the Byzantine pronunciation - phonetically: изл̊евъ (< τοῦ 'Ισραήλ) (**Sav.**, p. 75). The latter principle is applied more frequently in the classical texts.

As far as the Byzantine Greek cluster {sr} is concerned, IAG consistently represents it as -ср-. (The text from **Dečansko Evangelije**, however, published by Jagić in lieu of the missing initial pages of **Mar.**, uses the forms

юзром, юзрома (Matth. I.3).) Here is an example from
IAG: фаре́съ же ро́ди, ю́срома. е́сром (< 'Εσρώμ) же ро́ди
а́рама (p. 6 b, Matth. I.3). Without exception, the forms
of the word for Israel and its derivatives are spelled with
-ср-: І́сраи́лѣ (pp. 9, 140, 143, 210 b), І́сраилю (p. 141b),
І́сраилеви (p. 215), І́сраили (p. 24), І́сраилевъ(p. 216),
І́сраи́лтѣнинь (p. 216), etc.

4.2.2.9. The previous examples represent how IAG
reflects regressive assimilation. The corresponding
progressive assimilation is registered in IAG only for the
Greek cluster {nt}, pronounced [nd]: великыи вь стхъ
кѡнстандинъ цр҃ь (IAG, Postscript, p. 275); кѡнстанди҃н
десро҃т, зꙗ҃т велика҃г цр҃ѣ (IAG, p. 2 b).

4.2.3. On the morphonemic status of {θ}.[429]The orthographic rules applied in IAG cause serious problems in
determining the morphonemic status of the obstruent {θ},
written θ. The rules follow the Byzantine norm of pronunciation for the sound represented by the Greek letter θ:
this is obvious from the non-transliterative method used by
Slavic to render the Greek double theta: τθ (applied also
in Latin: -tth-). This must express a certain Greek phonological rule of dissimilation. There are two personal names
spelled in the Greek New Testament with double theta: Ματ-

---

429. Cf. the brief discussion of the spelling
alternations in IAG, in:
R. Scholvin, Einleitung in das Johann-Alexander -
Evangelium, mit drei photolithographischen Tafeln, Archiv
für slavische Philologie, VII, 1884, p. 53.

θαῖος and Ματθάν. In IAG they are spelled as: матѳе́и

мытарь (p. 30), матѳеа (pp. 27b, 94b, 153b); and матѳана

(p. 7b), матѳан же (p. 7b), матѳа́новⷮ (p. 146), матѳа́нов

(p. 146b).

    4.2.3.1. In addition, 26 different Greek words,
biblical personal and place names and Hebrew phrases are
spelled with the letter θ̲ in place of the Greek theta; their
frequency varies between one and eleven cases of occurrence.
Used only once: при авиа́ѳарѣ (p. 93b), виѳезда̀ (p. 224),
далманоуѳьⷭⷭскихⷤ (p. 108), еффаѳа̀ (p. 107), лиѳостратоⷩ
(p. 265), мааѳо́въ (p. 146b), марѳины (p. 244), на́ѳановъ
(p. 146b), сси́ѳовъ (sic) (p. 146b), талиѳа̀. коу́ми(p. 100b)
ѿ ѳамары (p. 6b), годъ ѳемïана (p. 137b), ѳеофиле
(p. 137b). Used twice (for convenience, some of those used
more than once will be given only in one of the forms used):
Ἰ̂ѡа́ѳам (twice on p. 7), маⷮтаѳі́евъ (p. 146) and маттаѳо́вь
(p. 146b), ѳадеи (pp. 30, 94b). Used three times: варѳѡ-
ломеи (pp. 30, 94b, 153b), голгоѳа̂ (pp. 82b, 131, 265),
салаѳïиль (pp. 7b (twice), 146b). Used four times: ѿ
а̂римаѳеѧ (pp. 84, 132b, 209, 267). Used six times: виѳ-
леюемь (pp. 8b, 9 (twice), 9b, 10b, 141b), наѳанаи́лъ (pp.
216 (4 times), 216b, 270). Used seven times: виѳсаида
(pp. 34b, 104, 108b, 164b, 169, 216, 248b). Used eight
times: ѳѡма̂ (pp. 30, 94b, 153b, 253) and also as ѳома̂
(pp. 94b, 244b, 269b (twice)). Used eleven times: вь
виѳани́ѧ (pp. 62, 116b, 117 (twice), 124b, 194b, 212, 214b,
245 (twice), 247b) and ма́рѳа (pp. 171 (four times), 244,

245 (four times), 245b, 246, 247b).

4.2.3.2. Against those numerous words always spelled with the letter θ̲, there are only five Hebrew words and names where one should expect the letter θ̲, but finds one or another kind of substitution: τοῦ Θάρα - фара́новъ (p. 146b), τοῦ Μαθουσαλά - матоусала́н' (p. 146b), σαβαχ-θανί - савахтани (p. 132, but on p. 83 written correctly as савахθани), Γεθσημανῆ - гетсимании (p. 77, but on p. 126b written correctly as геθсимани) and finally, the Hebrew place name Βηθφαγῆ, written in three different ways: въ витсфагі́ѧ (p. 60b), въ витфагиѧ (p. 116b), and - correctly - въ виθ︡᷄фагі́ѧ (p. 194b).

The last five words may be explained as indicating that the Greek text according to which IAG was revised, substituted phi and tau in these Hebrew words and names. But there are strong arguments against a presumption that the spelling oscillation in these few words in IAG reflects the scribe's own pronunciation:

First, the consistency in the spelling of the Greek sequence -θθ- as -тθ- (матθеи and матθан) suggests that the orthography reflects a Greek phonological rule of dissimilation; therefore, a phonological principle is being applied.

Second, all previously-given examples of the voicing of {s} before {m} and {d} in the Greek words, as well as the voicing of the cluster {nt} as -нд- reflected by the Slavic spelling, strongly suggest an application of the phonological principle rather than a simple transliteration of the Greek words.

Third, the Greek diphthongs are rendered in Slavic phonologically, according to their Byzantine pronunciation, which also implies a phonological spelling principle.

Fourth, an extralinguistic consideration may be borne in mind: the educated clergy and members of the court in 14th-century Bulgaria were bilingual, or at least had a good command of Byzantine Greek, which is easy to explain by historical and geographic factors[430].

4.2.3.3. It seems that the educated people of the 14th-century Tərnovo Kingdom who were fully competent in both literary Bulgarian (Church Slavic) and Byzantine Greek tried to establish in the Slavic literary language a norm of orthoepy and orthography for foreign words in accordance with Byzantine orthoepic norms. The fact that this attempt did not make itself felt in the Bulgarian dialects is no evidence against such an assumption. The literary language could have possessed a number of features which did not exist in any of the spoken dialects of the time.

---

430. A. F. Višnjakova, K voprosu o kul'ture i prosveščenii bolgar v XIV v., Vizantijskij sbornik, Moscow - Leningrad, 1945, p. 256-259.

4.2.4. On the morphonemic status of {ʒ} [431]. The Church Slavic alphabets, in addition to the letter з, use two other graphemes, ʒ and ѕ, indicating a sound different from that represented by the letter з, yet occurring in a largely predictable environment parallel to the environment where {c} appears. In fact, the letter ѕ occurs either in word-initial position or at morpheme boundaries with suffixes and desinences.

4.2.4.1. In word-initial position the letter ѕ is found in a limited number of words. Most typical is the word ѕѣло or ѕѣлѡ, which appears over 20 times in IAG and is always written with the letter ѕ (the letter itself was called "dzělo"). The word свѣзда appears 7 times and is also always spelled with ѕ: свѣзда (p. 9b), свѣзды (pp. 9b, 71, 123b), свѣзⷣх (pp. 9, 10) and свѣздахъ (p. 200). The word свѣрь is found only once, in the phrase й бѣ съ свѣрми (p. 89, Mark I.13).

But in certain lexical stems, the initial ѕ alternates with the letter з in a fashion which makes it difficult to state rules for the alternation. The infinitive form здати (p. 183b), the imperfect зидаахх (p. 190) and the substantive зданїе (p. 122), зданиа (pp. 69b, 122), all spelled with з, are opposed to сиждете (pp. 68b, 174b), сиждхщоу (p. 156) and сиждхщеи (pp. 64, 119, 197). The

_____

431. Cf. the extensive comparison of spelling variants in IAG in:
R. Scholvin, op. cit., p. 24-30.

prefixed stem shows a similar alternation: създѧ̀ (p. 156b),
създати (p. 79), създавшоу (p. 148b), създана (p. 218),
създанию (p. 123) versus съзиждѫ (p. 49b) and съзида
(p. 131b). The forms of the prefixed verb просѧбати are
written seven times with с, as in просѧбнеть (p. 123b) and
once with з: прозѧбошѫ (p. 39b).

If all these spellings in IAG are compared with
the corresponding words in the glagolitic texts, one observes immediately that IAG is far more consistent in the
usage of the letter с. But the words which appear in Mar.
as сьрѣти, оусьрѣти, съсьрѣти, while often written with с
(or ꙅ) in all the glagolitic texts, are always spelled with
з in IAG: не зрйши бо на лйце чл̅комь (p. 119b, Mark XII.
14); ꙗ̇ко да оу̇зрѧ̇т дѣла ваша добраа (p. 16b, Matth. V.
16); съзираахѫ же сѧ междоу собѫ оу̇ченици (p. 252, John
XIII.22).

4.2.4.2. At a suffix or desinence boundary in
lexical morphemes, the letter с may represent the phonological outcome of the so-called Third Slavic Palatalization of
*g. It may occur after the reconstructed Common Slavic *ĭ
or a front nasal vowel, resulting from *iN. In this environment, it seems that the writer of IAG is consistent in
the use of the letter с only in certain words.

The word кнѧсь is used 18 times in different grammatical forms, always spelled with с; пѣнѧсь is written in
all 14 occurrences with с, and once is replaced by the word
цѧты (p. 217b). The word склѧсь from the classical texts

(Matth. XXII.19) does not occur in IAG, which has instead
ѡбразъ (p. 65). And the word кладѧѕь, registered in some of
the classical texts (e.g. Zogr.), appears on p. 221 of IAG
as кладѧцъ. The word *jeȝā 'wound' is used three times in
IAG (pp. 15, 29b, 90b) and is consistently written with ѕ,
e.g.: й всѣкх ꙁ̄ѕх въ людѣхъ (p. 29b, Matth. IX.35). The
word *stiȝā 'path' appears three times (pp. 12, 88-88b, 145),
and is always written with ѕ: правы творите сътъѕѧ е̄го.
(p. 145, Luke III.4).

   But there are oscillations in the spelling of
*poliȝa 'use, benefit': three times its forms are written
with ѕ (pp. 50b, 99b, 109b): каꙗ бѡ полѕа ю̃ чл̃коу.
(p. 109b, Mark VIII.36); and three times with ȝ (pp. 165b,
231, 248b): ꙗ̈ко никоꙗ ж̃ ползa ю̃. (p. 248b, John XII.
19). The verb ползевалъ (pp. 46, 105b) is written only
with the letter ȝ.

   4.2.4.3. The so-called Third Slavic Palatalization may occur at a suffix boundary of a lexical morpheme
ending in Common Slavic *g preceded by *ǐ, *iN or *ъ and
followed by the imperfective suffix *āj. The examples found
in IAG give contradictory data. Again, it seems that the
scribe used different rules for different individual words.
Forms of the verb стѧѕати сѧ 'to question' are used 11 times
and always spelled with the letter ѕ: начѧшх стѧѕати сѧ съ
нимь (p. 108, Mark VIII.11). The substantive стѧѕание
'conflict, disagreement', is also spelled with ѕ: бѣ же
стѧѕание ѿ оꙋченикъ Їѡ̄ӓновъ (p. 220, John III.25). But

another derivative of the same lexical stem, и̂стѧꙃати (сѧ) 'to settle a question', although written three times with ꙃ (pp. 155, 176b, 194b) has two forms with з: и̂стазавъ (p. 206b) and и̂стѧзати сѧ съ ними о̂ словеси. (p. 73b, Matth. XXV.19).

The verb подвиꙃати сѧ 'to attempt', used twice (pp. 180b, 263b), is spelled with ꙃ: подвизаите сѧ вьнити (p. 180b, Luke XIII.24).

The root *-tr̥'g- with different prefixes shows an even larger variety of forms. It is spelled with ꙃ in: протрьꙃаахѫ же мрѣжѫ и̂хъ (p. 150, Luke V.6); тогда а̂рхї-ереи растрьꙃа ризы своѫ гла. (p. 79, Matth. XXVI.65) and растрьꙃавъ (p. 128b). But it is spelled with з in: вьс- трьзаахѫ о̂у̂ченици е̂го (p. 153, Luke VI.1). It is even spelled with г, without a trace of the Third Palatalization, in: растрьгах ѫзы. (p. 162, Luke VIII.29).

The root *-žĭg-/*-žĕg- before the imperfective suffix *-āj- was usually spelled as жиꙃ- in the OCS texts[432] but in IAG it is consistently rendered with г, with no in-

---

432. A different opinion is offered by Diels in his reference grammar of OCS. See:
    P. Diels, Altkirchenslavische Grammatik mit einer Auswahl von Texten und einem Wörterbuch, Heidelberg, 1963 (2nd edition), I, xvi + 309 pp.; II, 116 pp.
    In the brief vocabulary at the end of part II, Diels pairs the attested verb вьжешти, вьжегѫ, s-aor. вьжахъ - 'anzünden' (p. 65) with an obviously reconstructed form, вьжагати, -жагаѭ- 'anzünden' (p. 64). He refers to part I paragraphs 23,5; 51,3 (should be 50,3) and 121,1-2, where no forms indicating the existence of *-žĕg-āj- (for *вь- жагати) are offered (cf. pp. 94, 134, 246). Such a recon- struction of the imperfective stem as in *вьжагати is in- correct. The different stems of the verb are as follows:

dication of palatalization in the final stem consonant: и҆

ѡ҆гнемь съжига҄тъ (p. 42, Matth. XIII.40); ни вьжига҄тъ

свѣтилника (p. 16, Matth. V.15); вьжигаѥтъ (p. 184b).

4.2.4.4. The letter s̲ is also found as an alternate form of the morphoneme {g} at particular morpheme boundaries as a result of the Second Slavic Palatalization. On
all such morpheme boundaries, listed below, it is written
with the letter s̲ (there is only one exception with з̲):

a) The nominative plural of the masculine substantives and adjectives: {bog-} > ꙗ҆ко ꙗ҆зъ рѣхъ б҃си нѣ́сте

(p. 243b, John X.34); {vrag-} > и҆ ѡ҆бложѧ҄тъ враси твои

ѡ҆строгъ ѡ҃ тебѣ (p. 195b, Luke XIX.43); {drug-} > дроуѕии

бо мнѣхѧ, и҆м же ковчежецъ и҆мѣше І҆ѡ́уда. (p. 252b, John XIII.

29); {mnog-} > ꙗ҆ко бѣси мноѕи вьнидошѧ въ нъ. (p. 162,

Luke VIII.30).

b) The nominative-accusative of feminine substantives: {nog-} > неже двѣ рѫцѣ и҆ двѣ носѣ и҆мѧщоу.

(p. 53b, Matth. XVIII.8).

---

*-žēg- (attested as -жешти, -жегѧ) is the perfective stem
(infinitive and future); *-žĕg- (attested as -жахъ) is the
s-aorist stem, parallel to that of решти, рекѧ, рѣхъ; *-žĭg-
is the imperative stem, attested in Supr. and Sav. as -жьси,
parallel to рьци.
     The imperfectivization of this verb is also paral-
lel to that of решти: (нарешти > нарицати), -жешти > -жисати.
The latter form is attested (cf. the glossary of Mar.).
Diels's mistake obviously arises from his assumption that
the imperfectivization would be realized by lengthening of
the vowel of the infinitive stem *(*-žĕg- > *-žēg-), while
what actually occurs here is a lengthening of the *ĭ of the
imperative stem (*-žĭg-   *-žīg-), along with the change of
the following *g > *ʒ (according to the Third Palatalization)
and the addition of the imperfectivizing suffix *-āj-.

c) Dative singular of feminine and masculine substantives of the hard *-a-stem declension: {slug-} > й
сългнѫвъ книгы, въдастъ слоузѣ й сѣде. (p. 148, Luke IV.20).

d) Locative singular of substantives of the hard
declensions - masculine, feminine (no examples in IAG) and
neuter - as well as locative singular of the hard adjectives
in masculine and neuter (no examples of neuter in IAG):
{bog-} > да ꙗвꙗтъ сѧ дѣла его ꙗко о бзѣ сѫтъ съдѣлана.
(p. 219b, John III.21); {n,odvg-} > .ли. лѣтъ ймыи въ
недѫзѣ своюмъ. (p. 224b, John V.5); {po=dv,ig-} > й бы
въ подвисѣ, прилежнѣю молѣше сѧ. (p. 203b, Luke XXII.44);
{mnog-} > можааше бо се продано быти, на мнозѣ (p. 75,
Matth. XXVI.9). But the locative case of the word брѣгъ on
p. 270b is written with з: стꙗ ӏс при брѣзѣ (John XXI.4);
{drug-} > въ дроузѣмъ корабли (p. 150b, Luke V.7).

e) Genitive, dative, instrumental and locative
plural (all genders) of the new adjectival declension, different from that of OCS, were remodelled according to the
pattern of the hard pronouns. The only existing example of
the Second Palatalization in this environment is for the
feminine genitive plural: {mnog-} > не оубоите сѧ оубо
мнозѣхъ птицъ. лоучьши есте вы. (p. 175b, Luke XII.7).

f) In all previously-described cases (1-5), the
Second Palatalization was caused historically by the following vowel, the result of the monophthongization of a diphthong. IAG, however, offers in addition one significant

example of a substitution of the Second Palatalization for
the expected First Palatalization (caused by *ě̆₁ < *ē̆) in
the comparative adjective мьножаишиихъ (Mar.), rendered in
IAG as мносѣишихъ: начѧшѫ ... прѣстаати и о̇ мносѣишихъ
'(they) began ... to provoke him (to speak) about many
(things)' (p. 175, Luke XI.53).

g) In the verbal system, the Second Palatalization of velars is observed in the imperative (only the 2nd
person singular is attested in IAG) for verbal stems ending
in {g}: {vr̥'g-} 'to throw down' and {po=mog-} 'to help'.
For both verbs, the letters з and ѕ oscillate in the imper-
atives: врѣзи ѿ себе (p. 17b, Matth. V.29) vs. врѣзи сѧ
низоу (p. 13b, Matth. IV.6); нѫ а̇ще что можеши помози намь
(p. 111, Mark IX.22) vs. вѣроуѫ Ги, помози моѥмоу невѣриѥ̇
(p. 111, Mark IX.24).

h) The only example of prepositions and adverbials representing etymologically petrified locative case
forms, attested in IAG, is the very high-frequency preposition скоѕѣ 'through, across' (note the difference from the
OCS сквоѕѣ), which is spelled only with ѕ: хождааше Іс̃ въ
сѫботѫ скоѕѣ сѣаниа (p. 35b, Matth. XII.1).

The Bulgarian literary language of the 14th century, as has been demonstrated on the preceding pages (253 -
259), tries to preserve {з} as a morphoneme. This was the
ideal toward which the scribe of IAG aimed.

4.2.5. The occurrence of double consonants. In

IAG, double consonants are written in both Slavic words and biblical names.

4.2.5.1. In Slavic words only the letter н̲ can appear as a geminate at suffixal morpheme boundaries. There are two types of boundaries̄ where this can occur:

a) Where the derivational stem ends in the sonorant {n}, and the suffix is either the substantival {-#n,ik-} or the adjectival {-#n-}: in either case IAG offers a small spelling innovation, resulting from new rules for the vocalization of the formerly phonemic jers, which have become fleeting vowels. In the classical OCS texts the two letters н̲ were separated by a letter jer.

The substantival suffix {-#n,ik-} after stems ending in {n}: безаконьникома (Mar.) → и̇ съ безаконникома причьтенъ бы̄◌ (p. 131b, Mark XV.28); законьникомъ (Zogr.) → и̇ вамъ законникомъ горе. (p. 174b, Luke XI.46); инс-племенъникъ (Sav.) → тъкмо и̇ноплеменникъ съ̄и̇ (p. 189b, Luke XVII.18).

The adjectival suffix {=#n-} after a stem ending in {n}: врѣменьни (Mar.) → нѫ врѣменни сѫтъ (p. 96b, Mark IV.17); законьноумоу (Mar.) → по ѡ̃бычаю законномоу (p. 143, Luke II.27); истинънъı (Zogr.) → нѫ ѡ̃ц̃ъ мои даеть вамъ хлѣбъ и̇стинныи съ нбсе. (p. 229b, John VI.32); каменьнѣемъ (Mar.) → а̇ дроугое паде на каменныхъ (p. 96, Mark IV.5); многоцѣнънъı (Zogr.) → нарды пистикіѧ много-цѣнны (p. 247b, John XII.3); неповинънъıхъ (Mar.) → николи же бисте ос̃ѫдили неповинныхъ (p. 35b-36, Matth.XII.

Whenever the morpheme boundary coincides with the
end of a line, a letter ъ or ь is written according to the
general rule for the use of the jers: и̑ съберѫть ѿ цр҃ствиꙗ
ѥго всѧ съблазнь‖никы. (p. 42, Matth. XIII.41).

b) Past passive participles in {-n-}, when used
as substantives, are, in most of the cases observed, written
with double -нн-. Compared with the situation in the classical texts, this is a new phenomenon, very consistently
carried out in IAG. There are only a few examples where
these past passive participles used as subject or predicate,
or in direct address, are spelled with a single -н-. Examples are: мноѕи бо сѫть званни, ма́ло же и̑збранныхъ (p. 65,
Matth. XXII.14); бракъ ꙋ́бо готовь е̑сть, а̑ званнии не бишѫ
достоини. (p. 64b, Matth. XXII.8); ра҃уи̑ сѧ ѡ̑брадованнаа
гь҃ с тобоѫ. (p. 139, Luke I.28); ни посланныи, болїи
пославшаго и̑. (p. 251b, John XIII.16); рожденное ѿ пльти,
пльть е̑сть, и̑ рож҃еное ѿ дх҃а, дх҃ъ е̑сть. (p. 218b, John III.
6); слово сѣ́анноѥ въ ср҃цихъ ихъ. (p. 96b, Mark IV.15);
се̑ ѡ̑бѣдъ мои оуготовахъ и̑ юнци мои и̑ оу̑питаннаа и̑сколена,
и̑ всѣ готова приидѣте на бракы. (p. 64b, Matth. XXII.4).

4.2.5.2. In addition to the rules for writing a
double -нн- at these morpheme boundaries, in three instances
a double -сс- is written in the forms for genitive singular
and accusative plural of the Slavic word весь 'small town,
village': и̑ ю̑ мъ за рѫкѫ слѣпааго и̑зведе и̑ вънъ и̑з весси.
(p. 108b, Mark VIII.23); и̑ диви сѧ за невѣрие ихъ. и̑

ѿбхождааше весси ѻкр҇ⷭтныⷯ оуⷱѧ: (p. 101, Mark VI.6); йдѣмъ

въ ближнѧⷶ вѐсси й грады (p. 91, Mark I.38).   No reasonable

explanation for this spelling can be offered. On the other

hand, in 25 instances when this word is used, it is always

written with a single -с-: и̋же бѣхѫ приишли, ѽ всѣхъ весии

галилеискыхъ й їоудеискыхъ   (p. 151, Luke V.17).

4.2.5.3. In rendering the biblical personal and

place names, the translator tries to follow the Greek spel-

ling as far as double consonants are concerned. The follow-

ing are among the words, some of them very frequent, which

are usually written with a double consonant as in Greek:

авва, варавва, равви, е̇ффаѳа̃, аддиевъ, маттаѳѻвь, маⷵ҇таѳі́евь

Iеммаоусъ, не̋мманоуилъ, геіе́нна, I͠ѻа́нна, I͠ѻа́ннъ, Iоаннѣевь

манна, осанна, не̋ссеи.

The use of a double consonant in biblical names

and words so as to comply with the Greek norm represents, iⁿ

IAG, a more advanced stage than that of the known texts of

the classical period (up to the 11th century). In glagolit-

ic writings double consonants are used sporadically; Sav.

is more influenced by the Greek orthography, while IAG re-

presents an even further development in this direction.

Here, however, the scribe of IAG makes the most numerous

mistakes and allows inconsistencies. Approximately three

quarters of the biblical names are spelled according to the

Byzantine orthographic rules, while the others are either

spelled with a single consonant, or - in a few instances -

with a double consonant unmotivated by the Greek spelling.

There is no clue to the orthoepic norm of the words written
with a double consonant, except the fact that some well -
known words, although having a double consonant in the Greek
spelling, are in IAG always written with a single one (coinciding with the Church Slavic tradition). This list includes such words and names as: садоукѣи (Σαδδοθκαῖος),
used 11 times; ѐлини ("Ελλεν) - 4 times; генисаретскыи
(Γεννησαρέτ) - 3 times; гомороу and гоморсцѣи (τὰ Γόμορρα);
месꙗ (Μεσσίας) - twice; манасина (Μανασσῆς) - twice;
ѳадеи (Θαδδαῖος) - twice; гаваѳа (Γαββαθᾶ) ; сосáна
(Σουσάννα) ; сирофиникиса (Συροφοινίκισσα). The word
сѫбота (Σάββατον), used 53 times, is of course a much
older borrowing in Slavic, so altered in shape that one
would hardly expect it to mirror the Greek form.

The following words have a double consonant, while
the Greek orthography does not require it: ссиѳовъ
(p. 146b) - (τοῦ Σήθ); ссимовъ (p. 146b) - (τοθ Σήμ);
асаррїи (p. 32) - (ἀσσάριον); фаррисеисцїи (p. 214) -
(φαρισαῖος). The spelling mistake in асаррїи may have been
caused by the scribe's awareness that one of the consonants
in the Greek form is indeed doubled - the correct spelling
would be ассарїи. The misspelling of фаррисеисцїи occurs
only once out of 95 occurrences of this word in IAG.

It is quite possible that the scribe who wrote IAG
followed, in many instances, the spellings in his Greek
original. Since most of the words in which he failed (from

our point of view) to use the double consonant correctly are
of Hebrew origin, we cannot rule out the possibility that
his "errors" were also those of his Greek original. Our
authority for the Greek spelling is the glossary of the
Codex Marianus, compiled by V. Jagić from normalized Greek
editions of the 19th century; the orthography in this glossary may not, in every case, be that of Byzantine manuscripts in the 14th century. Such a hypothesis, if correct,
would only show how great must have been the dependence of
the medieval Slavic translator upon the quality of his Greek
original.

       4.2.5.4. A correct use (according to the Byzan-
tine rules) of double consonants also involved the double
gamma, representing the cluster {ng}. The glagolitic texts
render this consonantal combination with the letters –нҕ–
(in cyrillic transliteration), while Ostr. always uses –нг–,
н'г or ньг: аньгели, арҳанѓела, еван'гелиѥ. But the
cyrillic Sav. uses only аг͠гелъ and ев͡а, hence the latter
spelling does not indicate how the cluster {ng} would have
been written if it were not abbreviated.

      In this respect, IAG follows consistently the
tradition established by Sav.: the cluster {ng} in the
Greek words is always spelled with a double –гг–, in accordance with the norms of Byzantine orthography: а͒гглъ
(ἄγγελος); а͒рҳа́ггелъ (ἀρχάγγελος); еу͒аггέлїе, е͒ваггέлие
or ѥу͡лие (εὐαγγέλιον); и͒а͒ггέωвъ (sic) (p. 146b) (τοῦ
Ναγγαί).

4.2.6. Single letters representing consonantal clusters.

4.2.6.1. The Slavic alphabet, as listed in Xrabər's treatise, has the Greek letter Ψ (psi) for the cluster {ps}. IAG, however, follows the tradition established in the glagolitic writings: it uses only the combination of letters -пс-. The number of words where Ψ should appear is very limited. While the glagolitic texts twice use the locative singular form паропсидѣ (Παροψίς), in IAG it has been replaced by the word блюдоу (pp. 68, 68b). But the Greek word Ψαλμός is still used twice in IAG: й про͡рцѣхъ й пса‖лмѣхъ о͡ мнѣ. (p. 211b-212, Luke XXIV.44); сам бо д͡дъ г͡летъ въ книгахъ псаломскыхъ (p. 198, Luke XX.42).

4.2.6.2. The classical texts do not use the letter ξ for the cluster {ks} in Greek words. Xrabər's list of the alphabet includes the letter ξ, and it is used twice in the IAG text. The classical texts (glagolitic) and the cyrillic Sav. show certain peculiarities in representing the Greek word φοῖνιξ as финикъ. Most likely, the phonological restrictions in the language did not allow for a final cluster {ks}. IAG, in the only instance where this word occurs, follows the same established tradition: прияшѫ вѣ͡твїе о͡ финикъ, (p. 248, John XII.13).

But if between two vowels not at the morpheme boundary, the cluster {ks} is preserved and expressed in IAG

by the letter ξ: а̂рфаξадо́въ (τοῦ ’Αρφαξάδ) (p. 146b);
ὤπΟΥ але̂ξандровоу и̂ роуфовоу (p. 130b, Mark XV.21). Also,
in the postscript, as well as in the initial two pages of
dedication to the Bulgarian king, the scribe writes the
king's name as ц҃рь. І̂ѡ̃. а̂леξандрь.

4.2.7. Sometimes the phoneme {v} in foreign words
if rendered in Greek by the letter upsilon, is expressed in
the same way (that is, by the letter y) in IAG[433]. Except
when immediately followed by the phoneme {i} (graphically
expressed in Greek by either ι or ει), this upsilon is expressed in the OCS texts by either в or у. The more frequently used of the two is в: Mar. has авгоуста, Assem. -
августа, while Ostr. has аугоста. For this word IAG also
uses the letter в: и̂зыде повелѣние ѿ ке́сара а̂вгоуста
(p. 141, Luke II.1). On the other hand, IAG continues the
tradition of orthographic duality in the spelling of the
word εὐαγγέλιον: whereas when abbreviated it is always
written with y (ю̄е̄у⁀г҃лие, ю̄е̄у⁀г҃лие, е̄у⁀г҃лие or е̄у⁀г҃лие), in
the title pages of the four gospels, where the word is not
abbreviated, there are Е̂ВАГГЕ́ЛЇЕ (Matth., p. 6 and Mark,
p. 88), but Е̂ВАГГЕ́ЛИЕ (Luke, p. 137) and ЕВАГГЕ́ЛЇЕ (John,
p. 213).

The classical texts accord different treatment to
the Greek upsilon (υ) when followed by the letter ι or the

---

433. Scholvin mentions Greek "consonantal u":
R. Scholvin, op. cit.,p. 53.

diphthong ει. All glagolitic texts have a cluster [vg,] (transliterated in cyrillic as -вh- or -вьh-). For example, Mar. has нинeвѣ̓итомъ for Νινευίτης, параскeвѣ̓ии for παρασκευή, левѣ̓ии for Λευείς or Λευΐς, левѣ̓итъ for Λευείτης. Ostr. uses various means to express this combination, obviously difficult phonetically for the ancient Slavs: левъгиты, параскеӱги (both with an epenthetic /g/), but also леӱитъ and леуиѫ without the epenthetic /g/. Sav. uses either вь or оу for the Slavic equivalent of the sound rendered in Greek by upsilon, but always adds the epenthetic /g/: параскевьгиа, левьгиѫ, леоугитъ. Compared with all this, the spelling of these words in IAG is perhaps much closer to the Byzantine pronunciation of the 14th century: the epenthetic /g/ is never used, and the upsilon is replaced by the letter в: ꙗ̈ко же бо бы̑с їѡна̑ знамениѥ нинeви́тѡ̑ (p. 173b, Luke IX.30); и̓ сⷮтвори чрѣждениѥ велїе левїи ѥ̈моу; въ домоу своемъ. (p. 152, Luke V.29); такожде и̓ левить, бывъ на томъ мѣстѣ. (p. 170b, Luke X.32). The word παρασκευή, however, is always translated as пѧтокъ or пѧтькъ: понеже бѣ пѧтькъ, ѥ̈же ѥ̈сть кь сѫботѣ: (p. 132b, Mark XV.42).

4.2.8. Simplification of the cluster /zdn/. IAG uses a simplified spelling for the word праздникъ (written this way in all the classical texts): празникъ. This word is used 23 times in IAG, always with omission of the letter д: потрѣбѫ же имѣаше на всѧ празники ѡ̈поущати ӥмъ ю̈диного.

(p. 206b, Luke XXIII.17). The same orthographic principle
is employed in the substantivized adjective <u>не</u>празнаа
'pregnant', which is used three times in IAG: възыде же и̇
І̇ѿсифъ ... написати сѧ съ мариеѧ. о̇брѫченоѫ е̇моу женоѫ,
сѫщоѫ <u>не</u>празноѫ + +   (p. 141b, Luke II.4-5).

In Luke XXI.23, as against непраздънымъ in the
glagolitic texts, IAG uses the synonymous expression ИМѦЩИМЪ
ВЪ ѪТРОБѢ (p. 200). In празникъ and непразнаа, /zdn/ is a
cluster which does not alternate with /zden/ in any paradigmatic form (since непразнаа 'pregnant' is a substantivi-
zation restricted to the feminine gender). But if the same
cluster /zdn/ in one of the paradigmatic forms of the word
alternates with /zden/ (as in празденъ 'empty, idle'), then
the morphonemic principle is followed in the spelling, and
the nominative masculine plural adjective is written as
<u>праздни</u>, despite the phonological rules for simplification
of the cluster: что зде стоите весь д͞нь <u>праздни</u>   (p. 58b,
Matth. XX.6); и̇ пришедъ о̇брѧщеть и̇ <u>праздень</u>   (p. 38b,
Matth. XII.44). This is a very significant example of the
application of the morphonemic principle in the spelling of
IAG: as long as obvious semantic links between the meanings 'empty' and 'idle' exist, due to the polysemy of the
word празденъ, the writer follows the morphonemic principle.
But when the concept of the word празникъ came to involve
first of all a 'celebration, feast' and last of all a 'day
when one is idle', the scribe failed to recognize the mor-

pheme structure of the word. The same applies to непразнаа 'pregnant', which must have meant to the scribe «имѫщаа въ ѫтробѣ» and not a 'woman who is not empty'. When the scribe was not able to reconstruct the morpheme structure of a word, the phonological principle was applied. In this case it is realized through a simplification of the cluster /zdn/ into [zn].

No examples are provided by the spelling for the phonetic simplification of the cluster /stn/. But the phonological rule should have applied in both cases.

4.2.9. The epenthetic /l,/. None of the classical glagolitic texts is absolutely consistent in the use of the epenthetic /l,/ at a morpheme boundary between a labial and a jod. Sav. is especially consistent in using the epenthetic /l,/. Ostr. is an exception, but its correct use is reinforced by the East Slavic phonological rules. In the eastern South Slavic area (and particularly on the territory of Bulgaria and Macedonia), this phonological rule must have ceased to exist by the time the classical texts were copied.

The scribe of IAG is very concious about consistency in writing the epenthetic /l,/ in the proper position. If compared with the older texts from Bulgaria, the 14th - century gospel completely disregards the contemporary phonological rules in the living dialects and tries to reconstruct a correct literary language as far as the usage of the epenthetic /l,/ is concerned. Any older, strictly Bulgarian copy of the gospel, used for reference by the scribe of IAG, could hardly have had consistent use of epenthetic /l,/[434]. Still, this would not have been a hard task for an experienced grammarian, since the rules for insertion of the epenthetic /l,/ are relatively simple.

A statistical comparison of the spelling of the word корабль 'a ship' in the glagolitic Mar., cyrillic Sav. (both exemplifying the situation in the classical OCS with strong Bulgarian features from the 11th century) and with IAG shows the following: in Mar., the word is written with an epenthetic /l,/, as кораблъ, кораблѣ, кораблю, кораблемь, корабли and корабла altogether 17 times; without the epenthetic /l,/, as корабъ, корабъ, кораби - 23 times; in Sav., a shorter version of the gospels, this word is used only in 12 places: three times with the epenthetic /l,/, as корабль, кораблѣ and 9 times without the epenthetic /l,/, as корабъ, корабъ, кораби. So here the forms without the epenthetic /l,/ are exactly three times as frequent as those with it.

In IAG the same word is used 32 times, and, without a single exception, with epenthetic /l,/. As an additional proof of the fact that the epenthetic /l,/ was not only an orthographic, but also an orthoepic norm in the

---

434. H. Birnbaum, The Dialects of Common Slavic, in: H. Birnbaum, J. Puhvel, ed's., Ancient Indo-European Dialects, Berkeley-Los Angeles, 1966, pp. 168, 176, 187, 191.

literary language, there is the example on p. 228: и не оу̃
бѣ пришелъ к нимъ І͡с въ <u>корабъль</u> (John VI.17). The insertion of the letter <u>ъ</u> for a vowel after an obstruent and
before a final liquid was caused by a phonological rule of
the living Bulgarian dialects of that time, and represented
the actual pronunciation of the word according to the rules
of phonological restriction in the language.

Although there are a few isolated words in which
the scribe forgot to write the epenthetic /l,/, they represent an insignificant fraction of the total number in which
he used it: (<u>Mar.</u>) на землѭ —→ сѐ рекъ, плюнѫ <u>на</u> земѧ.
(p. 239, John IX.6); (<u>Ostr.</u>) ѥмлюте —→ а̃ше ли ни, за тѧ̀
дѣла вѣрѫ ѥ̃мете ми. (p. 253 b, John XIV.11); (<u>Mar.</u>) по-
кѫплѭтъ сѧ —→ и ѿ̃ коуплѧ а̃ше не <u>покѫпѧт</u> <u>сѧ</u>, не ꙗ̃дѧтъ.
(p. 105, Mark VII.4).

4.2.10. Other peculiarities in the spelling of
the consonants. The word for 'gall', злъчьѭ (<u>Mar.</u>),
злъчиѭ (in all other classical texts and <u>Ostr.</u>) is replaced in IAG by <u>жльчиѧ</u> (p. 82 b): и дашѫ ѥ̃моу пити ѡ̃цеть
съ <u>жльчиѧ</u> смѣшенъ. (Matth. XXVII.34). In this case the
word registered in IAG represents the more common old Slavic
dialectal variant because of the palatalized syllabic *<u>l</u>'
in the first syllable.

There are two instances - съребро (and its derivatives) and съдравъ (and its derivatives) - where the glagolitic texts and <u>Ostr.</u> insert a jer after the initial <u>c</u>-.

In Sav., however, сребро and its derivatives are never
spelled with a jer, although съдравъ and its derivatives
are spelled as in the other classical texts. The text of
IAG not only follows Sav. as far as сребро is concerned,
but further eliminates the jer in съдравъ (and its derivatives) from the consonantal cluster здр-, in which the
voicing is expressed by the spelling: и̊ по что не въдаде
сребро моѥ трѫжником̑Ѣ (p. 194 b, Luke XIX.23); и̊ а́бие
здравъ бы̑ꙅ чл҃къ (p. 224 b, John V.9); не трѣбоуѫтъ
здравїи врача. (p. 152, Luke V.31).

      4.2.11. Later corrections in the spelling of some
words. Three words in IAG were consistently corrected by another hand, most likely a Serbian reader of the manuscript.

      4.2.11.1. The word скосѣ 'through' was changed
to ск͏ᵖосѣ by adding a small р over the line: this occurred
16 times, while the word was left unchanged only once (on
p. 114 b): оу̊добѣѥ е̊стъ вельбѫдоу скосѣ иглѣнѣ оу̊ши
проити. (Mark X.25). The form originally written as скосѣ
is the Middle Bulgarian variant of сквосѣ. While both
forms are used in Mar. - 10 times сквосѣ and only 7 times
скосѣ, Sav. knows only the form скосѣ. The latter, however,
is not registered in Ostr.

      4.2.11.2. The word трѣва 'grass' was five times
corrected into трава, by erasing the letter ѣ and writing
instead an a. It was left uncorrected only on p. 41:
ѥгда же просѧбе трѣва, и̊ плодъ сътвори. (Matth. XIII.26).
This correction reflects old Slavic dialectal variants of

the word. The older Church Slavic writings from Bulgaria know only the form трѣва, but <u>Ostr.</u> uses трѣва only once, and the form трава twice.

4.2.11.3. The word всѣ was changed in 6 instances to <u>вса̂</u>; <u>всѣкъ</u> or <u>вьсѣ͡к</u> in four cases to <u>всакъ</u>; and <u>всѣка</u> - four times to <u>всака</u>. The change of ѣ into <u>а</u> is attributable to the existence of dialectal variants: <u>Ostr.</u> uses in free variation вьсакъ, вьсѣкъ, вьсıакъ and вьсѧкъ.

4.3. On the phonemic softening of the consonants: the vowel system. While the voiced/voiceless pairing of the consonants is expressed in the Slavic alphabet by the use of different graphic symbols, the pairing of soft/hard consonants is not reflected graphically by separate letters. This fact alone says nothing about the existence of such pairing (or the existence of phonemic softening of the consonants) at the time when the Slavic alphabet was created. The Slavic alphabet is too closely patterned after the Greek one, for us to expect such revolutionarily new features as special graphemes for both hard and soft consonants. However, it supplies a reasonable method for expressing the feature softness/hardness of the consonant: the character of the following vowel.

The spelling rules applied in IAG and in all other Middle Bulgarian writings do not provide proof for the existence of <u>phonetic</u> softening of the consonants in a position other than before a vowel. Yet, through the morphonemic alternations - vowel/zero alternation, the alternations at a morpheme boundary - one could successfully establish phonemically soft consonants. The only position for which one has no means of examination is a consonantal cluster in which no vowel/zero alternation is observed (for instance the {s} in the cluster /st,-n-/.

Thus, the phonemically soft consonants cannot be determined through the spelling without a detailed study of the vowels and their graphic symbols.

The vowel system of the 14th-century Bulgarian literary language, as it is revealed by the application of the complicated spelling rules in IAG, consists of six vocalic morphonemes. They are as follows:

{i}   {u}

                        {o}

                    {#}

                    {ṽ}

                    {a}

The alphabet provides 19 letters with which to express them:

4.3.1. The morphoneme {i}[435] can be expressed by five different letters, depending on its distribution and

---

435. Various spelling alternations of this morphoneme are treated in:
R. Scholvin, op. cit., pp. 24, 30-31, 40-41, 53-54.

the presence or absence of phonemic softness in the preceding consonant. The letters и and ї are used after a soft consonant, while ы is used after a hard consonant. The letter ы never occurs in absolute word-initial position, but alternates with и at the beginning of some lexical stems, depending on the preceding prefix: и̑скати ~ вьзыскати. This fact might help us draw a conclusion, that perhaps in absolute word-initial position the morphoneme {i} was always jotated, and that this was expressed by the exclusive employment of the letter и in that position.

The use of both letters и and ї after consonants, opposed to that of the letter ы, could be an indicator of the pairing according to softness of the preceding consonants.

It is possible to make a list of words in which the letters и and ы are never used in alternation.

{b} ~ {b,}   быти – 'to be' vs. бити –'to beat': добро и̑сть намь зде быти (p. 51, Matth. XVII.4); и̑ начнеть би́ти клеврѣти своѫ. (p. 72, Matth. XXIV.49).

In a few words, however, the scribe shows hesitation in the choice between и and ы after the consonants {b} and {b,} . The nominative singular form of the word for 'love' in the classical texts is always written as любъı. On pp. 17b and 70 of IAG this word is spelled as in the older texts, while on p. 260b it is written with и, which does not necessarily indicate softening of the preceding consonant, but rather a phonetic process of eliminating the opposition [i] ~ [y]: да люби ѩже мѧ нѐси възлюбилъ, въ нихъ бѫдетъ. (John XVII.26). In this particular case the problem also seems to involve the very existence of this word in the spoken language, where we might expect a generalized stem like {l,ubov-} for the nominative singular. The form люби could have been an artificial remnant in the literary language and then, the rare morphonemic alternation of {i} vs. {ov} would have been meaningless to the scribe.

Another instance of oscillation in the use of the letters и and ы after {b,} is in the paradigm of the verb быти in the conditional. The same confusion (or alternate spelling?) is known in the classical texts; for instance, both forms бышѧ and бишѧ are registered in Mar. IAG has examples like: аще ли бысте вѣдѣли. (p. 35b, Matth. XII. 7); аще бисте имѣли вѣрѫ нѐко зрѣно горчично. (p. 188b, Luke XVII.6). Again, this kind of spelling alternation most likely implies a morphological change in the language. On the one hand, aorist forms like быхъ, бы,etc. were fully replaced by the forms бѣхъ, бѣ, etc. Thus, the old aorist forms would have continued to exist but with a new function - replacing the old conditional paradigm бимь, би, etc. The period of coexistence of the older and newer forms of the conditional would have yielded contaminated forms like бихъ and быхъ, би and бы, etc. This coexistence might have continued in the living dialects for a long time. If analogy throughout the paradigm of the verb 'to be' had taken

place (as in Russian), eventually the form /bix/, spelled
with ы, would have taken over completely; but there was also
the possibility that the language would try to distinguish
the conditional (through palatalization of /b/ into /b,/)
from the rest of the conjugation. This force most likely
prevented Middle Bulgarian from establishing a single form.

{p} ~ {p,} снопы - 'bundles, sheaves' vs. пиръ -
'feast': и̂ свѧжате нα въ снопы (p. 41, Matth.XIII.30);
нѫ е̂гда твориши пиръ, зови нищαα. (p. 182, Luke XIV.13).

{d} ~ {d,} грады - 'towns' vs. дира -'rent, rip':
и̂дѣмъ въ ближнαα вѣсси и̂ грады. (p. 91, Mark I.38); и̂
горши дира бѫдеть. (p. 93, Mark II.21).

{t} ~ {t,} ты - (nom.sg.) 'you' vs. ти - (dat.sg.)
'you': рече е̂мȣ І̂с̃, и̂ди и̂ тӹ сътвори такожде (p. 170b,
Luke X.37); а̂зъ ю̈гда възвращѫ сα въздам ти (p. 170b,
Luke X.35).

{z} ~ {z,} ѕ̈зы - 'bonds' vs. ѕ̈зилище - 'prison':
не по̂дбааше ли раздрѣшити ѫ ѿ̂ ѕ̈зы сеѫ. (p. 180, Luke XIII.
16); І̂ѡ̂аннь же о̂услышавъ, въ ѕ̈зилищи дѣла х̂ва, (p. 33b,
Matth. XI.2).

{s} ~ {s,} бѣсы - (acc.pl.) 'devils' vs. бѣси -
(nom.pl.) 'devils': мѫжь ... и̂же и̂мѣ бѣсы ѿ̂ лѣтъ многъ.
(p. 161b, Luke VIII.27); и̂зъшедше же бѣси ѿ̂ чл̃ка
вьнидошѫ вь свиниѧ. (p. 162, Luke VIII.33).

{m} ~ {m,} мы̂таръ - 'publican' vs. милъ -'dear':
и̂ мнози мы̂таре и̂ грѣшници (p. 92b, Mark II.15); и̂ милъ
ю̈моу бы̂. (p. 185, Luke XV.20).

{n} ~ {n,} вины -(gen.sg.) 'guilt' vs. нива -
'lot, ground': никое же вины не о̂брѣтаѫ до чл҃ка сего:
(p. 205b, Luke XXIII.4); чл҃коу нѣкоюмоу богатоу, оу҅гобзи
сѧ нива. (p. 176, Luke XII.16). But the word for 'now',
always spelled in the classical texts as нынѣ or нынꙗ
(Sav.), is, in IAG, written without exception with и: нинѣ
or нинꙗ. A possible explanation is the fact that this word
does not take part in any morphonemic alternation, nor has
it a minimum pair for contrast. This indicates that the
process of merging of the soft and hard consonants of a
pair before {i} went in the direction of the soft member.
The words нинѣ and люби are a good indication of this.

{1} ~ {1,} злыѫ - (acc.pl.masc.) 'bad' vs. зли -
(nom.pl.masc.) 'bad': а̂ злыѫ вьнь и̂звръгошѫ. (p. 42b,
Matth. XIII.48); а̂ще оу҅бо вы злꙇ́ сѫще . (p. 172, Luke XI.
13). The only oscillation between {1} and {1,} , indicated
by a fluctuation between ы and и after the consonant, is in
the spelling of the personal name Magdalene: бѣ же тоу
марїа магдалыни. и̂ дроугаа мариа. (p. 84b,Matth. XXVII.
61); в них же бѣ марїа магдалини. и̂ марїа І̂а́кѡвлѣ.
(p. 83b, Matth. XXVII.56). This dual spelling of the name
is known also in the classical texts. The reason should be
found in the shape of the segment after the {1,} - it very
much resembles the Slavic suffix -in,- (which is never found
after a soft consonant), as in {bog-in,-i}, {rab-in,-i},
etc. IAG shows predominant spelling with и (11 times) and

only once with ы (on p. 84b), in contrast to the classical
texts, in which this word is spelled with ы in many instances.

{r} ~ {r,} рыбъ - (gen.pl.) 'fish' vs. ризы-(gen.
sg.) 'garment': обьѭшѫ множьство рыбъ, много (p. 150,
Luke V.6); да не възвратит сѧ вьспѧть възѧти ризы своѥѧ.
(p. 123, Mark XIII.16). But the verb stem {=rid-aj-} 'to
weep' is written once with the letter и after a hard {r}:
ꙗко вьсплачете сѧ и̃ възридаѥте вы̃. (p. 258, John XVI.20).
In all other cases it is spelled with an ы: рыдаахѫ же
вьси и̃ плакаахѫ сѧ ѥ̃х. (p. 163b, Luke VIII.52). This
spelling mistake, if connected with the numerous mistakes
in the spelling of {a} as a instead of ѣ in the grammatical
endings after {r,}, indicates a phonetic hardening of {r,},
erasing the difference between [r] and [r,] (especially in
consonantal clusters like [kr], [zr], [tr]). Some modern
dialects of the Christian population in the Phodopa Mountains in Bulgaria also show a hardening of the {r,} in all
positions[436]. And still, the literary language of the 14th
century tries to preserve the historically correct spelling
as much as possible.

---

436. St. Stojkov offers examples from the speech
of Moslems vs. Christians in the city of Smoljan and the
village of Kremene near Smoljan: /sr,ed,é/ vs. /srad,é/ <
*srĕd-ьj-o; /r,ōt/ vs. /rōt/ < *rĕd-ъ in Smoljan;/r,úka-m/
vs. /rúka-m/ < *rjuk-aj-ǫ 'to call, cry out' in Kremene.
See:
   St. Stojkov, Akan'e v bolgarskom jazyke, Obšče-
slavjanskoe značenie problemy akan'ja, Sofia, 1968,
p. 113-114.

Before a vowel, the glide {v} is paired with {v,} :
й текь нападе на вы̃ᴣ не̃го, й ѡблобыза и. (p. 185, Luke XV.
20); й бѣ написанїе вины его написано, (p. 131, Mark XV.
26).

The letters for the consonants ф̠ and θ̠ in borrowed words and names, always represent palatalized /f,/ and
/θ,/, if they precede an {i}. The letter ы̲ is never written after them. This rule applies absolutely for those ф̠
and θ̠ which are not at the end of the lexical morpheme, at
the boundary with the grammatical endings (such as nominative and accusative plural masculine). In this position,
the nominative plural masculine must be marked through palatalization of the final consonant of the stem. Theoretically
in the plural paradigm there must be an opposition like
*{..f,i Nom.pl.masc.} vs. *{...fi Acc.pl.masc.}. Such forms
happen not to be registered in IAG, but from the indirect
evidence of forms like the dative singular /ios,íf-u/ (Ιωсй-
фоу, p. 221) and the vocative /iós,if,-o/ (Ιὠсифе, p. 8),
one sees clearly that at a morpheme boundary with the grammatical endings the alternation /f/ ~ /f,/ appears at the
same places where any Slavic hard consonant would have had
such an alternation.

Thus hypothetically we may generalize: the morphonemes {f} and {θ} when followed by an {i} inside a lexical morpheme exist only as soft phonetic variants [f,] and
[θ,], but at the morpheme boundary with the case endings
before {i}, they are paired as *[f] ~ *[f,] and *[θ,] ~ *[θ]

in accusative and nominative plural masculine, respectively.

The velars {k}, {g}, {x} in Slavic words do not have soft pairs in any position, and can be followed only by the letter ⷶ (never и). But in Greek borrowings, inside the lexical morpheme, all three of the velars appear before {i} only as soft phonetic variants ([k,], [g,], [x,]) and are never followed by the letter ⷶ: ꙗ́ко же бо бѣ І꙲ѡнⷶ въ чрѣвѣ ки́товѣ (p. 38, Matth. XII.40); и́ бы꙯ ꙗ́ко приближи сѧ въ виѳ꙯фаги́ѧ. (p. 194b, Luke XIX.29); бѣ же хи́тонь нешⷡьвень. ‖ нѫ съ выше и́стъканъ (p. 265b, John XIX.23).

IAG does not offer masculine substantives of Greek origin with {k}, {g}, {x} before paradigmatic morpheme boundaries of the nominative or accusative plural. It is known, however, from other texts, that a word like {m#n,ix-} 'monk' has a nominative plural /m#n,is,-i/ with a /x/ vs. /s,/ alternation, and an accusative plural /m#n,ix-i/ with no alternation of the final consonant. Such a restriction in the distribution of the soft/hard variants of the velars before {i} in Greek borrowings, indicated by the use of the letters и and ⷶ - only the soft velar inside the lexical morpheme, only the hard velar at a morpheme boundary - in effect rules out any independent phonemic status for the soft velars. One must bear in mind a further possibility: that the spelling и inside the lexical morpheme of a Greek borrowing is determined by the Greek orthography, and does not express phonetic softening of the velars.

In a position other than before the grammatical endings, {ʒ}, {c}, {ž}, {š} and {č} can be followed only by the letter и (never by ы). At a morpheme boundary with the grammatical endings, the same spelling rule applies for all of the above, except {ʒ}. Only once in IAG, where an etymological *ʒ was to be expected but the scribe wrote з, the latter was followed by an ы: польѧ (Mar.) 'profit' vs. ѿ пльти нѣ︮с︯ никоеѧ же ползы. (p. 231, John VI.63). This must have been caused by the phonetic merging of the phonemes /ʒ/ and /z/. Not only does the letter ы follow the substitute letter з for {ʒ}, but a deeper morphologi-cal change is observed in this case: the entire paradigm of the word has shifted from the soft to the hard declen-sion. However, this is a single "mistake" in the entire book; the orthographic rules of the language prohibited writing ы after с in any position, while no such rule ap-plied for the letter з. This is a significant indication of the tremendous importance of the symbol-letter for the medieval writer: he tried to follow the orthographic rules as closely as possible.

4.3.1.1. The use of the letter ï for the morpho-neme {i} after a soft consonant is of low frequency. Graph-ically, it represents an abbreviated version of и, the two parallel strokes being represented by the two dots over a single stroke. Here and there this letter is used between two consonants or at absolute word end in order to save space: й испльнишѫ сѧ вси нáрѡсти на съб́ѡрïщи ихъ.

(p. 148b, Luke IV.28). But in most cases, the letter ï is
used after a soft consonant before {j} followed by another
vowel. Since the jod in this case is never indicated by a
letter, graphically the letter ï precedes another letter
standing for a vowel: {pr,i-j#d,-o}: й áбиѥ йзыде йзъ
сѣнмища, прïиде въ домъ ... (p. 90b, Mark I.29);
{mar,-ij-am-∅}: й й́мѧ дв̃ѣ и марïа́мъ (p. 139, Luke I.27).

4.3.1.2. The letter ӥ (usually written with the
Greek "smooth-breathing" sign) can exist only in initial
position in biblical names. Only in a few cases does ï
occur in this position.

4.3.1.3. The letter ʋ (or ỵ), indicating {i}
after soft consonants, appears only in Greek borrowings,
where it represents the Greek upsilon. But it is used very
rarely: въставъ поими ѳтрочѧ й м̃тръ ѥ́го й б́ѣжи въ ѥ́гупеть
(p. 10b, Matth. II.13). Just a few lines later the scribe
wrote: ѿ ѥгипта призвахъ с̃на моего: (p. 10b, Matth. II.
15).

4.3.2. The morphoneme {u}[437] is expressed by two
letters: оу after hard paired consonants and velars; ю after
soft paired consonants (after palatal consonants and the
clusters /žd/, /št/ special orthographic rules are applied).
Inside a lexical morpheme, this is the most restricted vow-

---

437. Some spelling variants are treated in:
R. Scholvin, op. cit., pp. 33, 41-42.

el in Church Slavic. But the sequential restrictions inside
a lexical morpheme and at a morpheme boundary are different.

Within a lexical morpheme, {u} never occurs after
{ʒ} or {c}, nor, in IAG, is it represented after /z/; it can
occur after hard paired consonants, jod and, among the soft
paired consonants, /l,/ and /r,/. (It is possible that the
epenthetic -l-, which replaces a {j} after the labials, was
first triggered before {u} as an assimilative process: {j}
→ /l/ after rounded consonant before rounded vowel. The
feature of rounding in the Slavic -l- can be seen in the
Polish realization of {l} as [w], the Serbocroatian - of
{l} as [o] and [u] in certain positions, the East Slavic -
of *TELT as tolot, and the Ukrainian - of {l} as [w] in
certain positions.)

The morphoneme {u} is written ю in the following
environments in IAG:

a)   after {l,} : любити   (p. 121), ключь   (p.175),
etc.

b)   after the morphoneme {j} following a labial;
{j} changes into /l,/: {bjud-} > /bl,ud-/: й принесе главѫ
ѐго на блюдѣ   (p. 102b, Mark VI.28); {pju-n-} > /pl,u-n-/:
сѐ рекъ, плюнѫ на земѧ, й҃ сътвори брение ѿ плюновениѩ.
(p. 239, John IX.6).

c)   after initial {j}: {jug-}: югъ   (p. 179).

4.3.2.1. Classical OCS shows a great oscillation
between the letters оу and ю in initial position. This

represents a Slavic isogloss which not only separates East
Slavic from the rest of the Slavic dialects, but passes
across neighboring dialects in the same linguistic group
(South Slavic). The classical texts clearly indicate the
optional character of the initial jotation of some words:
оуже and юже in Mar., for instance. What is worth noting
is the fact that no initial original Common Slavic *u < *ou
could take prothetic jotation in two cases: in words whose
morphological structure reveals that the initial {u} is a
prefix, and in a limited number of words, for example оу̑ши,
оу̑ста, оу̑дъ, оу̑чити, оу̑мъ, etc. (This is true for all
Church Slavic texts, including IAG.)

The difference between the classical texts and IAG
is that in IAG a given word is consistently spelled either
with оу or with ю, whereas in the classical texts there is
considerable oscillation in the spelling of those forms
which may be said to have an original prothetic jod[438]. In
the classical texts the particle оу 'yet' is written with
either ю or оу. In Mar. it appears twice as ю and once as
оу. IAG in the same paragraphs has only о͡у: не о͡у ли
слышите ни разоумѣете. (p. 108, Mark VIII.17). Mar. also
uses the form юже (34 times), while the form оуже is used

---

438. The Rila Glagolitic Leaflets have оуже
(V4, 27) and юже (114, 1).
    Codex Clozianus also has оуже (p. 5a) vs. юже
(pp. 1b, 7a, 7b, 8a).
    Psalterium Sinaiticum has ютрю (p. 165) vs. оутро
(p. 78), ютрьневати (p. 171) vs. оутрь(н)ѭѫ (p. 75b),
etc.

only 8 times. In IAG it appears only as о́уже: о́уже вы
чисти ѥ́сте. (p. 225, John XV.3). But all classical texts
and IAG spell the word о́убо with о́у. While <u>Mar</u>. uses only
о́у in the spelling of о́утрѣ̇, о́утрѣ̇и, о́утрьни дьнь, о́утриѭ̇,
the substantive о́утро 'morrow' is written with either ю̇ or
о́у. The word appears as о́утро 8 times, and as ю̇тро 7 times;
<u>Sav</u>. has each form once. IAG again uses only the form with-
out jotation: о̇баче по^дбаѥт ми дне^с и̇ ѡ̇трѣ (p. 181, Luke
XIII.33). In IAG, as in the classical texts, words like
ю́гъ (p. 179), ю̇жьска (p. 173b), ю̇ности (p. 114), ю̇ноше
(p. 157b), ю̇нци (p. 64b) are always written with the letter
ю. Only these words in IAG have initial {ju} rather than
{u}.

    4.3.2.2. The Hebrew name of Judas in IAG is never
written with the letter ю (as it is in the classical texts,
alongside the more frequent spelling июда). The spelling in
IAG resembles the Greek - this word is always written as
І̇о́уда (p. 76b). The same principle applies to words like
І̇о́удинъ (p. 146b), І̇о́удѡвъ (p. 139b), І̇о́удѣ̇и (p. 224b),
І̇о́удѣ̇иска (p. 130) and І̇о́удѣ̇а (p. 12).

    4.3.2.3. As has been noted on p. 284, inside a
lexical morpheme the morphoneme {u} appears after no paired
soft consonant except /l,/ and /r,/. This fact, although
of exclusive significance, has, to the best of my knowledge,
gone unnoticed in previous studies of the phonological system of Church Slavic, as well as in Common Slavic reconstructions.

The same phonological restriction does not, however, apply at morpheme boundaries. There, {u} can follow
not only the hard paired consonants, /j/, and /š/, /ž/, /č/,
but also /c/, /ʒ/, /št/, /žd/ and the soft paired consonants.
IAG is no different in this respect from the classical
texts. The only difference is in the orthographic representation of {u} as either <u>ю</u> or <u>оу</u> after soft or palatal
consonants or /j/. It is very interesting that while in
some instances, as we shall show later, the spelling rules
require the choice of a different vowel letter after a palatal consonant inside a lexical morpheme than at a morpheme
boundary, the morphoneme {u} is not affected:

a) After {ž} and {š} inside a lexical morpheme,
only <u>оу</u> is written in IAG: о̂дьжди <u>жо꙯упелъ</u> и ꙩгнь съ нбⷭе.
(p. 190, Luke XVII.29); и̂ поставитъ ꙩвца꙯ ѿ десн҃жа себе. а̇
козлища꙯ ѿ <u>шоу꙯жа꙯</u>. (p. 74b, Matth. XXV.33); да не чюєть
<u>шоуица</u> твоꙗ, что творитъ десница твоа. (p. 19, Matth. VI.
3); ѿ неначааніа <u>шоума</u> морскаго. (p. 200b, Luke XXI.25).
All these words were written with <u>ю</u> in the classical texts,
but with <u>оу</u> in <u>Ostr</u>.

The clusters /št/ and /žd/ do not occur except at
the morpheme boundary. The word <u>шоуждь</u> is not registered
in IAG.

At the morpheme boundary, IAG offers examples for
only /ž/, /š/ and /št/. In all cases the classical texts
use the letter <u>ю</u>. But the orthographic rules of IAG require

оу: а̂ще достоитъ м<u>жжоу</u> женж поустити. (p. 113, Mark X.2);

въси<u>навшоу</u> слнцоу   (p. 133, Mark XVI.2); <u>непьщоуж</u> ꙗ̂ко

ê̂моу же множае ѡдастъ. (p. 159, Luke VII.43).

     b) Inside a lexical morpheme, the letter <u>ю</u> is
always used after {č}. There are no examples in IAG for /č/
at a morpheme boundary: и̂ <u>чюждаахж</u> <u>сѧ</u> ꙗ̂ко съ женож гла̂аше.
(p. 222, John IV.27). The situation is the following in the
classical texts: <u>Sav.</u> uses only <u>чю-</u>; the glagolitic texts
use mostly <u>чю-</u>, but also sporadically <u>чоу-</u> (see, in <u>Mar.</u>,
<u>чюдишѧ сѧ</u> and <u>чоуждаахж сѧ</u>); Ostr. uses mostly <u>чоу-</u>, but
has one example with <u>чю-</u>: <u>чкдотворьца</u>.

     c) As already stated, {c} and {з} do not occur
before {u} inside a lexical morpheme. But they occur at the
morpheme boundary of the masculine dative singular, where
the spelling rules applied in IAG demand the letter <u>оу</u>:
е̂гда бо грѧдеши ... кь <u>кнѧзоу</u>   (p. 179, Luke XII.58);
приидошж на гробъ въси<u>навшоу</u> <u>слнцоу</u>. (p. 133, Mark XVI.2).
At this boundary, the classical texts use the letter <u>оу</u>
more frequently, but a spelling with <u>ю</u> is also possible
(see, in <u>Mar.</u>, <u>слъньцю</u> and <u>слъньцоу</u>).

     4.3.2.4. After a soft paired consonant at the
morpheme boundary of masculine dative and vocative singular,
both the classical texts and IAG use only <u>ю</u>: и̂   запрѣти
ѳ́гню и̂ ѡ̂стави ж. (p. 149b, Luke IV.39); <u>оу̂чителю</u>. вѣмы
ꙗ̂ко право гл̂еши. (p. 197, Luke XX.21); раду̂и сѧ црю
I̊оу̂деискыи. (p. 264, John XIX.3).

- 288 -

4.3.2.5. At a morpheme boundary after {j}, the spelling requires only ю. In the entire IAG there is only one example where the letter Ȣ stands in this position - {n,o=v,ár,-#j-u}: помози моюмоу невѣриȢ ‖ (p. 111, Mark IX.24). But in this peculiar case, at the end of a line, the use of an Ȣ (very narrow and long) was probably dictated by lack of space.

4.3.2.6. The morphoneme {u} in initial position and after hard consonants is usually expressed graphically by the digraph оу, as in Greek and classical OCS. Sometimes in initial or final position it is expressed by the ligature Ȣ (uk). This letter does not occur between two consonants. But when the consonant before {u} is written above the line, and a vowel letter stands in the line before the grapheme for {u}, then usually the {u} is expressed only by the letter у (without the preceding о), while the front part of the letter у overlaps the letter for the vowel on the line: раꙟ ют сѧ (p. 54), раꙟитѣ сѧ (p. 85b), etc.

4.3.3. The morphoneme {o}[439] can follow any non - vocalic morphoneme, either inside a lexical morpheme or at a morpheme boundary; in Slavic words, it can stand in word in- itial position or follow a vowel, provided a prefixal mor- pheme boundary separates the two vowels (as in приобрѣсти). The latter restriction does not apply to Greek words.

---

439. The spellings of the outcomes of this mor- phoneme are discussed in:
R. Scholvin, op. cit., pp. 24, 31-33, 42.

Depending on the environment - the preceding consonant, sonorant or glide - {o} has two phonetic realizations: a rounded middle vowel after hard consonants ([o]) and an unrounded middle vowel after soft and palatal consonants and the glide /j/ ([e]). The same restriction as for {u} applies here too: the feature [+SOFT] of non-vocalic phonemes (which, following Chomsky and Halle[440], can be determined as [+HIGH]) is incompatible with the feature [+ROUNDED] of the following vocalic morphoneme.

4.3.3.1. Graphically, the morphoneme {o} is expressed in IAG by the following letters: o̱, ω̱, ꝑ, ꙩ, e̱, ѥ, ѣ. In Slavic words, the letters o̱, ω̱, ꝑ and ꙩ stand for the phoneme /o/ in word-initial position or after a vowel across the prefix boundary, as well as after hard consonants (in the latter environment, written only as o̱ or ω̱). In Greek words, the environment also includes "after a vowel within a lexical morpheme". The letter e̱ represents the segment [e], which, since it does not have morphonemic justification, is represented by {o}. The morphoneme {j} is usually omitted by the spelling, which doubtless indicates a phonological fact: its phonemic redundancy after having changed the feature [+ROUNDED] of {o} into [-ROUNDED] - i.e., {o} > [e]. But in many cases after {j} in initial position or at a morpheme boundary, the ligature ѥ stands

---

440. N. Chomsky, M. Halle, The Sound Pattern of English, New York, 1968, p. 301-329.

or the combination of {j} and {o}. In a few instances the
etter **ѣ** is used for the morphoneme {o} after a soft conso-
ant (cf. below).

4.3.3.2. All consonants paired for softness/hard-
ess may be followed by the morphoneme {o}, represented
raphically as **e** or **o**, expressing the phonetic outcomes [e]
nd [o], respectively. The palatal consonants /ȝ/, /c/, /ž/,
'š/, /č/ and the clusters /žd/ and /št/ can never be fol-
owed by the [+ROUNDED] phonemic variant of this morphoneme
and thus, by the letters **o** and **ѡ**). This rule holds for
ooth inside a lexical morpheme and at a morpheme boundary.

In **Mar.** and **Zogr.** the word for 'ashes' is regis-
ered in the phrase въ попелѣ. This word does not occur in
:he Aprakos versions. In IAG it is written with **e**, indi-
:ating a soft initial /p,/ (resulting from IE ablaut).
These two variants represent an old Common Slavic isogloss:
*pepelъ ~ *popelъ: древле оубо въ врѣтищи и̂ пепелѣ,
покаали сѧ бышѧ. (p. 34b, Matth. XI.21).

4.3.3.3. The velars {k}, {g} and {x} are always
hard in Slavic words. Before {i} within lexical morphemes
in Greek or Hebrew borrowings, they appear only in their
soft allophones. But before {o} in these borrowings they
are paired as /k/~/k,/, /g/~/g,/, /x/~/x,/: и̂ изыде
... на ѡнъ полъ потока кéдръскаго (p. 260b, John XVIII.1);
въвръже двѣ лептѣ. е̂же ю̈ кондратъ. (p. 121b, Mark XII.42);
оубоите же сѧ ... дш҃ѫ и тѣло погоубити въ геéнѣ: (p. 31b,

Matth. X.28); ѿрадьнѣе бѫдеть содомоу или гомороу ...

(p. 101b, Mark VI.11); ꙗко архелаю цр҃твоуютъ въ Іоудѣи.

(p. 11b, Matth. II.22); горе тебѣ хоразінъ. (p. 169, Luke

X.13).

    While some of the glagolitic texts use a special
letter _ⰼ_ (in cyrillic transliteration - ħ) for the Greek
phoneme /g,/ inside lexical morphemes, IAG follows the tradition already established in Sav. and the rest of the older
Bulgarian Church Slavic texts: it uses only the cyrillic
letter г. The phonetic palatalization of the soft velars
inside the lexical morphemes of foreign borrowings, expressed graphically by the letter e, is best illustrated by
the use of the ligature ѥ, which in all other instances in
IAG always denotes the combination {jo} either in word -
initial position or at a morpheme boundary after a vowel.
Thus, the only exception to this consistent spelling in IAG
is: й віна й сікюера не ймать пѝти. (p. 138, Luke I.15).

    4.3.3.4. In IAG, despite an older phonological
restriction on the occurrence of two vowels in a row, the
morphoneme {o} as a [+ROUNDED] vowel may follow another
vowel in foreign words, where it is usually written with ω:
{(j)ios,if-∅} > Іѡсифъ, {(j)ioann-∅} > Іѡаннъ, etc. The
classical OCS texts and Ostr. often have the letter e in
such an environment: ердане (Mar., p. 116), ерданьсцѣі
(Sav., p. 145b), ерданьсцѣи (Ostr., p. 254c), иерданьсцѣи
(Ostr., p. 255d). The letters e and ѥ in word-initial
position may represent initial {j} followed by {o}, or

initial {j} followed by the fleeting vowel {#}. In both cases the spelling utilizes more or less alternate forms with e or ҍе.

The only Slavic words registered in IAG which have initial {j} followed by {o} are the derivatives of the stem {jod,in-} and the forms of the word {joz,or-}. These words in the East Slavic dialects are without initial {j}, but in South Slavic and in the Church Slavic writings from the South they never appear without initial jotation. These two stems and almost all Greek borrowings which, in Greek, are written with the letter η (eta) and are morphonemically understood in Slavic as having initial {jo}, have alternate spellings with e and ҍе: е́динꙗ (p. 56) and ҍе́дино (p.16b); е́зера and ҍе́зеро (both on p. 161b); ҍезекиа (p. 7); елеазаръ (p. 7b); е́линское and ҍе́лины (both on p. 234).

4.3.3.5. In only one morphonological environment do the orthographic and phonological rules reflected in IAG allow the phonetic feature [+ROUNDED] in the morphoneme {o} after {j}; the following two conditions must be present:

   a)   The morphonemes {j} and {o} are separated by a morpheme boundary;

   b)   Before the morpheme boundary not only a final {j} is present, but the entire sequence {Soft Consonant+oj-}.

There is no exception to this rule in the spelling of IAG: {alf,oj-ov-∅} > алфéωвъ (p. 30); {andr,oj-ov-a} > андрéωва (p. 216); { z,ov,od,oj-om} > съ зеведеωмь

(p. 15). In this environment the glagolitic texts, <u>Sav</u>.
and <u>Ostr</u>. often use the letter <u>o</u>, but alternate spelling
with <u>e</u> is not unusual. In addition, the classical texts
have <u>геωнѣ</u> (<u>Mar</u>., p. 11), в
иθлеωмѣ (p. 5). Such spellings
are unknown in IAG. The literary language of the 14th century in the version of IAG distinguishes absolutely clearly
the phonological (and orthographic) rules within a lexical
morpheme from those applied at a morpheme boundary. So far
it has been demonstrated that phonetic innovations occur
first within the lexical morpheme, while the rules of Slavic
morphonology are extremely conservative at boundaries.

Even in Contemporary Standard Bulgarian, the same
rule (preservation of rounding in {o} after a {j} at a morpheme boundary) governs the plural-formation of monosyllabic
masculine substantives ending in {oj}, {ej}: {brój-ove} >
бро́еве 'issues (of a periodical)' versus {zméj-ove} >
зме́йове 'dragons', {béj-ove} > бе́йове 'Turkish overlords'.

4.3.3.6. The word for 'oil' in Church Slavic is
a Greek borrowing - ἔλαιον. In the glagolitic texts and
<u>Sav</u>. it is represented as олѣи, always with the letter <u>jat'</u>
and initial {o} without jotation. In <u>Ostr</u>. it appears as
олеіа (p. 148c). In IAG the Greek word for 'oil' is translated five times with масло, while the Greek borrowing is
used only three times, in one of them - as the instrumental
singular є́леемь (p. 101b). This seems to contradict the
absolute character of the phonological and orthographic rule

or the rounding of {o} at a morpheme boundary after {Soft
onsonant + oj-}; *{jól,oj-om} should give the unattested
in IAG) form *ёлешмь. But the morphonemic representation
f this word as *{jol,oj-om} does not seem to be justified.
he glagolitic texts and <u>Sav.</u>, with no oscillation, write
he word with the letter ѣ (олѣи); this would rather sug-
est for IAG such a morphonemic representation as {jol,aj-
m}. In this environment the {o} in the morphological end-
ng {-om} should become phonetically unrounded - [e]. The
epresentation of the morpheme {a}, which follows the soft
onsonant, before a soft consonant or {j} in unstressed
osition, does not cause problems[441].

Bearing in mind the shape of this word in the
ulgarian dialects and standard language of today, one might
e tempted to offer another possible representation for this
ord - {jól,#j-om}. The Contemporary Standard Bulgarian
ord for 'cooking oil' is олио, which can only be derived
from an underlying *{ol,#j-}. However, such a representation for the 14th-century form attested in IAG is untenable,
ecause the fleeting vowel in *{(j)ol,#j-} should have been
expressed in IAG by means of the letter и (for <u>tense jer</u>),
which, however, did not happen in any of the three forms

---

441. Phonetically, this unstressed /a/ after a
soft consonant should yield a [-LOW], [-ROUNDED] vowel,
which may be expressed graphically by the letters ѣ, e, or
even и. For further discussion see 4.3.4.11.

registered in IAG. The modern Bulgarian word is most likely
a new borrowing, whose phonetic expression as [ól,ič] <
{ól,#j-o} follows rules not attested in the classical texts
nor in IAG. Thus, for instance, in <u>Mar</u>. (and the rest of
the OCS texts) words like илиевъ (p. 204) and краниево
(p. 108) are attested only with -ев-. In IAG, as in the
classical OCS texts, rounding of the {o} in this environment
is not allowed at all. By contrast, many modern Bulgarian
dialects have such forms as [ilíof], [ilíuf][442].

4.3.3.7. The glagolitic texts show a phonetic
alternation of [e] and [o] at a morpheme boundary after a
final {r,}, expressed in the spelling by the use of either
<u>e</u> or <u>o</u>: кесареви and кесарови (<u>Mar</u>.) It seems that here
the problem is a general tendency to harden {r,} into /r/.
IAG has only кесаре́ви (p. 65) for the dative singular, and
ке́саревъ (p. 197b) for the possessive adjective.

4.3.3.8. The rules for distribution of the let-
ters <u>o</u>, <u>ω</u>, Ⓞ and ф are very tentative. The letters ф and Ⓞ
are rarely used, most likely for decorative purposes, and
appear only in initial position: фстѣма (p. 33b), Ⓞчи
(p. 239) or for the preposition: ф них же (p. 175). The
most frequent use of the letter <u>ω</u> is in the preposition and
prefix {ot#-}, usually written as a ligature ꙩ, but in a few

---

442. St. Stojkov, <u>Bolgarska dialektologija</u>,
Sofia, 1962, pp. 66, 126.

cases, both as prefix and as preposition, written instead as
о̏тъ. In addition, ѡ̣ is written in Greek names, where the
letter omega stands in the Greek originals; in many cases,
however, when we find the letter ѡ̣ in the Slavic text, there
should be an omicron in the Greek original, and vice versa
(cf. below). In Slavic words the letter ѡ̣ is most often
written in word-initial position. Some words are always
written with omega: ѿставление (5 times, on pp. 76b, 88b,
141, 144b, 212); in others the scribe uses either о̣ or ѡ̣:
ѻбрѣте (p. 25) and ѡбрѣте (p. 55). The tendency in IAG
is to use the omega in initial position in Slavic words
much more frequently than in the older Church Slavic texts.
In a few instances omega may even be found in word-final
position: е̇гѡ (p. 81). It may also appear inside a Slavic
lexical morpheme: похѡти (p. 97). At a morpheme boundary
omega is used very frequently to render the first phoneme
of the suffix {-ov-} (with [+ROUNDING]): а̇лѳе́ѡва (p. 92b),
бѣсѡвьсцѣмъ (p. 29b), and in the grammatical endings,
especially if they follow a velar: и̇дохѡмъ (p. 57b),
тръжникѡмъ (p. 61b), etc.

    Sometimes the initial letter for {o} in the word
очи is decorated with a dot in the center: ѻ is known as
"о̣ о́чное"[443] (it even appears once with two dots, like a

---

    443. E. F. Karskij, *Slavjanskaja kirillovskaja
paleografija*, Leningrad, 1928, p. 196-197. Karskij states
that "о̣ о́чное" can appear also in positions other than
word-initial (for instance, as in Pskovskij Apostol of
1309). However, no such case is registered in IAG.

pair of eyes - ꙍ, p. 210): и̇ помаза ѥмоу о́чи брениемъ.

(p. 239, John IX.6). But this type of ornamentation can
hardly have made "о о́чное" a different letter; it occurs
mostly in the forms of the word о̲чи̲, yet its frequency even
there is much lower than that of the conventional letter о̲.

4.3.3.9. There is a case where the morphoneme {o}
after a soft consonant is represented by the letter ѣ:
{bṽd,-a-t,o}: бѫдетѣ [=бѫдѣте] въ коупѣ двѣ мелѧщи.
(p. 190b, Luke XVII.35). The reason for this mistake is
the phonetic change of {a} into [e], [ə], or even [i] between two soft consonants (including {j}) or in absolute
word-final position after a soft consonant. This change of
a [+LOW] vowel into a [-LOW] ([-LOW][-HIGH] or even [+HIGH])
vowel is caused by the phonological restriction, according
to which no [+LOW] vowel can occur in the environment between two [+HIGH] (i.e. soft) consonants, nor, when unstressed, between a [+HIGH] consonant and word end. In this
particular case the rendering of final {o} after a soft
consonant as ѣ is a hypercorrection, since final unstressed
{o} and {a} have merged into the same phonetic outcome - a
[-LOW] (perhaps even [+HIGH]), [-ROUNDED], unstressed vowel
There are two more examples in IAG of the rendering of a
final unstressed {o} after a soft consonant as ѣ in the
verbal ending of the third person dual aorist: ѿврѣзостѣ
сѧ о́чи и̇ма (p. 29, Matth. IX.30); о́чи же ѥю оу̲д̲рѣжастѣ
сѧ. (p. 210, Luke XXIV.16).

4.3.3.10. The letter ѣ always stands for the morphoneme {o} after {n,} in the negative particle {n,o} (which
in isolation is graphically expressed as не) when it precedes the present tense forms of the verb 'to be'. But the
initial morphonemic sequence of the verb, {j#-}, is always
truncated if it follows the particle {n,o}. Here what is
involved is a phonemic change due to the stress rule: syn-
tactically, the forms of the present tense of the verb 'to
be' behave as clitics and change their position in the syntagma. They are always found after a word with emphatic
stress, or if there is none, after the first stressed word
of the syntagma. (If the same syntagma contains other clitics such as ли, бо, же, ти, etc., and the particles да, не,
the rules for ordering the clitics become extremely complex,
as in modern Bulgarian, and cannot be adequately treated
except in a special study.) Examples are: а́зь ѥ̇смь бъ̑
авраа́мовь (p. 66, Matth. XXII.32); нѫ азь благъ ѥ̇смь.
(p. 59, Matth. XX.15); ꙗ́ко ѿц҃ь вашь нб҃сныи съврьшень
ѥ̇сть. (p. 19, Matth. V.48); оу̇нѣ̇ѥ ти ѥ̇сть да погыбнеть
ѥ̇динь оу̇дь твоихь. (p. 17b, Matth. V.30).

Thus the combination of the two unstressed morphemes {n,o} and {j#s-m,} causes the appearance of stress
on the first one, namely {n,ó-}. The morphonemic sequence
{n,ó + j#s-m,} behaves as one word with its own stress, and
its phonemic outcome is /n,ásm,/ (first person singular).
In addition, for example, {n,ó + j#s-mi} becomes /n,ásmi/

(first person plural), and {n,ó + j#s,-i} becomes /n,ás,i/
(second person singular). What one observes in these forms
is a reduction of {j} to ∅ with a subsequent change in the
new sequence: n,ó-∅#- into n,á-. This must represent a
change which had occurred in the Common Slavic dialects when
*e and *ě (the reconstructed forms are *ne and *ně rather
than n,o and n,a) were opposed only by length. But in the
14th century one cannot express synchronically this change
as the lengthening of {o} into /a/, or of /e/ into /a/ after
a soft consonant, because it is impossible to prove that the
distinctive phonemic feature in these pairs was length.
Since the change of {o} to /a/ in this environment ({n,ó +
j#s-}) is connected with the reduction of {j} to ∅, the combination of {n,o} and the form of the third person plural of
the present tense of the verb 'to be' ({s-ṽt}), where initial {j} is absent, should simply have stayed unchanged -
{n,ó + s-ṽt} > /n,ósṽt/, which would be written не сѫтъ.
The classical texts and Ostr. always have нѣсмь, etc., but
never a third person plural in *нѣ: не сѫтъ (Mar.,
p. 358), не сѫтъ (Sav., p. 125b). In IAG, however, all
forms of the present tense of the verb 'to be' with the
particle {n,o} are spelled with нѣ, including the third
person plural: а наюмникъ иже нѣ︠с︡ пастыр. ємоу же нѣсѫтъ.
(p. 242, John X.12). This seems to be a result of morphonemic levelling of the entire paradigm of this verb in the
negative form.

The environment {j#-} after the morpheme boundary following the negative particle {n,o} is not sufficient to create /n,a/ < {n,o-j#...}; it must be combined with assignment of stress on the negative particle. Proof of this is furnished by the negative forms {n,o + j#m,-ṽt} > и не имѧтъ чьсо ꙗ̣сти. (p. 48, Matth. XV.32) and {n,o + j#mj-o-t,o} > семоу вꙑ̈ вѣрѫ не ꙗ̈млете. (p. 226b, John V.38).

It is interesting to compare the situation in Contemporary Standard Bulgarian, where the verb 'to be' has its own stress (and thus ceases to be a clitic) only if it immediately follows the negative particle не: не é йдвал 'he has not been here' (but compare: не щé (да) e йдвал 'he most likely has not been here'). When followed by forms of the present tense of the verb 'to be' in the standard language, the negative particle is never stressed. But contrary to what is observed in IAG, the verb 'to have' now behaves the way the verb 'to be' used to behave in the literary language of the 14th century: ѝмам 'I have', but нѝмам (/n,ámam/ < {n,ó + j#m-aj-m}) 'I do not have'.

4.3.4. The literary language of 14th-century Bulgaria, as represented in IAG, has a morphoneme {a}[444] - a [+LOW], [-ROUNDED], [-FRONT] vowel, which can follow either a hard or a soft consonant, either inside a lexical

---

444. Spellings with and without expressed jotation are mentioned in:
R. Scholvin, op. cit., pp. 41, 42.

morpheme or after a morpheme boundary. In addition, like
the morphonemes {i}, {o} and {u}, it may be found in absolute word-initial position. But as will be shown later, by
the time of the writing of IAG the phonological rules of the
language produced a phonemic and phonetic outcome of this
morphoneme, in the environment after a soft consonant, different from that in the environment after a hard consonant
or in word-initial position.

4.3.4.1. No modern Slavic dialect in present-day
Bulgaria, Macedonia, Greece or European Turkey distinguishes
an original jat' (*$\check{e}_1$ or *$\check{e}_2$), reconstructed on comparative
Slavic evidence, from an original combination *$j\bar{a}$[445], nor
was such a distinction made explicit in the known cyrillic
- much less, glagolitic - texts of classical OCS, written
in the Bulgarian linguistic area or copied from a Bulgarian
original[446]. And yet, the cyrillic Slavic alphabet, although without strict graphic distinction, has even in the

---

445. N. van Wijk, Le développement des voyelles
ě, a, ja en bulgare, Revue des études slaves, 7, Paris,
1927, p. 7-21.
        Xr. Kodov, Ezikət na trakijskite i maloaziatski-
te bəlgari, Sofia, 1935, p. 35-37.
        B. Conev, Istorija na bəlgarskij ezik, I, Sofia,
1919, p. 303-333.
        St. Mladenov, Geschichte der bulgarischen
Sprache, Berlin-Leipzig, 1929, p. 89-99.
        K. Mirčev, op. cit., p. 105-109.
        Bl. Koneski, Istorija na makedonskiot jazik,
Skopje, 1967, p. 50-52.

446. P. Diels, Altkirchenslavische Grammatik,
Heidelberg, 1963 (2nd edition), p. 31-36.

older texts two letters for *ě and the combination *jā: ѣ
and the ligature ꙗ.   On the other hand, the glagolitic alphabet utilizes only one graphic symbol, Ⱑ for both etymological *ě and *jā. This very fact gives evidence that the
glagolitic alphabet was originally designed for a linguistic
system which did not know such phonetic distinction, while
the cyrillic was created for a linguistic system which phonetically distinguished original *ě and *jā. From the oldest preserved records of cyrillic literature in Bulgaria,
Codex Suprasliensis and Savvina kniga, it is clear that the
existence of two graphemes for one phoneme created serious
orthographic problems. The medieval men's reverence for
written symbols made it impossible for them to eliminate
either of the two letters. As the Bulgarian dialects further developed their own structural peculiarities, different
from Church Slavic (under the influence of the Balkan convergence area), increasing efforts were made by the grammarians to standardize the literary language, and above all
its graphic system. If here and there the orthography shows
oscillation under the pressure of the living language, the
forms influenced by the spoken language were undoubtedly
spelling mistakes, and had no chance of becoming the norm.
The conscious efforts of grammarians to disregard completely
the changes in the living Bulgarian dialects and to purge
out of the literary writings mistakes introduced under the
influence of the dialects, are exactly what made the Middle

Bulgarian literary language not only a supradialectal but also a supranational medium of written communication. This fact, of which modern linguists complain most in their efforts to unveil the history of the Bulgarian language[447], was the greatest asset of the Bulgarian literary language, making possible the transfer of the Byzantine literature translated into this language, as well as some literary works originally written in it, into 14th-century Serbia and 15th-century Moldavia, Wallachia, Russian Lithuania and Russia.

4.3.4.2. The efforts to normalize the use of the graphemes ѣ and ꙗ must have been seriously upset by the fact that none of the cyrillic texts existing in Bulgaria offered consistent data upon which a scribe might build a firm set of orthographic rules. Moreover, some of the oldest Bulgarian cyrillic texts are direct copies from glagolitic originals[448], and even when both letters are used, the letter ꙗ has a very insignificant frequency. In the extant fragments of Eninski Apostol[449], ꙗ appears only eight times as against hundreds of occurrences of ѣ. But the amazing fact is that even in the 11th century, the

---

447. K. Mirčev, op. cit., p. 144.

448. E. F. Karskij, op. cit., p. 211-219.

449. K. Mirčev, Xr. Kodov, ed's., Eninski Apostol. Starobəlgarski pametnik ot XI vek, Sofia, 1965, 263pp.
(Reviewed by: A. Minčeva, Izdanie na nov originalen starobəlgarski pametnik, BəlgEz, XVI, 1966, 5, p. 520-522.)

scribe of this book tried to make some system for the use of
the two letters: in the extant fragment of the manuscript,
the letter ꙗ is, in six of its eight occurrences, written
after ѣ, as in любодѣꙑаниѣ (p. 2b). The scribe did not use
this principle consistently, and forms like стоудодѣѣнии
(p. 5b) exist too[450].

When one compares the situation in Eninski Apostol
with that in Sav. - another very old Bulgarian copy from the
11th century - it becomes clear that the scribe of Sav. also
follows some basic rules in the distribution of the two letters: generally stated, the letter ѣ was written most of
the time after a consonant, and the ligature ꙗ - after a
vowel or in word-initial position. Such a tendency must
have been created not by chance: the reason behind it is
the different distribution of etymological *ě̃ and *jā̃ within the word. According to ancient phonological rules of the
syllable structure in Slavic dialects, *jā̃ cannot follow a
consonant inside a morpheme, but can occur in word-initial
position or immediately after a morpheme boundary. On the
other hand, *ě̃ (from *ě̃$_1$ or *ě̃$_2$) inside a morpheme occurs
only after consonants; it appears very rarely in word-initial position (*ě̃xa-ti, *ě̃s-ti), and its most frequent usage
as a desinence is after morpheme boundaries of the hard
nominal declension (where the stems must end in consonants).

---

450. K. Mirčev, Xr. Kodov, ed's., Eninski
Apostol. ..., p. 183.

Thus, in the prototype of Sav., the phonetic distinction
between *ě̌ and * jā̇ must have been made, reflecting a dialect
different from those of the writers of the glagolitic texts.
The letter ѣ must have occurred in most instances after a
consonant, and the ligature ꙗ - after vowels or in word -
initial position. Remnants of the etymologically correct
spelling of ѣ and ꙗ in Sav., despite such a general tendency in their distribution after consonants or vowels and in
initial position, are forms such as ближьнꙗго (3 times
with the correct ꙗ, although graphically following a letter
for a consonant), different forms of the verb ѣсти (written
6 times with initial ѣ), and the complete absence of the
letter ѣ in word-initial position for the original sequence
*jā̇. But still, as I have counted, other forms of the verb
*ěsti appear 28 times written with initial ꙗ, following the
general tendency in the distribution of *ě̌ and *jā̇. The
original combination *j-ā̇ across a morpheme boundary (in
*mǒrj-ā̇) is expressed as морѣ (p. 40b), because the letter
required should immediately follow a consonant letter.

4.3.4.3. The scribe of IAG applies very strict
mechanical rules for the distribution of the letter ѣ and
the ligature ꙗ. In his original text, the letter ѣ never
appears in word-initial position or after a consonant. In
the only example where the ligature ꙗ is written after a
prefixal morpheme boundary when the prefix ends in a consonant ({b}), the ꙗ is actually written not after the б,

but after a letter which expresses either a vowel or a word boundary - ъ: о̑бьꙗдѣнїемь (p. 200b). A letter ꙗ written by the original scribe in the final version of the book follows the letter н in only two instances: пад же оу̑бо рабъ т҃ клан наше сѧ е̑моу гла҃. (p. 55, Matth. XVIII.26); и̑ блажн ꙗхⱬ сѧ о̑ нѐмь. (p. 101, Mark VI.3). But here someone has erased the letter ѣ which was written between the letters н and ꙗ, traces of which are still visible. The words originally were written by the hand of Monk Symon as кланѣꙗше сѧ and блажнѣꙗхⱬ сѧ. Similar corrections were made in the original spelling of the word нинѣ; the letter ѣ was erased and ꙗ was written instead (p. 140, 114b, etc.). The person who corrected those few words, not understanding the system applied by Monk Symon, for some reason tried to improve on the spelling.

In a few instances, in grammatical endings, the letter ѣ, originally written after the letter р, was erased and replaced by the letter а. (We have previously described - on p. 272-273 - corrections in the spelling of the word трѣва > трава, where this change takes place in the root.) Examples are: бѣ корабль по срѣдѣ мора (p. 104, Mark VI. 47); и̑ бы҃ⷵ боу̑ра вѣтръна велиа. (p. 98, Mark IV.37); бы҃ⷵ же и ‖ пра҃ вь нихъ. (p. 202-202b, Luke XXII.24); бѣста бо рыбара (p. 89b, Mark I.16); не и̑мамы цара, тькмо кесара. (p. 265, John XIX.15). The same kind of substitution of the letter а for ѣ after the letter р is attested in the cyril-

lic <u>Sav.</u> and <u>Supr.</u>[451]. There is no way to identify the
place and time of "corrections" of the original spelling of
these words. One thing is clear: although before {i} within a lexical morpheme, the language of the original scribe
seems to have lost the opposition [r,] ~ [r][452], his spelling of the sequence <u>r,-a</u> across the flexional morpheme
boundary is determined not by the phonological rules, but
by the morphological type of the word: forms like accusative singular море (p. 89b), dative singular морю (p. 92b)
and especially the locative singular мори (p. 95b) - which
otherwise should have been *морѣ - must have indicated to
the scribe that this word morphologically belonged to the
soft declension type.

    4.3.4.4. The only word whose final {r,} the
scribe Symon treats as [r] in the spelling of the genitive
and accusative singular in all three existing examples, is
the word кесара (pp. 141b, 144b, 265): изыде повелѣние
ѿ кéсара ꙗвгоуста. (p. 141b, Luke II.1). The genitive -
accusative singular of this word is written also with -<u>a</u>
in <u>Sav.</u>, but in <u>Mar.</u> it appears twice with ѣ and once with
<u>a</u>. Comparison of the spelling of the other registered forms
and derivatives of this word in <u>Mar.</u> and IAG reveals the

---

    451. <u>Savvina kniga</u> has forms like мора [=морѣ],
распьра [=распрѣ], съмѣраетъ сѧ [=съмѣрѣетъ сѧ], etc.
    <u>Codex Suprasliensis</u> has forms like боура [=боурѣ],
сакелароу [=сакеларю], сътворꙗ [=сътворꙗ], покараемъ
[=покарѣемъ], etc.

    452. See the paragraph on {r} ~ {r,} under 4.3.1.

following: while in Mar. the dative singular is spelled three times as кесареви and four times as кесарови, the only form registered in IAG is ке́сареви < {k,о́sar,-ov-i} (pp. 65, 119b, 120, 197, 197b, 205b, 264b twice); while in Mar. the possessive adjectives are spelled twice as кесарев- and four times as кесаров-, the only registered forms in IAG are ке́сарев- ({k,osár,ov-}) (pp. 65b twice, 120 twice, 197b twice). Since there is no oscillation in the spelling of the same grammatical forms - only кесара (as of the hard declension) and only ке́сареви, ке́сарев- (as of the soft declension, or derived from a word ending in a soft {r,}), it may be concluded that this word was treated like a word of "mixed" morphological type; but because of the lack of other case forms, such as the instrumental or locative singular, in IAG, it is unclear exactly which cases in addition to the genitive-accusative were from the hard, and which from the soft, declension. In derivation, however, the word appears to be of the soft declension. Such words of "mixed" type are not unusual for Church Slavic (compare the declension of some substantives with the suffix {-stv-}, such as цр͠тво, цр͠твиѥ which can have two forms, e.g., for gen. sg. ({-stv-a} and {-stv-#j-a}), but which have only one registered form ({-stv-#j-i}) for the loc. sg.[453])

---

453. I was not able to find reference in the literature to this peculiarity in the declension of the words цр͠тво, цр͠твиѥ. P. Diels, for instance, in paragraph 70,1 discusses the variant spellings of instrumental singular and dative plural of substantives ending in -stv-, but no exam-

Yet words of "mixed type" could hardly have had support in the Bulgarian dialects of the 14th century, since the nominal flexion was seriously altered by that time[454].

4.3.4.5. A word which is always written with the letter <u>a</u> instead of ѣ in all Middle Bulgarian texts, including IAG, is <u>самс</u> < <u>сѣмо</u> 'here'. B. Conev[455] believes this spelling to represent a general tendency towards phonetic hardening of {s,}, {з} and {c}. K. Mirčev neither accepts

ple of locative singular is given. (P. Diels, <u>op. cit.</u>, p. 168-169). In paragraph 73,1 there are numerous references to the occurrence of the locative singular form цѣсарьстви (P. Diels, <u>op. cit.</u>, p. 172-173). I looked very thoroughly through the glossaries of <u>Mar.</u> and <u>Sav.</u>, as well as through the abundant textual variants cited by Jagić in the footnotes of <u>Mar.</u>, but I did not find a single example of the locative form *црствѣ.

In IAG the number of occurrences of forms like црⷭтва, црⷭтвоу has considerably increased at the expense of црⷭтвиꙗ, црⷭтвию, yet there is no single example of *црⷭтвѣ.

B. von Arnim, in his monograph on the origin of the alternation of the suffixes -je, -stvo, -stvije in the biblical texts, gives many examples of alternating forms derived from the same lexical morphemes, in {-stv-} and {-stv-#j-}. But, since he does not list the registered locative singular forms, one cannot tell from his data whether or not a whole class of alternating words shares the peculiarity of црⷭтво, црⷭтвиѥ. See:

B. von Arnim, Beiträge zum Studium der altbulgarischen und altkirchenslavischen Wortbildung und Übersetzungskunst. Ursachen des Wechsels zwischen den Suffixen -je, -stvo, -stvije in Evangelium, Apostolus, Psalter und einigen anderen Übersetzungen, <u>Sitzungsberichte der phil. - hist. Klasse</u>, 22 October 1931, Berlin, 1932, p. 952-1024.

454. K. Mirčev, Po vəprosa za sklonenieto v bəlgarskija ezik, <u>BəlgEz</u>, IV, 1954, 1, p. 61-64.

455. B. Conev, ed., <u>Vračansko evangelie</u> (Bəlgarski starini, IV), Sofia, 1914, p. 48.

nor categorically rejects this explanation[456]. It seems
erroneous to link the phonetic hardening of {ʒ} and {c} in
some modern West Bulgarian dialects (yielding [calúvam] <
цѣловати) with the hardening of the {s,} in сѣмо, which
happened in all Bulgarian dialects (the existing form is
насáм 'hither, towards me'). Besides this difference - a
narrow dialectal change versus an all-area change - it does
not seem very convincing to link the phonetic outcome of the
Second and Third Slavic Palatalizations with phonetic changes in a phoneme which never resulted from the palatalization of a velar. By its origin the word сѣмо is a composite
of the demonstrative pronoun *sь and the adverbial morpheme
*-amo, which appears also in камо 'whither', овамо'here',
тамо 'there', онамо 'over there', инамо 'elsewhere' and
ямо 'here'[457]. All these words form a microsystem in which
the morpheme {-amo} follows a hard consonant in five cases,
and a soft consonant in only one ({s,-amo}). The force of
analogical levelling within the microsystem must have been
the only decisive one, which changes {s,} into /s/. It is
also possible that this process was sped up by the hardening

---

456. Although K. Mirčev expresses reservations
by writing, "It is not certain, though, that we deal with
a phonetic development ...", he lists the change of /s,amo/
to /samo/ in the paragraph on the phonetic hardening of /c/.
But, on the other hand, he also accepts the possibility of
the influence of the word /tamo/. See:
    K. Mirčev, Istoričeska gramatika na bəlgarskija
ezik, Sofia, 1963 (2nd edition), p. 107.

    457. L. Sadnik, R. Aitzetmüller, Handwörterbuch
zu den altkirchenslavischen Texten, Hague-Hdlbg.,1955,p. 197.

of the {s,} in the fossilized demonstrative enclitic, as in
днесъ,'today'; this hardening, however, is difficult to date

4.3.4.6. In one instance the letter ѣ seems to be
replaced by an a in the form имали (which, according to all
the classical texts, should be имѣли): да бишѫ имали на
нь что гл͠ати. (p. 235, John VIII.6). However, here the
problem is not phonetic hardening of {m,}, but deeper morphological changes: the stem from the present paradigm of
the verb имѣти - имамъ, имаши becomes also the derivational
stem for the -l-participle.

4.3.4.7. The spelling of two words in IAG with ѣ
(instead of ь or и, as in all classical texts) likewise had
little to do with phonological change: стъклѣници ←
стькльници (Mar.), иглѣнѣ ← игьлинѣ (Mar.). The forms
with ѣ registered in IAG have a different derivation - with
the Common Slavic suffix represented in Russian by -jan-,
used in the formation of some relative adjectives.

4.3.4.8. The archaic first person singular of the
athematic verb вѣдѣти, вѣдѣ, a remnant of the old perfect
tense[458], appears only once in IAG (p. 237), as against the
form вѣмь in the same sentence in all other classical texts.
But in Mar., for instance, the form вѣдѣ is not registered
at all[459]. IAG has a new form - вѣдѧ - instead of the

---

458. N. Trubeckoj, O nekotoryx ostatkax isčeznuvšix grammatičeskix kategorij v obščeslavjanskom prajazyke, Slavia, 1, 1922-23, p. 12-21.

459. P. Diels, op. cit., p. 280.

regular first person singular present в҃ѣмь or в҃ѣмъ of the
classical texts. The word вѣдѧ appears in IAG 11 times (pp.
73, 180b twice, 233, 235b, 238b three times, 240b, 250b,
251b). An explanation that the letter ѧ in this instance
stands for a correct ѣ (as in вѣдѣ) is unlikely; the substitution of ѧ for ѣ and vice versa, although known in some
other Middle Bulgarian texts[460], is unusual for IAG. But it
is more likely that such a substitution might have taken
place in one of the older Slavic Gospel texts which Symon
the Monk had at his disposal while preparing his revised
edition. He was not able to see the relation between вѣдѧ
and the obscure correct form вѣдѣ, and misinterpreted вѣдѧ
as either the first person singular from the extended stem
{v,ad-} (as in the third person plural of the present, in
the infinitive and in the -l-participle), or as a new form
for the short present active participle in the nominative
singular masculine: вѣды and вѣдѧ, parallel to сы҃и and сѧ҃и.
The latter misinterpretation would not have been prevented
by the syntactic structure of some of the sentences, since
very often the participles were used incorrectly, in place
of a conjugated verb: и не познасте ѥ҃го. а҃зъ же вѣдѧ ѥ҃го.
и а҃ще рекѫ не вѣдѧ е҃го, бѫдѫ подобень вамь лъжь. нѫ вѣдѧ
е҃го, и слово е҃го съблюдаѫ. (p. 238b, John VIII.55).

---

460. A typical example is the 13th-century Aprakos Gospel #849 in the Bulgarian National Library (Sofia).
It has forms like вѣще [=вѧще] (p. 45b); прозрѧ [=прозьрѣ]
(p. 7b); and others. See:
M. Stojanov, Xr. Kodov, Opis ..., III, Sofia,
1964, p. 21-22.

4.3.4.9. The words кокотъ, коуръ, known from the classical texts, are not registered in IAG; neither is the word пѣтелъ with the letter ѣ. When this latter word is written in the original hand, it always has the letter ѧ instead of ѣ: й пѧтель възгласи. (p. 129, Mark XIV.68). In a few instances someone erased the letter ѧ and wrote an e, but these spellings are not by the hand of the original scribe. In the case of пѧтель, the letter for the nasal vowel, ѧ, is not a substitution for the letter ѣ in the form {p,at,-#1-}. The underlying form of this word in the IAG scribe's language must be {p,ṽt,-#1-}[461].

4.3.4.10. The verb прѣѣде (Mar., Zogr.) or прѣꙗде (Ostr., Sav.) is always rendered in IAG, as in Assem., by прѣиде. As has already been discussed, the question here is not one of phonetic change of {ja} to [i], but rather of semantic changes in the meaning of some verbs of motion. The verbal pair {jax-aj-t,i} ~ {jazd,-i-t,i} meant only 'to ride horseback', while the verb {j#d-t,i} had expanded its meaning into 'to pass over, cross; to arrive'. There is no doubt that the verb {jax-aj-t,i} ~ {jazd,-i-t,i} existed with the meaning 'to ride horseback' in the 14th - century Bulgarian literary language. In the Tale of Troy[462] the aorist of the verb {na=jazd,-i-t,i} 'to draw abreast

---

461. This word will be discussed in 4.3.5.5.

462. I. Dujčev, ed., Letopista na Konstantin Manasi, Sofia, 1963, p. 83-125.

- 314 -

with (someone) on horseback, overtake (someone) on horseback', is registered twice: и̇ на̇а̇здиста сѧ, и̇ дрва менелае
а̇ле̧ѯандра фарижа, и̇ лежаше ‖ въ троискомъ прасѣ ...
(p. 55b) 'And they drew abreast on their horses, and Mene-
laos attacked Alexander/Paris, and (Alexander) lay in the
dust of Troy ...'; и взѧ а̇йакшь каме͡н, кое̇го не
могѫтъ два витеза двигнѫти, ‖ и̇ на̇а̇зди и̇ о̇у̇дари е̇ктора
кралѣ ... (p. 55-55b) 'And Ajax picked up a stone, which
two knights could not move, and on horseback overtook and
struck King Hector'.

4.3.4.11. In a few instances the letter ѣ in
classical texts is replaced by e in IAG. The imperfecti-
vized form of the verb въмести∼въмѣтати 'to throw into'
should be spelled with ѣ because of the regular morphonemic
alternation {o} ∼ {a} (historically caused by lengthening
of the stem vowel): {v#=m,ot-t,i} ∼ {v#=m,at-aj-t,i}
(въмѣтати, въмѣтаѭ). The third person singular present of
this imperfective verb, however, is in one instance spelled
with e instead of ѣ in IAG, although in the rest of its
occurrences it has ѣ: ꙗ̇ко же ч͡лкъ въметаетъ сѣмѧ
вь землѧ. (p. 97, Mark IV.26).

Similar oscillation is known in the classical
texts. Mar. has the forms въмѣтаема (p. 157) and въме-
таемоу (p. 107). In contrast to the latter, Zogr. has the
correct въмѣтаемѫ. The alternation /e/ ∼ /ja/ in the different aspects of this verb exists in modern Bulgarian too:

да ме́тна (perfective) versus мѧта́м (imperfective). The
spelling with e̲, in both IAG and Mar̲., of an imperfective
form which should definitely have {a} after {m,} in its underlying morphoneme, suggests a phonetic outcome for this
{a} of [e], [i] or [ə] in unstressed position - generally, a
[-LOW] vowel. This phonological rule must have been in
operation already at the time when the glagolitic texts from
Bulgaria were written, the late 10th or 11th century (cf.
the above quoted example from Mar̲.). Yet only in a few
places did the writer of IAG write the letter e̲ for the underlying morphoneme {a} after a soft consonant in either
stressed or unstressed position before a soft consonant or
the glide {j}, or in absolute word-end position. Such mistakes involve the verbal endings (e.g. the third person dual
бѫдетѣ < {bVd,-át,o} (p. 190b)) and the comparative degree
of some adjectives (e.g. оунеѥ < {ún,a-jo} (p. 17b)).

4.3.4.12. Recapitulating the above, the following
orthographic rules can be formulated for the original text
of IAG, as regards the representation of the morphoneme {a}
after hard and soft consonants:

a) After hard (paired) consonants, {a} is represented by the letter a̲.

b) After soft (paired) consonants, {a} is represented in most words by the letter ѣ̲ (never by the ligature
ꙗ). The spelling of the genitive singular кесара with a̲
is an orthographic rule, although in the rest of its para-

digm this word has a soft /r,/. But there are a few orthographic errors, made by the writer in representing the underlying {a} after a soft consonant by means of the letter e
in the following environments: first, where {a} is unstressed; second, where {á} is stressed, before a soft consonant or {j} or in absolute word-final position. The number of misspelled words is minimal, which shows the overall
importance of the <u>morphonemic</u> <u>principle</u> in the spelling.

c) After /ž/, /š/, /žd/ and /št/, both within a
lexical morpheme and at a morpheme boundary, the morphoneme
{a} is represented only by the letter <u>a</u> (the same rule was
applied in classical OCS): видѣвше же оу́бо клеврѣти ѥго,
бывшеѥ. <u>съжалишѫ</u> си ѕѣло. (p. 55b, Matth. XVIII.31);
придѣте <u>й</u> видите мѣсто йдеже <u>лёжа</u> Гь. (p. 85b, Matth.
XXVIII.6); жестоко ѥ[ⓒ] слово сé, кто можеть е́го <u>слышати</u>.
(p. 231, John VI.60); по немъ <u>хѡ́ждаахѫ</u> <u>й</u> <u>слоужаахѫ</u> ѐмоу.
(p. 132b, Mark XV.41); ꙗ́ко к томоу не <u>вьмѣщаахѫ</u> сѧ ни
прѣдь дверми. (p. 91b, Mark II.2).

d) After /č/ both within a lexical morpheme and
at a morpheme boundary, the morphoneme {a} is represented
only by the letter <u>a</u>. In a few cases the letter <u>ѣ</u> may be
found in the same environment in the classical texts (<u>чѣсѣ</u>
in <u>Mar.</u>, p. 85b, vs. <u>часѣ</u> in IAG in the same sentence):
въ <u>часѣ</u> врѣменнѣ (p. 147, Luke IV.5); ѿ страха, <u>й</u> <u>чааниа</u>
(p. 200b, Luke XXI.26); не трѣбоуѫть здравïи <u>врача</u> нѫ
болѧщïи. (p. 27b, Matth. IX.12).

e) After {ʒ} and {c} within a lexical morpheme, the morpheme {a} is represented by the letter ě, while at a morpheme boundary - by the letter a or the letter ě, depending on the type of morphemic alternation. This complicated spelling rule is inherited from classical OCS, whose orthography distinguished /ʒ/ and /c/ of the Second Slavic Palatalization (by writing ě for a following {a}) from {ʒ} and {c} of the Third Slavic Palatalization (by writing a for a following {a}). (I have compared the situation in the various OCS texts and come to this conclusion.) It is very tempting to believe that, as S. B. Bernštejn[463] and R. Nahtigal[464] suggest, there were two different phonetic outcomes for the phonemes /ʒ/ and /c/: [ʒ] and [c] (for the results of the Second Palatalization) versus [ʒ,] and [c,] (for the results of the Third Palatalization). The Slavist ought to take into account a very important detail: lexical and grammatical morphemes ending in /ʒ/ and /c/ from the Third Slavic Palatalization were morphologically interpreted as belonging to the soft paradigms (*stār-ĭk-ŭ > *star-ьc-ь), and in derivation are followed only by the phonetic outcomes of the vowels that follow soft consonants (*pŏ=lĭg-ŏv-āj-tei > польѕевати). The phonetic hardening of /c/ and /ʒ/ in the South Slavic dialects before an orig-

---

463. S. B. Bernštejn, Očerk sravnitel'noj grammatiki slavjanskix jazykov, Moscow, 1961, pp. 201, 208-209.

464. R. Nahtigal, Die slavischen Sprachen, Wiesbaden, 1961, p. 32.

inal *ā is expressed by the spelling in OCS in the same
fashion as the Common Slavic change of original *ě₁, after
the results of the First Slavic Palatalization, into *ā
(*čě > *ča; *žě > *ža; *šě > *ša).

Thus the spelling rule of classical OCS for rendering the morphoneme {a} after /c/ and /ʒ/, applied by the
writer of IAG, is the following: first, when not at a morpheme boundary with a suffix or grammatical ending, only the
letter ѣ is written after the letters ц and ѕ; second, at
a morpheme boundary with the grammatical ending of the dative or locative singular or the nominative-accusative dual
of the hard declensions (which are morphologically marked
through softening of the last consonant in the stem), only
ѣ is written after the letters ц, ѕ (and occasionally з)
when they represent the soft allophones of the velars {k}
and {g}; third, at a morpheme boundary with a suffix or
with any other grammatical ending, only the letter a is
written after the letters ц and ѕ.

However, there is one word in IAG which marks the
beginning of the opposition /c/ ~ /c,/ within the lexical
morpheme: цара (corrected later from the originally-writ-
ten царѣ (p. 265)). The word цѣсарь (written also as
ц̃срь) in the classical texts is not registered in IAG; the
only abbreviation is ц̄рь, without the letter c). The Bulgarian language of today distinguishes /c/ from /c,/ within
a lexical morpheme - /car/ 'king' vs. /c,ar/ 'medicine'.

The spelling цаṛѣ is the earliest indication of this distinction. It must have been triggered by the merging of /3,
and /z,/in the dialects, thus establishing a symmetry: /z/
~ /z,/ and /c/ ~ /c,/.

4.3.4.13. The phonological rules of reconstructe
Common Slavic did not allow a word to begin with {a} except
the conjunction a 'and, but'. The oldest OCS texts offer a
long list of words whose spelling throughout centuries of
Church Slavic literature oscillates between initial a and
ꙗ. Words which always had initial a are foreign borrowings, as well as the forms алкати, алдии, in which it is
difficult to explain why the liquid metathesis did not take
place[465].

IAG indicates a development in the phonological
system of the language: some words are always spelled with
initial a, the rest always with initial ꙗ, while the number of words having alternate spelling with initial a or ꙗ
as in the classical texts has decreased to zero. Slavic
words which are always spelled with initial a in IAG are
the following: the conjunction а̇ (numerous examples, the
same as in the classical texts); а̇гнецъ (pp. 168, 215,

---

465. One explanation for this alternation,
accepted by many scholars, is based on the accentual peculiarities of these words. Cf.:
H. Birnbaum, The Dialects of Common Slavic,
p. 170.

215b, 271b); а̑зъ (scores of examples); а̑лчдш– (pp. 74b, 140, 154); а̑ше (numerous examples). Slavic words which are always spelled with initial ꙗ̑ in IAG are: ꙗ̑вити сѧ (numerous examples); ꙗ̑вление (pp. 97, 141b, 161, 210b); ꙗ̑вѣ (pp. 19, 19b, 80, 94b, 247); all grammatical forms of the verb ꙗ̑сти (numerous examples); ꙗ̑зв– (pp. 170b, 269b); ꙗ̑ицꙗ̑ (p. 172); ꙗ̑ко (numerous examples); ꙗ̑ма (pp. 36, 46b, 155b); ꙗ̑може (numerous examples); ꙗ̑рем–нича (p. 61); ꙗ̑рости (p. 148b); ꙗ̑ръ (p. 194); ꙗ̑сли (pp. 142, 142b, 180).

The word а̑годичинѣ (for сукаминѣ in the classical texts) was written by the hand of the original writer on p. 188b (Luke XVII.6), but another scribe erased the word сикоморих on p. 193 (Luke XIX.4) and wrote ꙗ̑годичинꙋ. Since the latter spelling does not belong to the original scribe, we can conclude that the spelling rules of IAG exclude alternate spelling of initial a and ꙗ in the same word. The word алдии–ладии, registered in OCS texts, is completely absent from IAG, which instead has корабль; the word агода (Sav.) is represented in IAG, as in the rest of the OCS texts, by плодъ (p. 37b).

4.3.4.14. As has already been stated, the morpho- neme {a} has no sequential restrictions in the language of IAG except after a vowel within a Slavic lexical morpheme. But in biblical names, {a} can follow {i}, {o}, {u} and {a}: е̑лиаки́м (p. 7b); і̑аи́ръ (p. 163); І̑ѡа́нъ (p. 215b);

силоуа́мл҄ѧ (p. 239b) and на́асс̆о̂н (p. 6b). Although this violates older rules of Slavic syllable structure, intervocalic {j} need not be inserted before the vowel {a} when it follows another vowel within a lexical morpheme, since such a {j} is not inserted before {o} either: otherwise it would have changed this {o} into an [e][466].

4.3.5. Traditionally, students of the history of the Bulgarian language and its dialects - most prominent among them St. Mladenov[467], B. Conev[468], K. Mirčev[469] and B. Koneski[470] - discuss the nasal vowels (in the plural) or the question of the redistribution, exchange, etc. of the nasal vowels in Middle Bulgarian literature[471].

For the language of those dialects which exhibit oscillation in the use of the letters ж and ѧ, one should

---

466. Cf. the discussion of the problem, 4.3.3.4.

467. St. Mladenov, Geschichte der bulgarischen Sprache, Berlin-Leipzig, 1929, xiv + 354 pp.

468. B. Conev, Istorija na bəlgarskij ezik, Sofia, I, 1919, x + 529 pp.; II, 1934, xvi + 560 pp.; III, 1937, vi + 505 pp.

469. For a bibliographic survey of relevant works of K. S. Mirčev up to 1962 (in addition to his historical grammar), see:
M. Sl. Mladenov, Naučni trudove na Kiril Mirčev, IzvIBE, VIII, Sofia, 1962, p. 13-23.

470. B. Koneski, Istorija na makedonskiot jazik Skopje-Beograd, 1965, 103 pp.; Skopje, 1967 (2nd edition), 241 pp.

471. The problem of the distribution of the nasal vowel letters, of their oscillation with each other and with letters representing non-nasal vowels, is discussed in:
R. Scholvin, op. cit., p. 42-53.

rather speak of a single nasal vowel morphoneme, whose phonetic outcome as back or front vowel is predictable in the environment after, respectively, a phonetically hard or soft consonant. The situation of this morphoneme $\{\tilde{v}\}$ is thus similar to that of $\{o\}$, which has two different outcomes - [e] and [o] - similarly motivated. But in word-initial position (with optional prothetic jotation) and at a morpheme boundary after $\{j\}$, the two nasal-vowel letters oscillate in their use, very much like the letters a and ꙗ in OCS and many Middle Bulgarian texts (though not in IAG). The merging of the two distinct etymological nasal vowels in the Middle Bulgarian period roughly parallels the merging of the nasal vowels in Polish, although the results were different in the two languages[472].

4.3.5.1. It should be stated plainly, that the term "nasal vowel" is absolutely conventional, and does not refer to the articulatory or auditory character of the vowel, but to its origin. There are reliable indications

---

472. T. Lehr-Spƚawiński, Les voyelles nasales dans les langues lechites, Revue des études slaves, VI-VII, Paris, 1926, p. 54-66.
    Z. Stieber, Dwa problemy z fonologii sƚowiańskiej, Lingua Posnanensis, 1, Poznań, 1949, p. 81-86.
            , Rozwój fonologiczny języka polskiego, Warsaw, 1952, 95 pp.
    Z. Klemensiewicz, T. Lehr-Spƚawiński, S. Urbańczyk, Gramatyka historyczna języka polskiego, Warsaw, 1964, p. 102-111.

that as late as the 13th century some Bulgarian dialects[473]

had a phonologically nasal vowel; as late as the 19th cen-

tury a peripheral dialect in Macedonia and southern Bul-

garia[474] had a nasal vowel too; and some scholars believe

that several Bulgarian dialects in today's Rumania had nasal

vowels in the 15th century[475], which are represented by an

oral vowel plus /n/ in the Slavic borrowings in the Rumanian

language from that period[476]. On the other hand, many Bul-

garian texts from the Middle Bulgarian period show that the

"nasal" vowel was already denasalized.

There were a few Bulgarian dialects which pre-

served distinct outcomes of the etymological *ę and *ǫ:

473. L. Miletič, Sedmogradskite bəlgari i texnijat ezik, SpBAN, 33, 1936, p. 1-181.
The Bulgarians of the Sedmogradsko region were
captured by the Hungarians in the second half of the 13th
century and settled as workers in Hungary. A number of
hymns were translated from German into their dialect in the
16th century.

474. K. Mirčev, op. cit., p. 104.
P. Draganov, Nosovye glasnye zvuki v sovremennyx
makedonoslavjanskix i bolgarskix govorax, Russkij filologičeskij vestnik, 19, Warsaw, 1888, p. 1-27.
St. Kabasanov, Star i nov nasalizəm v neproučen
dosega bəlgarski govor, Slavistični studii, Sofia, 1963,
p. 173-184.
R. Ekblom, Le développement des voyelles originairement nasalisées dans le moyen bulgare, Le Monde Orien-
tal, 12, Uppsala, 1918, p. 177-225.

475. K. Mirčev, op. cit., p. 71-72.

476. K. Mirčev, ibid., gives as examples: Rum.
dumbrava < дѫброва; rind < рѫдъ; grinda < грѫда, etc. Cf.too
I. Gələbov, Stari bəlgarski ezikovi areali na
dakorumənskata ezikova teritorija, Ezik i literatura, 16,
Sofia, 1961, p. 39-48.

these were the dialects in which etymological *ǫ yielded {u}. In the other Bulgarian dialects of the 14th century there was only one nasal vowel morphoneme, which we shall represent as {ṽ}. The feature of nasality was not neces- sarily present in the dialect of any particular scribe.

4.3.5.2. The following phonological developments - different in different dialects - caused the graphic chaos in the use of the letters ⱒ and ⱔ in the Middle Bulgarian period for the historically nasal vowel:

a) the merging of the nasal vowel {ṽ} with the vocalic realization of the fleeting vowel {#}, which was phonetically, after hard consonants, a mid-central, [-ROUND- ED] vowel ([ə]), but, after soft consonants and {j}, either this same [ə] or a mid-front [-ROUNDED] vowel ([e]). Graph- ically, this development is expressed by the indiscriminate use of the letters ⱒ and ⱔ, ъ and ь for the phonetic outcome of the morphonemes {ṽ} and {#}[477].

b) the merging of the nasal vowel {ṽ} with the morphoneme {a}, whose phonetic outcome was a [-HIGH], [-ROUNDED] vowel. Orthographically, this is expressed by substitution of the letters ⱒ and a (and also ъ, cf. point a) for either {ṽ} or {a} after phonetically hard consonants,

---

477. The earliest example is from <u>Codex Supras-</u> <u>liensis</u>: и ти сѣло вѣтрьı и вльнами мьчими [=мⱒчими] възвраштаахⱒ сⱔ въспⱔть. (p. 151).

and of the letters Ა, ѣ, ꙗ, е (and also ь) for either $\{\widetilde{v}\}$ or {a} after soft consonants or {j}[478].

c) the optional phonetic reduction of inter-vocalic and prothetic {j} to $\emptyset$ before $\{\widetilde{v}\}$, similar to the reduction of {j} to $\emptyset$ before the morphoneme {a} and before the phonetic realization [e] of the morphonemes {o} and {#}. This phenomenon made it difficult to distinguish graphically ѫ from Ა, the latter standing in place of the letters Ა, ѧ, ꙗ and ѩ of the classical texts.

d) the change in the morphonemic alternations in two consonant-stem verbs expressing movement, which were originally paired as *tręs- vs. *tros-i- and *męt- vs. *mǫt-i- . Here one can see morphological changes, rather than mere confusion in the use of the letters for the nasal vowel (cf. below).

e) the phonetic hardening of the palatal con-sonants. This affected the spelling rules for distribution of the letters ѫ and Ა in a fashion similar to that for the letters a and ѣ.

The authority of the spelling of the older Church Slavic texts, in which different rules governed the use of

---

478. There are numerous examples in <u>Vračansko Evangelie</u> from the 14th century: слоушаа̂ [= слоушаѫ] (p. 10b); дш͠ѫ моѫ въз'мѫти сᲐ [= дша моа] (p. 34); ис корабла [= кораблѣ] (p. 57b); честь [= чᲐсть] (p. 61b); пᲐндико(с) [= пендикость] (p. 200b), etc. For more examples see the text:
B. Conev, ed., <u>Vračansko Evangelie</u> (Bəlgarski starini, IV), Sofia, 1914, ix + 236 pp.

the letters Ѫ and Ѧ, caused inconsistencies in the scribe's application of his contemporary norms; although the new norms demanded the letter Ѫ after /š/, a spelling like бѣшѧ could appear sporadically, as a residue of an older phonological and orthographic tradition.

In general, one deals with the lack, over a 300 - year period, of national orthographic rules for expressing unambiguously the different phonetic outcomes of the single morphoneme $\{\tilde{v}\}$ in all possible environments: in word - initial position, after prothetic or intervocalic $\{j\}$, after a paired hard or soft consonant, after a palatal consonant, either within the lexical morpheme or at the morpheme boundary - all by means of the two graphic symbols Ѫ and Ѧ. The difficulties of the scribes were multiplied when, in the dialects, the phonetic outcomes of the morphoneme $\{\tilde{v}\}$ had already merged with the phonetic outcomes of $\{a\}$ and vocalized $\{\#\}$. What is peculiar to most of the Middle Bulgarian manuscripts, with the exception of those written in the northwestern territories[479] (such as the Vidin kingdom), is the presence of at least one of the letters Ѫ or Ѧ. This separates graphically most of the Bulgarian literary monuments of the 13th - 14th centuries from the corresponding

---

479. Dialects with *ǫ > /u/ are still found in the northwest regions of today's Bulgaria, in the counties of Belogradčik, Berkovica, Trən, Breznik, and partially Vidin. See:
M. Mladenov, Govorət na Novo Selo Vidinsko, Sofia, 1969, p. 192-193.

Russian and Serbian ones, where different orthographic systems of Church Slavic were originally applied.

4.3.5.3. The original scribe of IAG uses correctly at least one of the letters for the nasal vowel wherever a nasal vowel should appear. There are only a few examples of spelling mistakes in this respect: десете for десѧте (p. 101) and чѧтырн for четыри (p. 265b): й призвавъ ѡ̊ба на десете ... (p. 101, Mark VI.7); й створишѫ чѧтыри чѧсти (p. 265b, John XIX.23). In the latter example, however, the letter ѧ in чѧтыри may have been triggered by the first syllable of the next word, чѧ-сти,(other examples will be discussed below).

4.3.5.4. There is one word in IAG which is always spelled with the letter ѫ, contrary to the situation in all of the classical texts: нѫ (vs. нъ in the classical OCS texts). K. Mirčev[480] suggests that нѫ represents a case of emphatic duplication of the *nŭ which became нъ of the classical texts: *nŭ-nŭ > *nǫ. Such an explanation meets a serious obstacle - the monophthongization of the diphthongs occurred before the fall of the jers in weak position, and never took place before a vowel (e.g. the final *ŭ of *nŭnŭ). If there had been reduplication of the particle *nŭ, the result would have been *нънъ or *нонъ - forms which were never registered. The Middle Bulgarian form нѫ

---

480. K. Mirčev, op. cit., p. 104.

has the Russian parallel ну. It would seem that some Common Slavic dialects had two particles: *nŭ and *nǫ. Without apparent reason, in the Middle Bulgarian period the latter completely replaced the particle нъ used in the classical texts, while in Russian both particles survived (as но and ну), but with different syntactic functions. The presence of the particle нѫ in a given text is an absolute graphical indication that such a Church Slavic text is either of Bulgarian origin or copied from a Bulgarian original.

4.3.5.5. As already mentioned, the word for 'rooster' used in IAG is always written by the original scribe of IAG as пѧтелъ (numerous examples): и а̇бꙇѥ ѥ̈ще гла̄щоу ꙇемоу вьзгласи пѧтель. (p. 205, Luke XXII.60). But in a few cases, the original word in the text was erased and rewritten with the letter e instead of ѧ. For instance, on p. 203 everything after the first letter п of the word was erased, and the word changed by a different hand to петѣ́лъ. The consistent spelling of this word with a letter for the nasal vowel instead of ѣ (пѣтелъ) should not be treated as a spelling mistake. The word /p,int,él/ exists even today in a peripheral Bulgarian dialect, together with /mənglá/ for *mŭglā and a few other such items[481]. These are cases of secondary nasalization inside the lexical morpheme, re-stricted to a very few dialects in the Bulgarian linguistic

---

481. K. Mirčev, ibid.
P. Draganov, op. cit., p. 1-27.

area, which are difficult to explain. The exclusive use of the form пѧтелъ by Symon the Monk indicates only that he himself was a native speaker of a dialect with such a feature, or else that he got his education in a center other than Tərnovo, and that the dialect of that center, having such a feature, determined his orthographical norm. He had no opportunity to check the spelling of this word in older texts with correct usage of the letters for the nasal vowel since the word пѣтелъ is a lexical innovation, compared to the words кокотъ and коуръ, which were used in the classica period.

The secondary nasalization of the vowel in пѧтел cannot have been a feature of the Tərnovo dialect from the end of the 14th century. We possess a short text with a drawing of the city of Tərnovo by the king's beekeeper: азъ димитръ писх̃ъ ѿ мо̃сина п꙼еларъ цр̃овъ [482]. This semiliterate native of the village of Musina near Tərnovo, although using the letter ѧ correctly in the form братнѧ (accusative singular) or братнѣ, substitutes the letter ъ for the expected ѫ: ... понеже имѣхъ братнѧ и ѹ‖мрѣхъ

---

482. The drawing of 14th-century Tərnovo is on p. 78v (sic), and the few lines follow, as a postscript, the text of a Bulgarian Mineja for September, #34 in the library of the Orthodox Church of "St. Nicolae din Şcheii" in Brashov, Rumania. Detailed information and photocopies of both the drawing and the text by the beekeeper Dimitər can be found in the article:
St. Maslev, Neizvestni u nas bəlgarski rəkopisi v Brašov, Izvestija na Instituta za istorija, 19, Sofia, 1967, p. 195-217.

(=ОꙋмрѣхѪ, new aorist form) два азъ единъ ѡсхъ (=ѡстахъ)
и б҃къ (= бг҃ъ) да прости въ ‖ бѫдъшемъ (= бѫдѫщемъ) вѣцѣ[483].
A comparison of the spelling used by the beekeeper Dimitər
of Musina and the scribe of IAG shows how little of the
phonological peculiarity of the Tərnovo dialect is part of
the literary language. For from the few lines of Dimitər
and other contemporary writings of 14th-century Tərnovo[484]
it is clear that there was no nasality whatsoever in that
dialect, not to speak of secondary nasalization.

4.3.5.6. The scribe of IAG uses only the two letters Ѫ and Ѧ for the morphoneme {ṽ}. When following a consonant, they have the following distribution:

a) After hard paired consonants and the velars,
the letter Ѫ is used. There are only a few spelling mistakes in the entire text: тогда приидошѪ к І҃соу, иже
бѣхѦ (=бѣхѪ) ѿ І҃ерс҃лма ... (p. 46, Matth. XV.1); направи
ногы нашѦ на пѦть (=пѫть) съмиренииа. (p. 141b, Luke I.
79); и҆ бѣ слѦка (=слѫка), немогѫщи въсклонити сѧ ѿнѭдъ
... (p. 180, Luke XIII.11). The adjective слѦка 'bowed
together' should be spelled with Ѫ, as it is in the classical texts. Softening of the consonant {l} into [l,] before {ṽ} is impossible, since it comes in regular alterna-

---

483. St. Maslev, op. cit., p. 206-207.

484. Typical for the replacement of the nasal -
vowel letters by letters denoting oral vowels is the Moscow
copy of the Manasses Chronicle, written by the priest Filip.
It is kept in the State Historical Museum in Moscow, under
#Sinod. 20-38.

tion with the verb {kl,ṽk-} 'to squat down' (the same alter

nation as in слоучити са (/sl/) vs. ключити са (/kl,/)[485].

One possible explanation for this misspelled word is that i

had already disappeared from the living language, while the

scribe was influenced by the existing verb клакнѧти 'to

squat', registered in the Tale of Troy[486]: поклакна ёкторъ

(p. 55b).

The verbal form блѧдите (second person plural,

present tense) from the classical texts is always spelled

with ѧ in IAG: блѧ́дите [<блѧдите] не вѣдѧще писаниꙗ

ни си́лы бжиѧ̅. (p. 66, Matth. XXII.29). Here the problem

seems to lie in a different derivation of the verb. It is

not derived from the same stem as that of the substantive

*блѧдъ 'sin' (unregistered in IAG) and of the adverb блѧдно

'sinfully': и̇ тоу расточи и̇мѣние свое живы блѧдно

(p. 184b, Luke XV.13). The verb form блѧ́дите is rather

derived from the same stem as the adjective блѧ́дъ (spelled

the same way in the classical OCS texts): и̇ ꙗвишѧ сѧ

прѣд ними ꙗко блѧ́ди гли и̇хъ, (p. 210, Luke XXIV.11).

b) After a paired soft consonant, the letter ѧ

is used. There are a few spelling mistakes in the entire

text: и̇ ты бѧди надь пѫтиѧ (= пѧтиѧ) градъ. (p. 194, Luke

---

485. P. Ilčev, Iz bəlgarskata istoričeska leksi
kologija. Starobəlgarskoto KLJUČITI SĘ, IzvIBE, VIII, Sofia
1962, p. 117-129.

486. I. Dujčev, ed., Letopista na Konstantin
Manasi, Sofia, 1963, p. 110.

XIX.19). A similar mistake is made in <u>Mar.</u> (Luke II.44):
придете пѧть (= пѫть) дьне. 'they went a day's journey'.

The word тѧгота 'burden' of the classical texts
appears only once in IAG, where it is spelled with ѫ:
принесшиимь тѫготѫ дне и варъ (p. 59, Matth. XX.12). But
other derivatives from the same stem are written with ѧ:
бѣстѣ бо ѻчи ихъ тѧготнѣ (p. 127b, Mark XIV.40); бѣстѣ
бо ѻчи ихъ отѧгченѣ (p. 77b, Matth. XXVI.43).

The word мѧта 'mint' (Latin <u>mentha</u>) was spelled
correctly on p. 68: ꙗко ѿдесѧтствоуете мѧтѫ и пигань и
киминъ. (p. 68, Matth. XXIII.23). But on p. 174, where it
was originally written мѫ̃ы, someone later erased the letter
ы (but not the stress over it) and wrote вы: ꙗко десѧтинѫ
даюте ѿ мѫ̃вы (< мѫ̃ы) и пигана, и всѣкого зѣлиа.
(p. 174, Luke XI.42).

c) There are changes in the distribution of the
letters ѫ and ѧ in different grammatical forms of the two
pairs of verbs expressing movement: $\{-m\widetilde{v}t,i-\}$ vs. $\{-m,\widetilde{v}t-\}$
'to move (of emotions), change shape' and $\{-tr\widetilde{v}s,i-\}$ vs.
$\{-tr,\widetilde{v}s-\}$ 'to shake'. On p. 139b, <u>Sav.</u> has the phrase:
оуслышавъ же иродъ црь съмѧте сѧ. (Matth. II.3). The same
paragraph in IAG (p. 9) reads as follows: слышавъ же иродъ
црь, смѧти сѧ. и весь Іероусалимъ сь нимь. Here, obviously,
the scribe did not simply substitute the letter ѫ for the ѧ
of the classical text: he replaced the aorist of the stem
ending in a hard consonant with the aorist of the corres-

- 333 -

ponding stem, ending in a soft consonant. A similar change
was made in the passive past participle потрѫсънѫ 'shaken'
(in the classical OCS texts). In IAG the passage reads:
мѣрѫ ‖ добрѫ натканѫ и̇̇ потрѧсенѫ дадѧть на лоно ваше.
(p. 155-155b, Luke VI.38). While forms like смѧти сѧ (p. 9)
and смѧте сѧ (p. 138), възмѧти сѧ(p. 224b) and възмѧтошѫ̃с̃
(p. 104) are registered in IAG, indicating aspectual differences in the prefixed verbs with the prefixes {s#=} and
{v#z=}, it is impossible to determine whether aspectual
pairing of the verb потрѧсти ～ потрѫсити was achieved by use
of the different stems ({po=tr,$\widetilde{V}$s-t,i} vs. {po=tr$\widetilde{V}$s,i-t,i}).
or whether the prefix {po=} (with inceptive meaning) formed
only a perfective verb with no corresponding imperfective.

    4.3.5.7. Like the OCS texts, IAG has alternating
forms with ѧ versus e or ѣ for the non-past and imperative
stems of the verbs of body position *lęg- and *sęd-. While
Mar. has сѣдѣштемъ (Matth. XI.16), IAG in the same phrase
has сѣдѧщемь (p. 34), but in Luke XX.42 both Zogr. and IAG
(p. 198) have сѣди (2nd person singular imperative) versus
сѧди in Mar. The 2nd person plural of the imperative of the
same verb, however, is сѣдѣте in both Mar. and Zogr. (Luke
XXIV.49), while IAG has сѧдѣте in the same sentence (p. 212)

    The verb 'to deteriorate' in 3rd person plural
future, is in all OCS texts просѧдѧть сѧ (Matth. IX.17); in
the same verse IAG has the letter a instead of ѧ (or even
ѣ or e, as might be expected): ни вливаѫть вина нова въ
мѣхы ветхы. а̇ще ли же ни̇, просадат сѧ мѣси, и̇ вино пролѣет

c . (p. 28). This probably represents not a phonological development, but the realization of a distinct root shape: *sād- instead of *sęd-.

In most occurrences, the outcome of *lęg- is spelled with e in IAG, versus ѧ in the classical OCS texts: и възлегѫть вь цр͠ствии б͠жии. (p. 181, Luke XIII.29). But in one phrase, where all OCS texts have the form with e - възлежѧштемъ (Mark XVI.14) - IAG has ѧ instead: по слѣди же възлѧжѫщемъ имъ е́диномоу на де́сѧте ꙗави сѧ. (p. 134).

4.3.5.8. The morphoneme {ṽ} after /ž/, /š/, /žd/ and /št/ is expressed by the letter ѫ (as after a hard consonant): вьсѣкъ пиѫ҃и ѿ воды сеѧ̀, въжѫждет сѧ пакы (p. 221b, John IV.13); а́з же послах вы жѫти (p. 223, John IV.38); жѫтва оу́бо многа, а́ жѫтелеи мало (p. 168, Luke X.2); а́з же по срѣдѣ васъ ю̈́смь слоужѫ́и (p. 202b, Luke XXII.27). Thus the ending for 3rd person plural aorist, OCS –шѧ, becomes –шѫ, with only isolated exceptions, such as вьзашѧ, which are a manifestation of the strength of tradition: и пристѫпльше оу́ченици ю̈́го, вьзашѧ тѣло ю̈́го и погребошѫ ю̈́. (p. 44, Matth. XIV.12). Parallel to these few oscillating archaisms, the genitive singular and nominative/accusative plural feminine and the accusative plural masculine adjectival endings after /š/, which in OCS are written –шѧ, are in IAG usually written –шѫ, though there are still remnants of the traditional spelling: и ѿстави намъ длъгы нашѧ (p. 171b, Luke XI.4).

In most cases, the letter ѫ is written after жд: о̂трокъ мои ‖ лежить ... ꙗко <u>страждѫ</u> (p. 24 - 24b, Matth. VIII.6); блажени а̑лчѧщеи ‖ и̑ <u>жѧждѧщеи</u> правдѫ. (p. 15b - 16, Matth. V.6). After the ligature щ, representing either the combinations {z=č}, as in {j#z=čṽd,-#j-}, or {sk-j}, ѫ is usually written: и̑щѫдїа ю̈хиднова (p. 37b, Matth. XII.34); а̑ <u>и̑щѫи</u> славы послав̑шаго и, съ̑ и̑стиненъ е̑стъ (p. 232b, John VII.18). But in a few cases the letter ѧ is written after the letter щ, as in the older texts.

After /č/, represented by ч, either within a lexical morpheme or at a morpheme boundary, the letter ѧ is written: нѣсте ^{ли} чьли ꙗко сътворѧи вь <u>начѧлѣ</u> мѫжьскыи по́лъ ... (p. 56, Matth. XIX.4); блажени а̑лчѧщеи (p. 15b, Matth. V.6).

While only ѧ occurs after the letter ц, representing /c/, within the lexical morpheme (cf. <u>цѧта</u>), both ѧ and ѫ occur after ц at a morpheme boundary, with a certain tendency to distinguish different case endings: -цѫ for genitive and accusative singular feminine, but -цѧ for accusative plural masculine and nominative/accusative plural feminine: и̑ <u>срачицѫ</u> (gen. sing. fem.) не възбрани̑ (p. 155, Luke VI.29); о̑поусти ю̈м꙯ꙋ и <u>срачицѫ</u> (acc. sing. fem.) твоѫ (p. 18b, Matth. V.40); ꙗко Ѳбрѣтохъ о̑вцѫ (acc. sing. fem.) моѫ погыбш҄ѫѧ(p. 184, Luke XV.6); и̑ о̑вцѧ (nom. pl. fem.) гла҄ его слышѫтъ, и̑ своѫ о̑вцѧ (acc. pl. fem.) зоветь по и̑мени(p. 241 b, John X.3); ꙗко на новы мѣсѧцѧ (acc. pl. masc.) бѣсноуѥт сѧ (p. 51b, Matth. XVII.15).

4.3.5.9. In word-initial position, the letters ѧ and ѫ are used in free alternation to express *ǫ and *(j)ę. Such a spelling alternation must represent the normative Church Slavic pronunciation in 14th-century Bulgaria, based on a southwestern dialect, since in all modern Bulgarian dialects initial etymological *(j)ę and *ǫ are kept distinct by the presence of prothetic /v/ before etymological *ǫ: вѫже (Blg.)∿ jаже (Mac.) < *ǫže. The scribe of IAG treats initial etymological *ǫ in the same fashion as *(j)ę: и вѧзаахѫ ѐго ѫжи желѣзны (p. 162, Luke VIII.29); и ни ѫжемъ желѣзномь, никто же не можааше ѐгѡ свѧзати (p. 98b, Mark V.3). The forms of the word ѩзꙑкъ (as spelled in OCS) are in most instances written with initial ѫ, but spellings with ѧ also occur: въ свѣдѣниѥ имъ. и ѧзыкѡмь. (p. 31, Matth. X.18).

At morpheme boundaries after {j} the morphoneme {ṽ} is in most instances represented by the letter ѫ: тꙋ недѫгы нашѧ прижтъ (p. 25b, Matth. VIII.17); гѡре же непразнымʼ и дожщиимь въ тꙑ дни (p. 70b, Matth. XXIV.19). The use of the letters ѫ and ѧ for the nasal vowel {ṽ} in word-initial position (with or without prothetic -j-) and at morpheme boundaries after {j} is parallel to the use of the letters е and ѥ for {jo} in word-initial position and at morpheme boundaries. This must be related to certain phonetic properties, common to both [e] and /ṽ/:

[- BACK], [- LOW], [- HIGH], [- ROUNDED] vowels.

4.3.6. The letters ъ and ь [487] are used in free alternation, without any distinction, for marking boundaries after words ending in consonants, as well as for marking the end of a line after a consonant within a word - all orthographic boundaries; when they can be vocalized within a morpheme they represent the morphoneme {#}, but they may also appear between two consonants in an unexpected position; they usually follow the letters р and л before a consonant, thus expressing syllabic {r̥} and {l̥}.

4.3.6.1. A line ends either in a letter for a vowel or in a jer (ъ or ь), or, extremely rarely, in a paercik ('), which is an abbreviated jer. Although the letter ъ is used more often for marking the end of a line, the letter ь is also used in numerous cases where it is unjustified etymologically, so that no special rules can be observed. The only letters for consonants which can occur at the end of a line are с in the abbreviation ĩс̃ (which in all positions is spelled in this same fashion, in imitation of the Greek shape of the name) and the letter ч in the abbreviation реч̑ (for рече); in the latter case, however, the ч most often is superscribed between the letters р and е (р̑е) giving the graphic impression that the line ends in е. When the letter ъ is used at the end of a line, it is usually taller than the rest of the letters in that line: и̓деже

---

487. Scholvin includes examples of various vocalizations of the jers. See:
R. Scholvin, op. cit., p. 36-38.

чр҄ǂ ‖ въ ни тлѣ тлитъ (p. 20b).

The two letters ⸯъ and ь are written interchange-
ably after prepositions ending in an obstruent stop, as well
as after words ending in a consonant, thus marking preposi-
tion- and word- boundaries. Sometimes it seems that the
scribe wrote only ь in one line, and only ъ in another,
without respect to their etymological origins from *ь or *ъ,
reflected in OCS: йже ‖ приходѧтъ къ вамь въ ѡдежда‖хъ
овчинахъ. (p. 22b, Matth. VII.15). However, before the
monosyllabic enclitics же and сѧ, the jers are in most instances absent: ѻ҆н же (p. 65); да събѫдет сѧ (p. 61);
бойм сѧ (p. 63).

4.3.6.2. After prefixes and prepositions, the
letters ъ and ь, in free alternation, are used (or not used)
according to rules, stated in 4.2.2.3. In this respect,
besides a tendency to establish strict rules for the use of
a jer, IAG differs from the glagolitic texts in not using
the letter o instead of *ъ; here IAG follows the tradition
of the cyrillic Sav. and Supr., representing the normative
Church Slavic pronunciation in Bulgaria.

In no instance in IAG are the articles -отъ or
-осъ found, while the demonstrative pronouns тъ/ть and съ/сь
should be treated as enclitics rather than articles, since
no unusual phonetic changes are observed at the end of the
preceding word (cf. злиѡтъ рабъ in Dobrejšovo Evangelie).

4.3.6.3. Within lexical morphemes, the letters
ъ and ь (in free alternation) express the vocalic phonetic

outcome of the fleeting vowel {#}. In most instances the
morphoneme {#} appears in the environment before or after
the sonorants {m}, {m,}, {n}, {n,} or the glides {v}, {v,} :
ꙗко сътворитъ мьсть ихъ въ скорѣ   (p. 191, Luke XVIII.8);
й изгнашѫ же й вънъ,   (p. 241, John IX.35). However, since
the morphoneme {#} in a number of lexical morphemes appears
between two obstruents, one cannot eliminate the morphoneme
{#} altogether from the morphonemic representation simply
by introducing syllabic sonorants (similar to the syllabic
liquids {ᶉ} and {ḷ}): й дьскы тръжникѡмъ йспровръже
(p. 61b, Matth. XXI.12); дръзаи дъщи   (p. 163b, Luke VII.
48). There might still be a possibility of avoiding the use
of the morphoneme {#} in the abstract representation of 14th
century literary Bulgarian: if one could derive a complete
set of rules for the insertion of a vowel in certain consonantal clusters (for instance *{dsk-}; such an approach, although intriguing, has not been followed in this study,
because the Four Gospels text alone provides insufficient
material.

4.3.6.4. In the OCS texts, the imperative stems
of the verbs решти, пешти сѧ have ь: рьци, рьцѣте,   and
пьцѣте сѧ. In IAG, all attested imperative forms of the
verb пешти have /e/ as the vowel in the lexical morpheme,
while the change of the stem final /k/ to /c/ is preserved.
However, in its many occurrences throughout IAG, the imperative of решти stays рьци, рьцѣте: иди же ‖ къ брати моюи

и рьци имъ (p. 268b - 269, John XX.17); изшедше на
распѧтїа его, рьцѣте.   (p. 168b, Luke X.10); не пецѣте сѧ
како или что имате глати   (p. 31, Matth. X.19). The form
of the 2nd person singular does not occur in the Gospel text
but пецѣте сѧ occurs in IAG 7 times, and only in this one
shape. The conjugation of the verb решти preserves another
archaic feature as well: the forms of the root aorist in the
first person singular and the 3rd person plural, рѣхъ and
рѣшѧ. It is possible that the conjugation of this verb was
learned by the scribe of IAG as an exception to the rule for
the new spoken forms, represented by the imperative пецѣте
сѧ (vs. пцѣте сѧ, пьцѣте сѧ in OCS), with morphological
levelling of the imperative to the rest of the paradigm (no
root aorist *пѣшѧ - or any other aorist form of this verb -
occurs in the text of the New Testament).

   4.3.6.5. The letter ь (only in a few cases ъ) is
written in all words containing the suffix {-stv-} preceded
by a consonant. The rule is consistently employed, most
likely indicating not only an orthographic but a phonological Church Slavic norm. Examples are: вы сами
мнѣ послоушьствоуете, ꙗко рѣхъ нѣсмь азъ х͠с, (p. 220,
John III.28); и не створи тоу силы многы. за невѣрьствие
ихъ: (p. 43, Matth. XIII.58); разоумѣвъ же І͠с лѫкавьство
ихъ, ре͡ч. (p. 65, Matth. XXII.18).

   4.3.6.6. The morphoneme {#} in the suffixes
{-#n-}, {-#l-} , {-#c-}, {-#k-} is either realized as ∅ or,

when vocalized, is expressed by the letters e (in -елъ, -енъ
-ецъ) or o (in -окъ). The spelling ък/ьк appears in free alternation with -окъ, while for the other suffixes, the spellings -ьнъ, -ьцъ are seldom used in IAG and the spelling
-ьлъ is rare and most likely a correction by later scribes.
It is definitely a later correction in the forms пѣтьлъ
from earlier пѧтелъ, where it is easy to see on the microfilm copy the traces of the previous letters. Examples of
the vowel/zero alternation in these suffixes are: которааго
ѿ васъ ѻселъ, или волъ. въ стоуденецъ вьпадеть (p. 181b,
Luke XIV.5); сѐ црь твои грѧдеть тебѣ кротокъ и вьсѣдь на
ѻслѧ и жрѣбѧ... (p. 61, Matth. XXI.5); понеже бѣ пѧтькъ
(p. 132b, Mark XV.42); оубо пака ради (p. 267b, John
XIX.42); аще силенъ естъ (p. 183b, Luke XIV.31); нако
сътвори мнѣ величие силныи (p. 140, Luke I.49); и ѿкрылъ
еси сиа младенцемъ (p. 35, Matth. XI.25).

The graphic expression of the vowel/zero alternation in these suffixes in IAG is a spelling norm - an
orthographic innovation compared with the situation in the
classical OCS texts. The classical texts of the late 10th
and 11th centuries from Bulgaria, both glagolitic and cyrillic, rarely omit the letters ъ and ь from their etymological
positions; such omissions as do occur are in positions where
the jer's phonetic outcome would be ∅, indicating that the
vowel/zero alternation **was** already established in the language. That so few jers were omitted shows that the scribes

were attempting to reflect an older Church Slavic phonology
and spelling.

4.3.6.7. The very consistent spellings -рѣ-/-рь-
and -ль-/-лѣ- in IAG, together with the further development
in the Macedono-Bulgarian dialects suggest that these letter
combinations represented syllabic liquids {ŗ} and {ļ}.
Both letters (р and л are, in most cases, followed by ѣ
and ь in free alternation, but the spellings -рѣ- and -ль-
somewhat predominate: сѐ ѥ҃ крѣвь моа, новааго завѣта
(p. 126, Mark XIV.24); и҆ сѣде мрътвыи и҆ начѧть глати
(p. 157b, Luke VII.15); и҆ плодъ ѥ҃го зль҃. (p. 37b, Matth.
XII.33); е҆гда и҆спльни сѧ ѻ҃смь дн҃їи(p. 142b, Luke II.21).

In a very few cases, the letter р alone represents
the syllable {ŗ}: и҆ быш꙼ѧ ꙗ҆ко мрѢ҃и: (p. 85, Matth.
XXVIII.4). There are a very few instances where the letters
р and л are surrounded by two jers: народъ же запрѣти и҆ма
да оу҆мьльчѧть (p. 60, Matth. XX.31). The syllabic liquid
morphonemes do not form a syllable when followed by a vowel;
in such cases, the jers are usually not written: ѿ недѫ҃гъ
и҆ ранъ и҆ доухъ злыхъ (p. 157b, Luke VII.21).

4.4. On grammatical archaism and innovation
in IAG. The morphology of the Middle Bulgarian literary
language, reflected in IAG, is thoroughly studied by R.
Scholvin[488]. The morphological structure is generally the

---

488. R. Scholvin, op. cit., p. 161-219.

same as that of the OCS texts of the 10th - 11th centuries, with the same alternation of archaic and newer Church Slavic forms[489]. Grammatical forms representing further developments of the Middle Bulgarian period (12th - 14th centuries) are either very limited in number (cf. below) or not attested at all in IAG, in contrast to most of the other Middle Bulgarian texts[490]. The archaism of the grammar and the lim-

---

489. P. Diels, Altkirchenslavische Grammatik, part I, Heidelberg, 1963 (2nd edition), p. 148-282.
K. Mirčev, Istoričeska gramatika na bəlgarskija ezik, Sofia, 1963 (2nd edition), p. 47-52
I. Duridanov, Kəm problemata za razvoja na bəlgarskija ezik ot sintetizəm kəm analitizəm, Godišnik SU, LI, Sofia, 1955, 3, p. 156-249.

490. K. Mirčev, op. cit., pp. 52-56, 144-265.
_____, Analitični formi za sravnitelna stepen v dva srednobəlgarski pametnika ot XIV v., BəlgEz, I, 1951, 3-4, p. 215-217.
_____, Za smesvaneto na okončanijata v minalo-svəršeno i minalo-nesvəršeno vreme na glagolite v bəlgarskija ezik, BəlgEz, II, 1952, 1-2, p. 36-45.
_____, Za člennite formi v Dobrejšovoto evangelie, srednobəlgarski pametnik ot XIII v., BəlgEz, IV, 1956, 3, p. 223-228.
_____, Po vəprosa za naj-rannite primeri na analitičen datelen padež v bəlgarskite pametnici, Ezikovedski izsledvanija v čest na akademik Stefan Mladenov, Sofia, 1957, p. 37-46.
_____, Za člennite formi v srednobəlgarskite pametnici, IzvIBE, XI, Sofia, 1964, p. 231-234.
B. Koneski, Istorija na makedonskiot jazik, Skopje-Beograd, 1965, p. 99-173.
I. Duridanov, Edin slučaj na ranna upotreba na predloga na za izrazjavane na datelno otnošenie, BəlgEz, III, 1953, 1, p. 58-60.
A. Minčeva, Kəm vəprosa za pojavata na pritežatelnoto značenie na predloga na v bəlgarskija ezik, IzvIBE, VIII, Sofia, 1962, p. 93-110.
_____, Razvoj na datelnija pritežatelen padež v bəlgarskija ezik, Sofia, 1964, p. 21-114.
S. Bojadžiev, Kəm istoričeskija razvoj na predloga na v bəlgarskija ezik, IzvIBE, IX, Sofia, 1962,

ited number of morphological innovations seems to be the main reason that scholars in the historical development of Bulgarian have tended to ignore IAG. But this linguistic feature of the revised edition of the New Testament from 14th-century Bulgaria is very indicative of the direction taken by revisions in the language of the OCS translations from Greek. The fact that all attested grammatical forms from the cyrillic Sav. and Supr. are used in IAG suggests that the revision of the translation was made according to copies as old as Sav. and Supr. (the root aorist forms found in the glagolitic texts, except those of the verb решти, are not attested in IAG).

---

p. 211-296.
      D. Ivanova-Mirčeva, Razvoj na bədešte vreme (Futurum) v bəlgarskija ezik ot X do XVIII vek, Sofia, 1962, p. 28-191.
      J. Rusek, Za srednobəlgarskite vinitelni formi na anaforičnoto mestoimenie v ženski rod ex, exжe, нех, BəlgEz, 1-2, 1962, p. 100-103.
                , Deklinacja i użycie przypadków w triodzie Chłudowa, Wrocław-Warsaw-Cracow, 1964, p. 9-194.
                , Beležki vərxu razvoja na pričastijata v bəlgarski ezik, BəlgEz, XVI, 1966, 5, p. 477-490.
      I. Bojukliev, Šopov psaltir, BəlgEz, XIII, 1963, 3, p. 234-254.
                , Srednobəlgarski psaltiren otkəs ot XIV v. (Šopov psaltir), Trudove na Visšija pedagogičeski institut "Bratja Kiril i Metodi" vəv Veliko Tərnovo, II, Sofia, 1965, p. 49-94.
      N. Dilevski, Kəm vəprosa za proizxoda na "Germanovija sbornik" ot 1359, BəlgEz, XVII, 1967, 4, p. 307-322.
      K. Steinke, Studien über den Verfall der bulgarischen Deklination, Munich, 1968, p. 35-117.
      I. K. Bunina, Istorija glagol'nyx vremen v bolgarskom jazyke, Moscow, 1970, p. 45-219.
      E. V. Češko, Istorija bolgarskogo sklonenija, Moscow, 1970, p. 67-301.

4.4.1. Certain systematic morphological innovations are introduced in IAG:

a) new genitive and locative forms in {-(i)x} of the numerals from **three** to **ten**: да въ оӱстѣхъ двою или **трехъ** свѣдѣтель (p. 54, Matth. XVIII.16) and кто оӱбо тѣхъ **трїихъ** (p. 170b, Luke X.36); ӥ съберѫть ӥзбранныѫ ёго. ѿ **четырехъ** вѣтръ (p. 71, Matth. XXIV.31) and ӧ пѧти҇ хлѣбѣ (p. 87, Table of Contents to Mark); ӥ бы҇ по **шестихъ** днехъ (p. 50b, Matth. XVII.1); которомӧ ‖ ѿ **седмихъ** бѫдетъ женᷳ (p. 65b - 66, Matth. XXII.28); по немь ӥдошѫ на́роди мно́ѕи ѿ галилѣѧ ӥ **десѧтихъ** градъ (p. 15b, Matth. IV.25).

b) the ending for the first person plural of the non-past tense of the athematic verbs, always {-mi}, spelled —**мы**: ӥако зде на поустѣ мѣстѣ ёсмы (p. 164b, Luke IX.12); что ꙗмы или что пиюмь (p. 21b, Matth. VI.31); **дамы** ли, ӥли не **дамы** (p. 119b, Mark XII.14); мы вѣмы ӥако чл҃къ сь грѣшенъ ёстъ (p. 240b, John IX.24).

4.4.2. The syntactic structure represented in IAG reveals no significant changes in comparison with the classical OCS texts; the differences are in the use of different grammatical forms in the same verse of the New Testament. For instance, when in one phrase all the classical texts have the possessive genitive, IAG has the possessive dative, but in one where the classical texts have the possessive dative, IAG has the genitive.

Even the occurrence of double object in IAG is no

an innovation, as one might be led to believe by the dating
of the earliest attested occurrences to the 14th century[491].
While comparing the text of IAG with those of Mar., Sav.,
and the Russian Ostr., I found a few instances of the
double object in Mar. which have remained unnoticed by students of this text. Here are the occurrences of duplicated
accusative object in Mar.: зълъɪ зълѣ погоубитъ ѩ (Matth.
XXI.41) 'He will miserably destroy them the wicked men'. On
the duplication of the object through the use of the pronoun
form ѩ, Jagić notes in the fn. on p. 77 of Mar.: "ѩ is
a spelling error"; егоже азъ оусѣкнѫхъ иоана (Mark VI.16)
'I beheaded him John'; дѣла бо (ѣже дастъ мънѣ о͞тцъ) да
съврьшѫ ѣ (John V.36) 'the works (which the Father gave
me) to finish them'; вьсѣкѫ разгѫ не творѧштѫѩ плода.
ιзъметъ ѭ. ι вьсѣкѫ тво[тво]рѧштѫ плодъ отрѣбитъ ѭ (John
XV.2) 'Every branch not bearing fruit. He will take it away,
and every (branch) bearing fruit, He will prune it'.

In Mar. there is one instance of a possible double
dative: елисавети же исплъни сѧ врѣмѧ родити еи (Luke I.
57) 'The time for Elizabeth to give birth came for her'.
However, this phrase may be explained also in a different

---

491. J. Rusek, Po vəprosa za xronologijata na
udvojavane na dopəlnenijata v bəlgarskija ezik, BəlgEz,
XIII, 1963, 2, p. 141-143.
        K. Mirčev, Za xronologijata na osnovnite bal-
kanizmi v bəlgarskija ezik, BəlgEz, XVI, 1966, 4, p. 281 -
293.
        _____, Istoričeska gramatika ..., p. 60.

way: родити еи might represent dative plus infinitive, a
purposive construction - 'so that she would give birth' -
while елисавети is linked with врѣмѧ - 'the time for Elizabeth'; in this case the translation would be: 'Elizabeth's
time came that she should give birth'. It seems that either
interpretation is correct and possible.

The double dative is clearly expressed in **Mar.** in
one instance of a dative absolute construction: въшедъшоу
же емоу исви въ каперънаоумъ (Matth. VIII.5) 'When Jesus
he entered Capernaum'. In this phrase the insertion of the
enclitic же between the past active participle in the dative
case (въшедъшоу) and the duplicating dative personal pronoun
(емоу) makes the interpretation unambiguous. However, there
are many similar cases in OCS (including **Mar.**) where the enclitic же is absent; because of the spelling tradition of
non-separation of words, scholars prefer to see in such
cases not duplication of a participial by a pronominal form,
but simply a long form of the participle, for example,in **Mar**
пришедъшоуемоуІ͞сви (Matth. VIII.28), мимоходѧштюемоуІ͞с͞оу
(Mark II.23). These phrases are ambiguous, for the words in
them can be separated either way: пришедъшоуемоу І͞сви or
пришедъшоу емоу І͞сви; мимоходѧштюемоу І͞с͞оу or мимоходѧштю
емоу І͞с͞оу. If the second approach is accepted, the duplication of the dative through the addition of a personal pronoun will be additional evidence that the temporal dative
absolute was a living syntactic feature of the spoken Balkan

Slavic language at the time Mar. was written. But such an
altered view can be accepted only when more supporting data
from the classical texts has been collected.

An indirect proof that the double object, both accusative and dative, was an established syntactic Balkanism
in the Bulgarian language of the 10th - 11th centuries, is
found in the Russian copy of Sinajskij Paterik[492]. The occurrences of double accusative and double dative objects in
this manuscript of the 11th or early 12th century have gone
unnoticed, both by the publishers of the newest Soviet edition of the manuscript and by slavists who have studied the
text[493], perhaps because they were unaware of the existence
of such a Balkan syntactic feature. In a casual reading of
Sinajskij Paterik I found two clear cases of double object;
double accusative: тогда въставъ идохъ к'нигъ1 давъшю ми ıa
и рекохъ ıемоу. (p. 32b of the MS, p. 100 of the publication) 'then, after I got up, I went to (the person) who had
given me them the books and told him'; and double dative:
ıави же сѧ ıемх [=ıемоу] пакъ1 бѣсъ. затворьникоу и гла
ıемх [=ıемоу].   (p. 31b of the MS, p. 98 of the publica-

---

492. V. S. Golyšenko, V. F. Dubrovina, ed's.,
Sinajskij paterik, Moscow, 1967, 400 pp. + xi tables.

493. An exhaustive bibliography on the studies
of this manuscript, and review of the major findings by
scholars who have studied it, can be found in the preface
to the 1967 Soviet publication of the manuscript (cf. fn.
492), pp. 5-9, 16-36.

tion) 'and the devil appeared again to <u>him</u> <u>the hermit</u>, and
told him'.

The text of IAG also reflects the same Balkan syntactic feature of reduplication of the accusative and dative
objects, as does the text of <u>Mar.</u>, in some of the same phrases and in a few different ones. Examples of duplicated accusative are: всѣко <u>дрѣво</u>, не творѧщее плода добра,
посѣкаѫтъ <u>ѥ</u>, и̑ вь ѽгнь вьметаѫтъ (p. 23, Matth. VII.19)
'they cut <u>it</u> down <u>every tree</u>, not bringing forth good fruit,
and cast into the fire'. In this phrase the classical texts
do not have the accusative pronoun ѥ. The other five instances (in four sentences) of double accusative in IAG occur in the same verses as in <u>Mar.</u>: злыѫ злѣ погоубить ѧ̋
(p. 64, Matth. XXI.41); е̑гоже а̑зъ оу̑сѣкнѧхъ І̑ѡ́анна (p. 102,
Mark VI.16); дѣла ... да съврьшѫ ѩ̋ (p. 226b, John V.36);
вьсѣкѫ <u>розгѫ</u> ... и̑зметь ѫ̏. и̑ всѣкѫ... ѿрѣбить ѧ. (p. 255,
John XV.2). What is new in the orthography of IAG is that
in three of the six occurrences, the duplicating anaphoric
pronoun in the accusative has been stressed with the sign ̋
or ̏: ѧ̋ (p. 64), ѩ̋ (p. 226b), ѫ̏ (p. 255).

IAG does not offer examples of the double dative
in the dative absolute construction. But it has an indisput-
able double dative object at the beginning of St. Matthew's
Gospel for which we possess no parallel text in the classical glagolitic <u>Mar.</u> and <u>Zogr.</u> The double dative object in
Matth. IV.16 appears only in IAG; it does not exist in the

14th-century Bulgarian <u>Dečansko</u> <u>Evangelie</u>, published by

Jagić in <u>Mar.</u> in lieu of the lost initial pages of <u>Mar.</u> and

<u>Zogr.</u>. IAG has: людиѥ сѣдѧщеи въ тъмѣ видѣшѫ свѣтъ ве-

ликъ. ‖ й сѣдѧщимь въ странѣ й сѣни съмрътнѣи, свѣтъ

въсиꙗ имъ.(p. 14-14b) 'The people sitting in darkness saw

a great light, and <u>to those sitting</u> in the region and shadow

of death light sprang up <u>to them</u>'. In the same verse (Matth.

IV.16) both <u>Dečansko</u> <u>Evangelie</u> and <u>Sav.</u> have a nominative

plural <u>сѣдѧщеи</u> instead of the dative plural <u>сѣдѧщимь</u>, thus

showing syntactic disagreement in the sentence. <u>Sav.</u> has

the following phrase: й сѣдѧщеɪ въ странѣ. й сѣни съмрьтьнѣ

свѣтъ въсиꙗ имъ (p. 149b). The lack of grammatical agree-

ment between <u>сѣдѧщеɪ</u> and <u>имъ</u> in <u>Sav.</u> is not an argument

against the existence of a double dative object in its pro-

totype. In modern Bulgarian, phrases like на Петър му

говсря and Петър му говоря are in free alternation in col-

loquial speech and in the dialects, due to the inversion;

but *говоря му Петър is an impossible phrase. There is a

syntactic parallel between сѣдѧщеɪ... свѣтъ въсиꙗ имъ —

сѣдѧщимь... свѣтъ въсиꙗ имъ on the one hand and Петър му

говоря — на Петър му говоря on the other. Without duplica-

tion of the object (имъ in <u>Sav.</u>, му in the modern Bulgarian

example), both phrases (*сѣдѧщеɪ свѣтъ въсиꙗ , and *Петър

говоря) would be meaningless.

The above quoted examples of double accusative and

dative objects from <u>Mar.</u> and from the Russian copy of <u>Sinaj-</u>

skij Paterik, and even the one definite double dative in the dative absolute construction in Mar., indicate that the six instances of double accusative object and one of double dative object, attested in the text of IAG, are not syntactic innovations but rather archaisms in the language of IAG compared to that of some classical OCS texts from Bulgaria, both known (Mar.) and unknown (the prototype of the Russian Sinajskij Paterik). Thus all typical Balkan grammatical features, with the exception of the article, are present in the language of the 14th-century Bulgarian revised edition of the Four Gospels, in the same general quantity as in the classical OCS texts from 10th- and 11th-century Bulgaria (cf. fn. 287). It seems that the only Balkan grammatical feature which the 14th-century Bulgarians purged from their literary language as being foreign to Church Slavic, was the article, which definitely existed in the Bulgarian dialects of that time[494].

Balkanisms in OCS and in the Middle Bulgarian literary language, such as non-distinction of direction and location with the verbs of motion, establishment of only three cases - subjective, objective and dative - demonstrated by the incorrect use of the other cases and by generalization of the objective (accusative) case as a prepositional case,

---

494. K. Mirčev, Za člennite formi v Dobrejšovo evangelie, BəlgEz, VII, 1957, p. 223-228.

and duplication of the accusative and dative objects, seriously violate the grammatical structure of both literary
Russian and Serbian. Although the Serbian and Russian copyists of Old and Middle Bulgarian texts must have tried to
correct and interpret these "mistakes", a few of them penetrated into the Serbian and Russian literary monuments (cf.,
for example, 2.4.2.). The presence of such anomalies is
extremely useful as an indicator of an Old or Middle Bulgarian prototype for the Serbian and Russian copies. The
Balkan features in the Bulgarian language have come to the
attention of linguists relatively recently[495]. The most
detailed studies on the structural similarities of Bulgarian,
Macedonian, the Serbian Torlak dialects, Rumanian, the
Romance dialects in Macedonia, Albanian and some North Greek
dialects have been made at the synchronic level[496]. A

---

495. K. Sandfeld, Linguistique balkanique;
problèmes et résultats ("2e edition, un peu remaniée et
notablement augmentée de mon livre danois Balkanfilologien,
paru en 1929"), Paris, 1930, 242 pp.
    K. Sandfeld, P. Skok, Balkanski jezici, in:
Kniga o Balkanu, I, Beograd, 1936, p. 260-275.

    496. T. V. Civ'jan, Opyt opisanija form novo-
grečeskogo suščestvitel'nogo metodom analiza i sinteza,
VJaz, 1963, 6, p. 57-68.
                      , Imja suščestvitel'noe v balkan-
skix jazykax, Moscow, 1965, 194 pp.
    H. Birnbaum, Balkanslavisch und Südslavisch. Zur
Reichweite der Balkanismen im südslavischen Sprachraum,
Zeitschrift für Balkanologie, III, 1965, p. 12-63.
    Exhaustive bibliography on the subject is given
in the above-mentioned works. Cf. also:
    P. Ivić, Liens phonologiques entre les langues
balkaniques, Actes du 1er Congrès international des études
balkaniques et sud-est européennes, VI, Sofia, 1968,
p. 133-141.

diachronic comparative study is impossible, since the only early attested language of the group is Bulgarian. Nevertheless it would be incorrect to presume that it was the Bulgarian language which influenced Rumanian, Albanian and the North Greek dialects. The term "Balkan convergence area" is a most appropriate one for the territory on which, historically, the Daco-Thracian, Vulgar Latin, Greek and Slavic languages interacted, creating as a result a unique structural unity of languages and dialects different by origin[497].

4.5. When compared with the classical OCS Gospel texts, IAG reflects deep and serious lexical changes; in my study of these changes I discovered more than 1500 instances where a word was changed in IAG relative to the classical

---

497. T. V. Civ'jan, op. cit., pp. 15-16, 22, 183-189, 191-192.
        B. A. Uspenskij, Tipologičeskaja klassifikacija jazykov kak osnova jazykovyx sootvetstvij (Struktura jazyka-ètalona pri tipologičeskoj klassifikacii jazykov), VJaz, 1961, 6, p. 51-64.
        H. Birnbaum, On Typology, Affinity and Balkan Linguistics, Zbornik za filologiju i lingvistiku, IX, 1966, p. 17-30.
        _____, Slavjanskie jazyki na Balkanax i ponjatie tak nazyvaemyx jazykovyx sojuzov, Glossa, II, 1968, p. 70-92.
        G. Reichenkron, Der Typus der Balkansprachen, Zeitschrift für Balkanologie, I, 1962, p. 91-122.
        J. Matl, Das romanische Element am Balkan mit besonderer Berücksichtigung der italoromanischen Kulturausstrahlung, in: III. Grazer Balkanologen -Tagung 1968, Munich, 1968, p. 33-52.
        See also the bibliography in fn. 287.

texts. Many of these lexical changes occurred in the text
of the Psalter and in other Church Slavic texts as well[498].
For a better understanding of the change of the Church Slavic lexicon in Bulgaria from the 10th - 11th centuries until
the end of the 14th century, one must study in detail all
texts available in old and newer variants. My study of the
lexical changes in the Four Gospels text (IAG) indicates
that they are significant and should be reported in detail
in a separate work. Below will be given, in brief, as they
pertain to the theme of this dissertation, the general types
of lexical changes in the Middle Bulgarian literary language.

4.5.1. Although the revision of the text of the
Four Gospels must have been made so as to bring the Slavic
translation closer to the Greek original, Greek and Hebrew
lexical borrowings in OCS have been systematically purged
from the language of IAG. Here are examples: аромат́ъı →
воньми благо҂ханными (p. 267b); аромат́ъ т муро → вон҄ѧ
й помазание (p. 209); архиереи→старѣишны жрьтьскы(p. 197);
власфимиѧ → хоулѧ(p. 92); гнафеи → бѣлⷣилникъ(p. 110);
еⷩкение (in Mar.) is свѧштениіа (in the other OCS texts)→
ѡбновлениа (p. 242b); ỷпокрити → лицемѣрии (p. 65); катапе-
тазма → завѣса (p. 208b); кентѷриона → сѣтника (p.132b);
мисѣ → блюдѣ (p. 44); мироіѧ →мастиѧ (p. 159b);
мѷромь → мастиѧ (p. 159); олѣⷯи → масла(p. 72b); олокав-

_____

498. L. S. Kovtun, Russkaja leksikografija
èpoxi Srednevekov'ja, Moscow-Leningrad, 1963, p. 155-215.

томатъ ⟶ съжигаюмыхъ (p. 121); параклитъ ⟶ оутѣшитель
(p. 256b); параскевѣии ⟶ пѧтькъ (p. 132); паропсидѣ ⟶
блюдоу (p. 68); пирѫ ⟶ врѣтище (p. 203); пирѣı ⟶ въ лага-
лища (p. 101b); хризмъı нарѣдънъı пистикиѧ драгъı (Mar.)
⟶ масти нарды вѣрныѫ многоцѣнны (p. 124b); преторъ ⟶
сѫдище (p. 262b); равьвии ⟶ оучителю (p. 218), but
раввоуни is twice replaced by равви (pp. 116, 268b);
сѵкаминѣ ⟶ агодичинѣ (p. 188b); сѵкоморыѫ ⟶ ѩгоди-
чинѕ (p. 193, in a different hand); скандалъ ⟶ съ-
блазнь (p. 53b); сканьдѣлъı (Mar.) is съблазнъı in all
other OCS texts ⟶ съблазньникы (p. 42); скандалисаєтъ ⟶ съ-
блазнить (p. 53); скиниѧ ⟶ сѣни (p. 166); скинопигиѣ ⟶
потьчѣнїе кѫщъ (p. 231b, in a different hand); прıемъ
спирѫ ⟶ поюмъ воины (p. 260b); спира ⟶ воини (p. 261);
стадии ⟶ пьприщь (p. 245); стратигомъ ⟶ воюводамъ (p. 204);
тетрархъ ⟶ четврѣтовластьцъ (p. 43b); отъ вонѧ хризмь-
нъıѧ ⟶ ѿ маꚍти благовонныѧ (p. 248); литрѫ хризмъı ⟶
стъклѣницѫ мира (p. 247b); похризмити ⟶ помазати (p. 125);
хризма ⟶ масть (p. 124b); хризмьнаѣ ⟶ мастнаа (p. 124b).

    In the process of replacing the Greek and Hebrew
words with Slavic equivalents, the scribe once even translated a place name - that of the town of Decapolis: по
немь йдошѫ народи мнози ѿ галилѣѧ и десѧтихъ градъ (p. 15b,
Matth. IV.25). Later in the text, however, he left the
Greek name for the town unchanged: й иде й начѧть пропо-
вѣдати вь декаполи юлико створи ємоу Іс (p. 99b, Mark V.20).

This replacement process is well attested in the classical OCS texts, where most of the above listed Slavic substitutions occur in alternation with the foreign borrowings. In IAG it is almost completed; while a few doublets such as равви /оучителю, ипокрити/лицемѣрии still exist, most of the above listed foreign words are not attested at all in IAG (гнафеи, еӥкениѐ, кентѵрионъ, миса, олокавтоматъ, параклитъ, параскевѣӈии, паропсида, сѵкамина,скинделъ,etc.).

4.5.2. Another large group of words, attested in most of the classical OCS texts but systematically avoided in IAG, consists mostly of words unknown in today's Bulgarian dialects. Only a few of these words survived in Bulgarian, either with a somewhat different meaning (вратьникъ – 'gate' vs., in OCS, 'doorman'; заклепе – 'strike a bell' vs., in OCS, 'lock in') or with the same meaning as in OCS, but in only a few dialects (мѫдъна, наваждена, скриницѫ). Here given in their basic dictionary form, are words found in OCS texts but consistently replaced in IAG, most likely as archaisms or dialectisms; they are followed by their replacements in IAG and the page number of each: балии – врачь , (p. 92b) 'doctor'; вратьникъ – дверникъ , (p. 124) 'doorman'; врътъ – врътоградъ , (p. 260b) 'orchard'; гороушьнъ, горюшьнъ – гороушиченъ(pp. 52, 41b), горчиченъ(pp. 180b, 188b) 'mustard', adj.;доволъ – имѣнïе,(p. 183) 'cost, expense'; дрѧхлъ (Mar.) or дрѧселъ (Zogr.) — печаленъ, (p. 114) 'sad'; жалии (Mar.)— гробъ,(p. 26b) 'tombs';

заседьникъ — прѣлогатаи(p. 197) 'spy'; tспъ — горѣ,
(p. 246) 'up there'; клепити - назнаменовати, (p. 263)
'signify'; кънигчии - книжникъ, (p. 67b) 'bookman'; заклепе (Mar.) or заключи (Zogr.)- затвори, (p. 146) 'lock
in'; кокотъ, коуръ - пѫтелъ, (p. 77) ' rooster'; ладиа —
корабль, (p. 89b) 'boat'; маломошть - бѣдникъ, (p. 182)
or бѣденъ, (p. 112b) 'maimed, crippled'; мошьна - пира,
(p. 30b) 'skin for holding water'; мьнити - понижати.
(p. 220b) 'to shorten, make smaller'; мѫдьнъ - кьсенъ,
(p. 210b) 'slow, late'; натроути — накръмити, (p. 74b)
'to feed'; неврѣдоу сътворишѫ - не брѣгошѫ (pp. 64,197)
не вьсхотѣшѫ, (p. 119) 'reject'; подъпѣга, подъбѣга —
поушеница, (p. 18), поушена,(p. 56b) 'divorced woman';
прапрѫдьнъ, прѣпрѫдьнъ — багрѣнъ,(p. 263b) 'red'; пѣнѫжь-
никъ — трѫжникъ,(p. 194b) 'banker, usurer'; рыбытва —
рыбарь (p. 150) 'fisherman'; склѫбь, дѣло — ѡбразъ,(p. 65)
'relief, portrait'; скриница, рачица - ковчежець,(p. 252b)
'box'; соулѣе - оуне, (p. 224) 'better'; соулѣиши - лоучьши,(p. 175b) 'best'; соударъ — оуброусъ, (p. 268) 'ker-
chief'; ιѧдро — скоро (p. 182b) 'soon'.

Some of the words in this list had already been
replaced in some of the OCS texts, which indicates the existence of dialectal lexical variants in the oldest preserved OCS texts. In this respect IAG shows a further
development in this evolutionary process of removing from
the language obsolete and strictly dialectal words.

4.5.3. The bulk of the lexical replacements in IAG represent true or near synonyms, used in some instances in free alternation (ложе - одръ; печаленъ - скръбенъ), and in others interchanged to achieve a better, more precise translation (въ огнь вьметомо - вь пещь вьмѣтаюмо, p. 21). This is the most interesting type of lexical change in IAG, for it shows the slow but steady improvement of the OCS translations. The type of lexical replacement by synonymous or closely related words involved the following groups:

a) Words with different lexical morphemes, denoting identical or close concepts. Here are a few examples of these contextually-based changes: въздрастъ (all OCS) - ꙗко съмыслъ иматъ (p. 240b, John IX.23) 'he is of age'; глашаетъ (all OCS) - и своꙗ ѻвцѧ зоветь по имени (p. 241b, John X.3) 'call by name'; възгласитъ кокотъ (Mar.), коуръ (Zogr., Ostr.) - ꙗко прѣжде даже не вьспоють пѧтель, три краты (p. 205, Luke XXII.61) 'the cock crows'; пригласи (all OCS) - призвавъ же жениха архитриклинъ и гла юмоу. (p. 217, John II.10) 'call (someone)'; не зови (all OCS) - не глашаи дроугъ своихъ (p. 182, Luke XIV.12) 'invite, call'; исповѣдѣ (all OCS) - и ѻбѣща сѧ, и искааше подоⵊбна врѣмене да юго прѣдастъ без народа. (p. 201-201b, Luke XXII.6) 'commit oneself'; кънигъ (all OCS) - или сего писаниꙗ нѣсте чьли (p. 119, Mark XII.10) 'scripture'; льсть (all OCS) - разоумѣв же лѧкав'ство ихъ, рѣче имъ. (p. 197, Luke XX.23) 'craftiness'; а знамениѣ врѣменемь не можете

(all OCS) - не разоумѣ́ете (p. 49, Matth. XVI.3) 'understand, conceive'; недостоини (all OCS) - ꙗ́ко раби непо-
трѣбни ѥ́смы (p. 189, Luke XVII.10) 'worthless'; зо́лъ,
зъльꙁи (all OCS) - родъ лѫ́кавъ и́ прѣлюбодѣивъ, знамениꙗ
и́щетъ (p. 49, Matth. XVI.4) 'wicked, cunning'; съвѣдѣтель-
ствоуѥте (all OCS) - вы сами мнѣ послоушьствоуете. ꙗ́ко
рѣхъ нѣ́смъ а́́зъ х҃с. (p. 220, John III.28) 'to witness one'
words'; сътворѧтъ (и) ц҃рѣ (all OCS) - и поставѧты и́ ц҃рѣ
(p. 228, John VI.15) 'to make (one) a king'; въскрѣ́ситъ
сѣмѧ (all OCS) - въставить племѧ брата своѥго (p. 197b,
Luke XX.28) 'to resurrect the seed, reestablish the kin of';
тѣло (all OCS) - идеже троупъ, тоу и́ о́рли съберѫтъ сѧ:
(p. 190b, Luke XVII.36) 'corpse'; оужасаахѫ сѧ (all OCS)
- и́ дивлѣахѫ сѧ, и́ послѣдоуѫще, боꙗхѫ сѧ (p. 115, Mark
X.32) 'be amazed'; хотѧште (all OCS) - се҃ мт҃и твоꙗ и́
братиꙗ твоа вънѣ стоѧтъ и́скѫще гл҃ати тебѣ (p. 39, Matth.
XII.47) 'wanting, desiring'; шюмъ (all OCS) - и́ исхождаа-
ше слоухъ ѡ́ немъ въ всѣко мѣсто и́ странѫ. (p. 149, Luke
IV.37) 'rumor'.

   b)   Some of these changes, involving the use of
words with different lexical morphemes, are interesting in
that they occur within a group of words denoting the same
concept or object, from which the contextually-based choices
are different in IAG than in the OCS texts although no lexical morpheme is lost.   Here are two examples of this kind
of slight shift in the semantics of words: иночѧдъ - едино-

родень (p. 166b), while бештѧдъ is preserved, but with a different suffix, бесчѧденъ (p. 197b); however, не оставльше чѧдъ is changed to не ѻставльше сѣмене (p. 197b) and не възненавидитъ ... чѧдъ becomes не възненавидить ... дѣти (p. 183). In addition, дѣтищемъ is changed to отрочищемь (p. 34), while ѡтрокъı becomes дѣти (p. 10b). The second example: воеводами → влⷦ҇ками (p. 122b), while влкоѭ → властиѧ (p. 24b) but влⷦ҇ка → вождь (p. 9); власть → ѡбласть (pp. 213b, 242b), yet областъ → власть (pp. 118b, 196).

c) A great number of lexical changes involve only a change of the prefixes, which is both a lexical and a morphological innovation. Here are a few examples: възмѧти сѧ → смѧти сѧ (p. 24b); възвѣси сѧ → ѻбѣси сѧ (p. 80b); възвахъ → призвахъ (p. 10b); ищистити → ѻчистити (p. 24); положишѧ → възложишѫ (p. 82b); прогнѣвавъ сѧ → разгнѣвав сѧ (p. 55b); пропѧтъ → распѧть (p. 81b); пропѧтие → распѧтие (p. 82); прокопавъше → раскопавше (p. 91b); оусѣци → ѿсѣци (p. 17b); оустани → прѣстани (p. 98); сънѣдаѭтъ → изѣдаѭтъ (p. 198b). Some unprefixed words become prefixed: дѣлителѣ → раздѣлителѣ (p. 176); зъданию → създанию (p. 123); ѣдь → сънѣдь (p. 88b); in other words the prefix is introduced either after the first lexical morpheme in a compound (благо-волихъ → блⷢ҇го-из=волихъ, p. 146) or after the negative morpheme не (не-чааниѣ → не-на=чаанїа, p. 200b; не-оумѣхѫ → не-до=оумѣхѫ, p. 127b).

d) A relatively smaller group represents derivations from the same lexical morphemes as the words in the
parallel OCS phrases, but with different suffixes, which
sometimes cause phonological changes in the lexical morpheme
as, for example: четврътовласть<u>ник</u>ъ ⟶ четврътовласт<u>ец</u>ъ
(p. 146); с<u>ъ</u>прѣ ⟶ с<u>ъ</u>пер<u>ника</u>, (p. 190b); невѣрь<u>ство</u> ⟶
невѣрь<u>ствие</u>, (p. 43); невѣрь<u>ствию</u> ⟶ невѣ<u>рию̆</u>, (p. 111);
невѣръ<u>ство</u> ⟶ невѣ<u>рие</u>, (p. 101); об<u>ѣданиимъ</u> ⟶ об<u>ыадѐнїемъ</u>,
(p. 200b); слоу<u>хъ</u> ⟶ слы<u>шанїа</u>, (p. 122); призра<u>къ</u> ⟶ при-
зрѣ<u>нїе</u>, (p. 104); прокаже<u>ниѣ</u> ⟶ прока<u>зы</u>, (p. 150b).

e) There are many other kinds of lexico-grammatical changes in IAG, which will be united in this group
for brevity of exposition. Substantives are replaced by
substantivized adjectives (<u>слѣпецъ</u> ⟶ <u>слѣпыи</u>, p. 116; <u>грѣ-</u>
<u>шъникъ</u> ⟶ <u>грѣшень</u>, p. 240b; <u>недѫжьникъ</u> ⟶ <u>недѫжныѫ</u>,
p. 101); combinations of substantive with 'empty' verb are
replaced by verbs (<u>съвѣтъ сътворишѫ</u> ⟶ <u>съвѣщашѫ сѫ</u>, p. 75)
and vice versa (<u>трождаате</u> женѫ ⟶ <u>троуды даете</u> женѣ,
p. 75b); the verbs <u>творити</u> and <u>дѣати</u> are exchanged in combination with different substantives (прѣлюбъı <u>творити</u> ⟶
прѣлюби <u>дѣати</u>, p. 56b, while молитвѫ <u>дѣаше</u> ⟶ молитвѫ
<u>творѣаше</u>, p. 90b), etc.

In one instance the change in the text is purely
ideological, reflecting a changed interpretation of the
Christian ideal of poverty, and may have been triggered by
a like change in the Greek original. In Mark X.23, all OCS

texts read as in <u>Mar.</u>: ι възьрѣвъ ис҃ъ гл҃а оученикомъ
своимъ. како не оудобь <u>имѫщеи</u> <u>богатьство</u>. въ ц҃рствие б҃жие
вънидѫтъ. In IAG the phrase <u>имѫщеи</u> <u>богатьство</u> 'those who
have wealth' has been replaced by <u>оуповаѭщимъ</u> <u>на</u> <u>богатьство</u>
'those who rely on (their) wealth' (p. 114).

The extensive lexical changes in the text of IAG
greatly improved the quality of the translation. Compared
with the lexicon of the classical OCS Gospel texts, the lexicon of IAG is much more stabilized, with fewer foreign borrowings and fewer words used in free alternation, and with a
more precise contextual usage of those words attested in the
classical texts. There are almost no neologisms in IAG; on
the contrary, a great number of perhaps dialectal words in
the classical OCS texts has been systematically purged from
the language of IAG. There is no doubt, from the lexicolo-
gical point of view, that the language of IAG is far superi-
or to that of any of the classical OCS Gospel texts.

CONCLUSIONS

There have been many misconceptions in the traditional understanding of the causes of the second South Slavic influence on the Russian literary language and literature of the late 14th - 15th centuries, as well as of the extent of that influence and of the mechanisms behind it. In this dissertation, the prevailing authoritative opinions and arguments on the problem have been examined, and in many cases revised, with the aid of historical counter - arguments and data from the medieval Slavic literatures.

The Turkish conquest of the South Slavic countries - Bulgaria and Serbia - did not cause, nor even accelerate, the second South Slavic influence in Russia, but rather created obstacles to the cultural interchange among the Christian nations in the area and destroyed some prominent Slavic cultural centers in the Balkans. The historically unjustified linking of the Turkish conquest of Bulgaria and Serbia (which was accomplished from 1364 to 1459) with the second South Slavic influence in Russia was brought about by the assumption that there were Bulgarian and Serbian "refugees" in Russia in the late 14th - early 15th centuries. There is no historical evidence that such "refugees" existed; the appointment of two Bulgarians - Kiprian and Camblak - as Metropolitans of Muscovite Russia and Russian Lithuania, respectively, is in no way related to the Turkish

invasion of the Balkans. Only a very few Bulgarian manuscripts were brought to Russia before 1649 - 1655, when, in
connection with Nikon's reform, Arsenij Suxanov brought to
Moscow 700 Greek and South Slavic manuscripts.

The beginning of the second South Slavic influence
on Russian is connected with the efforts of the Russians
themselves to renovate their literature after two centuries
of Tatar domination, and to create a national Russian literary language devoid of narrow dialectal grammatical and
lexical features. In the initial efforts by Russians in
this direction, South Slavic revised editions of Church
Slavic texts were used as models, but their characteristic
orthographic, grammatical and lexical features were carefully avoided in the Russian copies. The establishment of the
Middle Bulgarian orthography - and, partially, grammar and
lexicon - as normative for the Russian literary language
at the end of the 14th and in the early 15th century, must
have been caused by two factors: the authority of the Russian Metropolitans of Bulgarian origin, Kiprian and Camblak,
who doubtless regarded the Middle Bulgarian language of the
second half of the 14th century as the best, most truly
supranational Church Slavic; and the prestige of the 14th -
century Bulgarian revised editions in the monasteries of
Constantinople and Mt. Athos. Almost all of the Middle
Bulgarian manuscripts were copied by Russians in these centers of Church Slavic literature. This gave Russian copy-

ists the opportunity to learn the meanings of various South Slavic words unknown in Russia, and then to replace them by Russian or OCS synonyms in their own copies. In the same way many morphological and syntactic innovations in the South Slavic prototypes were replaced either by Russian or by OCS forms. Thus even in the first Russian copies from South Slavic manuscripts, many local features of the language were eliminated, making it a very difficult task to establish the national origin of a certain Church Slavic text from the early period - and all the more from later periods.

By the first half of the 14th century, the Middle Bulgarian literary language had acquired the characteristics of a supradialectal and, in great measure, a supranational medium of communication. Most of the OCS translations from Greek were corrected and reconciled with the texts of the originals. The revision of the Middle Bulgarian texts and language was a process which must have begun with the political unification of Bulgaria under Ioan Asěn II (1218-1241) and the re-establishment of the Church Slavic liturgy in connection with the restoration of the Tərnovo Patriarchate in 1235. This process of revision of the Church Slavic books continued through the entire 14th century; by 1337 and 1355/56, when King Ioan Aleksandər's _Psalter_ and _Four Gospels_ (IAG) were written, the orthographic, grammatical and lexical norms of the 14th-century Middle Bulgarian literary language were firmly established. There is no single historical or linguistic evidence that there was ever an orthographic and linguistic reform initiated by the Tərnovo Patriarch Euthymius, or by the Hesychasts. Patriarch Euthymius was a very prolific Bulgarian writer, one of the many translators who participated in the revision of Church Slavic texts (the Služebnik, for instance), but his role in the development of the Bulgarian literary language was modest, and in the second South Slavic influence - negligible, since he wrote mostly vitae of Bulgarian saints not celebrated by the Russian Church. The role of the Bulgarian Hesychasts in the creation of a new South Slavic hagiographic genre has been much overstated, while the contribution of the 13th - 14th century Serbian hagiographic tradition has been underestimated by many scholars. The belief that the new South Slavic style was devised by the Hesychasts, and that it was confined to the vitae, is incorrect. It was actually the predominant style in the South Slavic literature of the 13th - 14th centuries, borrowed from contemporaneous Byzantine literature, and is to be found even in the language of Golden Bulls and chronicles.

Hesychasm was a mystical philosophical-religious movement, confined to the last decades of the existence of Bulgaria and Byzantium; it had nothing in common with the humanism of the Renaissance. Hesychasm never spread in Russia as a trend in the spiritual life of the country. The

Metropolitan Kiprian was never known as a Hesychast, while
the Metropolitan Camblak, at the time when he became head of
the Russian-Lithuanian Church, severed all ties with the
Byzantine Church and accepted the leadership of Rome, thus
bringing Russian Lithuania temporarily into the Western cultural sphere.

The Middle Bulgarian literary language of the 14th
century, in its best samples - books made for the King,
manuscripts in the prosperous monasteries in Constantinople
and on Mt. Athos - was a highly normalized system. Most
of the innovations in the orthography (relative to that of
the known OCS texts of the 10th and 11th centuries) are in
the direction of the firm establishment of morphonemic spelling rules and the avoidance, as much as possible, of phonological spellings reflecting typically Bulgarian features.
The only two instances in which the scribe failed to rise
above the Bulgarian phonological system were in the confusion of the letters denoting the two OCS nasal vowels, and
in the use of the letters ꙗ and ѣ to represent both etymological *ě and *ja. But in the latter respect, the Middle
Bulgarian texts are not very different from the OCS cyrillic
texts, with the exception that a new mechanical principle
of distribution is consistently applied to these letters:
ѣ after a letter denoting a consonant, ꙗ in word initial
position or after a letter denoting a vowel. In their
orthographical devices, the good Middle Bulgarian texts of

the 14th century strikingly resemble both the classical cyrillic OCS texts and the contemporaneous Byzantine texts; this made them attractive models for imitation by Russians seeking to revive the Church Slavic literature of the older period and to bring it up to the level of the Byzantine literature of their own time.

The grammar of the best Middle Bulgarian texts is little different from the grammar of the OCS texts from Bulgaria. There are very few instances of systematic grammatical innovation in the literary language, and most of the archaic and newer alternating forms are already registered in the OCS texts. The drastic grammatical changes in the structure of the Bulgarian dialects by the 14th century are very seldom represented in the literary language; they were easily avoidable, in copying, as "mistakes". But most of the Balkan structural features of Bulgarian, appearing sporadically as freely alternating forms in the literary language, cannot be considered innovations, since they are attested in the OCS texts from Bulgaria. Moreover, they are valuable tools in determining the Bulgarian origin of a Russian or Serbian copy, when a Bulgarian copy is lacking for comparison.

The Middle Bulgarian texts differ from OCS mostly in the lexicon. While there are few neologisms in the revised OCS translations, many archaic and dialectal words, as well as foreign borrowings, have been purged from the language, and the attested OCS words are used more precisely in different contexts, and less in free alternation, than in OCS. Thus the old translations were brought closer to the Greek originals, made more correct and improved stylistically. In the newer translations from Byzantine Greek, many neologisms, especially compound words, were created, following Greek derivational models and OCS tradition. But the problem of Middle Bulgarian word formation should be treated separately in a special study.

With all its orthographic, grammatical and lexical peculiarities, the language of the revised OCS translations, newer translations and original Slavic writings in 14th - century Bulgaria had unique qualities which made it acceptable, with slight modifications, as a supranational literary language. This is the main reason it played such a major part in the second South Slavic influence on Russian.

So far it has been impossible fully to determine the extent of the second South Slavic influence on the Russian literature of the late 14th and 15th centuries, because of the enormous number of manuscripts of the period, kept in Soviet libraries and museums. But while the influence of the Middle Bulgarian language - orthography, grammar, lexicon - has been established earlier by Sobolevskij and Lixačev, and the causes and mechanisms of this influence have been re-examined in this dissertation, any real influence of Bulgarian manuscript illumination in Russia is most improbable, as is the very existence of a Bulgarian school of manuscript illumination.

Bulgarian art and literature of the 14th century, in their best exemplars, definitely lack national characteristics: they were part of the Byzantine culture, and were prized by the Russians exactly for that reason. Thus the second South Slavic influence in Russia, generally speaking, served as a shortcut in raising the Russian literature and cultural and spiritual life to the level of their Byzantine counterparts.

APPENDICES

Appendix One:

ѐлма оу̑бо быстъ мановение б҃а ѡ҃ца и̑ г҃а нашего Ї̑исоу҃ хрїста. ходатаиствомъ сѫщыѫ и̑ истиньныѫ прѣчистыѫ и̑ прѣбл҃гословеныѫ вл҃дцѫ и̑ бг҃ородителницѫ, на ст҃ѣи горѣ а̏ѳон- стѣи еже быти въ неи пристанище сп҃сениоу въсѣкои д҃ши хрїс- тиан'стѣи паче же православнѣи̑. и̑ съ оу̑сръдиемъ прѣбѣгаѫщои въ неи. ѐ̑ѫже ради вины, и̑ въздвигошѫ троудолюбезнѣ мноѕи. дѡмовы стыѫ велики и̑ дивны. ц҃рие бл҃гочестивии. и̑ бѡголюбивии вельмѫже. и̑ прѣподобнии и̑нѡ́ци. и̑ оу̑красїшѫ и̑ ѡ̑бѡгатишѫ въсѣ- ко. камениемъ мнѡгоцѣннымъ и̑ бис҃рѡмъ златом же. и̑ сребрѡмъ и̑ имáн'ми и̑ инѣми правдами мнѡгыми. движимыми и̑ недвижимыми. ѐже быти въ довóльство и̑ и̑зобїлие сѫщимъ и̑ прѣбываѫщиимъ въ таковыихъ въсечестныи̑хъ и̑ бж҃ествъныи[х] дѡмовохъ. поѫщихъ и̑ славѧщихъ ѐдїного бг҃а въ трои̑ци славимаго. и̑ прѣчистѫѫ и въсепѣтѫѫ ѐго матере. поминати же и̑ православныѫ и̑ хрїсто- любивыѫ и̑ присно памѧтныѫ ц҃рѧ. и̑ прочаѫ блаженыѫ ктиторы и̑ въсѣкъ рѡдъ хрїстиансы. и̑бо. не ѿ ѐдїного рѡда тъчиѫ и̑ли ѿ двою̑. ѡ̑брѣтаѫт сѧ въ томъ ст҃ѣмъ мѣстѣ здáтеле, нѫ понеже ѡ̑бьщее сп҃сение въ немъ ѐст' и̑скаѫщиимъ ю̏. ѡ̑б'ще бѡ̏ бысть и̑ мѣсто благовольствоуѫщиимъ. тѡ́го ради. и̑ ѡ̑брѣтаѫт сѧ зда- ниа ѿ въсѣкого рѡда и̑ ѧ̑зыка православнаго. ѐже сѫтъ пръвѣе и̑ и̑зрѧднѣи̑шее. гръци. блъгаре. по тѡм же. сръбъе̏. роусси. и̑вере. въсѣкъ же и̑матъ памѧть протївѫ своѐмоу потроуждению̑.

паче же ръвениоу.

G. A. Il'inskij, <u>Gramoty bolgarskix carej</u>
(Drevnosti. Trudy Slavjanskoj kommissii Imperator-
skogo Moskovskogo arxeologičeskogo obščestva, V.),
Moscow, 1911 (Photoedition: London, 1970), p.21-22.

A p p e n d i x   T w o:

таковаа нѣкаа цвѣтнаа пъстрота н҃бо оукрашааше.

такова нѣкаа належааше н҃бсномоу лицоу· многозрачнаа и̇ радост-

наа и̇ доброзрачна красота· и врътоградъ новонасажденъ н҃бо

творѣше, е̇моу же врътоградаръ б҃ъ· ꙗ̇ко садовиа же и̇ ѿрасли,

и ꙗ̇ко цвѣтиа многоразличнаа, свѣздныꙗ свѣтлости. тогда пръ-

вѣе с҃лнцоу вьсиавшоу и̇ просъвтѣвъшоу сѧ. ꙗ̇вльши же сѧ кра-

сотѣ н҃бснѣи и̇ добротѣ дневнѣи, послоужишѧ повелѣнию сътвор-

шаго· и прѣклонии‖въ съвръши д҃нь четвръты̇· си̇це оубѡ съвръ-

шишѧ сѧ ꙗ̇же о̇ свѣздахъ· и̇ оучинено бы҃с с҃лнце свѣзда д҃нь

съдръжащиа: лоунное же бръвно просвѣщааше нощь·

I. Dujčev (ed.), <u>Letopista na Konstantin
Manasi</u> (Fototipno izdanie na Vatikanskija prepis
na srednobəlgarskija prevod), Sofia, 1963, pp.6,9.

A p p e n d i x   T h r e e:

ц҃рство таркі̇ниево, и̇же пѧтыи бы҃с ц҃рь по рѡмилѣ

въ римѣ· и̇ по томъ ц҃рствова таркиние, пѧтыи по рѡмилѣ, ни-

чим же е̇моу прилежꙗще пріемъ ц҃рство. и̇бо с҃новомъ достоино бѣ

ц҃рствовати, маркиа ц҃рѣ·

ц҃рство тилі̇ево·

и̇ по томъ зѧть таркиниевъ, тилие ц҃рств҃ва. иже изь

детьства ꙗ̇ко же г҃лѧтъ и̇ ѿ пръваго възраста, нареченъ бы҃с

- 373 -

сервие, ꙗко рѡдив сѧ ѿ рабы. тлъкоует бѡ сѧ ‖ сервие, рабъ
римлѣны. съи припрѧже дъщерь своѫ на бракъ съ цр҃евѣмъ сы-
нѡмъ· левкїа таркиниа. ею же единѣмъ съвѣтѡмъ и̇ разоумомъ
оу̇бииствнымъ· и̇ живота и̇ власти ѡ̇каанныи лишенъ бы́с. и̇
съвѣтѡмъ о̇пшиимъ, соупервъ наре꙳ сѧ· грѣдаго же по тлькоу
и̇хъ сице нарицаѫтъ.

            I. Dujčev (ed.), <u>Letopista na Konstantin
Manasi</u>, Sofia, 1963, p. 136-137.

A p p e n d i x   F o u r :

цр҃ство <u>василиа македѡнѣнина</u>:

съи абие фѡ́тїа и̇згна ѿ цркве. и̇ пакы ѿдастъ прѣ-
столъ и̇гна́тиеви. ‖ въсхотѣв же и̇ нарѡдоу и̇мѣние ѿдати. и̇
и̇зыскавъ домовы златохранѧщѧѧ. и̇же пръвѣе сътѧзаахѫ и̇мѣ-
нїѡмъ множъства. и видѣвъ въсѧ празны и ничьсѡ же и̇мѧщѫ.
скръбѣше: тѫжаше. печаловааше. оу̇нывааше. не и̇мѣше что сътво
рити си. ѿ въсѧдоу недоо̇мѣаше сѧ. цр҃ь бѡ не и̇мѣѭ и̇мѣниа
многобогатнаго, подобенъ е̇сть о̇рлоу прѣветхоу и̇ прѣстароу не
и̇мѧщоу перїа. и̇ ноктїа и клюна. сего ради и̇ василїе печаловааше и̇ тѫжаше. и̇бѡ цр҃ъ михаилъ въсѣ и̇стъщивъ и̇ глоумцемъ
раздавъ, съ и̇грѣцемъ своимъ и̇ съпирникѡмъ.

            I. Dujčev (ed.), <u>Letopista na Konstantin
Manasi</u>, Sofia, 1963, p. 328-329.

A p p e n d i x   F i v e :

        а кипрїѧнъ м҃трополитъ пс гречески гораздо не
разꙋмѣлъ и нашего ꙗзы́ка довольно не зна́лъ же. а̋ще и съ на-

ми единъ нашъ ꙗ̎зыкъ сирѣ̑ч҇ славенски. да мы̋ говори̑м҇ по
своѐм҇ꙋ ꙗзы́кꙋ чисто и шꙋ̎мко. а онѣ̏ говора̑т҇ моложано ...,
и в писа́нїи рѣ́чи на́ши с ними не схо́датсѧ. а̎ о̎нъ мнѣл'сѧ что
поправи̑л҇ ѱалмов по на́шемꙋ̎. а̎ болши неразꙋ̎мїе в ни̑х҇ напи-
са̑л҇ в рѣ́че̑х҇ и̎ слове̑х҇ все по сер̑б҇ски написа̑л҇. и ны́нѣ
мнѡ́гыꙗ оу нас и всѧ времѧ на кни́гы пишꙋ̑т҇. а̎ пишꙋ̋тъ ѿ нера-
зꙋ̎мїѧ все̏ по се́рбски ... гдѣ надобе̑т҇ по нашемꙋ̎ а, а по
сербски ѣ, и̎ли́ ѧ̑, по нашему ю, а по сербски ѧ, по нашемꙋ̎
ꙋ̎, а сербски ѧ̑, оу на̑с҇ ы, а сербски и, а рѣ́чи по нашемꙋ̎
не заме̑д҇ли, а сербски, и̎ли бꙋ̎де бо́лгарски не замꙋ́ди. по на-
шемꙋ̎ ко́сно ме̑д҇лленноѧзыченъ, или гꙋ́гни̑в҇, а̎ сербски мꙋ̎дноѧзы́-
че̑н҇. и прꙋ̎чїѧ рѣ́чи намъ неразꙋ̎мны. бохма, васнь, реснотивїе,
цѣщи, ашꙋ̎тъ. и мнѡ́го таковыхъ мы не разꙋ̎мѣемъ і̎но сербски,
а і̎но болгарски. и̎ сїѧ доселѣ недостане̑т҇. на̑м҇ лѣ́то на
повѣствованїе.

       Arximandrit Amfiloxij, Čto vnes Sv. Kiprian,
mitropolit Kievskij i vseja Rossii, a potom Moskovskij i vseja Rossii, iz svoego rodnogo narečija
i iz perevodov ego vremeni v naši bogoslužebnye
knigi?, Trudy Tret'ego Arxeologičeskogo s"ezda v
Rossii, byvšego v Kieve v avguste 1874 g., II,
Kiev, 1878, p. 231-232.

A p p e n d i x   S i x:
       слава въ тр҇о́ци, славимомоу б҇оу. съвръшаꙗ̑щомоу
вьсѣко начинаниѥ б҇лго. ꙗже ѡ немь начинаѥмомоу. и̎ даꙗ̑що-
моу, по нача́лѣ и̎ конецъ:

       писа сѧ сии животочный и̎сточникъ новыꙗ̑ блг҇д҇ти.
прѣсла̑д҇го оу̎ченїа х҇с҇ва, и̎ того бж҇с҇твныхъ самовидецъ, оу̎че-

ник же, и а̇п͡слъ. г͡лемыи четвороб͡лг̑овѣстникъ. не вънѣшнимъ

тькмо шаромъ. и̇ли златомъ. и̇ли ви̇сомъ прѣсоуканнымъ, и̇ли ка-

менї̈емь и̇ би̇сромь оу̇крашаѥмь, нж̑ вьнѫтрънимъ бж͡ствнаго сло-

ва, и̇злианїемъ и̇ таинъствнаго съмотренїа и̇спльнениѥ. ꙗ̇же

въ немь вл͡дчнѣго и̇ бж͡ствнаго вьчл͡ченї̈а. и̇ чюдодѣиства. ꙗ̇же

съврьши на͡с ради. мл͡рдї̈а же, и̇ мл͡ти. даже до кр͡ста и̇ по-

гребенїа. и̇ славнаго тридневнаго въскр͡сенї̈а. и̇ вьзнесенїа.

и̇ кто доволенъ порѧдоу и̇счьсти и̇ли и̇зг͡лати ꙗ̇же вь немь

въо̇браже‖ние дѣиствъ х͡свѣхъ. по и̇стинѣ ꙗ̇ко же и̇сточникоу

ꙗ̇вльшоу сѧ вь земли безводнѣи, и̇ жѫждѫи кто пиеть ѿ него,

не вьжѫж͡дет сѧ к томоу. точить бо строѫ, и̇ наслаждаѥть

д͡шж. веселить ср͡дце, въ коупѣ и̇ помышленїа. и̇ли ꙗ̇коже

скровищоу съкрꙑвеноу, на селѣ ср͡дечномь. сиѥ̇ вьзыскавъ ѡ̇б-

рѣте, бл͡говѣрныи, и̇ х͡столюбивыи. прѣвысѡкыи, и̇ б͡говѣнчанныи

самодрьжець І̇ѡ̇а́нь а̇ле́ѯан͡дрь ц͡рь. ꙗ̇коже свѣтилникоу положе-

ноу въ темнѣ мѣстѣ. и̇ забьвеноу и̇ въ нерадение положеноу

древними ц͡ри. ѥ̇го же бж͡ствнымь желаниемь и̇зъѡ̇брѣте съи

хр͡столюбивыи ц͡рь .І̇ѡ̇. а̇леѯандрь. и̇ и̇зложивъ прѣписа. и̇зь

е̇ллиньскы͡х словесь, вь нашж словѣнскѫѫ слогнѫ, и̇ въ ꙗ̇вле-

ние положи. сего и̇зьвьноу златыми дьсками покова́, и̇ вьн-

ѫтрѧ̇доу, животворными ѡ̇бразы вл͡дчными, и̇ того славныхъ

о̇ученикъ. шары ‖ свѣтлыми и̇ златомь. живо́писцы хѫдожнѣ оу̇кра

сивь. на отврѫждение своемоу ц͡рствоу. ꙗ̇коже великыи вь ст͡хъ

кѡнстандинъ ц͡рь сь м͡триж е̇ленож, и̇знесь и̇з боукоу земною

животворивыи кр͡стъ г͡нь, си̇це и̇ сь, сего четвороб͡лг̑овѣс͡тника:

съдрьжѫщоу тогда ски̇птра бл͡гарскаго, и̇ грьчькаго

цр͡ства. съ благовѣрнож и ͠бг͡овѣнчанно҄ж и новопросвѣ͡шно҄ж

ц͡рце҄ж своеѧ кира θео͡Дро҄ж. тьзоймет҄нож ͠бж͡и҄иемоу дароу. и съ

присныимъ и прѣвьзлюбленымь с͡номь своимь і͡ѡа҄номъ шишманомь

ц͡ремъ: вь славж творцоу все͡х҄, и того ͠бл͡говѣстьник҄ѡ͡м. матθе҄ю.

ма́ркоу. лоуцѣ. и і͡ѡа҄ноу. и҄х же молитвами. побѣдж да прїиме͡Т.

ѿ ͠ба, на врагы ратоуѧщихъ того. и главы ихъ ськрꙋ́ши͡Т по͡Д

носѣ сво͡и҄, с а́ми͡н +

        лѣтоу текжщоу, ҂ѕ͡ѡ͡ѯд͡. ͟индїкта ͡θ: ⁓

        + ра͠б же ͠гна моего ц͡рѣ, писавыи сиж книг҄ж, сїмѡнъ

мни͡х нарицает сѧ: ⤙

        IAG (microfilm copy of the manuscript), p.275-
276. This text is easily available only in modern
Bulgarian, in the translation by I. Dujčev in
Starobəlgarski stranici. Antologija, Sofia, 1968,
p. 456-457. The original was published by F. Uspenskij in Žurnal Ministerstva narodnogo prosveščenija, 199, St.Petersburg, 1878. Since Dujčev's
translation is extremely free, I have made the
English translation from the original, which is
quoted in this dissertation.

BIBLIOGRAPHY

BIBLIOGRAPHY

Of the Most Important Works Consulted for this Dissertation

AN SSSR (B. D. Grekov, ed.), <u>Dokumenty</u> <u>k</u> <u>istorii</u> <u>slavjano-</u>
  <u>vedenija</u> <u>v</u> <u>Rossii</u> <u>(1850-1912)</u>, Moscow-Leningrad,
  1948, 407 pp.

AN SSSR (Ju. V. Bromlej, I. S. Dostjan, V. G. Karasaev,
  S. A. Nikitin, ed's.), <u>Istorija</u> <u>Jugoslavii</u>, 1,
  Moscow, 1963, 736 pp.

AN SSSR, <u>Istorija</u> <u>Vizantii</u>, 3, Moscow, 1967, 507 pp.

Adrianova-Peretc, V. P., Drevnerusskie literaturnye pamjatniki v jugoslavjanskoj pis'mennosti, <u>Trudy</u> <u>ODRL</u>,
  XIX, Moscow-Leningrad, 1963, p. 5-27.

Aleksandrov, F., O značenijax i funkcijax mestoimenij
  "kotoryj", "iže" i "kyj" v osnovnyx pamjatnikax
  drevnebolgarskogo jazyka, <u>Slavističen</u> <u>sbornik</u>, I,
  Sofia, 1958, p. 145-163.

Andersen, H., The Phonological Status of the Russian
  "Labial Fricatives", <u>Journal</u> <u>of</u> <u>Linguistics</u>, 5,
  1969, p. 121-127.

Andreev, M., Kəm vəprosa za sključvaneto i səderžanieto na
  dogovora na dobrudžanskija vladetel Ivanko s genue-
  zite ot 1387 g., <u>Pravna</u> <u>misəl</u>, 1961, 3.,p. 79-93.

Andriotes, N. P., <u>The</u> <u>Confederate</u> <u>State</u> <u>of</u> <u>Skopje</u> <u>and</u> <u>its</u>
  <u>Language</u>, Athens, 1957, 68 pp.

Angelov, B. St., K voprosu o načale russko-bolgarskix literaturnyx svjazej, <u>Trudy</u> <u>ODRL</u>, XIV, Moscow - Leningrad, 1958, p. 132-138.

_____, ed., <u>Iz starata bəlgarska</u>, <u>ruska</u> <u>i</u> <u>srəbska</u> literatura, 1, Sofia, 1958, 238 pp. + viii plates; 2, Sofia, 1967, 279 pp.

_____, Apokrifi (in: <u>Istorija</u> <u>na</u> <u>bəlgarskata</u> <u>lite-</u> <u>ratura</u>, 1), Sofia, 1963, p. 178-192.

Angelov, D., <u>Agrarnite</u> <u>otnošenija</u> <u>v</u> <u>Severna</u> <u>i</u> <u>Sredna</u> <u>Make-</u> <u>donija</u> <u>prez</u> <u>XIV</u> <u>v.</u>, Sofia, 1958, p. 9-15.

_____, Kəm vəprosa za srednovekovnija bəlgarski grad, <u>Arxeologija</u>, 1960, 3, p. 9-22.

_____, Vəprosi na feodalizma v bəlgarskite zemi prez XIII - XIV v., <u>IstPr</u>, 1960, 6, p. 61-90.

_____, Svetogledət na gospodstvuvaštata klasa v srednovekovna Bəlgarija, otrazen v žitijnata literatura, <u>IzvII</u>, 14-15, 1964, p. 263-294.

Arxangel'skij, A. S., Bolgarskij "pesnivec" 1337 goda. "Poxvala" i otryvok psaltyrnogo teksta, <u>IzvORJaS</u>, II, 3, St. Petersburg, 1897 (Photoedition: Graz, 1964), p. 786-794.

_____, K istorii južnoslavjanskoj i drevne- russkoj apokrifičeskoj literatury. Dva ljubopytnyx sbornika Sofijskoj Narodnoj biblioteki v Bolgarii, <u>IzvORJaS</u>, IV, 1, St. Petersburg (Photoedition: Graz, 1964), p. 101-147.

Atanasov, P., Slavjanski kirilski inkunabuli v Bəlgarija,

BəlgEz, XIV, 1964, 2-3, p. 160-172.

Babinger, Fr. C. H., ed., Hans Dernschwamms Tagebuch einer
Reise nach Konstantinopel u. Kleinasien (1553-55),
Munich-Leipzig, 1923, 314 pp.

Bakalov, I., Materiali iz oblastta na bəlgarskata narodna
medicina, SbNUNK, XII, Sofia, 1895, p. 349-358.

Balasčev, G., Səštinski li e xrisovulət na car Konstantin
Tix (1258-1277)?, Minalo, II, Sofia, 1911, 5-6,
p. 178-179.

Beck, H. G., Theodoros Metochites. Die Krise des byzantinischen Weltbildes im XIV. Jh., Munich, 1952,
149 pp.

Begunov, Ju. K., Bolgarskij pisatel' X v. Kozma Presviter
v russkoj pis'mennosti konca XV - XVI vv., Trudy
ODRL, XIX, Moscow-Leningrad, 1963, p. 289-302.

Belić, A., Zametki o slavjanskom žitii sv. Pjatki-Petki
(s priloženiem), IzvORJaS, II, 4, St. Petersburg,
1897 (Photoedition: Graz, 1964), p. 1045-1057.

_____, Dialektologičeskaja karta serbskogo jazyka,
Stat'i po slavjanovedeniju, II, St. Petersburg,
1906, p. 58-59.

_____, O srpskim ili hrvatskim dijalektima, Beograd,
1908, 164 pp.

_____, Istorija srpskohrvatskog jezika (mimeographed
publication), Beograd, 1962 (2nd edition), II, 1,
271 pp.; II, 2, 212 pp.

Beneševič, V. N., Dva spiska slavjanskogo perevoda Sintag-
my Matfeja Vlastarja, xranjaščiesja v Spb. Sinodal'noj Biblioteke, IzvORJaS, VI, 4, St. Petersburg, 1901 (Photoedition: Graz, 1964), p. 150-227

Bernštejn, S. B., Razyskanija v oblasti bolgarskoj istoričeskoj dialektologii, 1, Moscow-Leningrad, 1948,
368 pp.

_____, K voprosu o periodizacii istorii bolgar-
skogo jazyka, IzvOLJa, 9, Moscow, 1950, 2,
p. 108-118.

_____, Očerk sravnitel'noj grammatiki slavjan-
skix jazykov, Moscow, 1961, 350 pp.

Bicilli, P. N., Glagolnata forma s -le v istorijata na
ruskija ezik, GodSU, 31, 7, Sofia, 1935, p. 1-15.

Birnbaum, H., Untersuchungen zu den Zukunftsumschreibungen
mit dem Infinitiv im Altkirchenslavischen (= Acta
Universitatis Stockholmiensis, Études de philologie slave, 6), Stockholm, 1958, 326 pp.

_____, Balkanslavisch und Südslavisch. Zur Reich-
weite der Balkanismen im südslavischen Sprachraum,
Zeitschrift für Balkanologie, III, Wiesbaden,
1965, 1-2, p. 12-63.

_____, The Dialects of Common Slavic (in: H. Birn-
baum, J. Puhvel, ed's., Ancient Indo-European
Dialects), Berkeley-Los Angeles, 1966, p. 153-197.

_____, On Typology, Affinity and Balkan Linguistics,

ZbMSFL, IX, 1966, p. 17-30.

_____, Grundkonzept und Aufgabenkreis einer ver-
gleichenden kirchenslavischen Literaturforschung
(in: Das heidnische und christliche Slaventum
(= Acta II Congressus internationalis historiae
Slavicae Salisburgo-Ratisbonensis anno 1967 cele-
brati)), Wiesbaden, 1967, p. 127-147.

_____, Slavjanskie jazyki na Balkanax i ponjatie tak
nazyvaemyx jazykovyx sojuzov, Glossa, II, Burnaby,
B.C., 1968, p. 70-92.

_____, Some Aspects of the Slavonic Renaissance,
SEER, XLVII, London, 1969, 108, p. 37-56.

_____, Byzantine Tradition Transformed: the Old
Serbian Vita (in: Aspects of the Balkans: Continuity and Change, H. Birnbaum, S. Vryonis, Jr.,
ed's.), Hague: Mouton p. 243 - 284.

Bogdan, I., Ein Beitrag zur bulgarischen und serbischen
Geschichtschreibung, AfSlPh, XIII, 1891, p. 481 -
543.

_____, Cronica lui Constantin Manasses. Traducere
mediobulgară făcută pe la 1350. Text şi glosar de
Ioan Bogdan. Cu prefaţa de prof. I. Bianu,
Bucharest, 1922 (Photoedition = Slavische Propyläen, 12, Munich, 1966), xx + 222 pp.

Boissin, H., La Manassès moyen bulgare: étude linguistique, Paris, 1946, ii + 124 pp.

Bojadžiev, S., Kəm istoričeskija razvoj na predloga na v
bəlgarskija ezik, IzvIBE, IX, 1962, p. 211-296.

Bojukliev, I., Šopov psaltir, BəlgEz, XIII, 1963, 3,
p. 234-254.

_____, Srednobəlgarski psaltiren otkəs ot XIV v.
(Šopov psaltir), Trudove na Visšija pedagogičeski
institut "Bratja Kiril i Metodi" vəv Veliko
Tərnovo, II, Sofia, 1965, p. 49-94.

Bordier, H. L., Déscription des peintures et autres ornements contenus dans les MMS grecs de la Bibliothèque Nationale, Paris, 1883, viii + 336 pp.

Bräuer, H., Der persönliche Agens beim Passiv im Altbulgarischen. Eine syntaktische Untersuchung,
Wiesbaden, 1952, 95 pp.

Budovnic, I. U., Slovar' russkoj, ukrainskoj, belorusskoj
pis'mennosti i literatury do XVIII veka, Moscow,
1962, 398 pp.

Budziszewska, W., Zapożyczenia greckie w historii języka
buɭgarskiego, Warsaw, 1969, 188 pp.

Bulaxovskij, L. A., Istoričeskij kommentarij k russkomu
literaturnomu jazyku, Kiev, 1958 (5th edition),
488 pp.

Burbury, J., A Relation of a Journey of the Right Honourable My Lord Henry Howard From London to Vienna,
and thence to Constantinople; In the Company of
his Excellency Count Lesley, Knight of the Order

of the Golden Fleece, Councellour of State to his
Imperial Majesty, etc., And Extraordinary Ambas-
sadour from Leopoldus Emperour of Germany to the
Grand Signior, Sultan Mahomet Han the Forth.
Written by John Burbury Gent. London, 1671,
225 pp.

Bunina, I. K., Istorija glagol'nyx vremen v bolgarskom
        jazyke, Moscow, 1970, 299 pp.

Bəlgarska Akademija na Naukite, Istorija na Bəlgarija, I,
        Sofia, 1961 (2nd edition), 551 pp.

Bəlgarska Akademija na Naukite (V. Velčev, E. Georgiev,
        P. Dinekov, ed's.), Istorija na bəlgarskata
        literatura, 1. Starobəlgarska literatura, Sofia,
        1963, 451 pp.

Çabej, E., Ältere Stufen des Albanischen im Lichte der
        Nachbarsprachen, Zeitschrift für Balkanologie,
        II, Wiesbaden, 1964, p. 6-32.

Camaj, M., Zur Entwicklung der Nasalvokale der slavischen
        Lehnwörter im Albanischen (in: Die Kultur Süd-
        osteuropas, ihre Geschichte und ihre Ausdrucks-
        formen), Wiesbaden, 1964, p. 18-25.

Chomsky, N., Halle, M., The Sound Pattern of English, New
        York, 1968, xiv + 470 pp.

Civ'jan, T. V., Opyt opisanija form novogrečeskogo suščest-
        vitel'nogo metodom analiza i sinteza, VJaz, 1963,
        6, p. 57-68.

————————, Imja suščestvitel'noe v balkanskix jazykax. K strukturno-tipologičeskoj xarakteristike balkanskogo jazykovogo sojuza, Moscow, 1965, 194 pp.

Conev, B., Kjustendilsko četveroevangelie - srednobəlgarski prototip na šesta pravopisna škola, PeriodSpBAN, LXVI, 1905-06, p. 536-561.

————————, Dobrejšovo evangelie, srednobəlgarski pametnik ot XIII v. (= Bəlgarski starini, I), Sofia, 1906, 264 + vi pp.

————————, Opis na rəkopisite i staropečatnite knigi na Narodnata biblioteka v Sofija, I, Sofia, 1910, 555 + xviii pp.; II (under the title Opis na slavjanskite rəkopisi v Sofijskata narodna biblioteka), Sofia, 1923, 552 + lii pp.

————————, ed., Vračansko Evangelie (= Bəlgarski starini, IV), Sofia, 1914, ix + 236 pp.

————————, Slavjanski rəkopisi na Bəlgarskata akademija, SbBAN, VI, 1916, p. 4-13.

————————, Istorija na bəlgarskij ezik, Sofia, I, 1919, x + 529 pp.; II, 1934, xvi + 560 pp.; III, 1937, vi + 505 pp.

————————, Slavjanski rəkopisi vəv Viena, GodSU, XXV, Sofia, 1929, p. 1-27.

————————, Edin srednobəlgarski pametnik ot 13 vek, GodSU, XXVII, II, 1, 1931, p. 1-50.

Cvetkova, B. A., Novye dannye o xristianax-spaxijax na Bal-

kanskom poluostrove v period tureckogo gospodstva,
Vizantijskij vremennik, XIII, Moscow, 1958,
p. 184-197.

Čaev, N. S., Čerepnin, L. V., Russkaja paleografija,
Moscow, 1946, 212 pp. + 19 plates.

Čerepnin, L. V., Russkaja paleografija, Moscow, 1956,
616 pp.

_____, Iz istorii eretičeskix dviženij na Rusi v
XIV - XV vv. (in: Voprosy istorii religii i
ateizma, VII), Moscow, 1959, p. 257-283.

Česko, E. V., Istorija bolgarskogo sklonenija, Moscow,
1970, 319 pp.

Čizevskij, D., History of Russian Literature from the
Eleventh Century to the End of the Baroque, Hague,
1960, 451 pp. + 34 plates.

_____, Comparative History of Slavic Literatures
(Translation of: Vergleichende Geschichte der
slavischen Literaturen), Baltimore, 1971, 225 pp.

Ćorović, V., Poslanica bugarskog patrijarha Jevtimija
Tismenskomu arhimandritu Nikodimu, JF, XIII,
1933-34, p. 162-165.

Dančev, G., Rilskata povest na Vladislav Gramatik i sporo-
vete okolo dvete ì redakcii, Trudove na VPI
"Bratja Kiril i Metodij" vəv Veliko Tərnovo, III,
Sofia, 1966, 1, p. 49-88.

_____, Vladislav Gramatik - knižovnik i pisatel,

Sofia, 1969, 147 pp.

Desnickaja, A. V., Slavjano-albanskie jazykovye otnošenija
i albanskaja dialektologija, Slavjanskoe jazykoznanie (VI Meždunarodnyj s"ezd slavistov), Moscow,
1968, p. 120-147.

Diels, P., Altkirchenslavische Grammatik mit einer Auswahl
von Texten und einem Wörterbuch, Heidelberg, 1963
(2nd edition), I, xvi + 309 pp.; II, 116 pp.

Dilevski, N., Kəm vəprosa za proizxoda na "Germanovija
sbornik" ot 1359, BəlgEz, XVII, 1967, 4, p. 302 -
322.

Dimitrievič, S. M., Est' li tonsury na golovax svjatitelej
v starom vostočno-pravoslavnom ikonopisanii?,
IzvBAI, X, 1936, p. 113-128.

Dinekov, P., Stara bəlgarska literatura, II, Sofia, 1953,
206 pp.

_____, Evtimij Tərnovski (in: Istorija na bəlgarska-
ta literatura, 1), Sofia, 1963, p. 285-306.

_____, Iz istorii russko-bolgarskix literaturnyx
svjazej XVI - XVIII vv., Trudy ODRL, XIX, Moscow -
Leningrad, 1963, p. 318-329.

_____, Literaturnijat život prez XIII v. (in: Isto-
rija na bəlgarskata literatura, 1), Sofia, 1963,
p. 254-266.

_____, Razkazi i povesti (in: Istorija na bəlgarska-
ta literatura, 1), Sofia, 1963, p. 164-177.

Dmitriev, L. A., Rol' i značenie mitropolita Kipriana v
   istorii drevnerusskoj literatury (k russko-bolgar-
   skim literaturnym svjazjam XIV - XV vv.), Trudy
   ODRL, XIX, Moscow-Leningrad, 1963, p. 215-254.

Dmitrieva, R. P., Svetskaja literatura v sostave monastyrskix bibliotek XV i XVI vv. (Kirillo-Belozerskogo,
   Volokolamskogo monastyrej i Troice-Sergievoj
   lavry), Trudy ODRL, Leningrad, 1968, p. 143-170.

Dobrev, I., Kəm istorijata na starobəlgarskata morfema že,
   IzvIBE, VIII, 1962, p. 111-116.

_____, Nepodkrepeno ot grəckija original povtarjane
   na predlozi v starobəlgarskite tekstove, BəlgEz,
   XVII, 1967, 6, p. 522-530.

Draganov, P., Nosovye glasnye zvuki v sovremennyx makedonoslavjanskix i bolgarskix govorax, RFV, 19, Warsaw,
   1888, p. 1-27.

Dragomanov, M. P., Slavjanskite prepravki v Edipovata
   istorija, SbNUNK, 1891, 5, p. 267-310; 6, p. 239
   - 310.

Dragova, N., Vtorata apologija na bəlgarskata kniga i nej-
   nite izvory (in: Konstantin-Kiril Filosof),
   Sofia, 1969, p. 315-347.

Drovnikova, L. N., Istorija čislitel'nyx dva, tri, četyre
   v russkom jazyke (in: Voprosy istorii russkogo
   jazyka. Sbornik statej), Moscow, 1959, p. 183-207.

Dubrovina, V. F., O leksičeskix grecizmax v original'nyx

i perevodnyx žitijnyx tekstax po russkim spiskam (in: Pamjatniki drevnerusskoj pis'mennosti, V. V. Vinogradov, ed.), Moscow, 1968, p. 117-136.

Dujčev, I.; Latinskite nadpisi po Vatikanskija prepis na Manasievata xronika, IzvBAI, VIII, 1934, p. 369 - 378.

_____, Car Ivan-Asen II, 1218-1241, po slučaj sedem-stotin godini ot negovata smərt, Sofia, 1941, 53 pp.

_____, Prinosi kəm istorijata na Ivan-Asenja II, SpBAN, LXVI, 1943, 3, p. 168-169.

_____, Iz starata bəlgarska knižnina. II. Knižovni i istoričeski pametnici ot Vtoroto bəlgarsko car-stvo, Sofia, 1944, xxxvi + 436 pp.

_____, Rilskijat svetec (Sv. Ivan Rilski) i negovata obitel, Sofia, 1947, viii + 432 pp.

_____, Legendarnyj motiv u Grigorija Camblaka, Slavia, XXI, 1952-53, p. 345-349.

_____, Edno nejasno mjasto ot Camblakovata vəzxvala za Evtimij, BəlgEz, IV, 1954, 2, p. 171-172.

_____, Estestvoznanieto v srednovekovna Bəlgarija. Sbornik ot istoričeski izvori, Sofia, 1954, 626 + 4 pp.

_____, Za knižovnoto tvorčestvo na Konstantin Koste-nečki, IzvIBL, II, Sofia, 1954, p. 223-231.

_____, Odna citata iz Manassievoj Xroniki v srednebolgarskom perevode, <u>Trudy</u> <u>ODRL</u>, XVI, Moscow - Leningrad, 1960, p. 647-649.

_____, À propos de la biographie de Joseph II patriarche de Constantinople, <u>Revue</u> <u>des</u> <u>études</u> byzantines, XIX, Paris, 1961, p. 333-339.

_____, Il problemo delle lingue nazionali nel Medio Evo e gli Slavi, <u>Ricerche</u> <u>slavistiche</u>, VIII, Rome, 1961, p. 39-60.

_____, Obrazi na bəlgarin ot XV v. vəv Florencija, <u>Izkustvo</u>, I, Sofia, 1961, p. 22-24.

_____, ed., <u>Miniatjurite</u> <u>na</u> <u>Manasievata</u> <u>letopis</u> (= <u>Pametnici</u> <u>na</u> <u>starata</u> <u>bəlgarska</u> <u>živopis</u>, I), Sofia, 1962, 138 pp.

_____, Bolgarskie licevye rukopisi XIV veka (in: <u>Bolgarskaja</u> <u>miniatjura</u> <u>XIV</u> <u>veka</u>, M. V. Ščepkina, ed.), Moscow, 1963, p. 7-19.

_____, Centry vizantijsko-slavjanskogo sotrudničestva, <u>Trudy</u> <u>ODRL</u>, XIX, Moscow-Leningrad, 1963, p. 107 - 129.

_____, ed., <u>Letopista</u> <u>na</u> <u>Konstantin</u> <u>Manasi</u>, Sofia, 1963, xxxiv + 415 pp.

_____, Racionalističeski probljasəci v slavjanskoto Srednovekovie, <u>IstPr</u>, 1963, 5, p. 86-100.

_____, Vrəzki meždu čexi, slovaci i bəlgari prez Srednovekovieto (in: <u>Čexoslovakija</u> <u>i</u> <u>Bəlgarija</u> <u>prez</u> <u>vekovete</u>), Sofia, 1963, p. 7-41.

_____, Zaraždane na naučnata misəl v srednovekovna Bəlgarija, _Arxeologija_, 1963, 2, p. 10-15.

_____, ed., _Bolonski psaltir_ (Photopublication of the manuscript), Sofia, 1968, 530 pp.

_____, Kuev, K., Bəlgarskata literatura prez XIV v. (in: _Istorija na bəlgarskata literatura_, 1), Sofia, 1963, p. 267-284.

Duridanov, I., Edin slučaj na ranna upotreba na predloga _na_ za izrazjavane na datelno otnošenie, _BəlgEz_, III, 1953, 1, p. 58-60.

_____, Kəm problemata za razvoja na bəlgarskija ezik ot sintetizəm kəm analitizəm, _GodSU_, LI, Sofia, 1955, 3, p. 87-272.

_____, Iz istorijata na pričastijata v bəlgarskija ezik, _BəlgEz_, VI, 1956, 2, p. 148-152.

_____, Beležki vərxu starobəlgarskija prevod na evangelieto s ogled na vlijanieto na grəckija sintaksis (in: _Ezikovedski izsledvanija v čest na akad. St. Mladenov_), Sofia, 1957, p. 225-235.

_____, Pətjat na bəlgarskija ezik ot sintetizəm kəm analitizəm, _BəlgEz_, VII, 1957, 1, p. 5-8.

_____, Za načenkite na analitizma v bəlgarskija ezik, _Rocznik slawistyczny_, 20, Cracow, 1958, p. 16-26.

Durnovo, N., _K istorii povesti ob Akire. Materialy i izsledovanija po starinnoj literature_, 1, Moscow, 1915, ii + 131 pp.

_____, Slavjanskoe pravopisanie X - XI vv., Slavia,

12, 1933-34, p. 45-82.

D'jačenko, G., Polnyj cerkovno-slavjanskij slovar', Moscow,

1900, xxxviii + 1120 pp.

Ekblom, R., Le développement des voyelles originairement

nasalisées dans le moyen bulgare, Le Monde Orien-

tal, 12, Uppsala, 1918, p. 177-225.

Eremin, I. P., O vizantijskom vlijanii v bolgarskoj i

drevnerusskoj literaturax IX - XII vv., Slavjan-

skie literatury (Doklady sovetskoj delegacii. V

Meždunarodnyj s"ezd slavistov), Moscow, 1963,

p. 5-13.

Evseev, I., Kniga proroka Isaji v drevne-slavjanskom pere-

vode, St. Petersburg, 1897, 1, ii + 168 pp.; 2,

145 + iii pp.

_____, Zametki po drevneslavjanskomu perevodu Sv.

Pisanija, IV, IzvORJaS, V, 3, St. Petersburg,

1900 (Photoedition: Graz, 1964), p. 788-823.

Filkova, P., Ranni svedenija za bəlgarskija ezik v Rusija,

BəlgEz, XII, Sofia, 3, 1962, p. 231-239.

Filov, B., Die Miniaturen des Ev. Iwan Alexanders in Lon-

don, Byzantion, IV, 1927-28, p. 313-319.

_____, Londonskoto evangelie na Ivan Aleksandər i nego-

vite miniatjuri, SpBAN, XXXVIII, Sofia, 1929,

p. 1-32.

_____, Starobəlgarskata živopis prez XIII i XIV vek,

BəlgIstBibl, III, 1930, 1, p. 87-89.

_____, Les miniatures de l'Evangile du roi Ivan
Alexandre à Londres (in: Monumenta Artis Bulga-
riae, 3),Sofia, 1934.

Fuchs, F., Die höheren Schulen von Konstantinopel im Mittelalter, Leipzig-Berlin, 1926, vi + 79 pp.

Gadolina, M. A., K istorii nekotoryx form ličnyx i vozvrat-
nyx mestoimenij v russkom jazyke XIII - XVII vv.,
Trudy IJa, 5, Moscow, 1954, p. 34-80.

Geanakoplos, D. J., Byzantine East and Latin West, New York
- Evanston, 1967, x + 206 pp.

Gečev, St. A., Kəm vəprosa za slavjanskija Fiziolog, Sofia,
1938, 127 + xxvii pp.

Georgieva, S., Po vəprosa za xaraktera na rannosrednovekov-
nata bəlgarska kultura, Arxeologija, 3, p. 1-5.

Gerov, B., Die griechischen, semitischen und lateinischen
Nomina im Altbulgarischen, GodSU, XXXIX, Sofia,
1943, p. 1-36.

Gianelli, G., Vaillant, A., Un lexique Macédonien du XVIe
siècle, Paris, 1958, 69 pp.

Glubokovskij, N. M., Sv. Kiprian, mitropolit vseja Rossii,
kak pisatel', Čtenija v Obščestve ljubitelej
duxovnogo prosveščenija, 1, Jan. 1892, p. 358-424.

Görner, F., Za nadrednite znaci v starobəlgarskite pametnici do XIII v., EL, 6, 1967, p. 53-58.

Gołąb, Z., Funkcja syntaktyczna partykuły da w językach

pd.-słowiańskich (bułgarskim, macedońskim i serbo-chorwackim), Biuletyn polskiego Towarzystwa Językoznawczego, XIII, Cracow, 1954, p. 67-92.

_____, Conditionalis typu bałkańskiego w językach południowosłowiańskich ze szczególnym uwględnieniem macedońskiego, Wrocław-Cracow-Warsaw, 1964, 202pp.

Golubinskij, E. E., Istorija russkoj cerkvi, II, 1, Moscow, 1900 (Photoedition: Hague, 1969), 919 pp.

Golyšenko, V. S., Dubrovina, V. F., ed's., Sinajskij paterik, Moscow, 1967, 400 pp. + xi tables.

Gorskij, A. V., Nevostruev, K., Opisanie slavjanskix rukopisej Moskovskoj Sinodal'noj biblioteki, Moscow, II.2, 1859, 637 pp.; II.3, 1862, 841 pp.; III.1, 1869, 584 pp.

Gošev, I., Car-Asenovijat nadpis nad krepostta Kričim, SpBAN, 33, 1945, p. 65-85.

Gudzij, N. K., Istorija drevnej russkoj literatury, Moscow, 1945 (3rd edition), 510 pp.

Guilland, R. J., Correspondance de Nicéphore Grégoras, Paris, 1927, xxii + 391 pp.

Gələbov, I. P., Stari bəlgarski ezikovi areali na dako-rumənskata ezikova teritorija, EL, 16, 1961, p. 39-48.

_____, Nadpisi kəm Bojanskite stenopisi, Sofia, 1963, 111 pp.

_____, Nastavkata -telъ i vəprosət za starite

ezikovi vrəzki na praslavjanski, IzvIBE, 16, 1968,
p. 55-63.

Halle, M., The Sound Pattern of Russian, Hague, 1959,
206 pp.

Haltzidakis, G. N., Zur Wortbildungslehre des Mittel- und
Neugriechischen, Byzantinische Zeitschrift, II,
Leipzig, 1893, p. 235-286.

Horálek, K., K otázce staroslověnského infinitivu, Pocta
Fr. Trávníčkovi a F. Wollmanovi, Brno, 1948,
p. 159-165.

_____, Evangeliáře a čtveroevangelia, Prague, 1954,
313 pp.

Hüttl-Worth, G., Problemy mežslavjanskix i slavjano -
neslavjanskix leksičeskix otnošenij (in: American
Contributions to the Fifth International Congress
of Slavists, 1), Hague, 1963, p. 133-152.

_____, K issledovaniju proisxoždenija russkogo
jazyka (Leksičeskie materijaly iz drevnix perevodov psaltyri), ZbMSFL, IX, 1966, p. 31-40.

_____, Rol' cerkovnoslavjanskogo jazyka v raz-
vitii russkogo literaturnogo jazyka. K istoričes-
komu analizu i klassifikacii slavjanizmov (in:
American Contributions to the Sixth International
Congress of Slavists, 1), Hague, 1968, p. 1-30.

Ilčev, P. St., Iz bəlgarskata istoričeska leksikologija.
Starobəlgarskoto KLJUČITI SĘ, IzvIBE, VIII, 1962,
p. 117-129.

_____, Za specifikata na starobəlgarskija "Dativus Absolutus", BəlgEz, XIII, 1963, 3, p. 211-233.

_____, Kəm razpredelenieto na dəlgite i kratkite pronominalni formi v starobəlgarski, IzvIBE, X, 1964, p. 235-248.

Il'inskij, G. A., Sofijskij Oktoix XIII veka, IzvORJaS, X, 4, St. Petersburg, 1905 (Photoedition: Graz, 1965), p. 204-228.

_____, Mittelbulgarisch "čьtomu = čemu", AfSlPh, XXVIII, 1906, p. 460-464.

_____, Manujlovskij Apostol XIII veka, IzvORJaS, XIII, 1, St. Petersburg, 1908 (Photoedition: Graz, 1965), p. 366-379.

_____, Značenie Afona v istorii slavjanskoj pis'mennosti, ŽMNP, XI, St. Petersburg, 1908, p. 1-41.

_____, Gramoty bolgarskix carej (= Drevnosti. Trudy Slavjanskoj kommissii Imperatorskogo Moskovskogo Arxeologičeskogo Obščestva, V), Moscow, 1911 (Photoedition: London, 1970), 159 pp. + 7 tables.

Isserlin, E. M., Leksika russkogo literaturnogo jazyka XVII v., Moscow, 1961, 80 pp.

Istomin, K. K., K voprosu o redakcijax Tolkovoj Palei, IzvORJaS, X, 1, St. Petersburg, 1905 (Photoedition: Graz, 1965), p. 147-184.

Istrin, V. M., <u>Aleksandrija</u> <u>russkix</u> <u>xronografov</u>. Izsledo-
vanie <u>i</u> <u>tekst</u>, Moscow, 1893, 378 pp.

_____, Odin tol'ko perevod Psevdokallisfena, a
drevnebolgarskaja enciklopedija X veka - mnimaja,
<u>Vizantijskij</u> <u>vremennik</u>, 1903, p. 1-30.

_____, Xronika Georgija Amartola v drevnem slavja-
no-russkom perevode, <u>Slavia</u>, II, 1923, 2-3,
p. 460-467.

Ivanov, J., <u>Severna</u> <u>Makedonija</u>, Sofia, 1906, 420 pp.

_____, <u>Bəlgarski</u> <u>starini</u> <u>iz</u> <u>Makedonija</u>, Sofia, 1908,
310 pp.; 1931 (2nd edition), 659 pp. + 10 plates.

_____, <u>Bəlgarite</u> <u>v</u> <u>Makedonija</u>. <u>Izdirvanija</u> <u>i</u> <u>dokumenti</u>
<u>za</u> <u>tjaxnoto</u> <u>poteklo</u>, <u>ezik</u> <u>i</u> <u>narodnost</u>, <u>s</u> <u>etnograf-</u>
<u>ska</u> <u>karta</u> <u>i</u> <u>statistika</u>, Sofia, 1917, v + 381 pp.

_____, <u>Sv</u>. <u>Ivan</u> <u>Rilski</u> <u>i</u> <u>negovijat</u> <u>manastir</u>. <u>S</u> <u>prilo-</u>
<u>ženie</u> <u>na</u> <u>pametnici</u> <u>i</u> <u>fotografski</u> <u>snimki</u>, Sofia,
1917, vi + 164 pp. + xix plates.

_____, <u>Bogomilski</u> <u>knigi</u> <u>i</u> <u>legendi</u>, Sofia, 1925, 387pp.

_____, <u>Starobəlgarski</u> <u>razkazi</u>. Tekstove, <u>novobəlgarski</u>
<u>prevod</u> <u>i</u> <u>beležki</u>, Sofia, 1935, vi + 322 pp.

_____, Žitija na sv. Ivana Rilski, <u>GodSU</u>, Ist.fil.fak.
32, 1936, p. 1-108.

_____, Bəlgarskoto knižovno vlijanie v Rusija pri
mitropolit Kiprian, <u>IzvIBL</u>, VI, 1958, p. 25-79.

Ivanova-Konstantinova, Kl., Ob odnoj rukopisi konca XIV v.
Pogodinskogo sobranija, <u>Trudy</u> <u>ODRL</u>, XXV, Moscow -

Leningrad, 1970, p. 294-308.

Ivanova-Mirčeva, D., Razvoj na bədešte vreme ("Futurum") v

bəlgarskija ezik ot X do XVIII vek, Sofia, 1962,

197 pp.

_____, Starobəlgarski, staroslavjanski i

srednobəlgarska redakcija na staroslavjanski (in:

Konstantin-Kiril Filosof), Sofia, 1969, p. 45-62.

Ivić, M., Iz problematike padežnih konstrukcija, JF, XXI,

1955-56, p. 165-214.

Ivić, P., Dijalektologija srpskohrvatskog jezika. Uvod i

štokavsko narečije, Novi Sad, 1956, 218 pp.

_____, Die serbokroatischen Dialekte. Ihre Struktur und

Entwicklung, Hague, 1958, 325 pp.

_____, O klasifikaciji srpskohrvatskih dijalekata,

Književnost i jezik, X, Beograd, 1963, 1, p.27-28.

_____, Liens phonologiques entre les langues balkaniques,

Actes du 1er Congrès international des études bal-

kaniques et sud-est européennes, VI, Sofia, 1968,

p. 133-141.

Jacimirskij, A. I., Iz slavjanskix rukopisej. Teksty i

zametki, Moscow, 1899, 166 pp.

_____, Grigorij Camblak. Očerk ego žizni, ad-

ministrativnoj i kniževnoj dejatel'nosti, St.

Petersburg, 1904, 480 pp.

_____, Slavjanskie i russkie rukopisi rumyn-

skix bibliotek, SbORJaS, 79, 1905, p. 721-723.

_____, Iz lingvističeskix i paleografičeskix nabljudenij nad slavjanskimi nadpisjami rumynskogo proisxoždenija, IzvORJaS, X, 3, St. Petersburg, 1906, p. 24-68.

_____, K istorii apokrifov i legend v južno-slavjanskoj pis'mennosti, IzvORJaS, St. Petersburg, 1910 (Photoedition: Graz, 1965), XIV,2, p. 267-322; XIV, 3, p. 103-159; XV, 1, p. 1-62.

_____, K istorii ložnyx molitv v južno-slavjanskoj pis'mennosti, IzvORJaS, St. Petersburg, 1913 (Photoedition: Graz, 1967), XVIII, 3, p. 1 - 102; XVIII, 4, p. 16-126.

Jagić, V., ed., Quattuor evangeliorum codex glagoliticus olim Zographensis nunc Petropolitanus, characteribus cyrillicis transcriptum notis criticus prolegomenis appendicibus auctum, Berlin, 1879 (Photoreprint: Graz, 1954), XLV + 175 + iii pp.

_____, Wie lautete ǫ bei den Bulgaren, AfSlPh, III, 1879, p. 312-357.

_____, ed., Quattuor evangeliorum versionis palaeoslovenicae Codex Marianus glagoliticus (Mariinskoe četveroevangelie s primečanijami i priloženijami), Berlin-St. Petersburg, 1883 (Photoreprint: Graz, 1960), XXX = 607 pp.

_____, Codex Slovenicus Rerum Grammaticarum (Razsuždenija južnoslavjanskoj i russkoj starini o

cerkovno-slavjanskom jazyke, Izsledovanija po russkomu jazyku, I, St. Petersburg, 1885-1895) (Photoedition: Slavische Propyläen, 25, Munich, 1968,
782 pp.).

_____, Kritičeskie zametki po istorii russkogo jazyka,
IzvORJaS, XLVI, 4, St. Petersburg, 1889 (Photoreprint: Graz, 1964), 171 pp.

_____, Bericht über einen mittelbulgarischen Zlatoust
des 13. - 14. Jahrhunderts, Sitzungsberichte der
philosophisch-historischen Klasse der Kaiser-
lichen Akademie der Wissenschaften, 139, Vienna,
1898, p. 1-72.

_____, Die slavischen Composita in ihrem sprachgeschicht-
lichen Auftreten, AfSlPh, XX, 1898, p. 519-556.

_____, Kritičeskie zametki k slavjanskomu perevodu dvux
apokrifičeskix skazanij (Apokrifičeskoe Pervoevan-
gelie Iakova, Apokrifičeskoe Poslanie Pilata v
Rim), IzvORJaS, St. Petersburg, 1898 (Photoedition: Graz, 1964), III, 2, p. 315-338; III, 3,
p. 793-822.

_____, Evangelium Dobromiri; ein altmacedonisches Denk-
mal der kirchenslavischen Sprache des XII. Jahrhunderts, Vienna, I, 1898, 138 + ii pp.; II, 1899,
140 + iii pp.

Jakobson, R., Remarques sur l'évolution phonologique du
russe comparée à celle des autres langues slaves,
Prague, 1929, 188 pp.

_____, On Slavic Diphthongs Ending in a Liquid,
Word, 8, 1952, p. 2-6.

Janin, R., Constantinople byzantine (= Archives de l'Orient
chrétien, 4), Paris, 1950, xxvii + 482 pp.,
15 maps.

Kabasanov, St., Star i nov nasalizəm v neproučen dosega
bəlgarski govor, Slavistični studii (Sbornik po
slučaj V Meždunaroden slavistичen kongres v
Sofija), Sofia, 1963, p. 173-184.

Kałużniacki, Em., Aus der panegyrischen Literatur der Südslaven, Vienna, 1901, 132 pp.

_____, Werke des Patriarchen von Bulgarien
Euthymius (1375-93), Vienna, 1901, cxxviii+450 pp.

Karskij, E. F., Očerk slavjanskoj kirillovskij paleografii,
Warsaw, 1915 (3rd edition), xvi + 518 pp.

_____, Slavjanskaja kirillovskaja paleografija,
Leningrad, 1928, xi + 494 pp.

Kazakova, N. A., Lur'e, Ja. S., Antifeodal'nye eretičeskie
dviženija na Rusi XIV - načala XVI v., Moscow -
Leningrad, 1955, 544 pp.

Kiselkov, V. Sl., Žitieto na sv. Teodosij Tərnovski kato
istoričeski pametnik, Sofia, 1926, lii + 32 pp.

_____, Sveti Teodosij Tərnovski, Sofia, 1926,
53 pp.

_____, Grigorij Sinait, predstavitel na misti-
cizma vəv Vizantija prez XIV v., Sofia, 1928,
32 pp.

_____, ed., Žitie na Sv. Paraskeva (ot patriarx Evtimij) (in: Bəlgarska istoričeska biblioteka, S. Slavčev, ed., III, 1), Sofia, 1930, p. 190-217.

_____, Mitropolit Joasaf Bdinski i slovoto mu za Sv. Filoteja (in: Bəlgarska istoričeska biblioteka, S. Slavčev, ed., IV, 1), Sofia, 1931, p. 167-206.

_____, Patriarx Evtimij, Sofia, 1938, 316 pp.

_____, Sv. Ivan Rilski. Žitija, Sofia, 1940, 88 pp.

_____, Prouki i očerti po starobəlgarskata literatura, Sofia, 1956, 400 pp.

Klemensiewicz, Z., Lehr-Spɫawiński, T., Urbańczyk, St., Gramatyka historyczna języka polskiego, Warsaw, 1964 (2nd edition), 596 pp.

Kniga Stepennaja carskogo rodoslovija; Polnoe sobranie russkix letopisej, XXI, 2, St. Petersburg, 1913, p. 343-708.

Kočin, G. E., Materialy dlja terminologičeskogo slovarja drevnej Rossii, Moscow-Leningrad, 1937 (Photoedition: Düsseldorf-Vaduz, 1969), 487 pp.

Kolesnikov, I. F., ed., Sbornik snimkov s russkogo pis'ma XI - XVIII vv., I, Moscow, 1913 (2nd edition), Table 15.

Koneski, Bl., Edna odlomka od XIII vek, spomenik od oxridskata skola, Godišen zbornik na filozofskiot

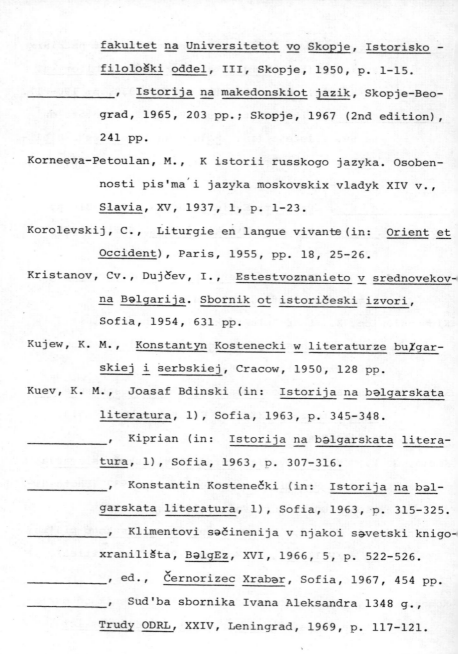
fakultet na Universitetot vo Skopje, Istorisko -
filološki oddel, III, Skopje, 1950, p. 1-15.

——————————, Istorija na makedonskiot jazik, Skopje-Beograd, 1965, 203 pp.; Skopje, 1967 (2nd edition),
241 pp.

Korneeva-Petoulan, M., K istorii russkogo jazyka. Osobennosti pis'ma i jazyka moskovskix vladyk XIV v.,
Slavia, XV, 1937, 1, p. 1-23.

Korolevskij, C., Liturgie en langue vivante (in: Orient et
Occident), Paris, 1955, pp. 18, 25-26.

Kristanov, Cv., Dujčev, I., Estestvoznanieto v srednovekovna Bəlgarija. Sbornik ot istoričeski izvori,
Sofia, 1954, 631 pp.

Kujew, K. M., Konstantyn Kostenecki w literaturze bułgarskiej i serbskiej, Cracow, 1950, 128 pp.

Kuev, K. M., Joasaf Bdinski (in: Istorija na bəlgarskata
literatura, 1), Sofia, 1963, p. 345-348.

——————————, Kiprian (in: Istorija na bəlgarskata literatura, 1), Sofia, 1963, p. 307-316.

——————————, Konstantin Kostenečki (in: Istorija na bəlgarskata literatura, 1), Sofia, 1963, p. 315-325.

——————————, Klimentovi səčinenija v njakoi səvetski knigo-
xranilišta, BəlgEz, XVI, 1966, 5, p. 522-526.

——————————, ed., Černorizec Xrabər, Sofia, 1967, 454 pp.

——————————, Sud'ba sbornika Ivana Aleksandra 1348 g.,
Trudy ODRL, XXIV, Leningrad, 1969, p. 117-121.

Kul'bakin, S. M., Materialy dlja xarakteristiki srednebolgarskogo jazyka. I. Bojanskoe Evangelie XII - XIII
veka, IzvORJaS, IV, 3, St. Petersburg, 1899
(Photoedition: Graz, 1964), pp. 800-868; II.
Otryvok Četveroevangelija Grigoroviča XIII - XIV
veka, IzvORJaS, V, 3, St. Petersburg, 1900 (Photoedition: Graz, 1964), p. 877-920.

_____, Oxridskaja rukopis' apostola konca XII
veka (= Bəlgarski starini, III), Sofia, 1907,
cxxxvi + 141 + viii pp.

Kurz, J., K otázce členu v jazycích slovanských se zvláštním zřetelem k staroslověnštině, Byzantinoslavica,
7, 1937-38, p. 212-340; 8, 1939-46, p. 172-288.

_____, and others, ed's., Slovník jazyka staroslověn-
ského. Lexicon linguae palaeoslovenicae, Prague,
1959 following.

Lascaris, M., Vatopedskata gramota na car Ivan Asenja II,
Sofia, 1930, 61 pp. + 1 plate.

_____, Influences byzantines dans la diplomatique
bulgare, serbe et slavo-roumaine, Byzantinoslavica,
III, 2, Prague, 1931, p. 500-510.

Lavrov, P. A., Obzor zvukovyx i formal'nyx osobennostej
bolgarskogo jazyka, Moscow, 1893, 109 pp.

_____, Zapis' v evangelii 1322 g. biblioteki Xilan-
darskogo Afonskogo monastyrja, IzvORJaS, I, 1,
St. Petersburg, 1896 (Photoedition: Graz, 1965),
p. 110-113.

_____, Oxridskij spisok pervoevangelija Iakova, IzvORJaS, VI, 1, St. Petersburg, 1901 (Photoedition: Graz, 1964), p. 9-36.

Lehr-Spł/awiński, T., Les voyelles nasales dans les langues lechites, RÉS, VI-VII, 1926, p. 54-66.

Leskien, A., Grammatik der altbulgarischen (altkirchenslavischen) Sprache, Heidelberg, 1919 (3rd edition), lii + 260 pp.

_____, Handbuch der altbulgarischen (altkirchenslavischen) Sprache; Grammatik, Texte, Glossar, Heidelberg, 1962 (8th edition), xxiv + 364 pp.

VIII letopisnyj sbornik, imenuemyj Patriaršeju ili Nikonovskoju letopis'ju, Polnoe sobranie russkix letopisej, XI, St. Petersburg, 1897 (Photoedition: Moscow, 1965), 254 pp.

Lightner, T. M., On the Phonology of Old Church Slavonic Conjugation, IJSLP, X, 1966, p. 1-28.

Lixačev, D. S., Kul'tura Rusi èpoxi obrazovanija russkogo nacional'nogo gosudarstva; konec XIV - načalo XVI v., Leningrad, 1946, 159 pp. + 1 plate.

_____, O istoričeskoj i formal'noj klassifikacijax spiskov drevneslavjanskix pamjatnikov (in: Slavjanskaja filologija. Sbornik statej, 1), Moscow, 1958, p. 264-274.

_____, Nekotorye zadači izučenija vtorogo južnoslavjanskogo vlijanija v Rossii, Issledovanija po

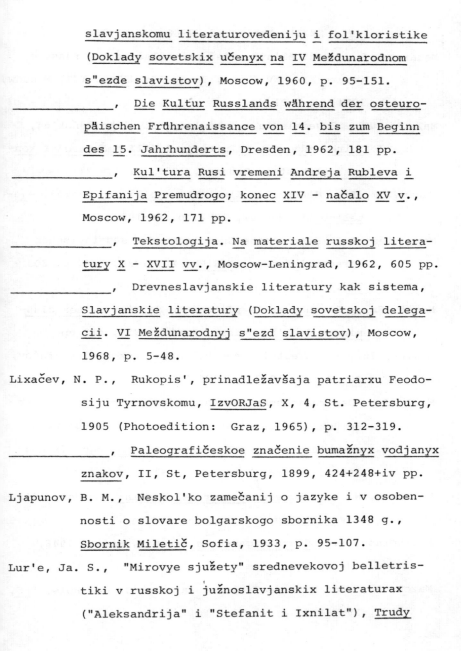

slavjanskomu literaturovedeniju i fol'kloristike
(Doklady sovetskix učenyx na IV Meždunarodnom
s"ezde slavistov), Moscow, 1960, p. 95-151.

_____, Die Kultur Russlands während der osteuro-
päischen Frührenaissance von 14. bis zum Beginn
des 15. Jahrhunderts, Dresden, 1962, 181 pp.

_____, Kul'tura Rusi vremeni Andreja Rubleva i
Epifanija Premudrogo; konec XIV - načalo XV v.,
Moscow, 1962, 171 pp.

_____, Tekstologija. Na materiale russkoj litera-
tury X - XVII vv., Moscow-Leningrad, 1962, 605 pp.

_____, Drevneslavjanskie literatury kak sistema,
Slavjanskie literatury (Doklady sovetskoj delegacii. VI Meždunarodnyj s"ezd slavistov), Moscow,
1968, p. 5-48.

Lixačev, N. P., Rukopis', prinadležavšaja patriarxu Feodo-
siju Tyrnovskomu, IzvORJaS, X, 4, St. Petersburg,
1905 (Photoedition: Graz, 1965), p. 312-319.

_____, Paleografičeskoe značenie bumažnyx vodjanyx
znakov, II, St, Petersburg, 1899, 424+248+iv pp.

Ljapunov, B. M., Neskol'ko zamečanij o jazyke i v osobennosti o slovare bolgarskogo sbornika 1348 g.,
Sbornik Miletič, Sofia, 1933, p. 95-107.

Lur'e, Ja. S., "Mirovye sjužety" srednevekovoj belletris-
tiki v russkoj i južnoslavjanskix literaturax
("Aleksandrija" i "Stefanit i Ixnilat"), Trudy

ODRL, XXIII, Leningrad, 1968, p. 16-26.

Makarova, S., Roditel'nyj padež prinadležnosti v russkom jazyke XI - XVII vv., Trudy IJaANSSSR, III, Moscow 1954, p. 7-31.

Małecki, M., Zagadnienia sporne lingwistyki bałkańskiej, Zbirka odgovora na pitanja 1 (III Međunarodni kongres slavista), Beograd, 1939, p. 216-217.

Mansvetov, I., Mitropolit Kiprian v ego liturgičeskoj dejatel'nosti, Moscow, 1882, p. 66-100.

Marguliés, A., Historische Grundlagen der südslavischen Sprachgliederung, AfSlPh, XL, 1926, 3-4, p. 203 - 208.

Masai, Fr., Pléthon et la platonisme de Mistra. Les classiques de l'humanisme, Paris, 1956, 419 pp.

Maslev, St., Neizvestni u nas bəlgarski rəkopisi v Brašov, IzvII, 19, 1967, p. 195-217.

Matl, J., Das romanische Element am Balkan mit besonderer Berücksichtigung der italoromanischen Kulturausstrahlung (in: III. Grazer Balkanologen-Tagung 1968), Munich, 1968, p. 33-52.

Matthews, W. K., Russian Historical Grammar, London, 1960, xiv + 362 pp.

Mavrodinov, N., Starobəlgarskata živopis, Sofia, 1946, 196 pp.

Mazon, A., Les Dits de Troie et la Parabole des Rois, RÉS, XV, 1935, p. 12-52.

_____, Le Dit d'Alexandre le Viel, RÉS, XX, 1942,
p. 13-40.

Meščerskij, N. A., Iskusstvo perevoda Kievskoj Rusi, Trudy
ODRL, XV, Moscow-Leningrad, 1958, p. 54-72.

Meyendorff, J., Introduction à l'étude de Grégoire Palamas,
Paris, 1959, p. 25-58.

Meyer, K. H., Der Untergang der Deklination im Bulgarischen,
Heidelberg, 1920, 75 pp.

_____, Altkirchenslawisch-griechisches Wörterbuch
des Codex Suprasliensis, Glückstadt-Hamburg, 1935,
ix + 302 pp.

Mičev, M., Beležki vərxu imeto i stopanstvoto na edno iz-
čeznalo selište ot epoxata na feudalizma (XIII -
XIV v.), Sbornik v čest na Jordan Zaxariev, Sofia,
1964, p. 141-150.

Miklosich, F., Monumenta linguae palaeoslovenicae e Codice
Suprasliensi, Vienna, 1851, 456 pp.

_____, Lexicon palaeoslovenico-graeco-latinum;
emendatum auctum, Vienna, 1862-65, xxii + 1171 pp.

Miletič, L., Dako-romənite i tjaxnata slavjanska pismenost,
SbNUNK, IX, Sofia, 1893, p. 211-390.

_____, Novi vlaxo-bəlgarski gramoti ot Brašov, SbNUNK,
XIII, Sofia, 1896, p. 3-152.

_____, Kəm istorijata na bəlgarskoto analitično sklo-
nenie, Makedonski pregled, IX, Sofia, 1935, 3-4,
p. 59-76.

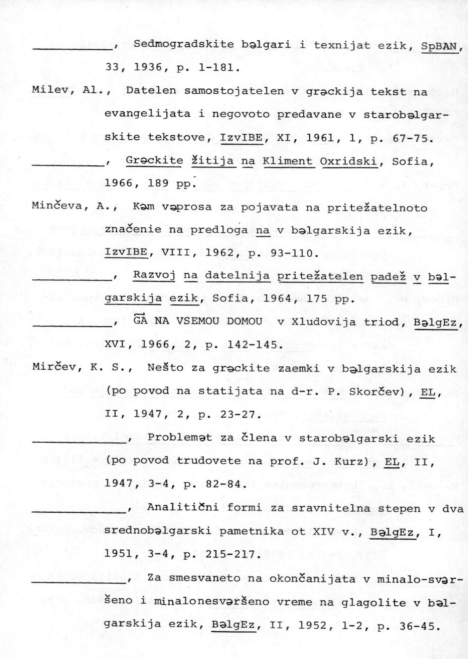

_____, Sedmogradskite bəlgari i texnijat ezik, SpBAN, 33, 1936, p. 1-181.

Milev, Al., Datelen samostojatelen v grəckija tekst na evangelijata i negovoto predavane v starobəlgarskite tekstove, IzvIBE, XI, 1961, 1, p. 67-75.

_____, Grəckite žitija na Kliment Oxridski, Sofia, 1966, 189 pp.

Minčeva, A., Kəm vəprosa za pojavata na pritežatelnoto značenie na predloga na v bəlgarskija ezik, IzvIBE, VIII, 1962, p. 93-110.

_____, Razvoj na datelnija pritežatelen padež v bəlgarskija ezik, Sofia, 1964, 175 pp.

_____, GA NA VSEMOU DOMOU v Xludovija triod, BəlgEz, XVI, 1966, 2, p. 142-145.

Mirčev, K. S., Nešto za grəckite zaemki v bəlgarskija ezik (po povod na statijata na d-r. P. Skorčev), EL, II, 1947, 2, p. 23-27.

_____, Problemət za člena v starobəlgarski ezik (po povod trudovete na prof. J. Kurz), EL, II, 1947, 3-4, p. 82-84.

_____, Analitični formi za sravnitelna stepen v dva srednobəlgarski pametnika ot XIV v., BəlgEz, I, 1951, 3-4, p. 215-217.

_____, Za smesvaneto na okončanijata v minalo-svəršeno i minalonesvəršeno vreme na glagolite v bəlgarskija ezik, BəlgEz, II, 1952, 1-2, p. 36-45.

_____, Koga vəznikva člennata forma v bəlgarskija

ezik, BəlgEz, III, 1953, 4, p. 309-328.

_____, Po vəprosa za sklonenieto v bəlgarskija

ezik, BəlgEz, IV, 1954, 1, p. 61-64.

_____, Za njakoi leksikalni osobenosti na bəlgar-

skija fiziolog ot XVI v., Sbornik v čest na aka-

demik Aleksandər Teodorov-Balan ... , Sofia, 1955,

p. 319-323.

_____, Za člennite formi v Dobrejšovoto evangelie,

srednobəlgarski pametnik ot XIII v., BəlgEz, IV,

1956, 3, p. 223-228.

_____, Za osmisljaneto na edin gərcizəm v sredno-

bəlgarskite pametnici, BəlgEz, VII, 1957, 6,

p. 540-541.

_____, Po vəprosa za naj-rannite primeri na anali-

tičen datelen padež v bəlgarskite pametnici,

Ezikovedski izsledvanija v čest na akademik Stefan

Mladenov, Sofia, 1957, p. 37-46.

_____, Za edna rusko-bəlgarska usporedica v razvoja

na mestoimenijata, Slavističen sbornik, I, Sofia,

1958, p. 73-78.

_____, Istoričeska gramatika na bəlgarskija ezik,

Sofia, 1958, 275 pp.; 1963 (2nd edition), 274 pp.

_____, Za novite morfologičeski čerti v Pražkoto

evangelie - srednobəlgarski pametnik ot XV vek

(in: Ezikovedsko-etnografski izsledvanija v pamet

na akademik <u>Stojan</u> <u>Romanski</u>), Sofia, 1960,
p. 231-237.

_____, Za člennite formi v srednobəlgarskite pamet-
nici, <u>IzvIBE</u>, XI, 1964, p. 231-234.

_____, Za xronologijata na osnovnite balkanizmi v
bəlgarskija ezik, <u>BəlgEz</u>, XVI, 1966, 4, p. 281-293

_____, Kodov, Xr., ed's., <u>Eninski</u> <u>apostol</u>. <u>Staro</u>-
<u>bəlgarski</u> <u>pametnik</u> <u>ot</u> <u>XI</u> <u>vek</u>, Sofia, 1965, 263 pp.

Mladenov, St., K voprosu o granice meždu bolgarskim i serb-
skim jazykom, <u>RFV</u>, 57, Warsaw, 1914, p. 383-403.

_____, <u>Geschichte</u> <u>der</u> <u>bulgarischen</u> <u>Sprache</u>, Berlin -
Leipzig, 1929, xiv + 354 pp.

_____, Kodov, Xr., Vakarelski, Xr., <u>Bit</u> <u>i</u> <u>ezik</u> <u>na</u>
<u>trakijskite</u> <u>i</u> <u>maloaziatskite</u> <u>bəlgari</u>, Sofia, I,
1935, viii + 496 pp. + 6 plates; II, 1936, 127pp.

Molnár, N., The Calques of Greek Origin in the Most Ancient
Old Slavic Gospel Texts, <u>Studia</u> <u>Slavica</u>, X,
Budapest, 1964, p. 99-146.

Mošin, Vl., K istorii vzaimootnošenij russkoj i južnoslavjanskoj pis'mennosti, <u>Slavjane</u>, Moscow, 1958,
1, p. 40-42.

_____, O periodizacii russko-južnoslavjanskix litera-
turnyx svjazej X - XV vv., <u>Trudy</u> <u>ODRL</u>, XIX,
Moscow-Leningrad, 1963, p. 28-106.

Mulić, M. I., Pletenije sloves i hezihazam, <u>ZbRZSF</u>, 7,
1965, p. 141-156.

_____, Serbskie agiografy XIII - XIV vv. i osoben-
nosti ix stilja, Trudy ODRL, Leningrad, 1968,
p. 127-142.

Mur'janov, M. F., Aleksej Čelovek Božij v slavjanskoj re-
cenzii vizantijskoj kul'tury, Trudy ODR , XXIII,
Leningrad, p. 109-126.

Načov, N. A., Tikveški rэkopis, SbNUNK, VIII, Sofia, 1892,
p. 369-418.

Nahtigal, R., Slovanski jeziki, Ljubljana, 1952 (2nd edition), 335 pp.; in German translation: Die
slavischen Sprachen, Wiesbaden, 1961, 270 pp.;
in Russian translation: Slavjanskie jazyki,
Moscow, 1963, 341 pp.

Nasonov, A. N., Moskovskij svod 1479 g. i ego južnorusskij
istočnik, Problemy istočnikovedenija, IX, Moscow,
1961, p. 350-385.

Nazarevskij, A. A., Bibliografija drevnerusskoj povesti,
Moscow-Leningrad, 1955, 192 pp.

Nešev, G., K voprosu o sostojanii bolgarskix cerkvej i
monastyrej v pervye stoletija Osmanskogo vladyče-
stva (in: Études historiques. V. À l'occasion du
XIIIe Congrès international des Sciences historiques, Moscou, août 1970), Sofia, 1970, p. 273 -
290.

Nikolaeva, T. V., K voprosu o svjazej drevnej Rusi s južnymi slavjanami (in: Soobščenija Zagorskogo gosu-

darstvennogo istoriko-xudožestvennogo muzeja-zapo-
vednika, 2), Zagorsk, 1958, p. 19-24.

Ohienko, I., Język cerkiewno-słowiański na Litwie i w
Polsce w wiekach XV - XVIII, Prace filologiczne,
14, Warsaw, 1929, p. 525-543.

Orlov, A. S., Bibliografija russkix nadpisej XI - XV vv.,
Moscow-Leningrad, 1936, 180 pp.

Orlova, V. G., Izmenenija v xaraktere razvitija russkogo
jazyka v svjazi s istorii naroda, VJa, II, 1953,
1, p. 52-70.

Pascu, Şt., Ionaşcu, I., Cihodaru, C., Georgescu, Gh.,
Istoria Medie a României. Partea întîi, Bucharest,
1966, 405 pp.

Penev, B., Istorija na novata bəlgarska literatura, Sofia,
I, 1930, 456 pp.; II, 1932, 411 pp.

Penkova, P., Sintaktični funkcii na starobəlgarskoto ěko,
IzvIBE, X, 1964, p. 249-279.

_____, Ilčev, P., K voprosu o makedonskom jazyke i
ego istorii, Balkansko ezikoznanie, XII, Sofia,
1967, p. 5-37.

Peretc, V. N., K istorii apokrifa i legendy. K istorii
Gromnika i Lunnika, IzvORJaS, VI, 4, St. Petersburg, 1901 (Photoedition: Graz, 1964), p.103-131.

_____, Materialy k istorii apokrifa i legendy. K
istorii Lunnika, IzvORJaS, VI, 3, St. Petersburg,
1901 (Photoedition: Graz, 1964), p. 1-126.

_____, K istorii teksta "Povesti ob Akire Premud-
rom", IzvORJaS, XXI, 1, Petrograd, 1916 (Photoedition: Graz, 1967), p. 262-278.

Petrov, P., Kəm vəprosa za avtentičnostta na Virginskata
gramota i dostovernostta na sədəržaštite se v neja
svedenija, GodSU, Filolog.Ist.Fak, I, 2, 1958,
p. 171-175.

_____, Kəm vəprosa za bəlgaro-vizantijskite otnošenija
prez vtorata polovina na XIII v., IstPr, 1960, 1,
p. 83-90.

Picchio, R., "Prerinascimento esteuropeo" e "Rinascita
slava ortodossa" (A proposito di una tesi di
D. S. Lichačëv), Ricerche slavistiche, VI, Rome,
1958, p. 185-199.

_____, Storia della letteratura russa antica (in the
series: Storia delle letterature di tutto il
mondo), Milan, 1959, 414 pp. + 1 map.

_____, Die historisch-philologische Bedeutung der
kirchenslavischen Tradition, Die Welt der Slaven,
VII, Wiesbaden, 1962, p. 1-27.

_____, A proposito della Slavia ortodossa e della
comunità linguistica slava ecclesiastica, Ricerche
slavistiche, XI, Rome, 1963, p. 105-127.

Pokrovskaja, V. F., Kartoteka akademika N. K. Nikol'skogo,
Trudy Biblioteki Akademii nauk SSSR, I, Moscow -
Leningrad, 1948, p. 142-150.

Polák, V., Die Beziehungen des Albanischen zu den europäischen Substratsprachen mit Rücksicht auf die balkanische Situation (in: Die Kultur Südosteuropas, ihre Geschichte und ihre Ausdrucksformen), Wiesbaden, 1964, p. 207-217.

Polívka, G., Paleographische, grammatische, und kritische Eigenthümlichkeiten in dem Makedonischen Praxapostolus, AfSlPh, X, Berlin, 1887, pp. 106-132, 417 - 483.

_____, Srednjebugarsko jevanđelje Srećkovićevo i njegov odnošaj prema ostalim crkveno-slovenskim versijama jevanđelja, Starine, XXIX, Zagreb, 1898, p. 95-256.

Popov, Xr. I., Evtimij, posleden Tərnovski i trapezicki patriarx (1375-1394). Po slučaj 500-godišninata ot smərtta mu (1402-1902), Plovdiv, 1901, 296 pp.

Popruženko, M. G., Sinodik carja Borila (= Bəlgarski starini, VIII), Sofia, 1928, clxxix + 96 pp. + iv tabl.

_____, Iz istorii religioznogo dviženija v Bolgarii v XIV veke, Slavia, VII, 1928-29, p. 536 - 548.

Poroxova, O. G., Zametki o novyx slovax v russkom jazyke XV - XVII vv. (in: Issledovanija po leksikologii i grammatike russkogo jazyka), Moscow, 1961, p. 145-167.

Potapov, P. O., Sud'ba xroniki Zonary v slavjano-russkoj

literature, IzvORJaS, XXII, 2, Petrograd, 1917
(Photoedition: Graz, 1967), p. 141-186.

Pravdin, A. B., Datel'nyj priglagol'nyj v staroslavjanskom
i drevnerusskom jazykax, UčZapIS, XIII, Moscow,
1956, p. 3-120.

Protič, A., Sveta Gora i bəlgarskoto izkustvo, Bəlgarski
pregled, I, Sofia, 1929, 2, p. 249-276.

Proxorov, G. M., Isixazm i obščestvennaja mysl' v vostočnoj
Evrope (in: Literaturnye svjazi drevnix slavjan),
Trudy ODRL, XXIII, Leningrad, 1968, p. 86-108.

Rabinovič, M. G., Tixomirov, M. N., Srednevekovnaja Moskva
v XIV - XV vekax, Moscow, 1957, 317 pp.

Radčenko, K. F., Zametki o pergamentnom Sbornike XIV veka
Venskoj Pridvornoj Biblioteki, IzvORJaS, VIII, 4,
St. Petersburg, 1903 (Photoedition: Graz, 1964),
p. 175-211.

Radčuk-Pavlenko, S. T., O nekotoryx osobennostjax razvitija
drevnerusskoj literatury XIV - XV vv. (in: Nauko-
vi zapysky Žytomyrs'koho derž. pedahohičnoho in-
stytutu im. I. Franka, VIII), Žytomyr, 1958,
p. 267-280.

Radojčić, Đ. Sp., Antologija stare srpske književnosti,
Beograd, 1960, 374 pp.

Reichenkron, G., Der Typus der Balkansprachen, Zeitschrift
für Balkanologie, I, Wiesbaden, 1962, p. 91-122.

Ringheim, A., Eine altserbische Trojasage (= Publications

de l'Institut slave d'Upsal, IV), Prague-Uppsala,
1951, 383 pp.

Romanova, N. P., Iz istorii otglagol'nyx suščestvitel'nyx
na -nie, -enie, -tie v russkom jazyke XVI v.,
SlMov, 2, 1958, p. 54-88.

Rozanov, S. P., Žitie serbskogo despota Stefana Lazareviča
i russkij Xronograf, IzvORJaS, XI, 2, St. Petersburg (Photoedition: Graz, 1965), p. 65-97.

Rozov, N. N., Južnoslavjanskie rukopisi Gosudarstvennoj
Publičnoj biblioteki, Trudy GPB, V, 8, Leningrad,
1958, p. 105-118.

Rusek, J., Za srednobəlgarskite vinitelni formi na anaforič
noto mestoimenie v ženski rod eǫ, eǫže, neǫ,
BəlgEz, 1-2, 1962, p. 100-103.

_____, Po vəprosa za xronologijata na udvojavane na
dopəlnenijata v bəlgarskija ezik, BəlgEz, XIII,
1963, 2, p. 141-143.

_____, Deklinacja i użycie przypadków w Triodzie Chłu-
dowa. Studium nad rozwojem analityzmu w języku
bułgarskim, Wrocław-Warsaw-Cracow, 1964, 209 pp.

_____, Beležki vərxu razvoja na pričastijata v bəlgar-
ski ezik, BəlgEz, XVI, 1966, 5, p. 477-490.

Sadnik, L., Aitzetmüller, R., Handwörterbuch zu den altkirchenslavischen Texten, Hague-Heidelberg, 1955,
xx + 341 pp.

Sakəzov, I., Novootkriti dokumenti ot kraja na XIV v. za

blgari ot Makedonija, prodavani kato robi, Makedonski pregled, VII, 1932, 2-3, p. 23-62 (#63).

Salmina, M. A., "Entinarij" v "Povesti o začale Moskvy",
Trudy ODRL, XV, Moscow-Leningrad, 1958, p.362-363.

Sandfeld, K., Linguistique balkanique; problèmes et résultats (2nd edition, augmented, of his Balkanfilologien, 1929), Paris, 1930, 242 pp.

_____, Skok, P., Balkanski jezici (in: Knjiga o
Balkanu, I), Beograd, 1936, p. 260-275.

Schefer, Ch. H. A., ed., Le voyage d'outremer de Bertrandon
de la Broquière, premier écuyer tranchant et conseiller de Philippe le Bon, Duc de Bourgogne,
Paris, 1892, lxxviii + 323 pp.

Scholvin, R., Einleitung in das Johann-Alexander-Evangelium,
AfSlPh, VII, 1884, pp. 1-56, 161-221.

Schultze, F., Georgios Gemistos Plethon und seine reformatischen Bestrebungen (= Geschichte der Philosophie
der Renaissance, I), Jena, 1874, xii + 320 pp.

Schultze, H., Untersuchungen zum Aufbau des Skazanie o
pismenehь von Konstantin von Kostenec (Doctoral
dissertation, Georg-August University, Göttingen),
Göttingen, 1964, 263 pp.

Schultze, W., Zur kirchenslavischen Orthographie, Fest-
schrift A. Bezzenberger zum 14. April 1921,
Göttingen, 1921, p. 144-147.

Sedláček, J., Sintaksis staroslavjanskogo jazyka v svete

balkanistiki, <u>Slavia</u>, XXXII, 1963, 3, p. 385-394.

Seliščev, A. M., <u>Slavjanskoe</u> naselenie <u>v</u> Albanii (with illustrations and a map), Sofia, 1931, iv + 352 pp.

Semenov, V., Drevnjaja russkaja Pčela po pergamennomu spisku, <u>SbORJaS</u>, LIV, 4, St. Petersburg, 1893 (Photoedition: Nendeln, Liechtenstein, 1966), p. 1-444.

Sever'janov, S., <u>Suprasl'skaja</u> rukopis' (Pamjatniki <u>staroslavjanskogo</u> jazyka, II), St. Petersburg, 1904 (Photoreprint: Graz, 1956), iv + 570 pp.

<u>Simeonovskaja</u> letopis'. <u>Polnoe</u> sobranie russkix letopisej (Izdannoe po vysočajšemu poveleniju Imperatorskoj Arxeografičeskoju komissieju; A. E. Presnjakov, ed.), XVIII, St. Petersburg, 1913, 316 pp.

Simoni, P. K., Pamjatniki starinnoj russkoj leksikografii po rukopisjam XV - XVII stoletij, <u>IzvORJaS</u>, XIII, 1, St. Petersburg, 1908 (Photoedition: Graz, 1965), p. 175-212.

Sinicyna, N. V., Poslanie konstantinopol'skogo patriarxa Fotija knjazju Mixailu Bolgarskomu v spiskax XVI v., <u>Trudy</u> ODRL, XXI, Moscow-Leningrad, 1965, p. 96-125.

Skok, P., O bugarskom jeziku v svetlosti balkanistike, <u>JF</u>, XII, 1933, p. 72-146.

Slijepčević, Đ., <u>Istorija</u> Srpske pravoslavne crkve, I, Munich, 1962, 528 pp.

Snegarov, I., Duxovno-kulturni vrəzki meždu Bəlgarija i
Rusija prez srednite vekove (X - XV v.), Sofia,
1950, 96 pp.

Sobolevskij, A. I., Russkie zaimstvovannye slova (Litografirovannyj kurs), St. Petersburg, 1891, 401 pp.

_____, Južno-slavjanskoe vlijanie na russkuju
pis'mennost' v XIV - XV vekax. Reč', čitannaja na
godičnom akte Arxeologičeskogo instituta 8 maja
1894 goda prof. A. I. Sobolevskim, St. Petersburg,
1894, 30 pp.; the second, revised edition of this
work appeared as: Perevodnaja literatura Moskovskoj Rusi XIV - XVII vekov (Bibliografičeskie
materialy), St. Petersburg, 1903, p. 1-37.

_____, Lekcii po istorii russkogo jazyka,
Moscow, 1907 (4th edition), 309 pp.

_____, Materialy i izsledovanija v oblasti
slavjanskoj filologii i arxeologii, SbORJaS,
LXXXVIII, 3, St. Petersburg, 1910, vi + 287 pp.

_____, Osobennosti russkix perevodov domongol'-
skogo perioda, SbORJaS, LXXXVIII, 3, St. Petersburg, 1910, p. 162-177.

Solovjev, A., Histoire du monastère russe au Mont Athos,
Byzantion, VIII, Brussels, 1933, p. 213-238.

Speranskij, M. N., Delenie russkoj literatury na periody i
vlijanie russkoj literatury na jugoslavskuju, RFV,
XXXVI, 3-4, Warsaw, 1896, p. 193-223.

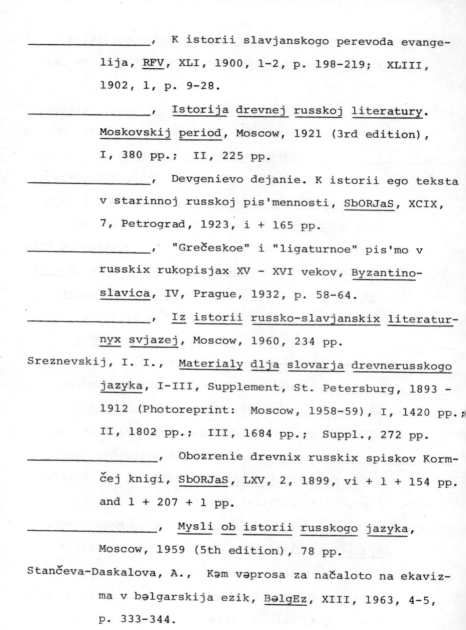

_____, K istorii slavjanskogo perevoda evange-
lija, RFV, XLI, 1900, 1-2, p. 198-219; XLIII,
1902, 1, p. 9-28.

_____, Istorija drevnej russkoj literatury.
Moskovskij period, Moscow, 1921 (3rd edition),
I, 380 pp.; II, 225 pp.

_____, Devgenievo dejanie. K istorii ego teksta
v starinnoj russkoj pis'mennosti, SbORJaS, XCIX,
7, Petrograd, 1923, i + 165 pp.

_____, "Grečeskoe" i "ligaturnoe" pis'mo v
russkix rukopisjax XV - XVI vekov, Byzantinoslavica, IV, Prague, 1932, p. 58-64.

_____, Iz istorii russko-slavjanskix literatur-
nyx svjazej, Moscow, 1960, 234 pp.

Sreznevskij, I. I., Materialy dlja slovarja drevnerusskogo
jazyka, I-III, Supplement, St. Petersburg, 1893 -
1912 (Photoreprint: Moscow, 1958-59), I, 1420 pp.;
II, 1802 pp.; III, 1684 pp.; Suppl., 272 pp.

_____, Obozrenie drevnix russkix spiskov Korm-
čej knigi, SbORJaS, LXV, 2, 1899, vi + 1 + 154 pp.
and 1 + 207 + 1 pp.

_____, Mysli ob istorii russkogo jazyka,
Moscow, 1959 (5th edition), 78 pp.

Stančeva-Daskalova, A., Kəm vəprosa za načaloto na ekaviz-
ma v bəlgarskija ezik, BəlgEz, XIII, 1963, 4-5,
p. 333-344.

_____, Za njakoi dialektni osobenosti vəv vlaxo-bəlgarskite gramoti, BəlgEz, XVI, 1966, 6, p. 556-563.

Stankiewicz, E., Worth, D. S., A Selected Bibliography of Slavic Linguistics, Hague-Paris, I, 1966, 316 pp.; II, 1970, 530 pp.

Stanojević, St., Die Biographie Stefan Lazarević's von Konstantin dem Philosophen als Geschichtsquelle, AfSlPh, XVIII, 1896, p. 409-472.

Steinke, K., Studien über den Verfall der bulgarischen Deklination (= Slavistische Beiträge, 29), Munich, 1968, 133 pp.

Stieber, Z., Dwa problemy z fonologii słowiańskiej, Lingua Posnanensis, I, Poznan, 1949, p. 81-86.

_____, Rozwój fonologiczny języka polskiego, Warsaw, 1952, 95 pp.

Stojanov, M., Kodov, Xr., Opis na slavjanskite rəkopisi v Sofijskata narodna biblioteka, III, Sofia, 1964, 497 + xi pp.

Stojkov, St., Literaturen ezik i dialekti, IzvIBE, II, 1952, p. 129-171.

_____, Palatalnite səglasni v bəlgarskija ezik, IzvIBE, I, 1952, p. 5-65.

_____, Akan'e v bolgarskom jazyke (in: Obščesla-vjanskoe značenie problemy akan'ja, V. I. Georgiev, ed.), Sofia, 1968, p. 93-116.

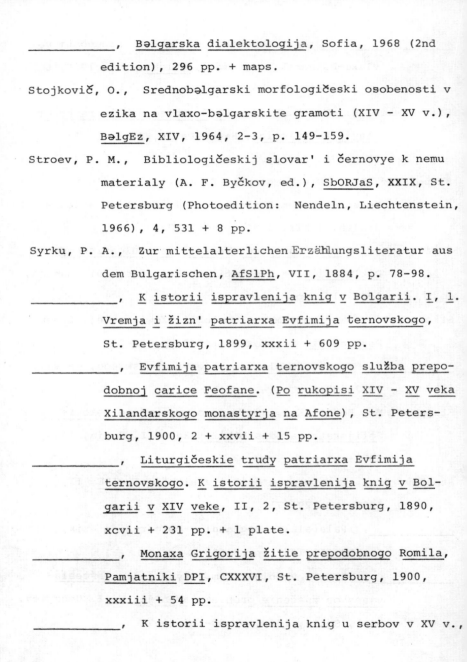

_____, Bəlgarska dialektologija, Sofia, 1968 (2nd edition), 296 pp. + maps.

Stojkovič, O., Srednobəlgarski morfologičeski osobenosti v ezika na vlaxo-bəlgarskite gramoti (XIV - XV v.), BəlgEz, XIV, 1964, 2-3, p. 149-159.

Stroev, P. M., Bibliologičeskij slovar' i černovye k nemu materialy (A. F. Byčkov, ed.), SbORJaS, XXIX, St. Petersburg (Photoedition: Nendeln, Liechtenstein, 1966), 4, 531 + 8 pp.

Syrku, P. A., Zur mittelalterlichen Erzählungsliteratur aus dem Bulgarischen, AfSlPh, VII, 1884, p. 78-98.

_____, K istorii ispravlenija knig v Bolgarii. I, 1. Vremja i žizn' patriarxa Evfimija ternovskogo, St. Petersburg, 1899, xxxii + 609 pp.

_____, Evfimija patriarxa ternovskogo služba prepodobnoj carice Feofane. (Po rukopisi XIV - XV veka Xilandarskogo monastyrja na Afone), St. Petersburg, 1900, 2 + xxvii + 15 pp.

_____, Liturgičeskie trudy patriarxa Evfimija ternovskogo. K istorii ispravlenija knig v Bolgarii v XIV veke, II, 2, St. Petersburg, 1890, xcvii + 231 pp. + 1 plate.

_____, Monaxa Grigorija žitie prepodobnogo Romila, Pamjatniki DPI, CXXXVI, St. Petersburg, 1900, xxxiii + 54 pp.

_____, K istorii ispravlenija knig u serbov v XV v.,

IzvORJaS, VII, 4, St. Petersburg, 1902 (Photoedition: Graz, 1964), p. 321-323.

Šaxmatov, A., Drevnebolgarskaja enciklopedija X veka, Vizantijskij vremennik, VII, 1900, p. 1-35.

Ščepkin, V. N., Cryillische Ligaturschrift, AfSlPh, XXV, 1903, p. 109-129.

_____, Savvina kniga (= Pamjatniki staroslavjanskogo jazyka, I, 2), St. Petersburg, 1903 (Photoreprint: Graz, 1959), vii + 235 pp.

_____, Bolgarskij ornament èpoxi Ioanna Aleksandra, Sbornik statej po slavjanovedeniju, posvjaščennyx prof. M. S. Drinovu, Kharkov, 1904, p. 153-158.

_____, Učebnik russkoj paleografii, Moscow, 1918 (1920), 182 pp.

Ševčenko, I., Études sur la polémique entre Théodore Métochite et Nicéphore Chumnos. La vie intellectuelle et politique à Byzance sous les premiers Paléologues, Brussels, 1963, viii + 330 pp.

Šklifov, Bl., Edin trud vərxu "makedonskata" leksika ot XVI v., BəlgEz, XVII, 1967, 4, p. 380-381.

Tal'berg, N., Istorija Russkoj Cerkvi, Jordanville, N. Y., 1959, 927 pp.

Tixomirov, M. N., Istoričeskie svjazi russkogo naroda s južnymi slavjanami s drevnejšix vremen do poloviny XVII v., Slavjanskij sbornik, Moscow, 1947, p. 125-201.

＿＿＿＿＿＿＿＿＿, Srednevekovnaja Moskva v XIV - XV vekax, Moscow, 1957, 318 pp.

Trifonov, Ju., Despot Ivan-Aleksandər i položenieto na Bəlgarija sled Velbəždkata bitka, SpBAN, XLIII, 1930, p. 61-91.

Trifunović, Đ., ed., Stara književnost, Beograd, 1965, 572 pp.

Trubeckoj, N. S., O nekotoryx ostatkax isčeznuvšix grammatičeskix kategorij v obščeslavjanskom prajazyke, Slavia, I, 1922-23, p. 12-21.

＿＿＿＿＿＿＿＿＿, Altkirchenslavische Grammatik. Schrift-, Laut- und Formensystem, Graz-Vienna-Cologne, 1968 (2nd edition), 197 pp.

Turdeanu, Em., Grégoire Camblak: Faux arguments d'une biographie, RÉS, XXII, 1946, p. 46-81.

＿＿＿＿＿＿＿＿＿, La littérature bulgare du XIVe siècle et sa diffusion dans les Pays Roumains (= Institut d'Études slaves, Travaux, 22), Paris, 1947, 188pp.

Uluxanov, I. S., O sud'be slavjanizmov v drevnerusskom literaturnom jazyke (Na materiale glagolov s pristavkoj "pre-") (in: Pamjatniki drevnerusskoj pis'mennosti, V. V. Vinogradov, ed.), Moscow, 1968, p. 19-71.

Uspenskij, B. A., Tipologičeskaja klassifikacija jazykov kak osnova jazykovyx sootvetstvij (Struktura jazyka-ètalona pri tipologičeskoj klassifikacii jazykov), VJaz, 1961, 6, p. 51-64.

Uxova, T. B., Katalog miniatjur, ornamenta i gravjur sobranij Troice-Sergievoj lavry i Moskovskoj duxovnoj
akademii, Zapiski Otdela rukopisej (GB SSSR im.
V. I. Lenina), XXII, Moscow, 1960, p. 104-145.

Vaillant, A., Manuel du vieux slave, Paris, 1948, I,
375 pp.; II, 125 pp. Russian translation, in
one volume, by V. V. Borodič, Rukovodstvo po
staroslavjanskomu jazyku, Moscow, 1952, 446 pp.

Valjavec, M., Trnovsko tetrajevandelije XIII vieka, Starine,
XX, Zagreb, 1888, p. 157-241; XXI, 1889, p. 1-68.

van Wijk, N., Taalkundige en historiese gegebens betref-
fende de oudste betrekkingen tussen Serven en
Bulgaren, Mededelingen der Koninklijke Nederlandse
Akademie van Wetenschappen, Afd. Letterkunde, 55,
A, 3, Amsterdam, 1923, p. 55-76.

_____, Le développement des voyelles ě, a, ja en
bulgare, RÉS, VII, 1927, p. 7-21.

_____, Geschichte der altkirchenslavischen Sprache,
I. Laut- und Formenlehre, Berlin-Leipzig, 1931,
v + 254 pp; Russian translation with supplemen-
tary bibliography: Istorija staroslavjanskogo
jazyka, Moscow, 1957, 368 pp.

Vasil'evskij, V., Vizantija i Pečenegi, ŽMNP, CLXIV, 1872,
2, p. 116-332.

Velčev, V., Grigorij Camblak (in: Istorija na bəlgarskata
literatura, I), Sofia, 1963, p. 326-344.

Verković, St., Narodne pesme makedonski bugara. Knjiga

    prva. Ženske pesme, Beograd, 1860, 337 pp.

Vinogradov, V. V., Osnovnye ètapy istorii russkogo jazyka,

    RJaŠ, 1940, 3, p. 1-15; 4, p. 1-18; 5, p. 1-9.

_____, ed., Obzor predloženij po usoveršenstvo-

    vaniju russkoj orfografii, Moscow, 1965, 450 pp.

Višnjakova, A. F., K voprosu o kul'ture i prosveščenii

    bolgar v XIV v., Vizantijskij sbornik, Moscow -

    Leningrad, 1945, p. 256-259.

von Arnim, B., Beiträge zum Studium der altbulgarischen und

    altkirchenslavischen Wortbildung und Übersetzungs-

    kunst. Ursachen des Wechsels zwischen den Suffixen

    -je, -stvo, -stvije in Evangelium, Apostolus,

    Psalter und einigen anderen Übersetzungen,

    Sitzungsberichte der phil.-hist. Klasse, 22 Oct.

    1931, Berlin, 1932, p. 952-1024.

Voskresenskij, G., Xarakterističeskie čerty četyrex redak-

    cii slavjanskogo perevoda Evangelija ot Marka po

    sto dvenadcati rukopisjam Evangelija XI - XVI vv.,

    Moscow, 1896, pp. 48-54, 258-291.

Vostokov, A. X., ed., Ostromirovo evangelie 1056-1057 g.

    S priloženiem grečeskogo teksta evangelij i s

    grammatičeskimi ob"jasnenijami, St. Petersburg,

    1843 (Photoedition: Wiesbaden, 1964), viii + 294

    + 320 pp.

Vryonis, S., Byzantium and Europe, London, 1967, 260 pp.

Vzdornov, G. I., Rol' slavjanskix monastyrskix masterskix
pis'ma Konstantinopolja i Afona v razvitii knigopisanija i xudožestvennogo oformlenija russkix
rukopisej na rubeže XIV - XV vv. (in: Literaturnye svjazi drevnix slavjan), Trudy ODRL, XXIII,
Leningrad, 1968, p. 171-198.

Worth, D. S., Phraseology in the Galician-Volynian Chronicle, Annals UAASUS, VIII, 1960, 1-2 (25-26),
p. 55-69.

Xodova, K. I., K voprosu o vyjavlenii leksičeskoj normy v
russkom literaturnom jazyke drevnego perioda (in:
Pamjatniki drevnerusskoj pis'mennosti, V. V.
Vinogradov, ed.), Moscow, 1968, p. 95-116.

Zaxariev, V., Ornamentalnata ukrasa na Radomirovija psaltir
ot bibliotekata na Zografskija manastir, Rodina,
II, Sofia, 1939, 2, p. 154-158.

Zlatarski, V. N., Žitie i žizn' prepodobnogo otca našego
Feodosija, SbNUNK, XX, p. 1-41.

_____, Istorija na bəlgarskata dəržava prez
srednite vekove, I, 1, Sofia, 1918, 479 pp.

_____, Tərnovskijat nadpis na Ivan Asenja II
(in: Bəlgarska istoričeska biblioteka, S. Slavčev,
ed., III, 3), Sofia, 1930, p. 56-64.

_____, Istorija na bəlgarskata dəržava prez
srednite vekove, III, Sofia, 1940, xvi + 637 pp.

Žukovskaja, L. P., Tipologija rukopisej drevnerusskogo

polnogo aprakosa XI - XIV vv. v svjazi s lingvis-
tičeskim izučeniem ix (in: <u>Pamjatniki</u> <u>drevnerus-</u>
<u>skoj</u> <u>pis'mennosti</u>, V. V. Vinogradov, ed.), Moscow,
1968, p. 199-332.